T0089079

come away rooting harder than ever for the kids and harder than ever against the basketball profiteers."

—L. Jon Wertheim, author of *Strokes of Genius*

"What happens when the nation's foremost investigative sports reporter spends eight years probing the fascinating underworld of grassroots basketball? You get a page-turning narrative that will absorb and repulse you at the same time. I thought I knew a lot about grassroots hoops, but the scope and depth of the reportage in this book just blew me away. *Play Their Hearts Out* is a must-read for anyone who has ever watched, played, coached, or otherwise worked in—and cared about—the sport of basketball."

—Seth Davis, author of *When March Went Mad*

"It's a brilliant and heart-wrenching journey, and a cautionary tale to any basketball player who thinks the path to the NBA is a slam dunk."

—*Publishers Weekly*

"By far my favorite book of the summer was George Dohrmann's book *Play Their Hearts Out.*"

—HoopsAddict.com

"An unflinching look at the world of AAU basketball."

—Deadspin.com

"Highly recommended for basketball fans and anyone looking for a well-researched, in-depth true story, *Play Their Hearts Out* will leave readers thinking, both about the grassroots system and professional sports in general."

—*The* Notre Dame *Observer*

"*Play Their Hearts Out* is a devastating examination of what happens when profit triumphs over heart."

—*The Dallas Morning News*

"Like other great works of sports journalism, the book whitewashes nothing and simultaneously makes you love the game all over again."

—Minneapolis *Star Tribune*

"Written with incomparable detail and insight, *Play Their Hearts Out* is a thoroughly unique narrative."

—WGN-TV, Chicago

"A well-told and engaging story."

—*Basketball Prospectus*

"It is a gripping narrative whose details are unsavory and alarming."

—*The Saratogian*

Play Their Hearts Out

A COACH, HIS STAR RECRUIT, AND THE YOUTH BASKETBALL MACHINE

George Dohrmann

BALLANTINE BOOKS TRADE PAPERBACKS

NEW YORK

A 2012 Ballantine Books Trade Paperback Edition

Published in the United States by Ballantine Books Trade Paperbacks,
an imprint of The Random House Publishing Group,
a division of Random House, Inc., New York.

BALLANTINE BOOKS TRADE PAPERBACKS and colophon
are registered trademarks of Random House, Inc.

Originally published in hardcover in the United States by Ballantine Books,
an imprint of The Random House Publishing Group,
a division of Random House, Inc., in 2011.

Library of Congress Cataloging-in-Publication Data

Dohrmann, George.
Play their hearts out : a coach, his star recruit, and the youth basketball machine /
George Dohrmann.
p. cm.
ISBN 978-0-345-50861-4
eBook ISBN 978-0-345-52316-7
1. Basketball—United States.   2. Youth league basketball—United States.
3. Keller, Joe.   4. Basketball coaches—United States.   5. Walker, Demetrius.
6. Basketball players—United States.   7. Basketball players—Recruiting—
United States.   I. Title.
GV885.D64 2010
796.3230973—dc22   2010015470

www.ballantinebooks.com

Book design by R. Bull

146119709

For my parents,
who encouraged and enabled grand pursuits

AUTHOR'S NOTE

This book is the result of more than eight years of reporting, and I witnessed most of the events and conversations depicted. I tried to avoid using material for which I was not present, though in some instances it was central to the narrative and had to be re-created through interviews with those involved. Relying on others to recall past events is an imperfect method of fact-gathering. I was left to trust that they would provide an honest version of what occurred. In cases where differing accounts were offered, I noted that in the text or went with the version relayed by the majority of those present.

PROLOGUE

Hunting
for Kids

Joe Keller

On a clear and warm Sunday afternoon in September of 1996, a basketball game was played in the gym at Riverside Community College in Southern California. No one from the school knew the game was scheduled, and the organizer, twenty-six-year-old Joe Keller, thought he would have to break into the gym and open the doors from the inside. At the last minute, a friend procured a key, but Keller was unable to turn on the scoreboard or the clock, so the score and the time were kept manually. There was no advance advertising of the game, no newspaper articles or Internet postings, yet fans filed in as soon as the doors opened. Estimates vary as to how many people filled the worn bleachers, but the crowd numbered at least 300 and might have been as large as 500, a considerable audience for a game in which none of the participants was older than fourteen.

Of the two teams playing that day, the Southern California All-Stars (SCA) were by far the most well known. Their coach, Pat Barrett, cut a wide swath in the world of grassroots basketball. Nike paid him more than $100,000 annually to assure that his players were aligned with that brand and gave him another $50,000 in shoes and other gear. His skills as a basketball instructor were limited, but his ability to identify and acquaint himself with the best young basketball players in Southern California was legendary. Given the considerable talent flowing annually from that part of the nation, this made him one of the most powerful figures in basketball, courted by college coaches, NBA scouts, and sports agents. A year earlier, after UCLA won the national title with a team that included several SCA alumni, including Final Four most valuable player Ed O'Bannon, the team's coach, Jim Harrick, gave Barrett a championship ring. A prominent UCLA booster also donated $200,000 to a nonprofit organization—Values for a Better America— that Barrett controlled.

Barrett had coached since the mid-1980s and operated teams in various age groups, but the team of seventh- and eighth-graders competing in Riverside that Sunday may have been the most impressive he'd ever assembled. There was Jamal Sampson (who would go on to play for Cal Berkeley and then the NBA's Milwaukee Bucks), Josh Childress (Stanford and then the Atlanta Hawks), Cedric Bozeman (UCLA and the Hawks), and Jamaal Williams (the Washington Huskies). The point guard, Keilon Fortune, was considered the best of the lot, even though he was a year younger than the other players. Two months earlier, SCA had claimed the 13-and-Under Amateur Athletic Union (AAU) national title, fueling talk that Barrett's assemblage of young stars was among the best ever.

SCA's opponent that day, the Inland Stars, was considerably less distinguished, and its coach, Joe Keller, paled in comparison to the mighty Barrett. A full-time welder and a part-time coach, Keller was considerably better at the former than the latter. When he started coaching a few years earlier, he couldn't even demonstrate a proper defensive stance. In his first season, his team played an SCA squad and lost by almost 100. While Barrett was flush with Nike money, financial stability constantly eluded Keller. He had only recently moved out of an apartment he shared with his mother in Riverside and often asked people he'd just met: "Do you know any rich people who could sponsor my team?"

Keller's squad in Riverside that Sunday was not without talent. Forwards Lance and Erik Soderberg—the sons of former Kentucky player Mark Soderberg—were capable players and would go on to earn college scholarships, as would the Inland Stars' best guard, Josh Dunaj. But they were no match for SCA's kids, and the swagger of Barrett's players was unmistakable as they entered the gym in matching Nike sweat suits. Keller's players—dressed in yellow uniforms he had borrowed from another coach—were already warming up when Barrett and the SCA kids arrived. They stopped and watched as fans streamed down from the bleachers to greet the recently crowned national champions.

Basketball games are often framed as battles between coaches, as if the players on the floor are chess pieces easily manipulated by the men on the sidelines. At the youth level, this is an especially foolish line of thought. Kids make mistakes. They act unpredictably. Coaching them requires an understanding of their fallibility. The biggest influence Keller and Barrett would have on the outcome of the game would come long before it began, in the procurement of players: The coach who assembled the most talent would likely win. Barrett had few peers in that regard, least of all Keller. If a bookie had set odds on the game, SCA would have been favored by at least 20, and it wouldn't have surprised anyone if Barrett's collection of future NBA players whipped the Inland Stars by more than 50.

But Keller would not have scheduled the game had he not believed in his team's chances. In the days before, he boldly predicted victory and became convinced that the game would be his defining moment as a coach. The reason for his optimism became apparent to the SCA players as they shed their sweat suits and began their pregame routine. Glancing toward the Inland Stars' end of the court, they saw the players that had long been part of Keller's team, but amid them was a boy they had never seen before. He was the tallest player in the gym, nearly six foot five, with impossibly long arms and a nimbleness unseen in a player so tall for his age. They watched as he executed a layup, jumping so high that it was clear he could dunk every time if he wanted. In a bit of showmanship scarcely seen from a player so young, he repeatedly surged upward toward the basket and, just as everyone anticipated him slamming the ball home, merely dropped it through the rim. He was letting the crowd and the SCA players—most of whom could not yet palm a basketball—know that dunking came so easily to him that he'd grown bored with it.

Questions about this boy spread quickly around the gym. *Who was he? Where had he come from? Was he really the same age as the other players?* Answers emerged slowly, passed from one person to the next in hushed tones. Keller had unearthed him after hearing rumors of a prodigal talent on the blacktops of San Bernardino. He had never played for an AAU team before. And, yes, he was only thirteen years old. His mere presence infused the game with an unexpected gravity. A boy of that size and obvious ability gave Keller's squad a puncher's chance. For the first time anyone could remember, a local team posed a threat to Pat Barrett and his Southern California All-Stars.

When the tall boy lined up against Sampson for the opening tip, the one advantage the Inland Stars had was obvious. Keller's center was several inches taller than Sampson, and his arms seemed twice as long. When the official tossed the ball skyward, the boy reached it at such a high point that Sampson appeared hopeless. He then sprinted upcourt, took a pass in the lane—catching the ball high above the reach of any of the SCA players—and flipped in a layup over Childress. On the sideline, Keller grinned and said to himself: "The rout is on."

No videotape of the game exists. The only stat sheet was lost. Keller does not remember the final score or how many points the tall boy scored, but he recalls never before seeing a more dominant performance by a player. The young boy swatted shots back at SCA guards brave enough to drive to the basket. He seemingly grabbed every rebound and scored at will. After Keller's team raced to an early 10-point lead, one of Barrett's assistant coaches was ejected for yelling at the officials. When the lead increased to 20 points with eight minutes left, Barrett was ejected too. Keller told the officials: "Let him stay. I don't want him to use that as an excuse for why he lost." Near the end of the game, Barrett sat down on the bench and put his hands on his knees, no longer wanting to watch the action on the floor. When Keller saw this, a feeling of immense satisfaction washed over him. With one game he'd gone from a coaching nobody to the guy who beat Pat Barrett.

At the final whistle, Keller ran onto the court and celebrated with his players; a few poured tiny cups of Gatorade on his head. The two teams never shook hands, and the SCA players quickly left the gym. Barrett was still shouting at the officials as he followed his players out the door. Keller had thought Barrett would be gracious in defeat, but it didn't dampen Keller's mood. "We beat the best team in the country," he told anyone willing to listen. Later that night, he told his wife that he thought his life was about to change.

A few days passed before Keller's premonition came true. Barrett called him and made a surprising proposition: He wanted to merge the best of the Inland Stars with SCA. The team would be called the Southern California All-Stars and be funded by Barrett, but Keller would be its coach. To Keller, this seemed like a sweet deal and he quickly agreed. He was short on money and coaching experience, and Barrett had both. He envisioned Barrett as something like a mentor, ushering him into a coaching career. He hoped Barrett would call his contacts at Nike and tell them about Keller and his talented new star. But Keller was naïve about the culture of grassroots basketball and how Barrett had built his youth-basketball empire. His life was indeed about to change, but not how he imagined.

I met Keller four years later, a few weeks before Christmas 2000. We met at an unremarkable brewpub just off Interstate 15 in San Bernardino. I was seated at a wide oval table watching a Los Angeles Lakers game on one of the restaurant's dozen televisions when Keller walked in. He wore jeans and a loose sweatshirt, and when I stood up to shake his hand, he ignored me and sat across the table and to my left, farther away than I expected. The mutual acquaintance who arranged our meeting had mentioned that Keller was afraid to talk with a writer from *Sports Illustrated,* and in that moment I felt that his paranoia had been undersold.

I was in Southern California, reporting on a story about Tyson Chandler, then an eighteen-year-old senior at Compton Dominguez High School, as he prepared to jump straight from high school to the National Basketball Association. The story was intended to expose the myriad of people (coaches, agents, relatives, friends) trying to align themselves with Chandler, which included Barrett. He had allegedly bought Chandler a Cadillac Escalade, moved Chandler's family from San Bernardino to a house closer to Barrett's in Orange County, and taken him on shopping sprees for clothes and shoes that often exceeded $5,000. If Chandler met a girl at an out-of-state tournament that he wanted to see again, Barrett bought her an airline ticket to California.

I had been told that Keller was Chandler's first AAU coach, until Barrett lured him to SCA and pushed Keller out of the picture. I was hoping Keller would give me some dirt on Barrett, but when I asked about him, he said only: "He is a powerful man in basketball." When I inquired why Barrett, not Keller, was coaching Chandler now, Keller got a pained look on his face. "Talking about that will only come back to hurt me." A frustrating argument followed. I suggested that if Keller hated Barrett, as I suspected, exposing his misdeeds in *Sports Illustrated* might put him out of business. Keller insisted that nothing I could write would ever push Barrett out of youth basketball and so tattling on him would bring Keller nothing but harm.

Keller was thirty when we met. He was two inches taller than me, about five foot ten, with wide shoulders but pale, skinny legs. He looked as if he'd been into weight lifting at one time but had stopped. A sparse goatee couldn't hide the acne scars on his face or detract from his two most striking features—deep-set blue eyes and a flattop haircut that seemed suited for a younger man. A narrow scar on the left side of his forehead ran into his hairline, making it seem as if his barber had tried to manufacture a part.

I didn't think much of Keller. For all his paranoia, he could be dismissive and arrogant. He asked when I thought Chandler would be selected in the NBA draft that June. I said somewhere in the top 15. "That's ridiculous. You don't know anything," Keller snapped. "He's top five, maybe top two." I spent an hour alternating between assuaging Keller's mistrust and enduring his insults before he consented to tell me the story of how he found Chandler.

During an Inland Stars practice in the spring of 1996, Keller was criticizing his players for not being tough enough, when one kid said almost matter-of-factly, "Then why don't you get that tall kid from San Bernardino?" Keller questioned the player, who knew nothing about the mysterious kid, not even his name. Keller called schools in the area, finally finding a teacher at Arrowview Middle School who thought he knew the boy and came up with a possible first name, Tyson, but nothing else.

Keller spent weeks cruising the roughest neighborhoods of San Bernardino, searching for the boy. He finally got a tip that led him to a low-slung house in one of the poorest areas of the city. During the 1990s, many African American families had fled inner-city homes in Los Angeles for nicer neighborhoods in the Inland Empire, the common name for the sunbaked cities of Riverside and San Bernardino Counties. But as Keller walked up a dirt driveway to the front door, he thought this family would have been better off staying in the ghetto. The house was originally painted white but was now gray. A falling chain-link fence surrounded a dirt-and-grass yard, which framed a porch of broken concrete. The neighboring houses were in the same shape or worse. Keller was a little afraid of what awaited him behind the front door, but then a lanky kid standing about six foot five answered. At first, Keller thought this was the older brother of the kid he had heard about, but the boy assured him that he was indeed just finishing the seventh grade.

"My God," Keller said, and for a moment he couldn't speak. He finally uttered, "Can you dribble or run or anything?"

"Yeah, I can dunk," the boy said.

Keller's mood softened as he told me the story and described how unbeatable his team became with Chandler. "And I can coach too," Keller added, a statement that seemed to be a criticism of other youth coaches. It felt like an opening to ask again about Barrett.

"So then why would Tyson want to go play for Pat Barrett?"

Keller frowned and shook his head, as if to say he wouldn't be tricked that easily. A short time later he said he had to get home to his wife and he left.

When the article, titled "School for Scandal," was published a few weeks later, I remember being greatly disappointed that it didn't cause more of a stir. There were rumors that Nike cut ties with Barrett because of it, but then I heard he signed a contract with Adidas. I had always known the world of youth basketball was an unregulated subculture where men like Barrett could get away with almost anything in their pursuit of talented kids, but I assumed that if a coach's dirty dealings were unveiled, the shoe companies and players would distance themselves.

Keller's ultimate contribution to the story was an insipid twelve-word quote, but I still called him after the article was published. I wanted to get his reaction to the unsavory moves by Barrett that I described, including selling Chandler to various agents. "That stuff from me was the best part of the story," Keller said when I reached him at his home. He wasn't joking. As for Barrett, he said, "Pat called me and said that since that article, he's had more parents calling him, wanting their kids to play for him, than ever before. That article helped Pat a lot."

His words stung. I was reminded of what Keller said during our meeting at the brewery: If an exposé in *Sports Illustrated* could do nothing more than increase the business of one of youth basketball's most controversial figures, then perhaps, as Keller said, I didn't know anything about the world in which Barrett operated.

I was in Los Angeles on assignment a few weeks later and I called Keller. I stressed that I no longer was working on a story about Barrett or Chandler but that I wanted to better understand the grassroots game. He agreed to meet, and I drove fifty miles east to Fontana, to the Inland Empire, and picked him up at the Citrus Grove Apartments, a complex that abutted train tracks, where he lived with his wife, Violet. We drove to a nearby Mexican restaurant and, after several Midori sours, Keller loosened up enough to tell me how he stumbled into coaching.

He was originally from Long Island and had moved to Riverside, California, with his mother before his senior year of high school. He had been a standout baseball player and dreamed of playing for the New York Yankees, but he tore his rotator cuff in his senior season and gave up the game. "After high school, I was the world's biggest fuckup," he said. He hung around guys who sold and smoked marijuana. He held several jobs, the longest for a year on the assembly line of a company that manufactured roofing tiles. He was still living with his mother when, in 1993, he applied for a job with the Riverside Parks and Recreation Department. The only opening was a $200-a-month job coaching ten- and eleven-year-old boys on a basketball team called the Bryant Park Lakers. "I needed the money," Keller said.

His first team was made up of "little rats," as he called them, short kids who hung around Bryant Park and had to scrap for every point. They wore black T-shirts with *Lakers* stenciled on the front, the words faded from too many washings. Keller showed me a picture of his first team. The boys are standing straight and stiff-armed, trying to look tough. Keller is at one end, slightly slouched, dressed in jeans shorts and a T-shirt. It is a typical photo, except for one detail: Keller slipped two fingers, the bunny ears, over his tallest player's head.

Through a mix of luck and dogged play, the Bryant Park Lakers won more games than they lost in Keller's first season, and in the spring of 1993 they played a regional qualifier for the state championships. When Keller arrived at a gym in Orange County for the game, he looked at his little players warming up and at their opponents and believed a mistake had been made. "Excuse me, I think we are in the wrong gym," he told Caynell Cotton, a woman who helped organize the tournament. "My guys are fifth- and sixth-graders." She pointed to the biggest of the boys on the opposing team and said, "That's my son, Schea, and he's going into the sixth grade. Welcome to AAU basketball."

Keller's motley bunch lost by almost 100, and Schea Cotton, who would go on to appear on the cover of *Sports Illustrated* as a high schooler and play at the University of Alabama, scored more than 30 points in the first half alone.

The night following the game, Keller called the coach of the team that had defeated him: Pat Barrett. He must have sounded naïve asking Barrett how he'd put together such a talented team. "It's simple," Barrett told him. "Go out and find the best players and hold on to them."

Keller was competitive and he was inspired: He hadn't known he could just go out and start a team of his own. After poaching the best players off the Bryant Park Lakers, he started an independent team, the Inland Stars. "I'd go to parks and rec centers, looking for kids, and talk to coaches at schools, asking if they had any players who starred during recess," Keller said. "Hunting for kids is the best part."

Most of Keller's energy over the next two years was spent trying to put together a team good enough to defeat SCA and Barrett, and by 1996 his team was almost ready. It lacked only a dominant inside player, someone to rebound and block shots and intimidate. "But then I found Tyson and it all came together." When SCA returned from Nationals, Keller called Barrett and laid the trap. He goaded Barrett, saying that if he'd had the money to take a team to the Nationals, he would have come home with the glass-bowl trophy.

When Keller described the game to me, his voice rose and adopted a dramatic rhythm. He was not a natural storyteller—he often left out vital facts—but his recollection of that September day included so many details that I believed he thought about it often. At the end of his description, after he talked about the boys pouring cups of Gatorade over his head, a look of gentle sadness settled in his eyes. He hadn't reconciled the joy that victory brought him with the betrayal he felt shortly thereafter. "That was a long time ago," he said, and then he fell silent, fingering his empty glass.

Keller wanted to stop there, but I wouldn't let him. I promised I wouldn't write in *Sports Illustrated* what he said but that I needed to know how Barrett ended up coaching Chandler. Before he answered, we moved from a booth to the bar. He ordered another Midori sour and also asked for a glass of olives, which he doused with so much Tabasco that there was more red than green in the glass. He began eating them vigorously. "You should try one," he said. I told him I couldn't think of anything I'd like to eat less. He insisted, and I felt as if this were a test, as if him telling me the story depended on me eating one of those soggy olives. I relented, swallowed one quickly, and the face I made delighted Keller. His laughter filled the nearly empty restaurant, and he slapped me on the back. "You're all right, George," he said, and then he began the story.

Immediately after he started to coach the newly merged team, Keller became uncomfortable with the attention Barrett showed Chandler. Barrett showered Chandler with gifts, shoes mostly, and would call Keller and ask if he could arrange for the three of them to go to dinner or the movies. About a month later, Keller got a call from George Raveling, the head of grassroots basketball for Nike. He asked for Chandler's shoe size and his address, and then a few days later approximately twenty pairs of shoes, all in Chandler's size, arrived at his house. Boxes of other gear—shirts, sweatshirts, bags—followed.

Coaching SCA was more work than Keller expected. He had gotten married only a year earlier, and he and Violet both worked full-time (Keller at a welding company, Artistic Iron; Violet as a clerk at the Riverside County assessor's office). Getting Chandler and the other boys to practice and games every day proved difficult. Chandler lived more than twenty miles from Keller's apartment, and other players lived as far away or farther. On weekdays, Keller woke at 4:00 a.m., worked until 3:00 p.m., and then either he or Violet picked up the boys and made the hour drive to a gym in Orange County near Barrett's home. After a three-hour practice, Keller or Violet carted players home, not returning to their apartment until well after 10:00 p.m. The weekends were just as bad. There was always a tournament in Los Angeles or San Diego or the

San Fernando Valley north of L.A. The hectic routine continued even after Violet got pregnant. On the few nights there wasn't practice or a game, Chandler would sleep at the apartment to avoid the commute the following day. Or he'd call and need a ride to the mall or the movie theater or elsewhere. Violet liked Chandler, but she felt they needed to start saying no to some of his requests. They had become chauffeurs and gofers for a middle schooler who wasn't even their own son.

One afternoon, Keller was seated at a desk in an office at Artistic Iron, looking over plans for a railing the company was welding, when owner John Robbins hurried into the room. "Joe, you need to go home right now," he said.

Robbins didn't want to be the one to break the news, but Keller said, "John, if you don't tell me what is going on, I am going to bust you in the face."

"I'm sorry, Joe. Violet just called. She had a miscarriage."

When Keller arrived at his apartment, Violet was lying on the sofa. Her brother, her mother, and one sister were there. He looked at them, saw the tears in their eyes, and began crying. He fell to his knees in front of the sofa and wrapped his arms around Violet. Her mother said over and over, "God just didn't mean for this baby to be born." Lying in bed that night, Violet settled on a more concrete reason for losing the child. "It was because of stress, Joe," she said. "You know it was the stress." So right then, while lying next to Violet in their small apartment in the spring of 1997, Keller decided to take a break from coaching.

Keller took more hours at Artistic Iron and made foreman. He ran a side business installing car alarms. He bought Violet an Explorer, the perfect car for the big family they planned to have. When Violet found out she was pregnant again, Keller seemed to be settling into a nice life.

"But I missed it," he told me. "I would go watch Tyson play once in a while. Violet was okay with that. But it wasn't the same as being the coach."

After giving birth to a son, Jordan, named after NBA star Michael Jordan, Violet agreed to let Keller coach again, and he immediately tried to get back in with SCA and Chandler. But Barrett had closed the door. There was an uneasiness when he called or visited Chandler, and he later learned that Barrett had whispered a hurtful lie into Chandler's ear. "Coach Joe abandoned you," Barrett told him, "because he didn't believe in you as a player."

"The funny thing," Keller said, "is at first I don't even think Pat realized what he had in Tyson. He knew he was good, but he kept talking about some of his other guys, like Keilon, kept saying they were better prospects. I told him, 'Forget those guys. Tyson is the best player you've ever had.'"

Exactly what Barrett had wouldn't be known until a few months after Keller and I met in Fontana. In June of 2001, Chandler, having grown to seven foot one, was selected number 2 overall in the NBA draft just a month out of high school. He signed a contract with the Chicago Bulls for $10.6 million and, according to Keller, gave Barrett $200,000 and pledged that, upon future contracts, his former AAU coach would receive even more. Keller watched this develop from a perch far away. He occasionally went to see Chandler play in high school, but he slipped into the gym quietly and left without being noticed. It was a shameful time for Keller. As Chandler ascended, Keller's estrangement from his onetime star became more noteworthy. In coaching circles, he became a laughable legend: the man who discovered Tyson Chandler, a once-in-a-lifetime talent, and then let Barrett steal him from right under his nose. He couldn't walk into a gym without someone pointing him out as the dupe who had lost a winning lottery ticket.

When I dropped Keller off at his apartment later that night, he told me: "You should keep in touch with me. Things are happening." When I pressed him for details, he claimed that he had recently started a new team and that it included at least five young players, none older than eleven, who would one day play in college or the NBA. "I am going to be in *Sports Illustrated* again someday. These kids are that good."

I was intrigued by the thought of such a robust collection of young talent, but I found the man touting them to be more fascinating. Keller had recently re-formed the Inland Stars and quit his welding job so he could devote all his attention to grooming a new generation of basketball hopefuls. He was staking his future and his family's on his ability to make a career out of coaching those kids. In other words, he was betting he could become another Pat Barrett, could land the shoe company contract and build himself into one of the most influential figures in the game. It was a basketball pipe dream, no different from a young boy insisting he would one day play in the NBA.

It dawned on me that Keller and his team presented an opportunity to get inside the world of grassroots basketball in a way never done before. Nearly every great American-born basketball player of the last ten years—from Kevin Garnett to Kobe Bryant to Tracy McGrady to LeBron James—has been a product of the AAU system, yet it remains a largely unexplored world. Stories about the grassroots game, such as the one I reported on for *Sports Illustrated,* usually focus on the kids who emerge from it to find a place in the NBA. What about the others, the kids who don't make NBA millions or land college scholarships? It is not in the best interest of the power brokers, men like Pat Barrett, for a light to be cast on their actions. The shoe companies, sports agents, college recruiters—they all have reasons for wanting the gritty details of how the machine operates to go untold. They won't let you inside, so the only way to unveil how the system works is to get inside without them knowing.

I called Keller a week later with a proposal: I would follow him and his team until the boys ended their time in AAU basketball, likely to be their senior year in high school. If he gave me complete access, if he kept no secrets, I wouldn't publish what I saw or heard until the boys were in college. I framed it as a form of basketball anthropology, a study of how children were raised within the sport. To my surprise, Keller agreed. "When the boys graduate from high school, I'll be rich and done with coaching," he said. "I won't give a shit what you write."

Another reason Keller approved the arrangement became clear later, when he said, "Mail me about thirty of your business cards." He intended to hand them out to the parents of the kids he scouted. "Having a guy from *Sports Illustrated* affiliated with my program will help with recruiting." So that was the deal we struck. Keller got a recruiting tool, and I got entrée into the underbelly of basketball.

Finding a group of kids at the beginning of their journey felt like a remarkable stroke of good fortune. What I didn't know was that at that moment a boy named Andrew was practicing his 3-point shot and a quiet forward named Rome was working on his mid-range game. I didn't know that a boy named Jordan was being urged by his father, John, to be more aggressive and drive to the hoop and that in Los Angeles a coach named Gary Franklin was starting his own team of tenyear-olds, some of whom would one day help determine Keller's fate. I didn't know that in Santa Barbara a guard named Roberto was learning the nuances of the game from his father, Bruce, or that across the Inland Empire, in Riverside, a tall boy named Aaron was kicking a soccer ball, not yet introduced to the sport he was destined to play.

I was also unaware how deep into the world of grassroots basketball my alliance with Keller would take me. I would encounter unscrupulous agents, college coaches, and the other profiteers just as they took aim at the best kids; I would sit with parents, good and bad, as they tried to manage the suddenness of childhood stardom; I would watch as men in boardrooms and locker rooms plotted the futures of the most gifted players. Through Keller and his team, I would come to understand why some kids made it and others did not and how the youth-basketball machine determined their fates.

None of that was apparent, however, when Keller agreed to let me follow his team. Most of all, I was intrigued by one of his players, a boy who would influence my charting of the world of grassroots basketball more than any other.

"Now that I can trust you, you need to know something," Keller had said in a phone call. Then he lowered his voice. "I just found a kid, a player so good you are not going to believe it. He's a phenom. He's going to be better than Tyson. He's going to be the best ever."

PART ONE

A Prized
Long-Term
Investment

1

(ROB BOCK)

Demetrius Walker (third from left) *at 10 years old*

The Frank A. Gonzales Community Center sits on the corner of Colton Avenue and E Street in a mostly Latino neighborhood in Colton, among houses with unkempt yards and low-sloped roofs and next to a baseball field with an all-dirt infield. Like many public buildings in the Inland Empire, it is less inviting the closer you get. The bottom third of the building is painted a reddish brown, the rest a dirty pink, and the whole rectangular structure appears in need of a good hosing. During a development spree in the 1990s, many similar structures were built—elementary schools, community centers, government buildings—and aesthetics were forsaken for speedy construction. All around the Inland Empire, these buildings rose along with cookie-cutter housing developments, each more soulless than its predecessor.

Standing outside the gymnasium, which takes up the left half of the center, you're most aware of how the thick concrete walls and steel doors mute the life inside. Sneakers sliding, a leather ball pounding on the wood floor, coaches urging players to get back on defense, parents shouting at their kids to take the open shot—you hear none of it. The milieu of Southern California abounds: cars speeding by on Colton Avenue, the zip of an air gun from one of two auto-repair shops across the street, a constant hum from Interstate 10. The sounds of its residents, meanwhile, remain locked within that windowless cement box.

Inside the gym, on the far side of the court, Joe Keller stood with his arms folded in front of a black golf shirt. He had positioned himself at midcourt, behind the scorer's table, which struck me as an odd place to stand. Fans seated behind him were forced to either end of the aluminum bleachers to gain a clear view of the court. Keller seemed oblivious to his obstruction, and it may have been intentional; it was like him to believe no one's view of the court was more important than his.

He watched intently a game between a team from Santa Monica and another from Orange County. The kids on the floor were no older than eleven, some as young as eight, and it was difficult to see basketball greatness amid the chaos on the court. In the time it took me to walk from the door to the far side of the court, one small blond boy had a pass go through his hands as if they were coated in butter and the center for the Orange County team had bounced a pass off a teammate's leg so strongly that the ball rolled into his team's bench. Looking at Keller, I wondered if he possessed a clairvoyance that enabled him to see the game and its participants differently, to find greatness in the folly of children.

Another AAU coach, only twenty-five and in his first year of coaching, stood next to Keller. They discussed the players on the court, beginning with the eleven-year-old point guard for the Santa Monica team, the only girl in the tournament. She deftly dribbled through defenders, slipping the ball through her legs and around her back with ease, and her outfit was equally refined. The red rubber band holding back her ponytail matched the red trim on her jersey and on the black Vince Carter–model Nikes she wore.

"That's Monica DeAngelis," Keller told the younger coach. "Her dad is smart playing her against boys. She'll be in the WNBA someday."

The last line was a definitive statement; most of what came out of

Keller's mouth was not up for discussion, not that the young coach would have disagreed. He was clearly deferential and at one point folded his arms in front of his chest and widened his stance, striking the same pose as Keller. Talk turned to the point guard for the team from Orange County, an Asian kid with whom the coach was clearly impressed.

"He's killing people," the coach said. "You like him?"

"I don't do Asians," Keller responded quickly, as if he'd anticipated the question.

"What do you mean?"

"Asians don't get tall enough. That kid is fast, sure, but how tall is he going to be? Not tall enough."

The young coach wasn't sure Keller was serious. "That kid is blowing by everybody, Joe. You wouldn't want him on your team?"

"Nope. I don't do Asians."

Keller liked the way that sounded and that he was enlightening a younger colleague. The guard again broke free for a layup, and Keller looked at the coach and while shaking his head said, "Still . . . no Asians."

One could sense the young coach taking notes in his head. He next brought up the portly center on the Orange County team, the tallest player on the court. This prompted a dismissive glance from Keller that suggested he had never heard a dumber question in his thirty years.

"That kid's a truck. He can barely move. Look at his legs. They're stumps. He'll be lucky if he ends up six foot two. If that kid was on my team, I'd tell his parents they needed to think about switching him to football."

As if on cue, the chubby kid missed a layup while alone under the basket and then knocked the ball out of bounds while trying to rebound his own miss.

"That kid might be retarded," Keller said, laughing, and he segued into a story. Six months earlier, in a tournament near San Diego, Keller's team had faced an opponent that included a center who was mentally disabled. "I mean, he was wearing a helmet. I'm serious. A fucking helmet. A couple times, my guys blocked his shot into the stands." Keller laughed vigorously for several moments, clapping his hands in front of him as if impersonating an alligator's bite. "What kind of coach sends a retarded kid out there? Why do that to a kid?"

There were only seconds left in the game, and Keller fell silent as Monica's team tried for the winning score. Coming off a high screen, she got free on the right wing for a clear, albeit distant, look at the basket. Her body scrunched downward like a jack-in-the-box; the elbow on her right arm dipped so low it seemed to touch her knee. She then sprang up and slightly forward in one sudden motion—more of a heave than a release—and it seemed unlikely a decent shot would emerge from such an ungraceful motion. Yet the result was a high-arcing shot with silky backspin. Monica hopped a little on her left foot as the ball floated toward the rim, and for a moment it looked good. But the ball grazed the front of the rim and rattled within the hoop before bouncing out.

As the Orange County team celebrated, Monica put her hand to her forehead and rubbed down her damp brown hair. She bent at the waist and placed her hands on her knees, staying there even as the next two teams to play circled the court, beginning their warm-ups. One of those teams, the Arizona Stars, wore white uniforms, and its players were a mishmash of gangly and squat, black and white, athletic and awkward. In short, they were a team of children, not unlike the two squads that had finished playing moments before. The other team, the Inland Stars, was something else. Every boy was African American, and they were bigger and taller. From just watching them circle the court twice, it was clear none possessed the clumsiness one associates with rapidly growing boys. They wore black warm-ups over black uniforms and black shoes, an intimidating ensemble that contributed to my first impression: There was no way they were in the same age group as the other team.

As Keller's team divided into two lines for a layup drill, one of the tallest players broke ranks and walked over to where Monica stood. She was still bent over, despondent over her miss, and at first she didn't notice him. He placed his hand on her back and she looked up. He said something only she could hear and pointed toward the basket, as if to show her how close her shot had come to going in. Monica straightened up and put her hands on her hips, listening as the tall boy, who wore number 23, went on. He was smiling the whole time, a wide smile that flattened his thick top lip, and he continually shifted his weight back and forth. Finally the boy said something and Monica shook her head, as if shaking off the defeat, and then she smiled too. The boy stuck out his right hand and Monica slapped it. Mission accomplished, he pivoted on his left foot and literally jumped away from her, bouncing back into line with his teammates.

Keller had pointed this boy out earlier. His name was Demetrius Walker, and Keller spared no hyperbole in describing his abilities. He was "the best ten-year-old in the country," so good "he could start for most high school teams right now," and "an NBA first-rounder for sure." This was the boy Keller believed would be better than Tyson Chandler, the child who would bring him success and riches.

At first glance Demetrius appeared to be unique. He had a large head and well-defined cheekbones, which could be evidence that he was taller and more athletic than other boys only because he matured earlier. But his arms, shoulders, chest, and legs were those of a prepubescent boy, smooth and lacking definition. Unlike his teammates, he didn't let his shorts sag to his knees. He pulled them up to his true waist, and that gave the impression that his legs bypassed his hips and connected directly to his chest. His arms were unusually long, and one could imagine opposing coaches describing him as a kid who was "all arms and legs." In other words, he looked like a kid with a lot of growing left to do. There were other indicators I learned about later, such as his shoe size (14) and the height of his relatives (his mom was six foot one, his uncle six foot eight), but at first I was not sure how to judge his potential. Few endeavors are less exact than trying to forecast athletic greatness in still-developing children. Keller *might* have unearthed something special, but how could anyone say for sure?

Keller sidled up to me as Demetrius and the rest of the Inland Stars continued their warm-ups. Away from the young coach he'd been schooling, Keller's demeanor changed. "Look, I don't know how we are going to play today," he began. He said the boys had been lethargic in practice the day before and a few were nursing minor injuries. He alerted me to a player he'd recently added to the team, a smallish guard named LaBradford Franklin. "The kid's got balls, but he is a year younger than my guys."

His remarks felt sincere—as if he was providing important information—but also calculated. He badly wanted me to see Demetrius and his players as he did, to validate his beliefs, but he was also ready with a bagful of excuses just in case I didn't. With the game about to start, Keller left me with one final caveat: "I know what you are going to say after the game, and so I'm saying now: Please don't say I'm crazy like Bobby Knight. I know that is what you're gonna think, but don't say it."

Just before the start, the Inland Stars gathered in a circle around Keller in front of their bench. As he spoke, he scowled and punched downward, as if he were hammering a nail with his clenched fist. "Take their hearts out!" he shouted. "Take their fucking hearts out!" His words reverberated around the gym, and no one—not his wife, Violet, who sat near the door, or the little kids playing under the bleachers—could have missed his directive. Apparently, Keller didn't see the rules painted high on the west and east walls of the gym, one of which read:

Many different age levels use the gym and Community Center.
Please consider your language — No Profanity.

Most of the Inland Stars had their heads down as Keller spoke, but Demetrius looked down the court, sizing up the Arizona Stars. They had two guards who looked athletic but otherwise didn't match up. This was most obvious when Demetrius stood facing their center for the opening tip. They were the same height, but the Arizona center had chunky legs accentuated by white socks pulled up to his knees. When the referee stepped between them and tossed the ball skyward, the center didn't (or couldn't) jump and just tried to swat at the ball. Demetrius exploded off the floor, getting to the ball more than a foot above the Arizona player's hand. He tapped the ball to a teammate, who cruised in for an uncontested score.

Keller's team set up in a half-court trapping defense, and as the Arizona Stars inbounded the ball, he jumped up and down, screaming something incomprehensible even from where I sat fifteen feet behind him. Whatever he said, it was clearly a command for the top two players in the press to trap the ball handler. His players reacted instantly to his barks, moving toward the opposing guard with such speed that they overwhelmed him. He panicked and aimed a pass across the court to a teammate, but Demetrius stepped in front of it and walked in for a layup. The next two possessions ended with similar results, and I began to wonder if Arizona would ever get the ball across half-court.

Despite his team's immediate dominance, Keller screamed nonstop, reacting negatively to almost everything. If one of his players missed a shot, even if it was a good attempt, Keller berated him. If an Arizona player made a miracle 3-pointer, Keller went ballistic. He reacted so strongly to perceived mistakes that he lunged forward as if he were going to run onto the court, grab one of his players by the jersey, and rip him out of the game.

After one of his forwards missed a jump shot from the baseline, Keller stomped his feet and screamed, "Goddammit, Rome!"

After the Inland Stars' point guard failed to see Demetrius open in the post and instead launched a long shot that missed, Keller wiped his face with his hands and shouted, "Drew, you're an idiot!"

After LaBradford turned the ball over, he bellowed, "Jesus Christ!" and turned and directed a cross look toward LaBradford's father in the stands.

This was all in the first four minutes of the game.

After each of those supposed mistakes, Keller pulled that player and substituted another. He ran players to the scorer's table so frequently, it became difficult to keep track of who was in the game. It was something I had never seen before: a coach who thought his team should never miss a shot, never give up a score, and never commit a foul. Even Bob Knight wasn't that unreasonable.

At the end of the opening quarter, with his team leading 18–5, Keller told his players, "Pathetic effort right there. Get a drink and sit down."

With his team ahead 33–13 late in the second quarter, Keller was whistled for a technical foul after running three steps onto the floor (toward a referee) while protesting a reaching foul.

Throughout the game, the officials reminded him to stay on the sidelines, and after each warning he snarled. "Pay attention to the game, not me!" he yelled at one official. Later, "Don't tell me what to do."

Near the end of the third quarter, the Inland Stars led 52–26 and it was clear the Arizona players were beaten; they even fought over who had to bring the ball up against the press. On one possession, however, Arizona was able to get the ball across the midline and settled into an offensive set. It was such a rare occurrence that the game slowed down and the possession took on an air of importance.

The Arizona guards swung the ball around the perimeter a few times before it ended up in the hands of the bulky center with the white socks. He was on the right side, his back to the basket and Demetrius. He slowly inched closer to the hoop by slamming his butt into Demetrius, whom he outweighed by at least thirty pounds, and then backing into the space created when Demetrius flew backward. It was a graceless three-stage motion—dribble, slam, back step—but effective. The Arizona center had started twelve feet from the hoop but butted his way to within a few feet. He then bumped Demetrius one more time and spun to his left, pushing up a shot while Demetrius was still falling backward.

With Demetrius off balance and out of position, this seemed a rare moment when an Arizona player would find success. But Demetrius sprang upward, not toward the Arizona center but slightly away from him, going with the inertia created from the bump he'd received. It was an odd scene—he jumped away from the ball—but he elevated so high and his reach was so long that he still managed to get the tips of his fingers on the shot, redirecting it upward. The ball lingered in the air between him and the Arizona center, and it appeared as if Demetrius had only given his opponent an easier shot. The bulky center would surely collect the ball and, as Demetrius descended, lay it in unobstructed. But as the Arizona player set himself to jump, Demetrius was somehow back in the air, corralling the ball with his left hand. Before the Arizona center knew what had happened, Demetrius had touched down, gone back up, and grabbed the ball, and then suddenly was on the ground again, turning up the floor.

The game had been played predominantly on Arizona's side of the court, and I hadn't had an opportunity to see Demetrius run the floor. He burst forward, breaking from a crowd around the basket with three dribbles and three long strides that put him near midcourt so quickly that only two Arizona defenders were able to get in front of him. Demetrius met the first defender after one more stride and simply pushed the ball to the left, a redirection of only a few degrees that befuddled the Arizona guard. By the time the guard reached for the ball, Demetrius was already past him. The final defender, another smallish guard, saw this and slid over, hoping to push Demetrius far to the left and buy enough time for other defenders to get back and cut him off. But Demetrius sliced sharply to the right, cross-dribbling the ball so close to his body that he reared up a little to avoid running into it. The move so surprised the Arizona defender that his legs crossed and he fell backward to the ground.

All that was left was the finish, and Demetrius didn't disappoint. Just inside the key, he jumped off two feet and twisted his body a little so he attacked the basket straightaway. He rolled the ball into the hoop when the fingers on his right hand were only a few inches from the rim.

To see a ten-year-old block a shot when he was out of position, retrieve the ball when others had a better line on it, and maneuver upcourt with such agility and speed—it was startling. Keller spun around and looked at me as Demetrius laid the ball in. He raised his chin a little and, though I tried not to react, he saw something in my eyes that delighted him. He clapped his hands as he turned back to the game, just in time to bark out orders as an Arizona Stars guard inbounded the ball.

The Inland Stars didn't give up a basket in the fourth quarter and won 80–26. After the teams shook hands, I approached the Arizona coach. I wanted to get his opinion of Demetrius, and I thought two of his guards had played reasonably well and guessed he'd like to hear a compliment after a rough defeat. "If you think my guards played well, then something is wrong with your eyes," the coach said, and he huffed away.

As Keller addressed his team behind one bench, I walked toward the exit, where Violet sat behind a metal folding table. She took the admission (four dollars for adults, three for kids) and carefully placed the money in a small metal lockbox, knowing exactly how much more she needed to make the $795 rent on their 750-square foot apartment. Also on the table were Gatorades and Skittles she sold for a dollar apiece. Violet had long, straight brown hair and a round face and brown skin and, on this Saturday afternoon, dark circles under her brown eyes. She had been at the gym since 7:00 a.m. setting up for the tournament, which Keller organized and tabbed the Super Showcase. Tournaments such as this were the family's primary source of income, which didn't sit well with Violet—her father, who was born in Mexicali, had worked at the same company for twenty-two years—but she was a dutiful wife. Asked if she was a basketball fan, she thought for a minute and then answered in carefully chosen words: "I would say I'm still learning to like basketball."

A beaming Keller found me a few moments later. When he was still ten feet away, he clapped vigorously and shouted, "Now you see it, now you see it. Is Demetrius the real deal or what?"

I shrugged, not sure how to respond. Keller stopped short and slowly looked me up and down. "You're crazy if you can't see it." He folded his arms and waited for me to say something. After a few long seconds, when he realized a compliment wasn't forthcoming, he broke into a wry smile and started nodding. "Okay, I see how it's gonna be. Now I see how it's gonna be. Well . . . you need to come with us to Portland, then. There is a tournament there with some of the best teams on the West Coast. Come to Portland and you'll see. After that, if you don't believe, well, then something is wrong with you."

2

Kisha Houston and her son, Demetrius Walker

Demetrius grabbed a ball and walked outside the 3-point line on the left side of the court. He wiped the bottoms of his shoes—a white Adidas model called Bromium II—with his hands and began mashing the ball into his right palm, rotating it slightly the way a sculptor does when working a piece of clay. As he searched for a good grip, his teammates moved to the outer edges of the court, creating a clear line to the hoop.

The gym at a middle school on the outskirts of Portland had two levels. On the upper court a game was in full swing; a referee's whistle and the occasional cheers from the crowd echoed throughout the gym. On the lower court, the Inland Stars warmed up before their game against Seattle Rotary Select. Their parents sat in the stands against one wall, looking tired from their flights into Portland late the previous night. Among them was Kisha Houston, Demetrius's mother, and she entertained the others with a description of her airline experience. "I'm afraid to fly, so when they closed the doors, I wanted to scream, 'Get me off of this thing!'" She spoke loudly and raised her right hand for emphasis, as if she swore her words were true. "No, I mean, I was really afraid. When the plane took off, I was sure that thing was going to crash." Other parents talked of delays and nearly missed flights, but then Demetrius retrieved a ball and slowly walked seven steps from the basket and everyone went quiet.

Demetrius had first dunked a month earlier—Keller had told me about it with the excitement of a father announcing a birth—but the novelty had not worn off. At the end of most practices he tried a few times, with teammates often throwing him alley-oops. He had yet to dunk in a game and converted less than a third of his attempts overall, so there remained some suspense when he lined up. Getting high enough was not the problem—Demetrius had been able to grab the rim since he was nine. The issue was his hands, which were still too small for him to palm the ball consistently. If he missed, it was usually because the ball came loose before he could slam it home.

After much searching, Demetrius settled on a grip and took a long breath. He held the air in and swished it between his cheeks and, after an exaggerated exhale, he sprang forward. He didn't dribble the ball, as he didn't want to jeopardize his grip; he held it in front of him with both hands. He looked odd, like a running back given a basketball rather than a football, but his first four steps were long and graceful. As he neared the basket, he took two smaller steps and then burst upward. As he swung his right arm down, the ball touched the front of the rim just a bit. He was still able to slam it through, but that graze threw him off balance and he landed awkwardly, on one foot and leaning backward, and he had to swing his arms to avoid falling. It made the dunk all the more impressive; he was like a gymnast who'd landed a difficult dismount.

Most of the Seattle Rotary Select players had stopped to watch him. A few of them slapped hands, as if to congratulate one another for being present when an eleven-year-old dunked. Others covered their mouths or exchanged looks of amazement. In a few minutes their game against the Inland Stars would begin, and they needed to win to advance to the next round of the Nike Invitational, but in that moment they were just giddy fans, awed by Demetrius's gifts like everyone else.

The only Seattle player who didn't stop to admire Demetrius's dunk was the team's point guard, Peyton Siva. It was often easy to identify the featured player on a team because of the special status he was awarded during warm-ups: He led the team as it circled the court and directed teammates on what drills to run at a given time. At about five foot two, Siva did not possess great height, but he wore his confidence. He walked with his chest puffed out, a little strut in his step. As Demetrius lined up for his dunk, Siva tooled around the 3-point line, firing up shots, making more than he missed. His teammates rebounded for him, promptly passing the ball back as if that were their only purpose. When they stopped rebounding to watch Demetrius, he yelled, "Hey!" snapping them back on task.

Siva wore his hair in what Demetrius termed "a Samoan Afro." It was wild and tall, what a different generation of kids might have likened to Buckwheat's hair, and was accentuated by a white headband Siva somehow stretched around his globe of hair nearly a foot in diameter. Before the game, his hair was widely discussed by the Inland Stars. They debated how he long he'd grown it and what product he used to style it. "Oh, but you know he can play," Demetrius counseled. "You don't wear your hair like that unless you can ball."

Siva could indeed ball. He was the best player on what was widely thought of as the top team in the Pacific Northwest. Darryl Hennings, Seattle's coach, was a veteran of the grassroots scene, having ushered several kids on to college. Like Keller, he had put his team together in the past eighteen months and planned to keep it together through high school.

Over the previous months, the Inland Stars had routed an assortment of foes all over Southern California. A common thread in all the games was the disparity in talent. They used their superior height and athletic ability to race to a big early lead, and games seemed over before they began. Seattle Rotary Select was the first challenger that at least looked up to the task. Siva's skill and confidence, combined with the height of his teammates, suggested the possibility of a real battle.

It was a possibility that existed for all of eleven minutes.

Early in the second quarter, with the Inland Stars already ahead

31–8, Siva took the inbounds pass after a Demetrius layup and turned up-court. He took a few steps forward and Keller screamed, "FIRE! FIRE!" and the top two guards in a 2-1-2 press Keller termed "Fist" jumped toward Siva, at which point Keller shouted, "DOUBLE! DOUBLE!" Siva cut to his left but lost his footing and fell down, and the ball bounced away. One of Keller's guards picked it up and slung a pass to Demetrius for yet another uncontested layup. It was Siva's third consecutive turnover, and as the Inland Stars reset in Fist, he stayed on the ground near the 3-point line. He wasn't hurt, but he sat with his head down, wiping his eyes.

Hennings didn't wait for the referee to halt the game before walking onto the court. He squatted down next to Siva and put his hand on his shoulder and whispered to him. It took time, but he talked the young boy to his feet, and Siva walked reluctantly toward the end line to receive the ball and try once again to crack Fist. There were still tears rolling down his cheeks as he turned with the ball to shouts of "FIRE! FIRE!" and then "DOUBLE! DOUBLE!"

"We've never lost like that," Hennings said after the game, a 96–29 drubbing. He was more shocked than angry. "My boys dominate every team where we live. I guess this will have to be a lesson for them on how they need to keep working." He paused, as if deciding whether to say what was really on his mind. "Look, they're studs. That coach has put together some real talent. It really helps when you got that number twenty-three. I've never seen a kid so big and agile at that age." He paused again, looking toward where Demetrius stood with his team-mates. "If that is his real age."

If that is his real age. It was the qualifier that followed much of the praise of Demetrius and the team. People couldn't believe he was that good *and* that young. Parents in the stands, coaches on the sidelines, even kids on the court, constantly questioned whether Demetrius was three or four years older than his stated age, and this led to a consensus that trailed the team wherever they went. Fans of opposing teams thought, Were the Inland Stars talented? Yes. Did they play hard? No doubt. Were they cheaters? Probably.

On the second day of the tournament, parents of the Arizona Wild-cats questioned Demetrius's age from the opening whistle. Then, with the Inland Stars up 83–26 in the fourth quarter, Arizona's coach turned to Kisha, who sat just above the scorer's table, and shouted, "No way I would disgrace my son and put him on that team when he is fifteen years old!"

"He is not fifteen!" Kisha yelled, and she stood up as if she were going to charge him.

"Kisha, stay there!" Keller ordered.

She sat down but chanted the date of Demetrius's birthday over and over.

Later in the day, during a rout of a Portland team, Demetrius tried to dunk in the third quarter with the Inland Stars ahead by 60.

"He's showboating," a woman yelled from the Portland section.

Kisha stood up, turned toward the woman, and yelled, "He's not showboating. But you know what? Now he's gonna really showboat." She turned back to the court. "D, showboat on them. Dunk it on them." She danced and paraphrased a line from the Mystikal song "Shake Ya Ass." "Show them what you're working with, son. Show them what you're working with."

Kisha's anger over those criticisms lingered after games ended, but they affected Keller the most. He took every comment as a personal affront. If Demetrius was too old, his coach was a cheater.

When told what Hennings said, Keller scanned the gym looking for him, as if he wanted to run up and punch him in the face. "He doesn't know what the hell he is talking about. He gets his ass whipped so he says I cheat. If he thinks D's too old, well, that's just stupid."

It was not stupid, however, and Keller's history with Demetrius bore that out. He would become the truest believer in Demetrius's potential, but when he'd first spotted him he thought, as many did, that he was too good to be true.

It was a summer afternoon in 2000, and Demetrius was playing in a rec-league game at the Carl Johnson Center Gymnasium in Rialto. The gym was more of a multipurpose area than a basketball facility; a net was draped down between two courts to keep errant balls from interfering with play. Kisha sat on the metal stands on the wall farthest from the door, watching Demetrius dominate the other nine-year-olds as usual, when a black man in his thirties walked into the gym.

Ladell Hill had coached at the AAU and high school levels and was famously known as the coach who let his wife sit on the bench during games. She even shouted out plays. Behind his back, Keller and other coaches would call him the most whipped coach in Southern California, but he was an agreeable sort and a good judge of talent and had recently agreed to help Keller evaluate kids for his new team. Earlier, Hill and Keller tried out a boy on one of the courts outside the Johnson Center. As Keller talked with the player's father, Hill wandered inside to see if there were any promising prospects in the rec games.

As he entered the center, Hill made a beeline for the bleachers where Kisha sat but stopped midway as he caught site of a player on the court, on a team wearing tattered gray jerseys. The boy was about five foot eight but not thick like some young boys that height. He was long and lean, and there was something in the way he moved, without a hint of clumsiness, that struck Hill as odd. *That boy's gotta be too old for this league,* Hill thought, and he walked farther down the baseline to get a closer look.

Arriving at the metal bleachers, Hill watched as the boy leaped high for a rebound and then, without any hesitation, sprinted upcourt with the ball, weaving around defenders. If this boy was indeed only nine or ten—and Hill had his doubts—never before had Hill seen a kid so young move with such speed.

Keller entered the gym fifteen minutes later, by which point Hill had identified Kisha as the tall player's mother, confirmed that he was indeed only nine, and begun telling her about the team his friend was forming. As Keller approached the bleachers, he guessed the player Hill was eyeing and before sitting down said loudly, "No way that kid is nine."

Kisha was used to people doubting her son's age, but there was something about the way Keller said it, with such conviction, that bothered her.

"Yes, he is nine!" she shouted, and she stood up. From her perch three rows up in the stands, she towered over Keller. "I'm his mother. He's nine. Nine years old."

Kisha had gotten in the habit of carrying her son's birth certificate to games but didn't have it that day. She wanted to thrust it in the man's face, show him where it said her son, Demetrius Walker, Jr., was born on September 6, 1990.

"I'm sorry," Keller said sheepishly, and he looked to Hill for help.

Hill talked Kisha into sitting down and then asked where she lived and where Demetrius went to school, anything to get her mind off Keller's remark. This gave Keller time to size her up. She was tall, just over six feet, with long, muscular arms and an athlete's build. She wouldn't have looked out of place lining up to run the 100 meters in the Olympics. Her face resembled that of the boy on the court. She had well-defined cheekbones and an angular chin. She was young, no more than thirty, and wasn't wearing a wedding ring.

During a break in the game, Demetrius walked over to where his mother sat. His calf muscles weren't clearly defined—that was what Keller noticed first. He took this to mean that Demetrius's exceptional speed and leaping ability were athletic gifts, not by-products of reaching puberty early. Demetrius's potential was not as easy to project as Tyson Chandler's, whose tremendous height was a giveaway, but Keller, like Hill, felt the boy possessed extraordinary athleticism.

While watching Demetrius play the second half, Hill and Keller took turns sweet-talking Kisha. They gushed about Demetrius's ability and talked about the team Keller hoped to build. Kisha was unmoved. Her first impression of the man she would later see as a surrogate father for Demetrius, as the shepherd of his dreams, was that he was trying to con her.

At the end of the game, Keller offered Kisha one of the business cards he'd recently had printed. On the drive home she showed the card to Demetrius, who said instantly, "I want to play for him."

"D, we gotta check him out first. I'm not going to let you play for someone I know nothing about."

The following week she called a woman whose son had played grass-roots basketball years earlier. The woman told Kisha that she had heard of Keller. "I am not sure, but I think he may be the guy who coached Tyson Chandler."

When Kisha informed Keller that Demetrius could play for his team, she added, "I can't take him to practice or pick him up. I can't drive him to games or take him home from games. I've got to work." Given Keller's goals, this was music to his ears. Anything he wanted to do to build a relationship with his precocious star was available to him. After less than two months, Demetrius saw more of Keller each day than of his mother or any of his classmates.

Demetrius was oddly comfortable around adults. Keller called him an "old soul," as if he'd been born that way, but his demeanor was polished by years of feigning maturity out of necessity. It began with the older boys who lived near his grandmother's house in South Central Los Angeles. As a four-year-old hanging around teenagers, kids who cut school and slung drugs, he learned to stay out of the way, keep his mouth shut, and laugh at the right times. It continued when they moved to Fontana. When Demetrius was six, Kisha did what many parents have done in the hopes of a better life for their children: drove away from Los Angeles until she found a neighborhood she could afford. Kisha worked two jobs—at a repossession company during the day and proofing checks for a credit union at night—to afford the single-story house in a middle-class neighborhood. There was no money for babysitters, so from the age of six Demetrius cooked his own dinner, put himself to bed, and got up and off to school on his own. He dreaded coming home to the empty house and would walk from room to room holding a steak knife, turning on every light and stabbing the knife into closets where he thought intruders might hide. "People don't know that you can handle being alone," Kisha told him, and he had no choice but to fulfill her faith in him.

It continued when Demetrius became the first member of the new Inland Stars. He spent day after day with Keller. They went to the gym together, or to dinner, or they just lounged at Keller's apartment playing marathon sessions of NBA Live on his PlayStation. Whether Demetrius realized it or not, thirty-year-old "Coach Joe" became his best friend.

It was a stunted childhood, but then again, that had been something of a family tradition.

Kisha's mother, Mary Ann Houston, was only seventeen when she gave birth to Kisha in 1969, the same year the Crips street gang was founded. Mary Ann attended Fremont High with the gang's founder, and several of Kisha's uncles ultimately joined the Crips. Relatives from another branch of her family were in smaller gangs that coalesced into the Bloods in the early 1970s, becoming the Crips' primary rival. "I had Crips on one side of me, Bloods on the other, and there I was, always walking in the middle waving a white flag, trying to keep the peace even when I was just a little girl," Kisha said. So many of her cousins, aunts, and uncles were arrested for a variety of crimes that she became the only family member from a specific generation without a criminal record.

By the time Kisha enrolled at Crenshaw High as a tenth-grader, she had been supporting herself for years. She worked at May Co., selling women's accessories, and also behind the counter at McDonald's; around Christmas she got a part-time job alongside Mary Ann at the post office. What she remembers most about that time of her life was the hours she spent on crowded city buses shuttling between school, home, and her jobs.

When Kisha was a seventeen-year-old senior, she attended a football game between Locke High and Jefferson High with her cousin, who was a cheerleader at Jefferson. She met a boy who had once been a star running back at the Pop Warner level and who would have played for Locke had he not repeatedly gotten into trouble with the law. He had the same almond-shaped eyes and defined cheekbones as Kisha, and from the neck up they could have passed for brother and sister. But whereas she was long and lean, he was stocky, about five foot ten, with huge biceps and abnormally wide forearms. After the game, he got Kisha's phone number from her cousin, and on their first date he took her to the Shakey's Pizza on La Brea Avenue. He was a year behind Kisha in school but seemed more mature and always had money to pay for dinner or other expenses. He worked occasionally at his father's heating-repair business but not enough to account for the money he carried. Kisha knew what that meant—"No job but always has money: He's dealing"— but she liked him, and he became her first real boyfriend. She called him "D" and, later, "Big D." He called her "Bay," short for "baby."

After graduating from Crenshaw High, Kisha took a job as a fax supervisor at a law firm in downtown Los Angeles and rented an apartment near her mother's. Big D moved in with her; although she knew he committed crimes, she treated it as a temporary lapse in judgment. "I remember he was very polite with his mom, and I was always told that if a guy really loves his mom, he will look out for you," she said.

On New Year's Day, 1990, she and Big D drove a rented car to Las Vegas and were married at the Candlelight Chapel. They drove home the same day. "We thought, well, we are living together and he loved me and I loved him and that it was the right thing to do." A month later, she found out she was pregnant.

On a Wednesday afternoon in the same month Kisha learned she was pregnant, Big D and a friend kidnapped another man and stole his car from an Exxon station in the San Fernando Valley. The man's bullet-riddled body was found later in an alley downtown, and his car had been stripped for parts.

On March 12, Big D was arrested and charged with murder and kidnapping for the purpose of robbery. It was not his first brush with the law; he had proposed to Kisha while in a California Youth Authority prison. This time, he got five years in prison for kidnapping, avoiding the murder charge for which his friend was convicted.

Kisha refused to discuss her husband's crimes; details of his offenses were culled from court and police documents. "There is no reason to talk about all that," she said whenever asked about Big D's past. She took the same stance with Demetrius. He did not know that his father missed his birth because he was in jail awaiting trial and did not know that, after he was released in 1993, he was arrested again a year later for robbery and assault with a deadly weapon, for which he was sentenced to four more years.

Demetrius did remember, however, the final appearance Big D made in their lives. It was 1998, and Big D moved in with them in Fontana after he was released from prison. He took a job at the Ontario Convention Center, doing ballroom setup, and it afforded him lots of free time with his son. Demetrius remembers riding around in Big D's Monte Carlo, staying up late playing video games with him, and admiring the large tattoos on his arms and chest. On his massive right forearm he had *Demetrius Jr.* and across the left side of his chest were the words *I am thankful for my wife Kisha.*

When Demetrius talked about this period of his life, he often inflated the length of time Big D lived with him, saying it was a year or longer. He spoke in a wistful tone, and you could sense some void had been filled when Big D was around.

They were actually together less than six months. On July 13, 1998, Big D was caught stealing several compact discs from the Virgin Megastore in the Ontario Mills mall. Because of his earlier convictions, this small crime was elevated to the charge of petty theft with a prior robbery conviction, which counted as a third offense under California's Three Strikes law. Nine days before Christmas 1999, Big D got the maximum: twenty-five years to life.

Kisha never took Demetrius to visit his father at Pleasant Valley State Prison near Fresno, and she never considered replacing Big D with another man. She invited Demetrius's uncle (Big D's younger brother) to the house and asked other male relatives to spend time with Demetrius. It helped, but the brightness she saw in her son in those few months when Big D was around slowly dimmed, and so her search for a stabilizing paternal figure for Demetrius continued.

Six months later, Joe Keller walked into the Carl Johnson Center and into their lives.

By the third day of the Nike Invitational in Portland, the atmosphere at games was hostile. Opposing coaches and parents criticized Keller and the team before games even began. The coach of the Sacramento Raiders delayed the tip-off of a semifinal because the father of one of the Inland Stars was keeping the official score book. "I'm not saying [the scorekeeper] will cheat, but I don't trust *him*," he said, pointing at Keller.

The Raiders stayed close in the first half because Demetrius got into foul trouble; they trailed only 27–17 at the break. Keller's response was to yo-yo his players in and out of the game. At one point he substituted four players on the court in a span of forty seconds and made twenty-eight substitutions in the first half alone. He made twenty-two more in the second half, the most astounding coming with 6:36 left. One of his guards had missed a long 3-pointer and, as usual, Keller erupted. He ran both hands through his hair and then grabbed a player off the bench by his jersey and shoved him toward the scorer's table. Once in the game, that player promptly threw his first pass out of bounds with the clock reading 6:31. Keller grabbed the player he had just taken out of the game and, before he had even sat down, sent him back to the scorer's table to reenter the game.

He pulled a player after only five seconds.

Demetrius dominated in the second half, and the Inland Stars advanced to the final with a 70–32 victory. Terrance Mitchell, the Raiders' coach, expressed admiration and disgust when asked about Keller and the Inland Stars. "That's the most talent I've seen on one team. We'll get to where they are someday. But we'll do it the fair-and-square route."

Before the finals, Keller strode up to the coach of Seattle Ice Vibe and offered to wager $100 on the outcome. The coach passed. "Okay, pizza, then. Let's bet pizza." Still, no bet.

It was a smart decision. The Inland Stars went up 7–2 without Demetrius scoring a single point. The Ice Vibe guards could deal with Fist, but once across half-court they found it difficult to score because of the Inland Stars' height. There were no open lanes to the basket, and Demetrius gobbled up every miss. Ice Vibe's defense was sound, but they just couldn't score enough to keep up.

As the Inland Stars moved further ahead in the second half, Ice Vibe's coach became more animated. After one of his guards was whistled for a foul, he tore a large silver watch off his wrist and hurled it into the stands. He then walked up the sideline, where the referee signaled the player's number to the scorekeeper, and slammed his palms on the scorer's table. The teenage girl operating the scoreboard jumped back in her seat.

"He smacked the table. You gotta give him a technical," Keller said to the official.

"I'll smack *you*," the Ice Vibe coach said.

"You try and see what happens."

The coach took a step toward Keller, but the official got between them. Demetrius echoed the sentiment of everyone when he loudly said, "Come on, let's just play."

There was a sense of relief when the game finally ended with the Inland Stars ahead, 67–31. The players shook hands after the game, but the coaches did not.

"Typical AAU coaches," one of the referees commented after the game. As for the play of the Inland Stars: "They play with a lot of intensity, but it's a controlled intensity. That coach has got control over every one of those kids. And I'll tell you, that number twenty-three is an amazing athlete."

As the ref spoke, Demetrius stood at midcourt, receiving a trophy as the tournament's most valuable player—having scored 26 points in the final—and Keller was off to the side, talking to a reporter from a local newspaper. "Demetrius is the best player his age in the country," he said. He spelled *Demetrius* for the reporter, then added, "We call him 'Sky Walker.' You should use that: Sky Walker."

3

(BILL FRAKES/*SPORTS ILLUSTRATED*)

Pat Barrett

At a practice not long after the team returned from its victorious trip to Portland, Keller introduced an inbounds play he dubbed "Red Sea." It was designed for when the team inbounded the ball on the baseline of an opponent's end of the court. Three players stood in a line in front of the guard inbounding the ball. After receiving the ball from the official, the guard slapped it with his palm, which was the cue for the three players to sprint either to the left or right. Demetrius was positioned atop the key, and upon hearing the slap he sprinted forward into the space created when his teammates parted to the sides. The guard then lofted the ball toward the rim, and Demetrius was supposed to rise up and dunk it with one hand.

It was essentially an alley-oop off an inbounds, and Keller did not borrow it from a college or pro program or a coaching guidebook. It was a Joe Keller original, and it was easy to see why others didn't employ it. It required Demetrius to complete a difficult dunk when he would likely be defended closely and with the strong possibility that even more defenders would obstruct his path to the hoop. The play also left no one to get back on defense to prevent a fast break if Demetrius missed and the rebound went long. It was a boom-or-bust play, with bust being the most likely outcome.

Keller worked on Red Sea for the entirety of that practice and parts of subsequent workouts. The fathers of a few players were present, some of whom had played high school basketball. Yet the absurdity of Red Sea, its total departure from what would be considered fundamental basketball, escaped them. When the play worked—and it happened only three or four times against ghost defenders—they slapped hands, celebrating along with Keller, who after one make wrapped Demetrius in a bear hug.

After the practice, Keller asked me what I thought of Red Sea, and I told him it was a pointless endeavor.

"You're stupid. People will go crazy when D slams off an inbounds," he said.

It would only work against the weakest of teams, if at all, I said. A well-coached team would surely mark Demetrius too closely and would not be fooled by the three players splitting to the sides and leave the basket unguarded.

"It doesn't matter who he does it against, only that he does it. What matters is that people hear how he pulled off a dunk like that."

This philosophy of Keller's was difficult to grasp. He often prioritized the perception of outsiders over matters a coach should consider more important, such as the development of the boys' fundamentals and their cohesion as teammates. It was as if marketing the boys, particularly Demetrius, was more important than coaching them.

We debated the issue often, most notably after the team's first game of the Nike Invitational in Portland. Their scheduled opponent had canceled at the last minute, so the Inland Stars were pitted against a fill-in local team, West Sylvan, which had no business being in the tournament. None of its players was taller than five foot seven, and all but one were white. They looked like the Orange County kids that Keller's bunch routinely intimidated and routed.

In the game's first eighty seconds, the Inland Stars scored 15 points, all off turnovers created by Fist, and at the end of the first quarter they led 28-0. I expected Keller to back out of Fist in the second quarter and slow the game down, but he kept the press on, and by halftime the score was 57-4. Surely, I thought, he would sit Demetrius and the other starters in the second half and call off the press. But Demetrius and the rest of the first unit trotted out after halftime and immediately lined up in Fist. Keller continued to implore his kids with shouts of "FIRE! FIRE!" and "DOUBLE! DOUBLE!" and the lead grew to 95-4. Keller finally sat Demetrius to start the fourth quarter, but his second unit—boys all more talented than the West Sylvan kids—continued with Fist. When the final buzzer sounded, the scoreboard read: *Inland Stars 116, West Sylvan 13.*

Never before had I seen a team so thoroughly humiliated, and it made me sick. Particularly upsetting was Keller's decision to reinsert Demetrius into the game with two minutes left, after he got word that the loud cheers emanating from the lower court came after the center for a team from Sacramento had dunked. Not to be upstaged, he ordered Demetrius to stand at half-court—a tactic known as cherry-picking—hoping he'd get a breakaway. Mercifully, Demetrius never got the chance to put one final stake in the hearts of the West Sylvan players.

When they left the floor at game's end, many of the West Sylvan kids were on the verge of tears. Coach Paul Walter went to each boy and offered encouraging words, but what could he say? I was reminded of something Amir Kermani, who ran the Orange County Shooting Stars, said about Keller: "Joe sets out not just to beat you but to break your will. If he gets up by fifty, he's still trapping and pressing and wants to beat you by a hundred. He wants a team to leave the game thinking, *If we have to play the Inland Stars again, we've got no chance.* He wants to break you. And he wants to let every other team out there know that if you play him, he's going to break your kids too."

Later that evening, Keller and I sat at the bar of our hotel near the Portland airport, and when asked why he ran up the score against a clearly hapless team, he indignantly slammed down his Corona.

"It's not my job to keep the score close. Don't blame me. Blame their coach."

For the next hour I explained the values of compassion and humility to Keller while he tried to make me realize that none of that applied to the grassroots game. Winning by 30 was not the same as winning by 103, he said. For a coach to rise up, he had to convince people that he had put together a special team, and there was nothing special about a 30-point victory. Though he couldn't articulate it clearly, Keller seemed to be saying that every game was a judgment and an opportunity to show he had elite players. He also made it clear that the feelings of the children, whether they were on the winning side or among the losers, didn't matter. There was no room for moral victories with the stakes so high. The world was too cutthroat for him to be worrying about the feelings of players who weren't "mentally tough." When I started to suggest that no eleven-year-old was truly mentally tough, he cut me off. "Demetrius is."

At one point he turned his chair toward me and said, "Look, this is the big time. I can't be worrying about how a kid feels when Demetrius dunks on him."

My instinct was to vehemently condemn everything Keller had said, yet he made at least one salient point: Before judging his actions, you first had to understand the world in which he operated.

When Keller returned to coaching, he had no illusions of supplanting Pat Barrett as Southern California's AAU kingpin. Other prominent coaches in the area, such as twins David and Dana Pump in the San Fernando Valley and Elvert "Kool-Aid" Perry in Riverside, were also out of reach. Like Barrett, they had shoe-company sponsorship and were so entrenched in their territories that they had de facto control over any talented high-school-age player who emerged from there. "They're big-time and I'm not," Keller said of the discrepancy between him and the others, "and I've got to find a way to become big-time."

In most urban centers, the shoe companies sponsored one or two coaches. In Southern California, the number was higher because of the concentration of talent, with around a dozen or more coaches paid as "consultants" by Nike or Adidas. The ratio of unsponsored coaches to sponsored coaches might be 20:1 in a hotbed like Los Angeles, which produces more Division I talent than any other metropolitan area, or it could be higher. There is simply no way of knowing. The AAU, Basketball Congress International (BCI), Youth Basketball of America (YBOA), and the United States Specialty Sports Association (USSSA) all register teams, but simply adding up their totals does not reveal the number of coaches operating across the country. There are an untold number of coaches who don't try to qualify their team for the national championships and thus never register with any organization.

There may be thousands of coaches, but the difference between the haves and have-nots is stark. On a map highlighting the percentage of the market controlled by the coaches in Southern California, Barrett and the Pumps would be identified by huge black dots blanketing all but a small portion of their regions. So many of the elite kids—those who will one day play for UCLA or Duke or some other top-tier pro-gram—are on their teams that the market share for the unsponsored coaches, even though they greatly outnumber their counterparts, would barely register. On the map, the unaffiliated coaches would be tiny red dots out on the periphery.

Keller was the quintessential red dot, and like all red dots, he dreamed of landing a shoe deal. But the landscape of the grassroots-basketball market worked against him. The power and the money were concentrated with the sponsored coaches, who, while they didn't col-lude, watched one another closely and employed the same tactics to dis-mantle the competition. It was a market dominated by just a few operators, an oligopoly, and Keller was out on what economists call the "competitive fringe." The barriers for entry into the market were almost insurmountable. Nike and Adidas didn't want to add coaches to their stables; they wanted the top kids to be with the coaches they already backed. The better Keller got at finding elite kids, the bigger a target he would become.

Barrett and the Pumps all had different styles, but the model for how they enticed players was largely the same. After identifying a spe-cial prospect, they offered free shoes, free travel to tournaments all over the country, and a chance to team up with the most heralded players. With parents, they talked of the "exposure" their son would need to land a college scholarship and how that exposure could come only from playing for a sponsored coach. They put a question to parents: Do you want to risk your son's future by letting him play for someone else? They rattled off the names of former players who had received college scholarships and sometimes had one of them call to support the coach's candidacy.

To Keller, the notion that a player had to be with a sponsored coach to be seen was absurd. "Would Tyson Chandler still have made the NBA if I'd kept coaching him?" Keller asked. "Of course. He was seven fucking feet tall." He also lamented the dubious marketing Barrett and others used to prop up their importance. For example, Barrett counted Baron Davis, who starred at UCLA and in the NBA with the Golden State Warriors, as an SCA product. But if you asked Davis, he would say his AAU coach was the unaffiliated Thaddeus McGrew. Yet because Davis played for Barrett in a few tournaments, Barrett claimed him. Parents never took the time to confirm these boasts because, as Keller put it, "If you're with Nike or Adidas, parents think you are legit no matter what bullshit you come up with."

This was maddening to Keller. He could recruit harder and coach better, but, in the end, his paradox remained the same: Without a shoe deal, it would be difficult to recruit and keep top players. And without great players, he would never get a shoe deal.

So Keller chose a tactic deeply rooted in the history of grassroots basketball. In 1978, John "Sonny" Vaccaro, who hosted an all-star game in his hometown of Pittsburgh called the Dapper Dan Roundball Classic, had approached Nike founder Phil Knight and proposed to help him break Converse's stranglehold on the basketball-shoe market. Vaccaro convinced Knight that, through his connections with college coaches, he could get the best collegiate players (and subsequently their fans) to wear Nikes. Vaccaro first signed a good friend, Jerry Tarkanian at UNLV, and then Lefty Driesell at Maryland, paying them to put their players in Nikes at a time when Converse was offering only free shoes and the occasional junket to Europe for speaking engagements. Vaccaro is best known for convincing Nike to sign then North Carolina sophomore Michael Jordan to a sponsorship contract in 1984, minting him as the foremost judge of an elite player's marketability, but it wasn't until a year later, at the 1985 Final Four in Lexington, Kentucky, that Nike's move into basketball was complete. Players for all four schools—Villanova, Memphis State, St. John's, and Georgetown—wore Nikes. "It was a seminal moment," Vaccaro said. "We had taken control of the market."

In 1991, Nike fired Vaccaro and a year later he landed at Adidas. He had a smaller budget but the same objective: to establish Adidas as a basketball brand. The best college programs, thanks to his earlier work, were with Nike, so "I had to go younger," Vaccaro said. "The only place I could do battle with Nike was at the youth level." He brokered spon-

sorship deals with top high schools and signed five of the most influential AAU coaches in America. The first was Gary Charles, coach of the
Long Island Panthers, who that summer controlled six-foot-eleven center Zendon Hamilton, considered the best prep player in the nation.

It hardly made a ripple at the time, but Adidas's move into the AAU
game changed basketball. Nike quickly followed Vaccaro's lead, align-
ing with high schools and forming its own stable of grassroots coaches,
which included Pat Barrett. Not long after Joe Keller discovered Tyson
Chandler in 1996, Nike and Adidas sponsored AAU teams in almost
every urban center in America.

Vaccaro's decision to go younger was followed by the drafting of
high schooler Kevin Garnett by the Minnesota Timberwolves with the
fifth pick in the 1995 NBA Draft. Garnett's early success, coupled with
Vaccaro's infusion of capital, fueled the rise of the AAU game. The
search for players who might one day become NBA stars moved from
college down to the prep-school level. The AAU season from April to
August became the most important time of the year for players to
showcase their skills.

Keller's dilemma when he returned to coaching was not unlike Vaccaro's when he arrived at Adidas. He couldn't compete for the older
kids, so he decided to go after the younger ones. In an oligopolistic market, a new operator must find a way to circumvent the barriers to entry.
One example commonly used by economics professors is the aluminum market, which for most of the twentieth century was controlled
by Alcoa. Competitors finally broke through by perfecting the process
of recycling aluminum and by discovering new sources of bauxite. Independent coaches like Keller often tried to build teams around recy-
cled players, kids that sponsored coaches had passed on or cast aside.
But that was hard work. You had to do more coaching and hope for a
late growth spurt or a sudden jump in ability that would push your
players into the upper echelon of prospects. Keller chose instead to find
a new entry point into the market. He theorized that if he cultivated a
strong relationship with kids and their parents long before the more
prominent coaches came after them, their loyalty to him would prevent
them from jumping to another team. Then, if the shoe companies
wanted access to his great players, they would have no choice but to give
him a contract like Barrett's, with the fat salary and all the free gear his
players wanted.

Keller's plan had some obvious flaws (foremost among them, everything banked on trust), but it was a plan nonetheless, and that was more than most coaches had. He first had to decide how young was young enough. How soon did he have to align himself with kids and their parents? He wanted to go only as young as he had to, since it would likely take until their freshman year of high school before his players would surface on the shoe companies' radar. Keller debated this for weeks, repeatedly asking himself the question: How many years would it take for him to build the kind of loyalty that Barrett and all his free shoes couldn't break?

He settled on an answer one night while sitting on the sofa in his apartment with Violet. They were talking about Joey, Keller's nine-year-old son from an earlier relationship, whom he rarely saw. "Maybe you should coach a team he can play on," Violet suggested. "It would be a way for you to spend more time with him." With little evidence to sway him otherwise, Keller agreed. Nine- and ten-year-olds would be the target. Though Keller's aims were grand, his intentions looked, on the surface, uncomplicated: He was merely a father starting a team for his son.

Shortly after he returned to coaching, Keller called Barrett and told him: "I'm getting back into the game. I'm gonna start up a new team."

The two men spoke periodically, but their dealings remained frosty. Keller would not normally discuss his plans with Barrett, but he laid out his vision for a team made up of the best fourth- and fifth-graders in Southern California. He then offered Barrett a proposition: In exchange for shoes and uniforms for his players, Keller would call his team the Southern California All-Stars.

Barrett was still with Nike and he had an abundance of resources. What Keller asked for was a pittance compared to what Barrett gave his older players. In exchange for so little, he got to expand his brand, and if Keller happened upon another player with the upside of Chandler, Barrett must have assumed that Keller would pass him off when he got older. There seemed no downside for Barrett, though that didn't stop him from making Keller work for it. He hemmed and hawed, and in the end, when he offered Keller twenty pairs of shoes and some money for uniforms, he framed it as if he were coming to the rescue of poor little Joe.

More than the shoes and money, what Keller believed he got in the deal was permission to dangle a tempting carrot in front of the kids and parents he recruited. SCA was a Nike-sponsored program, and, as a subsidiary, Keller considered his team to be Nike-sponsored as well. It was a loose application of the transitive theory, but because it aligned with Keller's motives it made perfect sense to him. He continued to call the team the Inland Stars, using SCA only in tournaments he knew Barrett would attend, but he wasn't bashful about throwing around his supposed ties to Nike. He created a flyer that he handed out to parents and posted in gyms, parks, and community centers. It included a giant Nike swoosh and read:

NIKE PRESENTS

SOUTHERN CALIFORNIA ALL-STARS

TRAVELING BASKETBALL TEAM

———

4th & 5th GRADERS

———

- *Sponsored Program*
- *Professional Coaching*
- *Team Discipline*
- *Fundamental Exercises*
- *Private Training*
- *Knowledge of the game*
- *Exposure for college*
- *Plays against top talent in the country*

———

FREE NIKE GEAR

He also paid for an advertisement in the sports section of the San Bernardino *Sun*. It read, in part: *The Southern California All-Stars, a Nike-sponsored traveling team, is looking for boys basketball players 10 and under. . . .*

No one at Nike's headquarters in Beaverton, Oregon, knew the name Joe Keller, but it is doubtful executives there would have protested had they learned of his actions. They had shown little interest in knowing what coaches like Barrett did with the gear and money given to them. "Other than making sure the coaches deliver the best players to our events, we don't care what they do," Vaccaro said. Because coaches were considered consultants, the shoe companies could always distance themselves if one did something unscrupulous that made headlines. "We could just say that the coach was operating on his own."

In such an environment, Keller's embellishments in the newspaper and on his flyers wouldn't even register. And if Nike wasn't going to stop him from calling his team a Nike-sponsored outfit, who would? The business cards he had printed up were white, with the SCA logo in one corner and, in the other, a giant black swoosh.

When Rob Bock, the coordinator of youth sports for the Rancho Cucamonga Parks and Recreation Department, saw Keller's ad in the San Bernardino *Sun,* he thought of the AAU coaches who held practices at the community center gyms around the Inland Empire. They yelled too much; they didn't know basketball; they never seemed to have children of their own. Rob had been so dismayed by what he saw that when his oldest son, Andrew, showed an interest in basketball, he decided to coach him rather than expose him to one of those men.

Rob was a large man with big cheeks. He had a dawdling gait and a sleepy way of speaking that reminded me of Droopy, the cartoon dog who used to appear in episodes of *Tom and Jerry.* He met his wife, Lisa, while they were students at Fontana High, and they married with the blessings of both their families, even though Rob was white and Lisa was black. Andrew looked like neither of his parents. He was light-skinned, with pastel-brown eyes. Even as a young boy he was constantly concerned about his hair, an obsession his parents could never explain. He changed hairstyles regularly, from short curls to a sheared look to a short Afro, chasing the latest trend. Years later, one of his teammates would watch him run the court during warm-ups, note that he had switched his hairstyle, and say, "Andrew's hair is his thing. His hair and that he can shoot."

At the time Rob spotted Keller's ad, Andrew was ten and stood five foot two. He had a reputation as one of the best young shooters in the Inland Empire. When he shot the ball, parents in the stands would shout "Good!" before it reached the basket and teammates would often start back on defense before the ball reached the rim. He played point guard for a rec team that Rob formed and immediately showed a feel for the game that coaches like to say can't be taught. He was also skilled at drawing fouls and getting to the free-throw line, where he rarely missed.

Rob had been a scrappy guard at Fontana High, a tenacious defender with an average outside shot. When Andrew began dominating rec-league games, Rob allowed himself to dream of Andrew starring at his alma mater and then landing a scholarship to UCLA or Arizona. He would catch himself entertaining this fantasy and remember how farfetched it was—only 3 percent of high school basketball players nationally get a scholarship. Yet as Andrew kept draining 3-pointers, Rob began to believe that one of his paternal obligations was to find out how good his son could be. At the time he spotted Keller's newspaper ad, he believed strongly that Andrew could be special if put on the right track.

A week later, Rob and Andrew met Keller at the Rancho Cucamonga Family Sports Center for an individual tryout. What Rob first noticed about Keller was what he held in his hand: a briefcase. *A basketball coach who carries a briefcase?* Rob thought, and in that moment Keller seemed more legitimate than any coach Rob had encountered. Keller asked Andrew to start shooting the ball, and for thirty minutes Andrew made 3-pointers, shooting off the dribble or off a pass. When hot, he could make six or seven in a row, and by Rob's guess Andrew made more than 60 percent of his attempts, an astounding rate for anyone, let alone a ten-year-old.

When the workout was over, while Andrew was off getting water, Keller told Rob: "I really like your son. He looks like he could one day play at the college level." Like any good salesman, Keller told Rob exactly what he wanted to hear at precisely the right moment. Keller talked of college coaches and NBA scouts he knew (a lie). He said his team would travel all over the country to play the best teams (an overstatement). He promised that Andrew would get unlimited free shoes and gear from Nike (an embellishment). Later, Keller added, "Being with a Nike team will help your son get exposure." Rob began to think that placing Andrew on Keller's team was like putting him on a bullet train toward a college scholarship, and Nike was picking up the fare.

The conjured Nike affiliation was a powerful tool, seductive in a way that exceeded even Keller's estimations. Even parents not prone to grand athletic dreams for their children were swayed by it.

Shortly after adding Andrew to the team, Keller met with Rome Draper, Sr., whose son played with Andrew. Tall and thin, Rome, Sr., looked like a black Vincent Price, with a narrow mustache that he trimmed from the top down. His son had the same proud cheekbones, disarming dimples, and thin lips, so it was fitting they shared a name: Romyandana Draper. It's a moniker that should have an interesting origin, should mean something in Cherokee or Swahili, but it was simply a mash of letters conjured up by Rome Sr.'s father, an army private during World War II who was in the South Pacific when Rome, Sr., was born. Rome, Sr., also joined the army and was a truck driver and mechanic at Fort Ord, then he worked truck maintenance for the U.S. Postal Service.

Rome, Jr., adopted his father's style—neatly ironed clothes, a short haircut—and also inherited his warmth, his acceptance of others regardless of whether they failed to meet his exacting standards. As Andrew Bock was known for his hair, Rome was characterized by his compassion. He instantly became a genuine friend to whomever he encountered, and Keller would come to gauge potential recruits on how they acted toward Rome. If a kid couldn't get along with Rome, that was a red flag.

Rome, Sr., did not love basketball as Rob did and never considered sports to be a possible future for his son. He had to be convinced by Rob that Rome was a talented player and that he should harvest his gift. When Rob showed him Keller's flyer, Rome, Sr., was instantly skeptical: "Nike is going to pay my son to play basketball?" Rob assured him that it was legitimate. "But these boys are only nine or ten. What would Nike want to do with my boy?"

A few days later, Rome, Sr., met Keller and stood on the sidelines as Rome went through an audition similar to Andrew's. Rome was not extremely tall for his age, about five foot five, but he had long arms. Rome, Sr., was six foot two, so Keller projected that Rome would be at least that tall. No one part of Rome's game stood out, but he had good hands and could rebound, dribble, and shoot, and Keller knew from Rob that Rome usually deferred to teammates on offense.

Keller gave Rome, Sr., the same pitch he had given Rob. He stressed how he could help Rome get a college scholarship. Rome, Sr., knew nothing about grassroots basketball. He didn't know that Keller knew more about welding than about how to get his son a scholarship. But his skepticism faded as he listened to Keller's pitch. Asked if he was ready to join the team, Rome, Sr., said eagerly, "Oh, yeah, we can do this."

Whereas Keller once struggled to find talented kids, the floodgates opened in the month or two after he first spotted Demetrius. Being able to tout his ties to Nike was a big part of it, but he also began to view kids differently, to see skills he might have undervalued before he had Demetrius. Andrew was the heady point guard who, when defenses collapsed around Demetrius, would make the open 3-point shot. Rome, with his amiable nature and willingness to do the small things, was the perfect complimentary player, and he could help Demetrius with his rebounding from the small forward spot.

After Andrew and Rome, Keller quickly filled out a roster of ten kids. Among the additions was Joseph Burton, a burly center who was part Native American—Keller took to calling him "Indian Joe"—and a quiet shooting guard named Jordan Finn. In his initial phone conversation with John Finn, Jordan's father, Keller mentioned his relationship with Nike so many times that John began counting. At the end of a twenty-minute talk, John tallied fourteen mentions. John worked for a mineral company and sold fertilizer to stores all over the West Coast. He believed that when someone sold something *too* hard, the product often didn't live up to the billing. Yet John not only agreed to let Jordan play for Keller, he eventually moved his family from Orange County to the Inland Empire to be closer for practices and games. Like Rob and Rome, Sr., he was convinced not by the power of Keller's personality or the breadth of his basketball knowledge but by the perception Keller created that the Inland Stars were an elite group with special status.

At the first practice he attended, John Finn marveled at how Keller instructed the boys on a complex offense known as "Flex," which involves a pattern of movements run continuously until a player gets open. Some high school coaches consider it too advanced, but John watched as Keller taught it to nine- and ten-year-olds. He was so awed that it wasn't until years later, when reflecting on his first impressions of Keller, that it dawned on him that never during that first workout did the boys practice ball handling, passing, or any other basic skills. Choosing style over substance was something legendary UCLA coach John Wooden cautioned against in *Practical Modern Basketball,* a book Keller never read but that is considered a bible in the coaching community. "The finest system cannot overcome poor execution of the fundamentals," Wooden wrote. "The coach must be certain that he never permits himself to get 'carried away' by a complicated system to the extent that it 'steals' practice time from the fundamentals." Keller would not disagree, but he would add that Wooden's teachings were less applicable to the grassroots game, where a coach's primary goals were to collect elite players and get people talking about them.

This was one of many areas where Keller's methods diverged from what would be considered normative coaching behavior. He never diagrammed plays, not during time-outs, during halftime, or even in practice. He never used a grease board or scribbled on a chalkboard. He also never recorded games to show them to his team later. Rob and John often taped games to show to Andrew and Jordan individually, and occasionally they tried to show Keller something they had recorded. Most often, he waved them off.

Keller also never used a whistle, a coach's most basic tool. It is an instrument of control, but in the right hands it can be a subtle tool, like a conductor's baton. Keller simply preferred to yell. To stop movement during the drilling of Red Sea, he just shouted "NO!" so loudly that it startled the boys to a halt. He then dragged a player by his jersey to the spot where he should have been and shouted "AGAIN!" to restart the sequence. As the mistakes mounted, so did the number of times Keller shouted "NO!" After the third time he screamed: "NO! NO! NO!" Keller's players probably would have welcomed a whistle, as it produced a gentler sound.

Keller took the boys to the movies and shopping at the Ontario Mills mall, but he did not take them to basketball camps or one-day clinics. Keller was passionate about his team, and his affection for some of the boys ran deep, but he was not drawn to teaching. He did not devour books on basketball, watch instructional videos, attend coaching clinics, or even pick the minds of more seasoned colleagues. Keller bragged that he learned by doing and not by studying, but it would be more accurate to say he didn't like learning at all.

Don't misunderstand: Keller talked a lot about basketball. As he watched the 2002 NCAA Championship game with Demetrius at a restaurant in Ontario, Keller loudly debated the NBA potential of the players. Demetrius, meanwhile, seemed to realize that he and the players on television played the same game. When a Maryland player caught the ball on the right block, Demetrius pieced together his moves as if he'd discovered the answer to a riddle. "Fake high. Spin low. Finish. Good." He turned to Keller and exclaimed, "Coach Joe, that's just like what I do!" Busy pondering the NBA potential of players he would never meet, Keller acted as if he didn't hear him.

Keller once said, "I model my program after Coach K's at Duke." Yet he never read Mike Krzyzewski's *Leading with the Heart: Coach K's Successful Strategies for Basketball, Business, and Life.* In that book, Krzyzewski spends several pages explaining two metaphors. "There are five fundamental qualities that make every team great: communication, trust, collective responsibility, caring, and pride. I like to think of each as a separate finger." Later in the book, he writes, "I look at the members of our team like the five fingers of a hand," and says he strives to make all five players on the floor "fit together into a powerful fist." For Krzyzewski, the fist was a metaphor for sportsmanship, integrity, and teamwork. For Keller, Fist was a defense he used to crush weak teams.

If Keller had a model as he built the Inland Stars, it was the Southern California All-Stars, despite the fact that Barrett was one of the poorer basketball minds among the top grassroots coaches. Barrett sat first chair when SCA played, but he usually had a parent or another person seated near him who ran substitutions and called plays. At a tournament in Las Vegas, Barrett deferred to the father of one of his players in every game. He even checked with him before calling a time-out.

Barrett couldn't school Keller on the technical side of basketball, but from his example Keller took a vital axiom: In the grassroots game, perception mattered most. The mistake in questioning Keller's teaching of Red Sea and criticizing him for running up the score on West Sylvan was thinking that he was only the coach of a basketball team. First and foremost, he was the architect of an image. Red Sea, if the Inland Stars ever pulled it off, would get people talking about Demetrius. Breaking the will of the West Sylvan boys, no matter how undersized and unskilled they might have been, was good for the brand.

4

(ROB BOCK)

The Inland Stars at the 2002 Nationals

arly in the summer of 2002, Keller and Demetrius went to Crabby Bob's, a restaurant near the Ontario Airport. It was part of the trinity of chain restaurants, along with Outback Steakhouse and Benihana, that Keller frequented. They chose a blue faux leather booth just off the bar. Two plastic lobsters, a miniature ship's wheel, and a shiny boat hook sat on a shelf above their booth. Keller ordered oysters to start and then shrimp and steak. Demetrius ordered ribs.

"How did I know you were gonna get ribs?" Keller said.

Demetrius shrugged. " 'Cuz I always do."

"Black people and ribs, I don't get it," Keller said. It was not the first time he'd made this comment, but Demetrius chuckled nonetheless.

"You eat so many ribs, you *are* a rib," Keller said, another well-worn joke.

Demetrius shook his head. "Coach Joe, you're sooo dumb."

Keller cocked his head back and furrowed his brow. His face was stone, and he seemed to be staring through Demetrius when he said, without a hint of sarcasm, "I'm gonna run you so hard tomorrow."

"Ha!" Demetrius shouted, and then he exploded into laughter.

Demetrius had a fantastic laugh. It started with that "Ha!" as if he'd tricked you and then ascended into machine-gun giggles. It was usually accompanied by some physical display. He'd jump up and down or cover his face. If something was truly funny, he'd run out of the room. At Crabby Bob's, he rolled onto his side in the booth and laughed for half a minute, his giggles muted somewhat by the tabletop. It was easy to forget how young Demetrius was, but if you made him laugh, the reward was an endearing reminder.

Demetrius was still recovering from his laughing spell when the waitress arrived with Keller's oysters. She was a sprightly high schooler named Kimberly, who wore her blond hair in a ponytail.

"How old do you think he is?" Keller asked her, and pointed across the table at Demetrius, who suddenly sat up straight and smiled.

Kimberly brought a notepad to her mouth, appearing to give the question serious thought.

"I'd say he's in high school. Maybe a junior."

"Nope. Wrong," Keller shouted, and he clapped his hands.

Keller's excitement bewildered her. "How old is he?"

"I'm eleven," Demetrius announced proudly.

"No way."

"Yep, he's eleven," Keller said. "And look at his feet. Size fourteen."

She went through the motion of glancing under the table. "When you said he wasn't in high school, I thought I offended him, that he was really in college."

Keller clapped again and sent Kimberly off for a Corona. Upon her return, Keller said, "He is the number one basketball player his age in the country."

She seemed impressed. "Well, then dessert is free. If he wants one."

"Oh, I want dessert," Demetrius said. "I want that chocolate cake thing."

As Kimberly left, Keller lowered his voice. "If you were taller, I could get the whole meal for free."

"Ha!" Demetrius shouted, and the giggles started. Soon he was back on his side, laughing like he couldn't stop.

No one could make Demetrius laugh like Coach Joe. At the mall, on the long drives to tournaments, during those NBA Live showdowns, they joked with each other the way brothers do. One evening, Keller disagreed with Demetrius's assessment that the Los Angeles Lakers were better than the Chicago Bulls on NBA Live. He tried to prove him wrong, but Demetrius, playing as the Lakers, beat him, so Keller did what an older brother would do: He wrestled Demetrius into submission on the rug.

Moments like that made their relationship difficult to quantify. They were father-son and coach-player, but they were also like friends or partners working toward a common goal. It was all blurred lines, and at Crabby Bob's the many facets of their relationship were on display.

"How can you eat those things? That's just gross," Demetrius said as he watched Keller pop an oyster in his mouth.

"How do you know? You've never tried one."

"And I never will."

Keller slid an oyster in a half shell onto his bread plate and passed it across the table. "Try it."

"No way."

"D, how do you know you don't like something if you don't try it? You gotta try new things."

Demetrius protested some more but eventually picked up the oyster gingerly, inspected it from all sides, and then closed his eyes and dropped it into his mouth.

He immediately gagged, spit the oyster back into his hand, and hurled it under the table as if it were hot to the touch.

"It's horrible."

He sucked on a slice of lemon he retrieved from Keller's plate.

"Well, now you know for sure that you don't like oysters."

Later, while munching on a rib, Demetrius mentioned a girl at school who had a crush on him. "I don't know about girls. I try to like them and I guess I kinda do, but I don't know."

"What did I tell you? Don't get serious," Keller said. "If I hadn't gotten serious with a girl and gotten her pregnant, I'd be playing professional baseball right now. I'd be playing for the Yankees or some team like that. Girls will fuck things up, D. Stay away from them."

Near the end of the meal, Kimberly brought dessert. ("For the number-one player in the country.") It was a massive slice of chocolate cake topped with vanilla ice cream and crushed Snickers and Oreos and a six-inch mound of whipped cream. It would have been a sufficient meal for three people. As Demetrius, spoon in hand, sized up where to launch his attack, Keller said, "D, that is going to make you sick. Don't eat too much or it will upset your stomach."

Demetrius spooned an oversize piece of the cake into his mouth. Then another and another.

"D, you're gonna get sick."

"No I won't," he mumbled.

"Okay, if you finish that and don't get sick, you don't have to run at practice tomorrow. If you do, you have to run double."

About fifteen minutes later, with two-thirds of the dessert gone, Demetrius hurried out of the booth and ran to the bathroom. He remained there for twenty minutes and then emerged, ashen, with his hand on his stomach.

"You, okay?" Keller asked.

"No."

"Let's go. Get ya home."

"I may need to go again."

They sat there for another twenty minutes, and when Demetrius rushed back to the bathroom, Keller followed a few minutes later to check on him. "We just gotta get you home, D, so you can lie down," he kept saying.

In that hour-long dinner, Keller filled a variety of roles. He was Demetrius's friend, teasing him about his love of ribs. He was his coach, promoting him to Kimberly, building up his profile. He was like an older brother, counseling him on girls. And he was a father, urging him to try new foods and worrying when he got an upset stomach. If asked, Keller would say that the constant was "I am always honest with D," but he was also uncensored. When Keller saw a pretty woman, he told Demetrius, "Man, I love my wife, but if I wasn't married right now . . ." If Keller wanted to cut a player, Demetrius heard about it first. When he was upset with a parent, Demetrius knew why. Whether Keller was a father figure or a friend or a coach was not a conscious choice. He was winging it, and whatever he felt in the moment was what Demetrius got.

It was most accurate to think of them as partners working to close a deal that would mutually benefit both parties. And if there was a moment when that partnership took shape, it was a late-summer afternoon at Truman Middle School in Fontana not long after Keller discovered Demetrius. It was the first day of a week of workouts that Keller called "Hell Week." The team met at the school's track, and Keller timed the players as they ran 100-meter sprints and then 400-meter sprints, making them run again if they didn't finish in under a certain time. When Keller thought they were exhausted, he made them run the stairs that divided the wooden stands.

"That was the warm-up," Keller said, a wry smile on his face, just before he ordered the boys into the gym. "Now practice can start."

For Rome, Andrew, and Jordan, the running was difficult but not extraordinary. They had known demanding coaches before Keller. But Demetrius had never had to work so hard.

Once in the gym, Keller organized some light basketball drills, but it was a mere respite before running the team some more. After less than thirty minutes he shouted, "On the line!" and the ten boys lined up along the baseline. "Do any of you know what a Rambo is?" Keller asked, and ten boys shook their heads. A Rambo was Keller's variation on a common conditioning drill. Players sprint continuously from the baseline to the free-throw line and back, from the baseline to midcourt and back, from the baseline to the far free-throw line and back, and then from the baseline to the opposite end line, finishing in a tired huff against the opposite wall of the gym. Keller's version doubled the running. It was a special kind of torture, and when he finished describing it, a collective moan rang out from the boys.

"How many we gotta do?" one player asked.

"As many as I want," Keller said, and the team moaned again.

Demetrius ran the first Rambo under protest. He was last to cross the line at the end. "Come on, D, there is no reason you should be last!" Keller shouted. After the second Rambo, when Demetrius again brought up the rear, Keller ordered, "You better pick it up, D." After the third Rambo, when Demetrius's last-place finish was probably because of fatigue, Keller had seen enough. "Until Demetrius finishes in the front, we're going to run all day long."

Demetrius was bent over, his hands grasping the front of his shorts. Without straightening himself, he yelled back, "Well, maybe I'll quit, then!"

Keller pointed to the twin doors leading to the parking lot. "Get the hell out of my gym."

Demetrius didn't know how to respond. He stood up straight and let go of his shorts. Keller stared crossly at him, his finger still pointed toward the doors. "Get out of my gym," Keller repeated. "You're a quitter."

Demetrius took a few slow steps forward, still believing Keller would drop his demand. Around the free-throw line, he sped up and veered to the left. He retrieved his backpack from up against a wall and then moved swiftly toward the doors. He slammed into them with his right arm and shoulder, and light from the outside slipped into the gym for a second. Then the doors swung shut and an impassive Keller turned toward the nine boys who remained.

"On the line. We're not done."

Outside, Demetrius stood alone in the parking lot, unsure of what to do. He could call his mom, but there was no guarantee she'd be able to pick him up; he would also have to explain why he'd been kicked out of practice. He leaned against the gray exterior wall of the gym, trying to decide whether to wait for practice to end so Keller could drive him home or to walk the five miles to his house. As Demetrius pondered his options, Keller came out of the gym.

"What are you going to do?" Keller asked.

Demetrius turned his back and quickly wiped his cheeks.

"I don't know," he said, "but I don't want to do all of this."

Keller's tone changed. It was softer, warmer.

"Look, Demetrius, you gotta make a choice. You can be a failure or you can succeed in life. Do you want to be somebody who quits or somebody who succeeds?"

Demetrius fingered the cell phone in his hand, the phone he could have used to call his mom.

"D, I will never lie to you. Believe me. I never will. And I'll tell you this: You can be a great player. You can be great if you want to, but you have to work for it."

He took a step toward Demetrius.

"I want to tell you something, and I mean this. You can make a living playing basketball. I mean that. You can make it to the NBA someday if you work hard enough and stay focused. But you have to decide: Do you want to be somebody who makes the NBA, who can take care of his mom, or do you want to be a lowlife?"

Up to that point, Keller had done much for Demetrius. He picked him up from school and drove him to and from practice, bought him meal after meal. He and Violet helped him with his homework, and Keller argued with principals and teachers who said Demetrius was unruly. When Demetrius scored well on a test, Keller took him to the Ontario Mills mall and bought him the newest Nike Air Jordans. Keller also doled out punishment when Demetrius deserved it. He grounded him for staying out too late and took away his Nintendo when he talked back. Much of what he did was very ordinary, but it was what was absent from Demetrius's life. On nights when Kisha worked, he escorted Demetrius into the house and helped him search the rooms and closets for intruders, and he lobbied Kisha until she brought home a cocker spaniel named Sierra, a dog whose bark signaled to Demetrius that it was safe inside that dark house.

More significant than all of Keller's noble deeds in his first year with Demetrius was what he said to him outside the gym at Truman Middle School. It is doubtful he knew the weight his words would have to a young African American boy, but he had made Demetrius a promise. Before that day, "I was just playing basketball for fun. I didn't know it could affect my life," Demetrius would say later. Now Demetrius had a goal, something to strive for, and, just as important, he had someone offering to guide him. If Demetrius did what he was told, he could make the NBA. That was the promise Keller had made.

After a few moments pondering Keller's words, Demetrius stepped away from the wall and wiped the last tear from his cheek.

"I don't wanna quit," he said.

Keller put his hand on Demetrius's back. "Come on," he said, and together they walked back into the gym.

Going forward, Demetrius followed Keller's orders unconditionally. As they spent day after day together, Demetrius's view of the world changed. He loved his mom, but Coach Joe was his mentor. Coach Joe was in charge.

The affection was mutual. When Joey, Keller's son from his earlier relationship, decided after one season he no longer wanted to sit at the end of the Inland Stars' bench, he was allowed to move back in with his mother full-time. "We just don't have much in common," Keller explained. He next moved Violet and Jordan from their apartment in Riverside to Fontana, just a few miles from Demetrius's home.

To Violet's family, it seemed strange that they would relocate to be closer to a boy on the Inland Stars, but, as Keller explained: "D is like my son."

In the summer of 2002, their partnership reached a critical moment. Keller took the team to the AAU Nationals, the biggest of the tournaments that crowned a national champion in various age groups. Winning the tournament, held that year in Cocoa Beach, Florida, was the stated goal, but Nationals also presented Keller with the chance to market Demetrius on the grandest stage. If his young star outperformed the pack at Nationals, it would help build a consensus that he controlled the country's top sixth-grader.

Teams advance to Nationals by winning qualifiers within their association, which comprises an entire state's worth of teams or, in the case of California, half a state. (California is divided into the Pacific and the Southern Pacific regions.) At Nationals, ninety-two teams are split into pools of four and play three games within their pool. The top two teams from each pool (forty-six total) advance to bracket play, where a single loss eliminates a team from contention for the glass-bowl trophy given to the winner.

The team arrived in Cocoa Beach riding its success in Portland and at a tournament in Arizona in June. Keller's confidence should have been at a peak, but he was a ball of nerves at the team's hotel before the start of pool play. Talking to John Finn about the team's first game, Keller went on about what Demetrius "needed" to do for the Inland Stars to be victorious.

"Joe, do you talk to D like that?" John asked.

Keller didn't answer.

"If you talk to D like that, you are really messing with his head."

Keller stared at John, genuinely puzzled.

"Joe, an eleven-year-old kid is not prepared to deal with something like that. Kids perform better when you teach them how to execute, teach them the little things, show them how doing those things will help them win. My experience is that if you put pressure on them, that makes them play bad more often than good."

"I don't tell D those things, so don't worry," Keller said, but John didn't believe him, and rightly so. Before the team left for Nationals,

Keller had told Demetrius: "If you don't take over, we don't have a chance."

The Inland Stars' performance during pool play helped settle Keller's nerves. They eased to victories over the Severna Park (Maryland) Green Hornets, 57–31, the Yakima (Washington) All-Valley Elite, 78–20, and the Caroline (Virginia) Foxes, 76–32. The script leading to each victory was the same the team had used in Portland. They pressed teams madly with Fist and used their athleticism to intimidate and score easy baskets. On the rare instances when they set up in a half-court offense, they passed the ball inside to Demetrius, who usually jumped higher than his defender and scored easily. When teams double- or triple-teamed Demetrius, Andrew or Jordan made open 3-point shots.

As elimination play began, it was more of the same: 56–33 over the Louisiana Panthers, then 44–26 over Municipal Gardens (Indiana) Gold. Nothing from the first few days of the weeklong tournament discounted the notion that the Inland Stars were the best team in the country, yet Keller grew more and more nervous. At the hotel the night before the quarterfinals, he sidled up to John again and said, "If D doesn't play well tomorrow, we can't win."

It was natural for Keller to be anxious, but John didn't share his opinion, which he felt was symptomatic of a larger problem. With the exception of Demetrius, Keller had little faith in his players. A good coach trusts that if he puts his kids in a position to win, they will execute as he has taught them. In a way, Keller's worrying hinted at his insecurity over his skills as an instructor. But it also led to some hurt feelings among the kids. They had lost only one game all year, yet many of them wondered if Coach Joe really believed in them. Keller created more discontent right before Nationals when he added a new guard, Justin Cobbs, to the roster, just under the deadline for him to be eligible. He was a good player, strong and adept at driving to the basket, and the boys liked him, but they bristled at Keller's claims that he was the "missing piece."

The Inland Stars' quarterfinal opponent, Indianapolis-based Hoosier Hoops, worried Keller on two levels. First, they were talented enough to beat the Inland Stars. But his greater fear was that Demetrius would be outplayed by the Hoops star guard, Rolandan Finch, whom everyone called "Deuce." Throughout the tournament, opposing players and coaches praised Deuce. He was shorter than Demetrius, about five foot seven, but stockier; he had to weigh 165 pounds. His biceps and calves were well defined, hints that his athletic prowess was the result of hitting puberty earlier than other boys. His arms and legs were also on the short side and, depending on the height of his parents, one could conclude he would never be tall enough to be an elite prospect. Had Keller spotted him at some park in the Inland Empire, he might have passed on him because his upside was debatable. But in Cocoa Beach, enough people talked about Deuce that it threatened the perception that Demetrius was the best player in the country.

Hoosier Hoops was not a one-man gang. Kevin Bloom, a five-foot-eight forward, could shoot from the outside and play in the post, and six-foot center Stephan Van Treese might have looked like the slow white kids the Inland Stars routinely dominated, but he wasn't a plodder. He could get off the floor and had range on his jump shot. Hearing Keller talk before the game, it would have been easy to conclude that if Demetrius outplayed Deuce, the Inland Stars would win. But anyone sitting in the stands in the gym during pregame warm-ups could tell that the Hoosier Hoops were as talented as the Inland Stars.

On the opening tip, Demetrius jumped higher than Van Treese and tipped the ball to Andrew, who gave Demetrius a quick return pass, and he sliced through the key for a layup. The Inland Stars quickly set up in Fist, and as the ball was inbounded to Deuce, Andrew and Jordan converged on him.

Unlike Peyton Siva or the countless other guards who were quickly overwhelmed by the Inland Stars' pressure defense, Deuce calmly knifed to his left, around Jordan and Andrew, hitting a gear that surprised them. Demetrius tried to rotate over, but Deuce cut across court and blew past him, resulting in a three-on-two advantage that ended with a layup that tied the score.

A possession later, when it appeared Jordan and Andrew had Deuce pinned to the sideline, he spun out of trouble and snapped a pass cross-court to an open Van Treese for an easy layup. On the Hoops' next possession, Andrew and Jordan approached Deuce with more caution, looking to contain rather than trap him, and he just power-dribbled right through them, drawing a foul on Andrew.

The Inland Stars' formula of flustering the opposition's point guard with Fist wasn't going to work against Deuce. In fact, it was a major liability. Once he broke the press, Deuce didn't allow the Inland Stars to get set on defense. He went to the hoop and either scored, was fouled, or dished to a teammate for an open shot.

On offense, the Inland Stars struggled to get the ball to Demetrius in spots where he could score. Bloom and Van Treese double-teamed him, pushing him farther from the basket and denying him the easy layups he was accustomed to getting. In the past, when teams had doubled Demetrius, Andrew and Jordan made them pay by knocking down 3-pointers. But neither of them was quick enough to create their shot off the dribble against Deuce and the Hoops' other guard.

The only adjustment Keller made was to scream more and more as the game slowly slipped away, acting, as John put it, "Like an emotional dad too worked up about how badly his son was playing to do what needed to be done to help the team win."

In the end, the Inland Stars lost 44–34, although the score was not an adequate indicator of how thoroughly Deuce and the rest of the Hoosier Hoops dominated.

Back at the hotel later, Keller sequestered himself in his room with Demetrius, and they didn't join the parents and kids who gathered in the lobby and later at a restaurant to break down what had happened. That group quickly reached a consensus: Keller had been outcoached. Staying in Fist and refusing to consider offensive options other than Demetrius had cost them the game. Not surprisingly, Keller placed the blame elsewhere. His conclusion was, of course, delivered unedited to Demetrius, his partner.

"I need to get you more help," he said. "The players around you aren't good enough."

5

Gary Franklin instructing the Runnin' Rebels

After the loss to Hoosier Hoops, Keller returned to California and holed up in his apartment, talking to almost no one about the disappointment at Nationals. His living room was like a hermitage. He sat on the sofa watching television and eating McDonald's, pondering the grander meaning of the devastation in Cocoa Beach. After a few weeks, he emerged and entered the team into a few local tournaments. The competition at each was mediocre, but that was the point. Keller needed to see his boys dominate again, to create some distance from the memory of what Deuce and the rest of the Hoosier Hoops had done to his team. He was like a struggling Major League Baseball player who gets sent down to the minors: Against lesser pitching, he rediscovers his confidence and then returns to the big leagues with renewed swagger. It took until the fall, but eventually Keller's assuredness returned. "Joe Keller is back. He's new and improved," he called to announce. The underpinning of insecurity was unmistakable, but on the surface he was more blustery than ever.

The "new and improved" Keller included one obvious modification: more vitriol. He had always preferred an us-against-the-world approach, particularly toward opposing coaches. He searched for anything that he could use to hate his counterparts. He would claim he heard secondhand that a coach had questioned Demetrius's age or had tried to lure away one of his players. He wouldn't use the information to motivate the team, only himself. If he couldn't find an insult to stir his fury, he'd make one up. Once, after hearing a positive comment about another coach, Keller searched for a reply for several moments before settling on: "I heard he beats his wife."

He sorted people into two distinct camps. There were "Friends of Joe," those true believers who never questioned his moves or motives, and "Enemies of Joe," which included just about everyone else. There were plenty of vultures in the grassroots game, and it was neither unwise nor uncommon for an unsponsored coach to view the populace this way. After all, blind trust had cost him Tyson Chandler. But after Nationals, Keller's cynicism spiked and his actions reflected this mood. He hinted at tactics that he said he was reluctant to use before but that were now unavoidable. "I've got to take care of my family," he said.

Prior to Cocoa Beach, Keller had what could be called a professional relationship with Gary Franklin, Sr., the coach of the Los Angeles–based Runnin' Rebels. Composed of mostly inner-city kids, the Runnin' Rebels played Keller's team four times in 2002, and their last two meetings were among the Inland Stars' toughest games that year. They posed the most prominent challenge to the Inland Stars' supremacy in California, yet Keller never spoke ill of Gary, Sr. Maybe he recognized that Gary, Sr., was one of the nicest and most virtuous men on the AAU scene. Perhaps they were so different that Keller didn't know how to attack him. Or maybe being kind to Gary, Sr., served a purpose that had yet to reveal itself. Whatever it was, Gary, Sr., was an abnormality, a threat to Keller's station who hadn't yet been moved under the banner of "Enemy of Joe."

Unlike Keller, Gary, Sr., had a basketball pedigree. He had been a star guard at Dorsey High in the 1990s and then played basketball and football at Los Angeles Valley College. After two years there, he got a scholarship offer to play football at the University of Idaho but turned it down because he learned that his girlfriend was pregnant with a boy. He took a job as a pest-control technician and worked later for Airborne Express but was never truly at peace with how his athletic dreams had gone unrealized.

When his son, also named Gary, was five, the boy's mother "just kind of left." Gary Sr.'s father had abandoned him at about the same age, and he had no model for how to father little Gary. He got a better job doing marketing for a multimedia company and began to play basketball again, dragging Gary along, making sure the young boy saw how good a point guard his father was even as he approached thirty. But by his own admission he wasn't a great father. He drank and stayed out too late and was not a commanding influence in his son's life.

In 2000, one of Gary Sr.'s close friends from Dorsey High became the preacher at Church of the Harvest International in Los Angeles and talked him into attending a service. His friend preached that day of "being in the world but not of this world," a sermon that Gary, Sr., felt had been written and packaged specifically for him. "You need to let the world see your light and your walk," he homilized. "We need to give our young people something to say 'yes' to. Always saying 'no' this and 'no' that to your kids. Give them something to say 'yes' to."

Later, his friend told Gary, Sr., of a gathering at the Los Angeles Convention Center called ManPower. "You should go," he said. "And take your son."

Gary Sr.'s recollection of ManPower and the sermon by T. D. Jakes, a popular author and preacher based in Dallas, was more vivid than his memory of any touchdown he'd ever scored, any winning basket. "He spoke about the man-child, about how the father is like a shadow. As he was saying things about how fathers have to be careful what they love, because their sons will love it, too, I thought about my own father and how he left my mom and me. I would never leave little Gary, but I also knew I could be a better father. I could love him more and set a better example. All around us, fathers and sons were hugging. With some families, there were three generations of men hugging and crying, and little Gary and I hugged too. It wasn't the first time we hugged, but it felt like the first real hug."

The energy born of Gary Sr.'s spiritual awakening was immense. He became the "shadow" Jakes preached about, and it was rare to see him apart from his son. One of their many shared activities came in 2000 when Gary, Sr., took Gary to Rancho Cienega Park in Los Angeles and signed him up for a ten-year-old team in a basketball league. Before the AAU scene exploded, the best kids played on park teams near their homes. The teams at "Rancho" included kids from Crenshaw, Compton, Dorsey, Baldwin Hills, and, finally, Baldwin Village, a square mile of apartments and condos known as the Jungle. Gary, Sr., had played on a Rancho team when he was a boy, and he considered it a mecca for young basketball talent. Though they lived in Inglewood and there were a number of parks closer to their home, Gary, Sr., believed that if his son could star for a Rancho team he could play anywhere. He offered to help with Gary's team and was surprised by how much he enjoyed coaching. The next year he took some of the best kids and started the Runnin' Rebels.

Gary, Sr., was six feet tall, with a dark complexion and a mustache he trimmed thin. He was built like a snowman, with a round face, head, and waist. He and his son shared some physical attributes—dark skin, huge cheeks dotted with dimples—but had contrasting demeanors. Gary, Jr., was talkative and a bit of a jokester. Gary, Sr., was reserved, grumbling out words as if he were reluctant to part with them. Only when he discussed one of his passions—such as basketball or his faith—did he speak clearly. His calm manner stood out in the grassroots world. He didn't yell. He talked about school and God as much as basketball. He spent entire practices preaching the fundamentals. At Rancho, the coach that Gary, Sr., had assisted told the players that only guards should dribble and shoot from the outside and that big men must stay close to the basket. Gary, Sr., watched college and NBA games endlessly and knew the game was changing: Kids had to be multifaceted. At the Runnin' Rebels' first practice, Gary, Sr., announced that everyone would work on their ballhandling and outside shooting and learn to play multiple positions.

Gary Sr.'s most talented player was a skinny forward named Jordan Hamilton, who had immense talent but a bad temper: He would sometimes punch opposing kids in the stomach or arm if they fouled them. Gary, Sr., spent hours trying to change his ways, and for a while it worked, but Hamilton's outbursts resumed and so Gary, Sr., let him leave for another team. A willingness to part with gifted players if they threatened the cohesiveness of his team was yet another trait that separated Gary, Sr., from other grassroots coaches.

The Runnin' Rebels core included Gary, Jr., and Justin Hawkins, a shooting guard from Baldwin Hills, and Terran Carter, a bulky kid who lived in the San Fernando Valley. Justin had a questionable outside shot when he joined the Runnin' Rebels. Terran had bad hands and was reluctant to use his strength against similar-size players. Under Gary Sr.'s guidance, they got better and smarter. Practices in the gym at Manual Arts High School were unique if only because of how Gary, Sr., took the time to explain how each exercise would make the players better. After one session, Justin returned home and told his mother, "Coach Gary just makes us think through everything."

Not long after the team's inception, the Runnin' Rebels played the Inland Stars in a tournament in the San Fernando Valley. Demetrius dominated, and the Inland Stars won by more than 30. Terran was stronger and wider than Demetrius, but he backed away rather than challenge Demetrius's shots. Fist gave Gary and Justin problems, and Keller seemed to send in wave after wave of long and athletic kids. "The boys were intimidated," Gary, Sr., said. "You can't win when you're scared."

The starkest contrast between Keller and Gary, Sr., was in how they assigned blame. After the loss, Gary, Sr., concluded that he hadn't put his players in a position to win. He paid $1,600 and went on a two-week tour with a team through Central America, playing with the team but also mentoring under the coach. He volunteered as an assistant on a Pro-Am team based in Los Angeles and headed by a former college coach. He went to coaching clinics, including one at Long Beach State, and joined the Positive Coaching Alliance, a nonprofit that conducted workshops on positive coaching and goal-setting. Gary, Sr., adopted a philosophy rare among AAU coaches: It is not hard to motivate kids to score, as they will naturally give maximum effort when success is measured in points scored, but truly successful teams make stopping the opposition their foremost objective. He hammered this message home practice after practice, drill after drill. His lessons did not differ greatly from what Keller or another coach would teach, but he was more successful at getting the boys to buy into his plan.

Justin exemplified how effective a player can be when he is totally committed on defense. He cut off passes, always kept his man in front of him, and contested every shot. He was rarely the team's leading scorer, but so many of his teammates' baskets came as a result of balls he stole or tipped that his influence on the game was unmistakable. It was the little things that made him so effective: He always had his hands up, stayed in a low defensive stance, and didn't reach unnecessarily for balls that might put him off balance. He also was wise beyond his years in his knowledge of how physical he could be without drawing the referee's attention. To the uneducated eye, Terran's size or Gary's quickness might have looked like the reason the Runnin' Rebels won most games. But their mastering of the fundamentals and effort on defense were what set them apart.

The Runnin' Rebels met the Inland Stars the second time at a tournament near Dana Point in south Orange County. Keller's bunch won by 8, but to Gary, Sr., it felt like an achievement. Without adding new players, he had cut the Inland Stars' margin of victory from the first game by more than half. As long as he continued to find ways to make his players better, it was only a matter of time before they'd break through.

A few months later, the two teams met again in the Inland Empire. Keller would come to refer to the game as an "unofficial loss," and when he talked about his team's unbeaten record in 2002 he left out that defeat. A tight contest ended when Jordan Finn missed a 3-pointer at the buzzer, giving the Runnin' Rebels a two-point victory. But Demetrius had missed the game while nursing a knee injury, and in Keller's mind that nullified the loss. "This game has got an asterisk on it, or whatever you call it," Keller told Gary, Sr., after the game. "You can't win if Demetrius plays."

In June, just before Nationals in Cocoa Beach, the two teams traveled to a tournament in Arizona. Both squads easily advanced to the finals, which was held at a gym on the Arizona State campus. Before the game, Keller teased Gary, Sr. ("Demetrius is playing this time"), and even taunted some of his players. Gary, Sr., had never felt more confident. Keller's antics, he believed, belied his fear. "Leave everything you've got on the floor," Gary, Sr., told his team before the game. "You do that and I know we will win."

Justin, Terran, and little Gary never played harder or better. Gary broke Fist easily, and Terran battled Demetrius for rebounds and stepped in front of him on drives, forcing two charging calls. Justin harassed Rome and Andrew and Jordan; he guarded each of them at different points in the game. The Inland Stars led by 8 with two minutes left, but a steal by Justin and a turnover forced by Gary led to baskets that cut the lead in half. With seventy seconds left, Terran partially blocked a shot by Rome and collected the ball, and Gary scored on a drive on the other end. With fifty seconds left, the Runnin' Rebels trailed by a single basket and had the momentum. As Andrew brought the ball upcourt, the crowd was on its feet, most of the people urging on the Runnin' Rebels. Their defensive intensity was palpable, and Justin and Gary seized on Andrew as he crossed half-court. Andrew tried to get the ball to Jordan on the left, but Justin's hand was in the passing lane. He tried to go right, but Gary slid over and cut him off. He picked up his dribble and Gary was all over him, swinging his arms wildly to block his view. With no other option, Andrew leaped backward and heaved the ball toward Demetrius on the block. He threw it higher than normal, counting on Demetrius to get to it before anyone else did. Terran had fronted Demetrius on the block, just as Gary, Sr., had taught him, and he was in a better position to catch the pass. But when the two boys went up for the ball, Demetrius negated that advantage by jumping higher than Terran. He reached his arm over Terran's shoulder and tipped the ball over his head, effectively passing it over Terran to himself. Before Terran or anyone else could react, Demetrius collected the ball, landed, then turned and with one step laid the ball in for a score.

There were still twenty seconds left, but the game was over. The Inland Stars made a few free throws that upped their margin of victory to 5, but the game was lost on that single possession. The Runnin' Rebels had played perfect defense, had done everything necessary to get the defensive stop that would have put them in a position for the tying score. But Demetrius's athletic gifts spoiled it all. After the game, Demetrius went up to a few of the Runnin' Rebels and told them, "Nobody plays us as hard as you guys." Justin remained near midcourt, his fingers interlaced and resting on the top of his head. He kept looking at the end of the court where Demetrius had scored the decisive basket, as if he was searching a catalog in his head of all that Gary, Sr., had taught him for what he could have done to change the outcome. But there was nothing. They had played perfectly, and they had lost.

After the earlier defeats to Keller, Gary, Sr., was invigorated. He knew instantly how his team could get better and couldn't wait to get back to practice. Walking out of the gym in Arizona, he didn't know what more he could do. He had been around athletics long enough to know that the deserving team didn't always win, but he also knew that many of his kids and their parents wouldn't accept that reasoning. The parents of his best kids would soon ask themselves (if they weren't asking themselves already) if Gary, Sr., was really the best coach for their sons. When he lost that game, he lost their faith, and for that there would be consequences.

In Arizona, Keller approached Gary, Sr., after a coaches' meeting and told him, "You're never going to beat us, so why don't you join us?" Keller had intimated before that Gary, Sr., should merge the best of the Runnin' Rebels with his team, but this was the most serious overture.

Gary, Sr., ignored him. "He was probably right," Gary, Sr., said later. "But I didn't want to believe that then."

At the end of the summer, Gary, Sr., gave his players a few months off. Gary was playing Pop Warner football, and Gary, Sr., wanted to coach his son. Keller forbade his kids to play other sports, and thus the Inland Stars' season never ended. In September, Rachel Carter, Terran's mother, called Gary, Sr., and asked if Terran could play for Keller while the Runnin' Rebels were off. "I couldn't tell her that Terran couldn't play for Joe when we weren't playing," Gary, Sr., said. A short time later, Gary, Sr., learned that Justin Hawkins was also playing for Keller. Their moves became permanent, although neither Rachel nor Carmen, Justin's mom, called Gary, Sr., to tell him.

"It would have been nice if they called, but I didn't expect them to," Gary, Sr., said. "That's just how it works."

After the loss at Nationals, the boys of the Inland Stars returned to school, most of them now in the sixth grade, and Keller began to remake the team. He replaced everyone except for the four players—Demetrius, Andrew, Rome, and Jordan—he called "my core." From another LA-based team, he lured a smallish point guard, Darius Morris, believing he'd be a good change of pace when Andrew wasn't on the floor. ("I like to think of him as a prized long-term investment," Keller said.) He also brought back Pe'Shon Howard, a stocky guard who had played for the team for a few months but left after his father, Bill Howard, feuded with Keller over Pe'Shon's playing time. Bill was a Hollywood hairdresser and wore large sunglasses at all times, including in the gym while he watched his son play. Keller thought Bill was arrogant, but he believed Pe'Shon was the perfect player to guard Deuce should the Inland Stars meet the Hoosier Hoops again. To get Pe'Shon back, Keller promised Bill: "Next to Demetrius, Pe'Shon will be the lead guy."

Bloom and Van Treese, the Hoosier Hoops' inside players, were on Keller's mind when he courted Terran and again later when he targeted six-foot-one Xavier Whitfield, the center for the Sacramento Raiders, one of the teams the Inland Stars had defeated in Portland. Keller called Terrance Mitchell, the Raiders' coach, and pitched an arrangement that sounded a lot like the one Pat Barrett had offered Keller in 1996 when he was after Tyson Chandler. "Joe said that I should add Xavier and two other good players I had to his team," Mitchell said later. "I shot it to my parents and the kids, and they thought it was a good idea. They knew Joe had a good team."

Keller paid for Mitchell, Xavier, and two other players to fly from Sacramento to Ontario for a workout. Afterward, Keller told Mitchell he was interested only in Xavier. Mitchell was angry, but Keller sweetened the deal by promising shoes and gear for a younger team Mitchell coached. "We even signed this little bullshit contract," recalled Mitchell, who didn't learn until almost a year later that Keller wasn't officially aligned with a shoe company.

Keller's final addition to the team puzzled most parents. At first glance, Tommy Stengel seemed the antithesis of the typical Keller recruit. He was short and white and, though he possessed an outstanding outside shot, was neither quick nor strong nor had a natural feel for the game. He was bullish on the court—football seemed a more natural pursuit—and his parents weren't particularly tall. In Keller's business of projecting athletic ability, Tommy was as likely a candidate for the Inland Stars as the Asian kids he refused to consider. He did, however, have one thing going for him: His father was rich.

After the 2002 Nationals, Keller was broke. Joe Burton left the team, depriving Keller of what he called the "Indian money" (Burton's parents had donated generously to the team), and taking the team to Nationals and other tournaments had cost nearly $40,000. The Inland

Stars needed a benefactor, and Keller had heard from another coach that Tom Stengel, Sr., was generous to the coaches who worked with his son.

Keller reached out to Tom before Nationals, saying he was interested in Tommy and that they should talk when he got back from Cocoa Beach. Shortly after the loss to Hoosier Hoops, Keller called Tom and told him, "We really could have used Tommy at Nationals." He continued to call and repeat the same message: Tommy was what the Inland Stars were missing. After a few weeks of planting that seed, Keller unexpectedly backed off. He told Tom he wasn't sure Tommy was good enough to play with Demetrius and the rest of his kids. It was the perfect ploy to use on an overachiever like Tom. He was a grunt, a guy who outworked you, and his son played basketball the same way. Keller built Tommy up and then out of the blue questioned his ability. Tom started thinking that Tommy *needed* to be on Inland Stars. He would show Keller that his son was good enough.

Tom had red hair, trimmed to a spiky crew cut similar to Keller's. He had pale skin and freckles and legs shaped like bowling pins. His calves were so thick they appeared bigger than his thighs. Tommy was a miniaturized version of his father—the same build, hair, fair skin, and freckles. Tom worked as a laborer for a concrete company out of high school and then started his own company, Team Finish, a few years later. He bid on concrete jobs like parking garages and office parks, then assembled teams of laborers and paid them a rate he negotiated. His was a skill in high demand in the stone jungle of Southern California, and he made millions in a hurry.

Much of that money was spent helping Tommy improve athletically. He had separate trainers for weight lifting and plyometrics (workouts designed to improve muscle ability), and Tom hired a former guard at Cal State Fullerton to work Tommy out one-on-one. Tom also installed a hyperbaric chamber—a capsule that creates an oxygen-rich environment—in Tommy's bedroom, in which he slept after grueling workouts.

A father willing to go to such lengths to make his son a better player wasn't going to back away when Keller suddenly said Tommy might not be good enough.

In the fall, Tom took Tommy to an open tryout for the Inland Stars, held at a gym in Colton. Watching his son struggle against Keller's elite athletes, Tom thought, *No way is he ready for this.* But Keller lauded Tommy's performance and extended an invitation to join the team. Tom went home and discussed it with his wife. She wanted Tommy to stay with the Orange County Shooting Stars and had been warned about Keller by the parents of Chris Cunningham, a center who had left the Inland Stars the previous year. Keller was not trustworthy, they told her. But Tom dreamed of Tommy playing college basketball and thought he needed to stop playing for "pussy Orange County teams." He had to compete with and against black kids, Tom believed. After a few more days of deliberating, Tom took Keller up on his offer.

By the end of 2002, Keller and Tom were close friends, eating every dinner together during away tournaments and after practices. Keller put Tom on the bench as an assistant coach. They spent many nights sitting in the backyard of Tom's home in the hills above Fullerton. Tom had landscaped the yard himself. A bean-shaped pool was surrounded by concrete of various textures and colors, and huge concrete boulders were stacked against a fence. In one corner was a concrete bar with Dos Equis on tap, covered by a cabana with concrete pillars. One evening not long after Tommy joined the team, Keller and Tom sat in the back-yard around a gas fire pit. Tom compared Tommy to Michael Gerrity, a star guard at powerhouse Mater Dei High in Santa Ana, who would go on to earn a scholarship to Pepperdine. Sipping his beer, his feet resting on the edge of the fire pit, Keller listened attentively. He did not project Tommy to be as good as Gerrity. In fact, he doubted Tommy would ever be tall enough to start on a good high school varsity team. But Keller lied through his teeth. "I think Tommy can be as good as Gerrity. That's a good comparison." This pleased Tom immensely, and he would be-come the archetypal "Friend of Joe."

A short time later, Tom agreed to contribute $20,000 to the Inland Stars for the season, with the potential for more. It was a tremendous coup for Keller. In just a few months, he had added size to his front-court (Terran and Xavier), got stronger and tougher in the backcourt (Justin and Pe'Shon), added quickness (Darius), and solved his finan-cial woes.

Indeed, Joe Keller was back.

6

(CARMEN HAWKINS)

Carmen and Justin Hawkins

Keller and Demetrius were at the Rancho Cucamonga Family Sports Center early in 2003 when a young man Demetrius guessed to be about twenty years old entered the gym. Demetrius did not recognize him, but Keller hurried over and they hugged, and he then led the young man to where Demetrius sat lacing his shoes.

"D, this is Keilon," Keller said. "He used to play for Pat. He's going to work out with you."

Demetrius looked at Keilon, more than a little confused. Keilon was a man, with several tattoos on his arms and a chiseled physique. *Why is he going to work out with me?* Demetrius thought. But he didn't say anything. If Coach Joe wanted him to work out with Keilon, there must be a good reason.

Demetrius and Keilon loosened up and ran a bit, but eventually the practice turned into a prolonged game of one-on-one. It was, however, the most lopsided game of one-on-one in history. Keilon was the quickest guard Demetrius had ever seen, with the sweetest handle, and he could drive past Demetrius whenever he wanted. They were about the same height, so when Demetrius had the ball he couldn't just back in and shoot over him. When he tried to dribble past, Keilon either cut him off or robbed him of the ball.

During one possession, Demetrius tried a crossover move, but Keilon easily picked the ball from him. "You can't show the ball like that. Do it like this," Keilon said, and he yo-yoed the ball to the right, then quickly to the left, and then burst past Demetrius for a layup. Later, Demetrius tried to drive, but Keilon slid in front of him, so Demetrius threw up a soft runner in the lane. "You can't get away with that bullshit against good players," Keilon said. "Go strong to the basket. You've got to be fearless."

His comments were not mocking but instructional, and Demetrius soaked them in. He began looking forward to the individual workouts with Keilon, rushing into the gym and quickly lacing up his shoes, eagerly waiting for Keilon to arrive. Over the next month and a half, as they continued to work out together, Demetrius learned bits of information about Keilon's past. He had played on the SCA team that lost to Tyson Chandler and Keller in 1996. He attended Compton Dominguez High with Chandler but was sent to Camp Kilpatrick in Malibu, a state-run juvenile detention school, where he also played basketball, and in 2001 was named the Southern Section Division V co-player of the year.

"It's just part of growing up where I did," Keilon told Demetrius about why he had been sent to Camp Kilpatrick. "Sometimes you've got to do things to protect yourself."

Demetrius did not hear that Keilon escaped from Camp Kilpatrick after an all-star game in May 2001. (He was eventually caught, his sentence at Kilpatrick extended.) Demetrius was also unaware that Keilon was trying to catch on with a junior college team because no Division I schools wanted him, due to poor grades and his criminal past. He did not know that Keilon needed money and had called Keller, who agreed to slip him a few bucks if he worked out his young star.

During one session, another former Barrett player arrived at the gym. He was six foot four and was introduced to Demetrius as "Olujimi." He was several years older than Keilon but they were friends, and Olujimi took a turn instructing Demetrius. "Man, he is just so strong," Demetrius told Keller after the practice.

Keller did not tell Demetrius that Olujimi had verbally committed to UCLA in 1995 as a junior at Santa Ana Valley High but that poor grades and a Pacific 10 Conference investigation into a car he'd received from Barrett soured the Bruins' interest. Demetrius did not hear how Olujimi tried to get back on track at the junior college level but that by 2003 the NBA dreams of a player once likened to Oscar Robertson were all but dead.

Demetrius came to view Keilon and Olujimi as mentors, older brothers, and he was heartbroken when the pair suddenly stopped showing up for workouts. One day they were there, teaching him all their tricks, and the next they were gone, with no explanation from Keller as to why. He wondered if they'd tired of hanging out with a twelve-year-old, if he wasn't a good enough player or wasn't cool enough for them. Eventually they washed from his memory, ghosts from his grassroots past, great players forgotten until someone brought them up one day much later and he said, "Man, Keilon and Olujimi could ball. Whatever happened to them?"

When they plunge into the grassroots world, parents and kids are bombarded with success stories. From Keller, they learn how he found Tyson Chandler. From Barrett, they hear how NBA players like Tayshaun Prince and Josh Childress wouldn't be in the NBA if it weren't for him. Other coaches have their own tales, and the message is the same: Trust me, and your son can also achieve basketball riches.

There are no disclosure rules in grassroots basketball, and thus parents rarely hear about the flameouts. Barrett never talks about Keilon Fortune and Olujimi Mann and the other seemingly surefire stars who flopped under his tutelage. He doesn't mention the directionless lives they led after they failed to reach the heights he'd promised them, how as adults they continued to ask him for money as they had as teenagers, and how he continued to give them handouts because he didn't know another way to help them.

Even if parents were aware of these unhappy endings, it is doubtful they would boycott AAU basketball, because they know how vital it is to their children's chances of landing a college scholarship. When they first look into placing their kids on a team, parents are confronted with a chicken-or-egg question. It begins with an irrefutable fact agreed upon by everyone: that the majority of American players who go on to play in college and the NBA pass through the grassroots system. Proponents of the system say that pitting talented kids against one another forces them to play the game at a higher level, thus developing them into college and pro players. Critics of the system believe that if you abolished grassroots basketball, the same kids would still get scholarships, because they possess the most talent. The argument can be reduced to this question: Do kids become elite by playing AAU basketball, or are they top players already and AAU coaches just latch on to them?

For parents, the debate is meaningless. They have no choice but to put their sons into the grassroots machine. They do, however, have a choice on which coach they choose and how much they trust them. One can't help but wonder if parents would still choose Barrett if they heard the tales of Keilon and Olujimi and other Barrett-led flops like Schea Cotton. Would he remain the most powerful coach in Southern California if, when parents were deciding between him and another coach, they were told the story of Kenny Brunner?

A stocky guard with bulging calves and a bowlegged gait, Brunner preceded Chandler by three years in the SCA pipeline. His quickness and toughness were unmatched by other lead guards in Southern California at that time, and he became one of the nation's top prospects. Just as with Chandler, Barrett lured him from another AAU team when he was thirteen and eventually sent him to Compton Dominguez High. "That Nike contract allowed Pat to do a lot of things other programs couldn't do," Brunner said. "Every kid wants Nikes. When I was thirteen, he gave me a care pack of shoes. That's what we called it, a 'care pack.' It was five pairs of shoes and all the jerseys and the T-shirts you needed to be the prettiest basketball player."

Like Chandler, Brunner had reservations about going to run-down Dominguez High, which is situated in one of the worst areas of Los Angeles. He grew up in Inglewood and wanted to go to Dorsey High with his neighborhood friends. But he was a Nike kid with SCA, and Barrett pushed him to attend a Nike-sponsored high school. From a basketball perspective, Dominguez was good for Brunner. He led the team to state titles in 1996 and 1997 and played in tournaments all over the country. Coupled with his travels with SCA in the spring and summer, he was seen by every major college and landed a scholarship to Georgetown. That should have been reward enough—a full ride to a great school in the Big East Conference—but for Brunner it felt like a step back. When he played for Barrett, he could do whatever he wanted, because the only aim was to keep him happy. Barrett took him on shopping sprees that ended with Brunner owning hundreds of dollars in shoes and clothing. When he needed money for food or to take a girl on a date, he asked Barrett and was never turned away. Barrett bought him a car and gave him gas money; he even paid an insurance deductible when Brunner got into an accident.

At Georgetown, Brunner had trouble adjusting to playing for tuition only and didn't respond to authority. To no one's surprise, he left after a dispute with the coach over playing time. He enrolled at Fresno State but was dismissed after he and another player were famously charged with robbing another student with a samurai sword. Later, he was accused of robbing a junior college coach at gunpoint, though he said he was only demanding money that he was promised. Although he was eventually cleared in both incidents, Brunner never played Division I basketball again.

Certainly all of Brunner's misdeeds can't be blamed on Barrett. But Brunner believes his basketball career was destined for failure the moment Barrett entered his life. "I went for years where I could do whatever I wanted, and then I was supposed to go to college and change? Now I understand why so many kids who played for Pat have left colleges. With Pat, there is no stability, because, if you remember, it started with him taking us off other teams. . . . If you look at every player—you look at me, you look at Olujimi, the best point guard I've ever seen, you look at Schea and Keilon—we were all blue chippers, great, great players. But Pat corrupted our minds. I'm not saying it's all Pat's fault, but I've been a professional since I was thirteen years old."

Coaches like Barrett give and give, and some people will see nothing wrong with that. Shoes, nice clothes, a car—Brunner and many SCA players might never have had such things if not for Barrett's generosity. Barrett also gave them a goal—the NBA—and is it so wrong to give a young life a purpose? Viewed only through a broad lens, the actions of coaches like Barrett can appear reasonable, even altruistic. But from the age of thirteen, Brunner believed unequivocally that he would make the NBA. Barrett, the closest thing he ever had to a father, had told him so. NBA riches became a guarantee, not the reward for sacrifice.

The greatest crime committed by Barrett and coaches like him is that they bleach the drive out of some of America's most gifted players by failing to teach them that the foundation for success is a catalog of failures. These coaches' fates and fortunes are so tightly tied to their players, they never chance them being disappointed or angry or sad, which could prompt a defection to a rival coach. Rather than push their players, rather than make them work to improve, Barrett and his ilk coddle them, and in doing so fail to teach one of the realities of basketball: Those who succeed are usually the hardest workers.

Eventually, players like Brunner or Mann or Cotton or Fortune either fold at the first sign of real adversity or avoid challenges altogether. They never become better players than they were at the moment when Barrett discovered them, and they drift from the basketball scene. Their legacy becomes the woebegone gym talk of AAU coaches comparing failures. "Kenny Brunner was one of the best point guards I ever saw," a coach will say. "Too bad he didn't have his head on straight." It goes unmentioned how his head got twisted in the first place.

In 2000, Brunner was playing for a newly formed American Basketball Association franchise in San Diego, clinging to one of the bottom rungs of minor-league basketball. "Please don't make me look like a misfit," he said when I asked him to talk about Barrett. He was worn down from all the negative press he'd received, which began after he departed Georgetown ("The biggest mistake of my life"). Sitting in a chair on the sideline of the court at the San Diego Sports Arena, he watched as his teammates warmed up before a game. Among them was Lloyd Daniels, once a streetball legend in New York, nicknamed Swee'Pea. Though he spent a few seasons in the NBA, drug abuse and other missteps prevented Daniels from ever reaching his full potential. He was widely viewed as a player who could have been so much more, and Brunner, only twenty years old when we spoke, had a similar aura hovering over him. He was adrift in the basketball netherworld; after the ABA would come the CBA and the NBDL—all the acronyms except the one that Barrett had promised him long ago.

When asked how he might have avoided becoming a victim of the grassroots machine, Brunner gave a simple answer: "Help."

"When Pat found me, my dad was around but not around. Mom—she was not involved in my basketball activities. Grandma was too old. So I did the whole process by myself."

None of the Inland Stars was in Brunner's predicament, but the level of help they received varied. By 2003, Kisha was at best a peripheral figure in Demetrius's basketball life. She stopped attending away tournaments and made fewer locals ones as well. When Keller bragged to other coaches, "I make the decisions about Demetrius," he wasn't exaggerating. The same was true for Terran Carter. Not long after he defected from the Runnin' Rebels, he was spending nights at Keller's apartment or sleeping at Demetrius's house. The two boys became close—Terran the dutiful sidekick to Demetrius's bandleader—because of the volume of time Terran spent in the Inland Empire. Rachel Carter lived more than seventy miles away in Chatsworth and had two other children. Leaving Terran with Keller was easier than spending three hours in the car shuttling him back and forth to practice and games. Soon, Keller spoke of directing Terran's future the same way he did of Demetrius's. "I'm thinking about holding D and Terran back a year in school," Keller told me. "They're young for their class." When I asked what Kisha and Rachel thought of this, he said, "It only matters what I think."

Rob and Rome, Sr., were more involved and knew most of what happened with their sons, but they possessed a naïveté perilous in the grassroots game. This manifested itself most obviously in how they trusted that Keller would always do right by their boys simply because they had been with the team since its inception. After Pe'Shon, Justin, and Darius joined the team, I assumed the men would be concerned that their sons' playing time would be cut. In fact, I didn't see how it *wouldn't* be cut. Yet Rob said, "We've been with Joe since the beginning. He wouldn't treat us like that."

John Finn was more suspicious of Keller and, for a while, was the only father who possessed what most would consider a healthy dose of skepticism. But John was more obsessed than the others with how to best position his son to get a college scholarship, and that was his blind spot. If convinced that something was in the best interest of Jordan's future, he would endure a lot to stay the course. It was John, after all, who so believed in Keller's initial salesmanship that he moved his family from Orange County to the Inland Empire to be closer to the team's base.

While not exactly exposed in the way that Kenny Brunner had been, Demetrius, Terran, Rome, Andrew, and Jordan appeared, at the least, to be in harm's way if the hopes their parents had for Keller turned out to be misplaced. Hope that he would be a good father figure, hope that he would be loyal to the kids he started with, hope that he held the key to a college scholarship—so many futures riding on a man who to that point had accomplished little more than the printing of a flyer full of falsities.

The one player who seemed safely insulated from the dangers of the grassroots machine, who would remain unscathed should Keller turn out to be more harmful than he initially appeared, was Justin Hawkins. The difference between him and the other boys was how his mother, Carmen, handled Keller. Much of what she did was just responsible parenting. She attended every game and practice, always questioned Keller's plans for the team, and monitored who he brought around the boys. But there was shrewdness to her approach. After Justin had been on the team less than six months, I asked Carmen what she thought about playing for Keller. She responded flatly: "Joe is going to use my son to get what he wants, and I'm going use Joe to get what Justin wants."

When Keller recruited Justin to the Inland Stars, he no doubt thought Carmen would be another Kisha, another single mom who'd see him as a respite from the overwhelming grind of life, who would essentially turn her child over to him. To an outsider, Carmen fit the image of the burdened inner-city mother. She had too many kids (two) and too few fathers (zero) around to help her raise them. When she began vigorously pursing a college basketball scholarship for Justin, her oldest, she was easily reducible to a cliché: the African American mom hoping basketball gets her son (and her) out of the ghetto.

But Carmen was no overburdened mother. She was a Georgetown-educated litigator for the Los Angeles City Attorney, an ambitious over-achiever going back to when she was a little girl growing up in Compton, where she drummed up jobs around her neighborhood—cutting lawns, washing cars, running errands for the elderly—to earn extra money. She would accompany her mom to bowling alleys and sell her scorekeeping skills to opposing teams for sixty cents a game. If a player got three strikes in a row, she got a bonus, usually a milk shake or a soda. In high school at Long Beach Poly, she took so many college courses taught by professors from nearby Cal State Long Beach (now

Long Beach State) that she graduated in 1973 with almost enough credits to qualify as a college sophomore. True to her nature, she also played basketball and volleyball, ran track, and was a member of the Black Student Union, the World Friendship Club, the student council, and the Polyettes, one of the school's cheerleading squads. She left Poly with a 3.5 grade point average and a full scholarship to the University of California at Santa Cruz, a considerable achievement considering she worked at the May Co. in Lakewood until 10:00 p.m. almost every day.

UCSC was less than ten years old and, with about 3,000 students, smaller than Poly the year Carmen enrolled. By her count, the school had fewer than 100 black students, but she didn't feel isolated. Santa Cruz was a progressive place—something of a satellite stage for the counterculture revolution based in San Francisco—and she found several mentors, including J. Herman Blake, the dean of her college. "UCSC gave the appearance of being this liberal arts, laid-back, Earth Shoe–wearing kind of environment. But the professors there were East Coast, Ivy League–educated. So even though they were walking around with a beard down to their knees and in sandals, you had to remember that they were smart."

After Santa Cruz, she studied international law at Georgetown and was offered a job at the Justice Department before she graduated. "But then Carter lost and Reagan came in and rescinded the offer." She returned to Los Angeles and did probate and family law for a sole practitioner, but after a few years she tired of hustling for clients and not having health insurance. She took a job as a litigator for the city and bought a flat-roofed house in Baldwin Hills. It overlooked the Jungle, the apartments near Rancho Cienega Park, but had three bedrooms and a pool and, on a clear day, she could see the skyscrapers downtown.

Carmen was thirty-five years old and financially stable when, in 1990, she gave birth to Justin. She dated his father for a year and they were engaged briefly, but they broke up just before Justin was born. He was also a lawyer and tangentially involved with his son early on, but then he moved to Atlanta. Two years later, Carmen had Marcus by a different man. "Being older when I had the boys and being economically independent, I looked at the world differently," she said.

Her style of parenting was much like her approach to school or work: Do the research; stay organized; work harder than everyone else.

When Marcus said he wanted to be an actor, she signed him up for every summer theater workshop that would take him and enrolled him in acting classes in Beverly Hills. He ultimately landed a small part in *Akeelah and the Bee* and appeared in a few commercials. When nine-year-old Justin said he wanted to be the next Magic Johnson, Carmen signed him up for camps and trainers and, once she realized that the best players were on AAU teams, she placed him on Triple Threat.

Carmen moved Justin from Triple Threat to Basketball Mathematics to the Runnin' Rebels to Keller's team. Some coaches and other parents were put off by her directness, but they'd have been wise to listen to her. Like any good lawyer, she did her research before exposing Justin to the grassroots game. Carmen knew that in the year before Justin joined the Inland Stars, AAU basketball was under scrutiny after Myron Piggie, a Nike-funded coach based in Kansas City, Missouri, was sentenced to thirty-seven months in prison for wire fraud and other crimes. His case received widespread media attention because it was revealed during the federal investigation that he had paid Corey Maggette, Kareem Rush, and Korleone Young (all future NBA players) to play for his grassroots team. He also had earlier been indicted for dealing crack cocaine, which Nike officials claimed to have had no knowledge of when they gave him a lucrative sponsorship deal. Carmen was also aware that the development of basketball players in the country had become a charged issue. In September 2002, the United States placed sixth at the FIBA World Championships, its worst finish in a major international event. A few months earlier, a record seventeen foreigners, including the number-1 overall pick, were selected in the NBA draft. Those developments prompted discussion about the health of basketball in this country, with some of the sport's power brokers claiming it was in decline. If you believed the naysayers, the sport was on the brink of ruin, an American institution like General Motors or Ford that might soon be pushed into irrelevance by overseas competitors.

NBA commissioner David Stern laid some of the blame on the grassroots game. There was a systematic problem with how we developed young basketball players, he said. Unsavory individuals concerned only with making money preyed on kids and failed to teach them fundamental basketball. As a result, the players who would come to wear the red, white, and blue were less prepared than their predecessors to meet challengers from abroad, and many talented kids never made it to the NBA or were so corrupted when they got there that they never reached their full potential. "There is something totally wrong with the developmental system for young players," Stern said. "There is something out of whack that these world-class athletes get exploited or exposed all the way up." Stern cited street runners, summer teams, summer camps, and the apparel companies as the exploiters. "It's a whole industry and everyone knows who the kids are. They're out there doing things for them, giving them things. . . . They ultimately get to us, but by that time . . . they are developed in their ways."

It was hard to believe that the root of all American-hoops evil was a coach like Joe Keller, that a former welder and car-alarm installer living in a tired apartment complex in the Inland Empire was what ailed basketball, but Carmen took note. At the very least, she understood that landing a spot on a team like the Inland Stars or SCA didn't guarantee success. She might not have known the story of Kenny Brunner, but she understood the factors that led to his downfall. "Parents assume these coaches will do right by them," she said. "They should assume the opposite."

Carmen had long, wild black hair that she usually hid beneath a baseball cap. She often wore sweatshirts or T-shirts with the team's logo on them. She talked loudly, was rarely without a Bluetooth headset in one ear, and always seemed to be carrying on three conversations at once. She'd be arranging an audition for Marcus while talking to a trainer about working out with Justin while conferencing with a colleague. She drove Justin from Baldwin Hills to Rancho Cucamonga every day after school, forty-five miles that she covered without complaint, and she often stayed long after practice, tagging along as Keller went to dinner with another parent or insisting she be allowed to sit in on a coaches' meetings. "How else am I going to know what Joe is up to?" she said. "He is not going to tell me."

Carmen had been something of a den mother with the Runnin' Rebels, and she tried to assume the same role on the Inland Stars. She devised a comprehensive academic-support program, which included collecting academic progress reports from the players each semester and creating reference binders for them containing relevant information, such as the NCAA's requirements for being eligible to compete as a freshman in college. She would review class schedules and advise parents if their son missed an opportunity to take a core requirement early. If a player was struggling in a class, she would help him find a tutor.

It required little effort from Keller, and he green-lighted the arrangement. "Carmen is going to be an academic adviser to the program," he said. But when it came time to actually implement her ideas, Keller failed to get progress reports for Terran and Demetrius and didn't push them to comply. He would brag about his new academic-support program to kids and parents he courted but then brush Carmen off when she asked for his help. Eventually she let the program die, although she continued to make annual binders for Justin, which lined a shelf in his bedroom.

Carmen organized tours and informational lectures in the cities the team visited. Before away tournaments, she researched what colleges were nearby so the boys could visit them. You never knew if one day they might be up for a scholarship to one of those schools, she figured. She also told Keller about museums and landmarks worth visiting. "I would tell him about the former slave plantation the boys should see and he would say how great that sounded, but then we'd get there and he'd take the team go-cart racing instead." She dragged Justin to the colleges and the museums anyway. "I knew what was best for my son, and it wasn't playing video games in a hotel room all day."

Keller initially tolerated Carmen, then he just ignored her. She wondered if Keller hated women and was surprised to hear that, like many of the players he would go on to coach, Keller was raised by a hard-working single mom. Diane Keller was twenty and still living with her mother in East Islip, New York, when, in 1970, she gave birth to Joseph Albert Keller. Keller never met his father. He knew his last name, Pellegrino, like the sparkling water, and that he was Italian. Diane told her son that he looked and acted nothing like his father, as if that side of Keller's DNA had been dormant.

One story Keller enjoyed telling about his mother occurred when he was in the eighth grade. "I had this baseball coach—he was a hell of a coach, but, man, he would rip into you. One game, I did something—I don't know what it was, but it was probably my fault—and he grabbed me by my jersey and just started cussing me out. I mean, this guy could yell. My mom was over by the snack bar. She was buying some snacks or something, and she saw him and just went crazy. She grabbed this ice chest and carried it over to the field where the coach was and she threw it at him. She threw it onto the field. It was crazy, but I loved it."

Before Keller's senior year, Diane followed her older brother to Riverside and got a job at General Dynamics, the defense-industry contractor. Keller continued to live with her even after he graduated from high school, and she regularly attended family events, including the birth of his first son, Joey. She eventually retired and moved to Victorville, a desert town between the Inland Empire and Las Vegas, and Keller saw her less, but they talked on the phone regularly. "I owe her everything," he would say. "No one could love their mom more than I love mine."

Given the environment in which he was raised, one would think that Keller would have a fondness for strong-willed single moms. If his favorite story was about the time his mom threw an ice chest at his coach, it was reasonable to believe he could appreciate Carmen's dedication. But when he said, "The perfect team is a team of all single moms," he meant moms like Kisha. Carmen was a thorn in his side, always around, always asking questions, always making sure the grass-roots machine didn't devour her son.

Justin, like all newcomers, experienced an initial rush upon joining the Inland Stars. Routing opponents, winning tournaments, bringing home trophies, that was part of it, but there was also the gear. Each player received what Brunner would have called a care pack: two sets of uniforms and warm-ups, two pairs of shoes (one white and one black), and several T-shirts. The uniforms were better quality than what they'd worn on previous teams, and Justin liked how Keller bought everything extra large, knowing the boys liked baggy shorts and long jerseys.

The schedule of tournaments the team would attend included events in Portland, Arizona, Baltimore, Las Vegas, and Nationals, which in 2003 would be held in Newport News, Virginia. Most 12-and-Under teams didn't have the funding to make two of those trips.

Joining the Inland Stars felt like stepping under the bright lights. "It's like going from the [Milwaukee] Bucks to the Lakers," Justin said. Larger crowds attended their games, more people knew their names, and Keller claimed they were being watched at all times by scouting services, college coaches, and even sports agents. Justin went from simply playing basketball on the Runnin' Rebels to feeling as if he were playing for his future every time he stepped on the floor.

At a tournament in 2003, the team entered the gym at Chandler (Arizona) High School during halftime of the preceding game. The two teams on the floor were in the middle of halftime warm-ups, and fans stood talking at the base of the bleachers or lined up at a table where a young girl sold snacks. As Demetrius led the team into the gym and up the first set of stands, almost everyone turned to watch. Players on the floor stopped shooting until the Inland Stars were seated, and parents pointed at Demetrius or Xavier, who was the tallest boy at the tournament.

During the tournament's second day, Billy Donovan, coach of the University of Florida, watched the Inland Stars play before his son's team, the New York Gauchos, took the floor. Later he told Keller how impressed he was with his squad.

"I'll take three of your kids right now," Donovan said, half joking. He pointed to Demetrius, Xavier, and Rome.

Keller called Demetrius over.

"What schools do you like?" Donovan asked him.

"Florida, Coach, of course." He was smiling; he knew to be diplomatic.

Donovan laughed. "You aren't just saying that, are you?"

"Of course not, Coach. Florida is *one* of my favorites."

"Good to hear," Donovan said, and he shook Demetrius's hand.

Justin saw Keller and Demetrius hobnobbing with Donovan, and it made him feel, to borrow one of Keller's favorite phrases, "big-time." Just as Coach Joe had said, important people were watching.

Teaming with Demetrius was better than Justin had imagined. Defenses keyed on Demetrius, which led to open jump shots and clear lines to the basket. Demetrius was also egoless and unselfish, focused as much on making the perfect pass as the picturesque shot. But what Justin and the other new players liked most was how they felt around Demetrius. He was so much better than everyone else that he had to be destined for college or the NBA. Teamed with him, they felt unique. Teamed with him, they felt closer to their dreams.

Against the San Diego Golden Stars on the final day of the tournament, Demetrius broke out after a turnover by a San Diego guard and caught the ball around midcourt, with no one between him and the basket. He ran at the hoop from straightaway and then rose up and dunked the ball one-handed. It was the first time he had dunked in a game, and when he landed he didn't immediately run back on defense. He stood under the basket, a little stunned that he had pulled it off.

Keller quickly called a time-out and ran onto the floor, along with most of the Inland Stars. They crowded around Demetrius, slapping his back and hands. Keller kept rubbing the top of Demetrius's head.

"How did that feel?" Keller shouted as the mob moved toward the sideline.

Demetrius was confused. "It feels just like any of the other butt-whippings, Coach."

"No, D, the dunk. How did it feel to dunk in a game?"

"Ooohhhhh. I gotta say, it feels pretty good. I actually thought it would feel even better. Still, it feels pretty good."

The San Diego players huddled at their end of the court. Their coach lectured them, but they weren't paying attention. Among them were a few players Keller had scouted and passed on, and they glanced longingly at the joyous display down the sideline. Given the choice, they would have traded places with Justin or Terran or Xavier or any of the Inland Stars. Given the choice, they'd have preferred to be associated with greatness over a 60-point loss every time. Like most children, they saw only the glory. It was up to the parents to see what lurked behind it.

(ROB BOCK)

Joe Keller yells at Rome Draper while Rome Draper, Sr.,
and Tom Stengel, Sr., look on.

L ess than twenty-four hours before the biggest game of the season, before the hyperbole and hope were exposed as either fact
or folly, Keller sat in a booth at an Outback Steakhouse on the
outskirts of Baltimore, doing what he always did before monumental
games: explaining how his team would probably lose.

Keller was not bound by tradition or routine or superstition. Many
of his actions seemed improvised, which could be maddening to those
affiliated with the team. He scheduled or canceled practice at the last
minute or pulled the team from or entered it in tournaments with only
a few days' notice. "I like to keep people on their toes," he said, as if even
his procrastination and disorganization were planned. The one custom

Keller followed with some consistency was to grow nervous and contemplative before a big game and to be less guarded about his fears and hopes. You learned the most about Keller by talking to him before an important game. Mostly, he worried how a loss would derail his dreams.

"We're going to get killed tomorrow. It won't even be close," he said in Baltimore. "We played worse today than I've ever seen. Demetrius, I don't know what the hell is wrong with him. He played like shit today. So did everyone else." Keller bent forward until his forehead rested on the knotty wood table. "I'm not ordering a steak. I'm going to order a noose so I can hang myself."

At first, predicting doom came across as Keller's way of managing expectations. If the team won, if he was proven wrong, the significance of the triumph would make whether or not he predicted it a minor quibble. But if they lost, well, he knew it all along, so it lessened the blow. Also, to be wrong was to appear weak, and Keller couldn't afford to come across as unknowing—not even on his team's chances of winning—when his advancement relied so heavily on perception. By the time of the team's trip to Baltimore in March 2003, his behavior was clearly less about his ego or managing expectations than it was about control—or, rather, his loss of it the moment the boys took the floor. So much of his life was spent building the team, tuning it, but when it came time for his work to be judged, for the boys to come through on a big stage, he had very little say in the matter. The way Keller worked a game—calling every offensive set, setting the defense, always putting new players on the floor—was suited more for football, where a coach's influence factors in almost every play. Basketball, according to Phil Jackson, the Chicago Bulls' and Los Angeles Lakers' coach, is more like jazz, because of its improvisational nature. "If someone drops a note, someone else must step into the vacuum and drive the beat that sustains the team," he said. That someone could not be the coach, and that caused Keller great stress.

Every time the boys took the court, Keller's future was in play, and the prospect of a setback—even if it was remote—exposed a vulnerability that he'd otherwise buried. This did not happen prior to games against the Runnin' Rebels or another team he knew a lot about, as even he couldn't sell himself on the idea of a loss. But if he knew little about an opponent or, worse, if the opponent had talent, he became almost paralyzed by fear. He couldn't sleep. He drank more. He treated the boys even more irrationally. "He gets himself all worked up," Tom said. "But most of the time he doesn't know what he's getting worked up about."

In Baltimore, the source of Keller's anxiety was clearly defined. The following evening, in the semifinals of a tournament called Bang With the Big Boys, the Inland Stars would face Team Maryland. After Hoosier Hoops had defeated the Inland Stars at the 12-and-Under Nationals, they lost to Team Maryland in the finals, leaving no doubt who was the best team in the country. Before the team left for Baltimore, I'd asked Keller to name the five best sixth-graders in the nation, and he answered without a second of thought: "Deuce, Chad, Leshon, Pe'Shon, and D." Deuce was, of course, Rolandan Finch of Hoosier Hoops. Chad Wilson was Team Maryland's lead guard, and Leshon Edwards played for another Baltimore team. Keller's evaluation of Wilson before the tournament was: "He's strong, but I don't know how good he is going to end up being. I'd take Pe'Shon over him, because I think Pe'Shon is going to be taller." At Outback, when Keller was deciding between a noose and a T-bone, Wilson became "the best guard we've ever played against, better than Deuce." Keller knew next to nothing about what offense Team Maryland ran or what defense the Inland Stars would face. Still, he assertively denounced his team's chances for a victory. "We won't win, and we might lose by fifty."

Contributing to Keller's worries was the Inland Stars' performance in the first game of the tournament. They had defeated the Mitchellville (Maryland) Trail Blazers, a group of white kids with a distinct size disadvantage, by only three points. There was a simple explanation for the poor showing: jet lag. The boys had not arrived at their hotel until after 10:00 p.m. EST on Thursday night, and because of the time change some weren't able to fall asleep until after midnight. To make a 9:00 a.m. tip-off Friday morning, they woke at 7:00 a.m. (which felt like 4:00 a.m.). During warm-ups, they looked like sleepwalkers. "Poor Rome," his mother, Sharon, said just before tip-off. "I don't think he even knows what day it is." Their performance in an afternoon game seemed to confirm this theory. After a round of naps back at the hotel, they shredded Florida Gulf Coast 53–28. Justin and Pe'Shon limited Kenny Boynton, Florida's star guard, to only 4 points, and Demetrius scored 14 in the first half when the Inland Stars pulled away. That should have calmed Keller's nerves, but at a team meeting back at the hotel on Friday evening, he focused only on the first game. "We fly across the country for the biggest tournament of the year, and you guys come out and play like shit," he said. He stood next to a kitchenette in his hotel room, looking back toward the door and the boys, who were strewn on the floor and still in their warm-ups. Tom and Rome, Sr., stood to Keller's left, nodding at his criticisms. "Why the hell did we fly out here, then? So you could embarrass yourselves?"

Team meetings always dragged on too long. A "short" meeting was thirty minutes. Most lasted at least an hour. Keller's speeches were rambling, repetitious outbursts, followed by more of the same from his assistant coaches. A sampling of Keller's remarks during the meeting in Baltimore, which lasted forty-two minutes: "If you don't take this shit seriously, you are going nowhere in life. . . . Terran, you have become D's little sidekick, and you need to make sure he is in line and D needs to make sure you are in line. That's what being teammates is all about. . . . If I or Coach Rome or Coach Tom say something and I catch you looking the other way or rolling your eyes, I will sit you the whole damn game. I don't care who it is. . . . Don't be staying up all night playing NBA Live. I want everyone in bed by eleven p.m. . . . When I was a young guy, I got mixed up with the wrong girl and had a kid and got into trouble. That's the shit you guys have to avoid. . . . Who here doesn't have money for food? Terran? How the hell do you not have money? I gave you forty dollars yesterday. . . . Rome, I love you. You bust your ass and never complain. As long as I am a coach, you are welcome on my team. . . . Shit, it stinks in here. Who took their shoes off? Justin, put your damn shoes back on!"

Tom spoke after Keller. In a soft voice, he asked the boys to stay focused and play "their game," boilerplate stuff. He then turned to Demetrius, who was seated below the window next to the door, and without naming him said loudly, "Tomorrow I don't want to see or hear any of you complaining to the officials. The more you talk to them, the less fouls they are going to call for us. Keep your mouth shut and play." He took a step farther into the middle of the room, puffed out his chest, and leaned over Demetrius. "You know, real men don't complain. Grow some hair on your balls and be men. If you are not going to start acting like men, you might as well get a slit down there."

Keller cussed at the boys every day, but this was more graphic. The players looked at one another, wondering how to react. Justin pulled the front of his sweatshirt over his face to cover his smile. Little Rome looked up at his father, who was as startled by Tom's words as any of the boys were. Tom was dead serious, but the boys were holding back laughter. Finally, Rome, Sr., said, "Tom, come on, man," and the boys erupted. Demetrius screamed, "Ha!" and rolled onto his side and Terran piled on top of him. Keller even smiled. But once the laughter subsided, he quickly put the team back on point.

"Listen, if you don't take this shit seriously, you are going to get killed tomorrow," Keller said. "I mean that. They will run you out of the gym."

K eller needed to know.

In the six months leading up to Bang With the Big Boys, the Inland Stars had defeated every team they faced, all but a few by whopping margins. They won events all over Southern California and cruised to the title of the Nike Invitational in Portland once again. Pe'Shon appeared to be the strong guard the Inland Stars needed. With Terran and Xavier added to Demetrius, the team had three players five foot ten or taller, when most teams were lucky to have one. In Keller's opinion, there was not a more talented team in the nation, and Demetrius was the best sixth-grader in the country. Still, doubt lingered in the back of his mind. He had believed his team was unbeatable before the 2002 Nationals, and Hoosier Hoops embarrassed him. He had thought Demetrius would dominate the Hoops' big men, but the opposite occurred. Was there a weakness he didn't see? Was there a flaw that could be exploited that would once again leave him and the boys short of their goal? He could wait until July and the 2003 Nationals in Newport News, Virginia, to find out, but patience was not his strength. He needed know if he was making progress toward his dream.

John Finn needed to know too.

If Bang With the Big Boys was Keller's moment of reckoning, for John it offered the chance to answer an important question: Was Keller doing more harm than good? In the months leading up to the tournament, John and Keller had feuded regularly. Since Justin and Pe'Shon joined the team, Jordan's playing time had been reduced, and that was the foundation for their disputes. On several occasions before the team left for Baltimore, John raised the issue with Keller in contentious talks that ended with each man taking a hard line: John believed Keller was being unfair to his son by favoring the new kids. Keller believed John was inflating his son's ability. He also said John pushed Jordan too hard, to the point that Keller predicted, "One day, Jordan is going to quit basketball just to get back at his dad."

Certainly, Keller favored new players, and he should have rewarded Jordan, Rome, and Andrew for their loyalty. Without question, John was the team's most demanding father. He came across as the consummate Little League dad living vicariously through his son, and his history bore that out. Growing up in Ohio, he had been a good enough offensive lineman to earn a football scholarship to Northwestern, but his first love was basketball, and he regretted not chasing a college career in that sport.

In an episode that illustrated John's obsession with his son's basketball development, John watched as Jordan played several uneventful minutes to start one of the earlier games in Maryland. When Jordan walked off the floor and sat on the bench, John said from across the court, "Jordan, drink some water." When his son didn't immediately find a water bottle, John raised his voice. "JORDAN, drink some water." At six foot four, John was an imposing man. He had a thick mat of dark hair and a goatee that made him look the villain in an action film. But his most intimidating feature was his voice. It was as if he had a megaphone built into his throat. Even a simple instruction to drink some water could come across as a booming directive from above.

John continued to demand that his son drink water, and Jordan continued to sit there unmoved. John assumed Jordan must not have access to water; it couldn't be that he was disobeying his command. John sent his youngest son, Tanner, to the bench with a bottle. Jordan took it from him but then set it on the floor under his seat without taking a sip. John spun around, looking at the other parents in disbelief. At this point, every person in the gym wondered: *Will Jordan take a drink?* Rare is it when a twelve-year-old takes such a public stand against his father. And, anyway, their contest of wills was far more interesting than the game. John paced back and forth along the far sideline of the court. If he suddenly charged the team's bench and forced water down Jordan's throat, no one would have been surprised. Instead, he took a few steps toward the bench and found a decibel level unavailable to most humans.

"JORDAN, YOU NEED TO DRINK SOME WATER!"

There was a period of silence that lasted maybe five seconds, but it felt longer. An entire gymful of people awaited Jordan's move. Rome, who sat three seats down the bench, leaned forward and looked at Jordan, and that triggered something. Without taking his eyes off the game, Jordan reached down and leisurely picked up the plastic bottle from beneath his chair. He held it in his lap for another several seconds and then put it to his mouth and drank barely enough water to fill a keyhole. John returned to where the other parents were seated and, in an exasperated tone, stated, "I don't want him getting dehydrated." All the parents nodded; a few even sipped from their water bottles just to be safe.

Clearly, John was fanatical, but his obsession meant he was constantly scrutinizing Keller's actions and their effect on Jordan. If Keller yelled at Jordan for missing a shot or chastised him for a turnover, Jordan often became less assertive, slipping into the background of the game. A great player's belief in his abilities never wavers. John knew this from his time playing college football. Demetrius and Pe'Shon—they had that attitude. No matter what Keller said or an opposing fan yelled, their mind-set remained the same: *I'm going to score.* Jordan had that instinct once, John believed, but it dulled as he spent more time around Keller.

Driving to the gym on Saturday, John raised several questions—but not because he wanted answers. Putting his thoughts out in the open was not easy for him. He was jittery and unnerved, and he shifted in his seat as if he couldn't get comfortable. "Do you think Joe is a good coach?" he asked me. "Do you think Joe cares about the kids the way a coach should?" He talked about the coaches he had growing up. Some of them were bastards, but he didn't question their understanding of the game, whether it was football or basketball. "You know, when we first joined the team, I thought Joe was a pretty good coach. He didn't focus on the fundamentals enough, I see that now, but he worked hard on making the boys better. But I think he has regressed. He's never gotten better than the first day we joined the team."

As the team's cavalcade of rented minivans pulled into the rotunda of The Boys' Latin School of Maryland, and the players hurried down a tree-lined path to the gym, John lagged behind, walking slowly with his hands stuffed deep into the pockets of his sweat suit. "I'll catch up in a minute," he said. He walked over to a perch overlooking a football field, a brooding look in his eyes, questions swirling in his head.

Moments before the start of the game against Team Maryland, Demetrius called his teammates to the free-throw line on the Inland Stars' end of the court. He put his arms out wide, as if he were showing off his wingspan, and Rome slid under his left arm and put his right arm around Demetrius's shoulder. The other boys followed suit, wrapping their arms around one another until they formed a tight circle. As a group, they leaned forward and the circle tightened, like a flower closing its petals. They began swaying back and forth and Demetrius started a chant, a simple "Oh . . . Oh . . . Oh." With each word the volume increased, as did the speed of the chant. Nothing during Keller's short pregame speech hinted that the game was different from others, but this was something they had never done before. Chad Wilson and the rest of the starting five for Team Maryland stood near midcourt, waiting for the game to begin, but like everyone else they were stunned into silence by this tight group dressed in black, chanting and swaying. Later, Demetrius would admit to improvising it on the spot, but the only hint of this came at the end. The chanting went on so long, it became apparent that the boys didn't know how to finish. The referee finally came over and tapped Demetrius on the back. When he looked up, the rest of the boys dropped their arms and the chanting stopped. Demetrius clapped his hands twice, walked to the center of the court, and stuck his hand out to Aristide Murdock, Team Maryland's center. It wasn't a cordial greeting; they were like two fighters touching gloves.

Demetrius wiped the bottom of both shoes and looked around at his teammates. Terran was to his right, Rome to his left. Andrew was behind him, and Pe'Shon stood behind Andrew, near the Inland Stars' free-throw line. Demetrius nodded at Pe'Shon. If he won the tip, he was going to send it all the way back to him. Murdock was as tall as Demetrius, and it was preposterous to think Demetrius would jump so much higher than Murdock that he would be able to get his whole hand on the ball and send it ten feet backward to Pe'Shon. Yet when the referee tossed the ball skyward, he did exactly that. Pe'Shon quickly pressed the ball upcourt and pulled up for a 14-foot jump shot that he knocked down for the game's first basket. Keller thrust a fist in the air, and for a brief moment it appeared as if the Inland Stars were going to win with ease.

But the defending national champions were well coached, and on offense they patiently swung the ball around the perimeter as Murdock and another forward, Javorn Farrell, fought Demetrius and Terran for position inside. Farrell was tireless, and when he got the ball he unleashed a series of post moves rarely mastered by a player so young, spinning and drop-stepping his way to a layup. Wilson scored on a drive and made a free throw, then another guard, Kendall Marshall, drove past Andrew to put Team Maryland ahead 7–2. Team Maryland's half-court trap prevented the Inland Stars from getting easy baskets, and they never got into a flow. Keller spent most of the opening quarter frantically searching for a solution, and, as usual, he resorted to aimless substituting. He pulled Andrew and put in Justin. He pulled Rome and put in Jordan. When Jordan missed a layup, he yanked him (after a mere forty seconds on the court) and inserted Darius.

After Team Maryland's initial flurry of baskets, the first quarter settled into a sloppy rhythm. It was ugly basketball, with missed shots and turnovers galore, but it was more a testament to how evenly matched the teams were than poor execution. They battled to a draw on almost every possession.

Just before halftime, Demetrius caught the ball on the right block and backed in against Murdock. He leaned into him with his left shoulder and, when he felt Murdock was overplaying that side, he spun right and flipped in a shot over his right hand. He repeated the move a possession later, and Murdock was completely fooled. He simply backed away in frustration as Demetrius gave the Inland Stars the lead, 14–12, going into halftime.

Keller led the team toward an anteroom that separated the gym from a hallway and blasted open the steel door with his right arm and held it open. "Get the fuck in there and sit down!" he shouted. One by one the players walked past him, their eyes downcast as Keller scowled at them. Volleyball nets and poles were stacked on one side of the tiny room, and the boys tripped over them as they tried to find open space. A few leaned against the wall and others sat on the nets. They left an opening in the middle of the room, into which Keller stepped.

"Jesus Christ! What the hell is happening?" he yelled. "You're letting these guys beat you to the ball! You're letting them beat you on the glass! What the hell is wrong with you guys? Jesus Christ!"

Keller paced in the small space, taking two steps forward, turning, then taking two steps back, as if he were caged. His gray golf shirt was dotted with sweat, and he was breathing heavier than any of the boys.

"This is the biggest game of the year. This is it. Team Maryland. Team fucking Maryland, and you come out and play like that. Jesus Christ!"

Demetrius squatted down, leaned back against the concrete wall, and closed his eyes. He didn't need to see Keller. He was not diagramming plays on a grease board. There was no talk of strategy. The entirety of Keller's message during the five-minute speech was: Stop fucking up. Demetrius and the others had heard it before. As Keller finished, Demetrius opened his eyes and stood up and put his hand on his coach's shoulder. "Coach, we got this. We got this."

The measure of a great player often comes after halftime, when the opposing coach has adjusted his defense. Team Maryland's coach had decided during the break that he would no longer let Demetrius go one-on-one versus Murdock. On the Inland Stars' first offensive possession, Murdock was still guarding Demetrius, but another Team Maryland player cheated off Rome or Justin or Terran—whoever was the closest—whenever Pe'Shon looked to get Demetrius the ball. The plan was for two players to deny Demetrius the ball and, if he did get it, to double-team him. The Team Maryland coaches didn't know that Demetrius was also the Inland Stars' best passer and more than willing to play facilitator for his teammates. He immediately recognized what Team Maryland was doing, and he moved two steps farther from the basket, creating more space between him and the defender rotating over to double him and more room for whichever of his teammates was left open. In a 9–2 run to start the second half, Demetrius didn't score a single point, but he figured in every score. He twice dropped the ball to Terran for easy layups, and when Justin's defender came at Demetrius, he snapped a crosscourt pass that found Justin open for a 3-pointer. Finally, he set a screen for Pe'Shon that opened a lane toward the basket.

As the fourth quarter started, the Inland Stars led 25–20. On the sidelines, Keller looked as if he'd been in a fight. His gray shirt was now completely soaked and untucked in the front, as he kept using it to wipe sweat off his face. With about four minutes left, after a Demetrius

8-footer extended the Inland Stars' lead to 7, a Team Maryland guard hit a 3-pointer from the left side. It was an incredible shot. Andrew had a hand in his face, and the guard was drifting slightly to the left when he released the ball. On the ensuing possession, Demetrius missed a shot inside. Team Maryland raced down and a smallish guard hit a driving layup before the Inland Stars could get set on defense. The insurmountable 7-point lead was down to 2, with just over three minutes remaining.

Pe'Shon was fouled on the next possession and converted one of two free throws to get the lead back to 3, but then Team Maryland scored to pull within 1 with 1:28 left. After a time-out, the Inland Stars inbounded the ball. Pe'Shon broke the trapping defense and settled the team into its offense. He dribbled high on the right side, killing time but with an eye on Demetrius down low. Demetrius was trying to free himself from Murdock, but when he managed to seal him off to receive the pass, another Team Maryland player slid over and got in front of him, forming a defensive sandwich that even Demetrius couldn't overcome. Pe'Shon reacted to this the way any good point guard would. He faked as if he were going to get the ball in to Demetrius and, when the second defender committed, he threw a skip pass across the court to Rome.

Standing at the 3-point line on the left side, Rome caught the ball and had as open a look at the basket as any player had all game. He could have held the ball and let more time run off the clock, but that went against everything he'd been taught over the last two years. In Keller's offense, if you were presented with an opportunity that good, you took the shot. Rome rose up and released a beautiful, high-arcing shot. Had it gone in, Keller would have been talking about Rome the hero for months, but it missed badly, gracing only the front of the rim and falling to Farrell. He quickly sent an outlet pass to Wilson, who caught it at midcourt and raced past Pe'Shon for a layup.

Keller should have called a time-out and settled his team. There were twenty seconds left and the Inland Stars trailed by only a single point, 29–28. There was plenty of time for a final shot. But he was so distressed over Rome's miss and Farrell's go-ahead layup that he turned away from the court. He didn't see Andrew throw an errant inbounds pass to Pe'Shon, which slipped off his fingers and went out of bounds.

Keller spun around at the sound of the whistle. "DAMMMMITT!"

he screamed, and he thrust his hands to the side of his head, pulling at his hair.

Team Maryland's coach called time-out, and the Inland Stars walked with their heads down to the sideline. Rome was last to reach the bench, and Keller jumped in front of him before he could sit down. "Jesus Christ, Rome! Where is your head? Where is your head? Damn, Rome. What the hell were you thinking?" Rome stood in front of him, head bowed, and didn't say a word. Keller's rant ended only when the referee's whistle called the teams back onto the court. As Rome turned, Keller pushed him in the back.

The game was over; that was what Keller thought. Why else would he spend an entire time-out berating poor Rome? But Pe'Shon saw it differently. He knew Team Maryland would look to get the ball to Wilson, and he believed they would try a tactic they had used all game. Wilson was so strong that, if he stood next to Pe'Shon and used his body to shield him off, he made it almost impossible for Pe'Shon to get in front of a well-thrown pass. In effect, he boxed Pe'Shon out of a space and then the ball was passed into that space, where only Wilson could get it. As Murdock took the ball from the referee, he immediately looked toward Wilson, who had his butt against Pe'Shon, blocking him from the space back toward Team Maryland's goal. If Murdock threw the ball high enough and far enough into that space, only Wilson could get it. But as Murdock tossed the ball, Pe'Shon used his right hand to grab Wilson's jersey. He chose that hand because it was opposite from where the referee stood. When Wilson jumped toward the ball, he barely got off the ground, thanks to Pe'Shon's hold. Pe'Shon then pushed off Wilson and jumped, managing to tip the ball back to the middle of the court, where he quickly snared it and called a time-out.

The plan Keller devised during the time-out was for Pe'Shon to get the ball to Demetrius on the right side; it was the one play that had worked consistently all night. After Rome inbounded the ball, Pe'Shon dribbled to the right of the top of the key and looked toward Demetrius. Two Team Maryland players defended Demetrius; one stood in front of him, and Murdock was on his back. A third player inched closer, ready to triple-team him if necessary. Demetrius tried to get Pe'Shon to just toss the ball in the air and let him go up and get it, but Pe'Shon wisely aborted the plan and drove to his left. He bumped into Wilson and managed to get a step on him, but as he reached the free-throw line, Rome's defender moved into the lane and cut off his path. There were ten seconds left, and Pe'Shon had only one option: He drew Rome's defender farther inside and then bounced a pass back out to the wing, where Rome stood unguarded.

Under normal circumstances, Rome would have been as good a choice as any to take the final shot. He could take a step or two toward the basket and launch an open 16-foot jumper. "Rome's game is all mid-range," Demetrius often said. "He loves those mid-range jumpers." But Rome's earlier miss and Keller's tirade left him in a fragile state. When he caught the ball, he dribbled in two steps but didn't immediately go up for the shot. He was afraid of failing again, of drawing Keller's ire. By the time he realized that he *had* to shoot, his defender had recovered and rushed at him. He got a piece of Rome's shot, causing it to fall far short of the goal, but in a stroke of luck it fell to Terran, who was near the low block on the left side. Two defenders swarmed, including Murdock, who left Demetrius, and Terran was unable to even turn toward the hoop. Keller screamed at him to shoot as the clock ticked from :06 to :04, but how could he shoot if he couldn't turn around? He finally jumped and spun in midair, heaving the ball toward the basket. At first it looked like a desperation shot, but he sent the ball so far over the goal and threw it so high, it was clear that he was putting it where he hoped only Demetrius could get it. Demetrius rose up and met the ball with the fingertips of his right hand. He corralled the pass, and when he came down, he was alone at his favorite spot on the right block. Murdock rushed back across the key, so Demetrius jumped toward the baseline, to the side of the rim, and flipped the ball over his head, a kind of half hook shot that assured that Murdock couldn't block it. As the final buzzer sounded, the ball touched the backboard softly just to the right of the square, caught the front of the rim, and fell through the net.

The Inland Stars on the court and on the sideline and several of the parents jumped in the air. Keller stomped up and down the sideline, his arms flailing and legs kicking upward in what looked like a modified Russian dance. He knocked several boys back into the bench; one blow sent Andrew flying onto the court behind him. The first to reach Demetrius was Pe'Shon, and then Terran and then Justin. Demetrius was quickly at the bottom of a large pile of gleeful eleven- and twelve-year-olds. In a corner where the parents stood, Sharon and Lisa hugged so hard that Lisa almost fell off her chair. Rob went to shake Rome Sr.'s hand, but Rome, Sr., hugged him instead. As those parents celebrated, others fumed. John was across the court, that same searching look on his face, and Darius's father scowled. Jordan and Darius had not played in the second half.

Little Rome did not pile on Demetrius with the others. He stood alone for a few moments on the spot where his shot had been deflected, on the same side of the court where earlier in the game he had missed the 3-pointer. As the celebration began to die down, he walked toward Keller, who was shaking hands with the Team Maryland coaches. At first, Keller didn't notice Rome, but when he turned, Rome surprised him by leaning forward and resting his forehead against Keller's chest. He stayed there for several moments, sobbing into Keller's sweat-soaked shirt.

"We did it. We're the number one team in the country. We did it," Keller told the team when they gathered in the anteroom later. "And you know what? We are probably going to have to play them again tomorrow. And this time, we're going to beat them by twenty."

The restaurant on the outskirts of Baltimore was warm and inviting. A tan carpet embroidered with a large white orchid covered the floor near the entrance. Nearby, a small stone fountain plugged into the wall gave off the soothing sound of a mountain stream. On the tables closest to the door, white cloth napkins sat upright, folded to resemble swans. Hugging the north and east walls were elaborate hand-painted screens, one of a young Japanese girl picking flowers, another of a woman holding a nursing baby. Into this peacefulness walked Keller, only a few hours removed from his big victory. He walked past a young Japanese girl holding menus and snared one of the tall stools at the sushi bar. "What kind of beer do you have?" he said, even before Tom found a stool. A diminutive sushi chef looked up from the narrow counter he had just wiped clean, perhaps believing his work was done for the night. It was almost 11:00 p.m., and few people frequented a sushi place tucked into a strip mall at that hour.

"We don't serve alcohol," the chef said, and he braced for Keller's response.

"What?" Keller said too loudly. "What kind of restaurant doesn't serve alcohol? How you gonna have a restaurant and not serve alcohol?" He pounded his open hand on the bamboo mat in front of him. After asking the chef to repeat himself several times, Keller pushed himself up on his stool and peered over a glass case filled with cuts of seafood. "Who owns this place?" Keller said. "Get me the owner."

A Japanese man even shorter than the chef appeared moments later. He wore tiny round eyeglasses and a clip-on tie. He walked out from behind the bar and stood behind and slightly to the left of Keller's chair.

"Sir, you have a question?"

Keller glanced over his shoulder, paused, and then shot Tom a smile.

"Yes, I have a question. Do you know who Joe Keller is?"

The owner's face went blank as Keller roared.

"So, you don't know who Joe Keller is? What about Demetrius Walker? Do you know who Demetrius Walker is?"

More laughs, more blank stares from the owner.

"Demetrius Walker? No? Well, you will."

Keller got up from his chair and put his arm around the owner, who now realized he was the butt of a joke. "I do have a question," Keller said. "And I hope you know the answer to this one. Where around here can we get some alcohol?"

A relieved smile spread across the owner's face. He gave directions to a liquor store less than a mile away, and fifteen minutes later Keller had a beer in his hand. It was a night of celebration, so Keller didn't hold just any beer. While Tom held a normal-size bottle, Keller drank from a forty-ounce Corona.

"Can you believe Pe'Shon? What a play," Keller said, once a feast of sushi was before them. He loved California rolls and had two platters full. "That was a big-time play. NBA players don't make that kind of play."

They replayed other moments from the game: Demetrius's last shot, his spinning layup to end the first half, Justin's 3-pointer early in the second. The only pause during a half hour of replay came when the sushi chef, comfortable that Keller was done ordering, turned on a small television to his right, near the bamboo curtain from where the owner had appeared. He settled on CNN, which was reporting that Elizabeth Smart, kidnapped nine months earlier from her home in Utah, had been found.

"They found that Smart girl? Incredible," Tom said.

"Who?" Keller asked.

"Elizabeth Smart. The girl who got kidnapped in Utah. Do you know who that is?"

"All I know is basketball."

Keller talked about meeting with John and Darius's father after the game and how they complained about their sons' lack of playing time. "We just win our biggest game ever and they are complaining," Keller said. "Unbelievable." He then raised his forty-ounce beer, as if to toast his critics.

The conversation turned to the next day's game. Team Maryland and Severna Park would play in the finals of the losers' bracket, and the winner would meet Inland Stars in the championship game. Team Maryland would certainly win, setting up a rematch. When Tom mentioned this, Keller waved him off. "We're not playing tomorrow." He said he would use the excuse of an early flight to get out of playing the finals. Tom didn't understand. Hadn't Keller told the boys in the anteroom that they would defeat Team Maryland by 20 next time? "Why would we play them again?" Keller said. "What is there to gain? If we beat them again, well, we already beat them once. If we lose, then people will say that our first win was a fluke. See, there is nothing to gain."

Tom was still as confused. "I don't know if that is sending the right message to the boys," he said.

Keller shook his head. "Too much to lose if we play them again." Then he popped the last California roll in his mouth. "Let's get out of here."

Keller had every intention of following through with his plan, but at some point between leaving the restaurant and having to tell tournament organizers he was skipping the final, he came upon a grand idea. He would play the final, but with a team that didn't include Demetrius and several other players. He would claim he wanted to get his second-stringers some experience, but his real motivation was twofold. If he lost, he could say it was because he didn't play some of his best kids. It also gave him a chance to spite the parents who had been complaining about their sons' playing time. "I'm going to teach them all a lesson," he said. "They are going to see just how good their kids are without D and the others."

Keller informed Demetrius of his decision as the team loaded into cars at the hotel. "I don't understand. Why don't we just go out and beat them?" Demetrius asked. Justin, Terran, Andrew, and Pe'Shon echoed his comments.

"D, you gotta trust me," Keller said. "I'm doing what is best for you."

The gym at The Boys' Latin School had been reconfigured from three courts to one. Wooden bleachers were pulled out from the walls, and people quickly filled them, anticipating a repeat of the exciting semifinal from a day earlier. In the small anteroom where Keller had said a day earlier that the Inland Stars would defeat Team Maryland by 20, he again gathered the team. There was no emotional send-off; he just named the starters, which included Jordan and Darius.

Team Maryland's coach sent out the same starting lineup as the day before. As those boys took the floor, the coach kept looking over at the Inland Stars' bench, at Demetrius, Pe'Shon, and the rest, waiting for them to enter the game. Keller had told Team Maryland's coaching staff before the tip-off that he would be playing only his backups, but no one believed him. For most of the first half, they expected Keller to insert Demetrius and the others at any moment. Keller made almost no substitutions and barely spoke to the boys during time-outs. He spent most of the first half whispering and laughing with Tom. With only a few minutes left before halftime, Team Maryland's coach realized Keller was not bluffing and pulled Murdock and Wilson and his other starters. At the time, Team Maryland led 20–10; at halftime it was 24–15.

At the intermission, as the boys filed into the anteroom, Keller remained outside for several minutes, perhaps searching for the right words to say. Grassroots coaches wield amazing power over their players. Much of their influence comes with the words they deliver during the pinnacles and pits kids encounter when they dedicate themselves to a sport. What does a coach say after a great victory? That's an easy one. What does a coach say when his team is beaten? That's harder. Harder still: What does a coach say when he wished for the beating? When he orchestrated it? That was Keller's dilemma, though he didn't spend much time searching for the precise words. He might as well have told Jordan and Darius: *This is what your fathers get for questioning me.* When he stepped into the middle of the room, Keller slowly looked at each of the boys who had played in the first half. Xavier's hands were on his knees, his big head jutting into the middle of the team circle. Even after five minutes of halftime, he still struggled with every breath. Darius held his skinny arms at his waist and nervously grabbed at the front of his untucked jersey. Jordan was on one knee with his head facing down. Those boys had struggled against Murdock and Wilson and the rest of Team Maryland's starters, yet they had outscored the second team 5–4. It was a silver lining Keller could have focused on. Instead, his speech began, "What the hell is wrong with you?" and he went on and on and on.

As they took the floor to start the second half, the boys looked beaten, with one exception: Jordan. He bounded over to the referee holding the ball. John, standing across the court, urged his son on: "Jordan, be aggressive! Don't let up!" On the opening possession, Jordan made a 3-pointer from the left side. A few possessions later, he got the ball on the left wing and drove to the basket, flipping in a layup while getting fouled. When he made the free throw, it seemed to be a turning point. Not in the game—Team Maryland was scoring at will inside against a tired Xavier and led 33–23—but for Jordan. Against Team Maryland's zone defense, he repeatedly got the ball on the wing and slashed toward the basket and drew fouls.

By the fourth quarter, Jordan was exhausted, but he kept competing, the only Inland Stars kid who did. On the final play of the game, he dribbled atop the arc, looking for a seam to the basket. For the Team Maryland players, the game had long been over. They settled into a tight zone, essentially telling Jordan that if he wanted to shoot a long shot he could. He moved back and forth, looking for a teammate to cut to the basket or pop into some open space, but they had decided it wasn't worth the trouble. Out of options, Jordan dribbled to the top of the arc and, with his feet just inside the 3-point line, he used his last bit of energy to heave a final shot as the buzzer sounded. In one sense, there was not a more meaningless shot attempted all tournament. What was the difference between a 14- or a 16-point loss? But, given all that weighed on John's mind, it might have been the most important moment of the tournament. As Jordan's heave fell through the net, John clapped vigorously and shouted, "Way to go, Jordan! Way to keep fighting!"

Keller had challenged Jordan, and he had passed the test. Yet no one congratulated him after the game. His teammates didn't pile on him when his final shot hit home or applaud him for being the one player on his team to shine in a game rigged against him. His coach didn't put his arm around him and say he'd never been prouder of a player, as Keller did with Demetrius in the mayhem after the victory a day earlier. The Inland Stars lost, but why was Jordan less worthy of praise? In the anteroom afterward, Keller didn't even mention the game. He reviewed the team's plans for the rest of the day: back to the hotel, pack, a quick dinner, and then the ride to the airport. It was as if the game, as if Jordan's quiet triumph, had never happened.

Outside the gym later, John pulled Jordan aside and told him he was proud of him. "You were the only one who could score against those guys," John said. But Jordan was upset, and he pulled away from his dad and walked off, joining teammates in a waiting minivan.

In the parking lot in the front of the school later, John posed another question to me: "What did Joe teach the boys today?" His voice was low. He kept pulling his hands in and out of his pockets. There was nothing intimidating about him. Then John said: "Today, Joe taught the boys that if he wants to, he can humiliate them. What a lesson."

8

(VIOLET KELLER)

Clark Francis

I n the spring of 2003, stories about the prodigious ability of twelve-
year-old Demetrius Walker spread throughout the Southern California basketball community and beyond. His name appeared on
message boards at SoCalHoops, a prominent website among hoopniks,
and he got his first piece of recruiting mail, a form letter from the University of Miami (Florida). His performance in Maryland had created
some buzz, but it was mostly the result of Keller's tireless promotion of
his young star. For years he had told anyone who would listen—parents,
journalists, high school coaches, college recruiters—that Demetrius was
a once-in-a-lifetime talent, and some were now convinced enough to
pass the word along.

One man spreading the Gospel of Joe was forty-three-year-old Clark Francis, a dowdy former journalism student at Indiana University who had built himself into one of the most quoted and curious figures in basketball. Since 1983, Francis had operated a recruiting newsletter, The Hoop Scoop, out of his Louisville apartment, building a following among basketball diehards. His bulletins, which began as black-and-white mailers, consisted of pages and pages of notes on the players Francis scouted at tournaments or camps, overwrought flattery of college and grassroots coaches, and "scoops" that weren't really scoops at all.

Francis did not play college basketball, which is apparent the minute you meet him. He is built like a Weeble, one of those egg-shaped toys that always rights itself because of the weight in its base. He is pale from the many days he spends in gyms across America—more than 200 a year by his estimate—and talks so fast he can be difficult to understand. Francis's lack of basketball experience did not make him unique among early followers of recruiting. He had an opinion and the means to distribute it, which was all anyone needed to become a recruiting analyst.

The bread and butter of most recruiting services, The Hoop Scoop included, are the rankings of high school players. The first person to compile such a list was Dave Bones in 1957. From his home in Toledo, Ohio, Bones sent out a questionnaire to high school coaches and then whittled that information into a briefing called "Cage Scope," which he passed on to colleges. Bones was the first, but Howard Garfinkel brought the practice into the mainstream. A New Yorker who ate at Manhattan's Carnegie Deli three times a week, "Garf" published the High School Basketball Report (HSBR) in 1964 and marketed it to college coaches recruiting in the greater New York area. It wasn't an instant success—between seven and nine copies sold the first year—but Garf refined the HSBR over the next few years and it became popular with recruiters. Garf ranked players on a scale of 1 to 5, with a 1 indicating a player who would one day contribute to a small-college team and a 5 being a player who by his second season would be a major contributor to a top 20 program. He limited his lists to kids in the East— from Maine to West Virginia—because he didn't feel comfortable ranking players he couldn't see several times a year. In 1965 he created the Five-Star Camp, a kind of scouting bazaar, and invited college coaches to work as counselors (and get a close look at the kids). The NCAA banned college coaches from working camps in 1984, but the Five-Star Camp remained, along with the HSBR, a valuable resource for recruiters.

In the 1980s, analyst Bob Gibbons in North Carolina rose to national prominence. Like Garf, he would eventually run a camp and put out a newsletter, All Star Report, but he differed from Garf in that he marketed to fans, not coaches. His lists, such as the top-100 seniors or top-100 underclassmen, were immensely popular. Fans wanted to know how the players their school signed stacked up against their rivals' recruits. If North Carolina got the number-1 player and Duke ended up getting number 7, that was ammunition a Tar Heels fan could use to prove his school's superiority.

Francis arrived on the scene after Gibbons and adopted his penchant for lists. But whereas Gibbons would stop at the top 100 or 150, Francis's rankings seemed to go on until he ran out of names. "He'd have a list of the top underclassmen, and it would go to 966," says Tom Konchalski, who took over HSBR from Garf in 1984. "We all chuckled at that. It was like he was taking every name a coach gave him and putting it out there in the hopes it would stick."

Konchalski and other veteran recruiting analysts liked Francis, but they drew a distinction between what they did and what he did. "Clark was more of a popularizer," Konchalski says. Garf or Konchalski felt their reputations were on the line when they ranked players—the college coaches who were their customers would know if they ranked a kid a 5 and he couldn't play a lick—and they resisted doing national rankings. "We wanted to be able to see a kid over a period of a few years, see a pattern of development physically and also how their skills developed," Konchalski says. "One person can't do that nationally." But for Francis, there was no consequence to ranking 966 kids or putting a guard from Arizona he'd never seen play in his top 50, and in his early years he did so with impunity.

Eventually Francis assembled a team of "editors" around the country to help him with rankings and his newsletters. Some were qualified independent scouts, but others were grassroots coaches, which created an obvious conflict of interest. For a spell, Francis's "California editor" was Dinos Trigonis, the long-time coach of the Belmont Shore Basketball Club. Not surprisingly, kids from his team appeared in Francis's rankings. In one newsletter in 2001, Francis wrote: "When our California Editor Dinos Trigonis goes against the consensus and ranks (Jamal) Boykin over 6'9" Soph Amir Johnson from Los Angeles (Verbum Dei) CA, as the #1 sophomore in California, we think it is more than justified." Nowhere does Francis mention that Boykin played for Belmont Shore and Johnson did not. Konchalski recalls another year when the father of a player Francis ranked highly was one of The Hoop Scoop's editors.

Francis would likely have remained among the minor recruiting gurus had he not moved to differentiate The Hoop Scoop from other scouting services. He was the first to rank the top eighth-graders in the country and in doing so passed a hard deck that others had been loath to cross. Veterans like Konchalski and Gibbons never stooped to that level, in part because the NCAA doesn't deem a player a recruitable athlete until the tenth grade. They also considered the evaluation of kids before they reached high school too inexact a science. The further out you tried to project a player's ability, the more of a guess it became. But like Sonny Vaccaro before him, Francis saw gold in going younger. He continued to push the limits, ranking sixth-graders and then even fourth-graders. Combined with the advent of the Internet, this innovation boosted the online Hoop Scoop's popularity and Francis's profile. He would eventually charge $495 for a year's subscription and claim that during the busy AAU months of June and July, his site got nearly one million hits.

Francis's lists of elementary-age kids were famously inaccurate. His first ranking of fourth-graders in 2004 had Kaleb Farrell of Indianapolis as the number-1 player. One problem: Kaleb was a second-grader and the younger brother of the player Francis meant to put number 1. Mistakes such as those didn't stop people from reading The Hoop Scoop, and it became the *National Enquirer* of recruiting, a hoops junkie's guilty pleasure.

Francis's justification for ranking kids so young varied depending on the day. In one interview, he sounded a lot like Joe Keller when he said, "Some kids can handle [the rankings] and some need to be sheltered. That's not my responsibility. That's the responsibility of their parents or coaches or teachers or counselors." But in that same interview he offered what came across as parental advice: "What's worse, to shelter a kid throughout most of his growing-up career and suddenly throw him to the wolves all at once, or to do it in increments and see if he can handle it? That's what happens with some players—they get to be sophomores and juniors in high school and are good enough to play on national AAU teams, but they're sheltered all their lives. Has someone done them a disservice?"

Francis repeatedly presented to me the classic drug pusher's defense: "I am just providing a service people want." To those who consider what he does harmful to children, it is a cop-out. "I like Clark, but I think ranking kids so young is a subtle form of child abuse," Konchalski says. "Pedophiles want child pornography. Does that mean we should cater to them? . . . The pressure it puts on kids is immense. But even with so many people saying it is a mistake, it is not illegal and he is not going to stop."

Among the largest subset of people who followed Francis's rankings were AAU coaches, and not only because some of them were on his payroll. Rankings of any kind, from any scouting service, regardless of its credibility, were instruments with which to measure one's importance. If a coach had the number-1 player in the country or several kids in the top 50, his value to the shoe companies, his popularity with college coaches, and his ability to recruit new kids was enhanced. To Keller, Francis was the most important opinion-maker in America, the key to creating a national groundswell about Demetrius and the team. Upon re-forming the Inland Stars in 2000, Keller made courting Francis a top priority. He called Francis regularly with "tips" about the great players on his team, and eventually Francis took the bait.

In April of 2001, in a report prior to the Kingwood Classic, a well-attended tournament in Houston, Francis wrote on his website: "The Inland Stars in the 10-Under Division might be worth a look as well, because this top-rated team includes tremendous size with . . . 5'8 Joseph Burton . . . 5'8 Demetrius Walker . . .and 5'5 Rome Draper." In a newsletter dated three days later, Francis wrote: "Now let's move to the 10-Under Division, where we made a point to watch the Inland Stars. The last time the Inland Stars were this good at so young an age, they had 7'0 Tyson Chandler from Compton (Dominguez) CA, 6'6 Josh Childress from Lakewood (Mayfair) CA, 6'5 Cedric Bozeman from Santa Ana (Mater Dei) CA, and 6'11 Jamal Sampson from Santa Ana (Mater Dei) CA. But this team promises to be better. As a matter of fact, Joe Keller has come out of retirement to coach this group. Their best player is 5'8 Demetrius Walker . . . Sure some Tyson Chandler comparisons are in order, but just like we told our buddy Pat Barrett, who is Chandler's mentor and club team coach, Walker plays a lot harder. Also, Walker's father is 6'8 and his mother is 6'1. So his potential for growth is scary. But right now we're talking about an outstanding athlete who is very fluid and impossible to stop at this level. . . . Unfortunately, we only got to see this team for about a quarter, because we had to go to the 15-Under Championship game."

The errors in Francis's report are numerous. Chandler, Childress, Bozeman, and the rest never played together on the Inland Stars, only on SCA, and Chandler did not play for Keller when he was a ten-year-old. Demetrius's father was not six foot eight—not even close. But the most astounding (and telling) aspect of his report was that after watching Demetrius play for only a quarter—about eight minutes—he likened him to Chandler, who at the time was months away from being selected in the first round of the NBA draft.

Seven months later, Demetrius made The Hoop Scoop again. In a tease of Trigonis's rankings of the top players in California, from seniors down to fifth-graders, Francis wrote that Demetrius was Trigonis's pick as the top sixth-grader in the state. "Speaking of Walker, his father is 6'9, his mother is 6'2 and he's already being touted as the next Tyson Chandler. So you might want to remember the name!"

Francis can be forgiven somewhat for taking erroneous information straight from Keller's mouth and plopping it into his report. How could he know Keller would lie to him about Demetrius's father's height or Kisha's? But comparing Demetrius to Chandler revealed an iniquitous truth about his mission. Francis would say he ranked and evaluated kids, but he was really in the business of hype. College coaches did not consider his rankings when they chose the kids they recruited. Whether they signed a player or not didn't hinge on Francis's opinion. He was writing only to titillate the rabid fans who made up his readership. Howard Garfinkel scouted kids; Clark Francis promoted them. He was a salesman, and he wrote what he thought his readers wanted, which was whispers of greatness in a kid still shy of middle school.

As Konchalski pointed out, this puts immense pressure on players very early in their lives. From the moment Francis compared Demetrius to Chandler, the bar was set. Demetrius *had* to become the next Tyson

Chandler. If he didn't, he would fail to live up to his potential. It didn't matter that his potential had been determined after only eight minutes by a man with no real experience playing or coaching basketball. Fans didn't know Francis's qualifications or his true motive. They knew only what they read: Demetrius was as talented and worked harder than a player who would ultimately be the second pick in the 2001 NBA draft.

Francis continued to listen as Keller gushed about Demetrius's ability. After the Inland Stars defeated Team Maryland in Baltimore, Keller called with the news and urged Francis to watch the team play in April at the Las Vegas Easter Classic. "Demetrius is the best player in the country," Keller told him. A few days later, just before the tournament, Francis wrote on his website: "Speaking of the 12-Under Division, we're especially anxious to check out SCA/Inland Stars, which features 6'2 Demetrius Walker from Fontana, CA, who is widely considered the best 6th grader in the nation." After the tournament, which Keller's team won easily, this appeared on The Hoop Scoop's website: "[Demetrius] Walker, who had 18 points in the game we attended, deserves special mention, because he had incredible moves, athleticism, and skills for somebody his age and, as a result, is the best 6th grader in the nation."

For three years Keller had been selling the idea of Demetrius as the top player in his class, and finally someone had put it into the recruiting lexicon. Keller could print out Francis's words and mail them to coaches, parents, and reporters. He could email a link to The Hoop Scoop posting all over the country, and he could use it to sway other recruiting analysts when the time was right ("Clark Francis has Demetrius number 1; why don't you?"). Keller believed no one was better than Demetrius, and so Francis's posting felt more like validation than deception. He didn't view what he'd done as lobbying. He'd merely tipped Francis off to a great kid, and Francis had confirmed with his own eyes that Demetrius was special.

When Demetrius heard what Francis wrote, he was characteristically unmoved: "That's great and all, but that doesn't mean nothin' if we don't win Nationals." But to Keller it meant everything. It substantiated the course he'd set for himself and his family. He always talked as if Demetrius's stardom were a foregone conclusion, but strands of uncertainty existed. Following Francis's stamp of approval, all qualifiers were removed. Demetrius was the next Tyson Chandler, and Keller was going to make millions. Case closed.

In addition to labeling Demetrius as the best player in the nation, Francis also printed, at Keller's request, the names of several of the Inland Stars, tagging them as players to watch. Jordan, Rome, Andrew, and even Tommy were listed, and the pride John and the other parents felt at seeing this cannot be overstated. They imagined coaches at UCLA, Arizona, and Duke scribbling down their son's name, making a note to check out Joe Keller's team of phenoms. The mention in The Hoop Scoop helped heal the wounds from Maryland, and the parents and kids turned their attention toward Nationals. "With Joe, it might be hard to see sometimes, but the good outweighs the bad," John said.

A few weeks after Francis proclaimed Demetrius the best player in the country, LeBron James signed a $90 million contract with Nike, despite having yet to graduate from high school. News of the deal reached Keller at his apartment, and he quickly called me to confirm the details. He then brought Demetrius on the line in a three-way call.

"D, did you hear? LeBron got ninety million dollars from Nike."

"That's nice," Demetrius said. "Good for him." He was chewing on something, and in the background a video game could be heard.

"Ninety million dollars. Ninety million. Wow," Keller said. "I've got to say, I would be happy if D got half that when he goes pro."

"I wouldn't," Demetrius said.

"D, what the hell are you talking about? You wouldn't be happy with forty-five million dollars?"

"Not if it's half of what LeBron got."

"D, are you crazy? Forty-five million? We're talking about forty-five million dollars. You're out of your mind if you wouldn't take that."

After a long pause, Demetrius answered, although reluctantly: "Okay, I guess I would take that. But I wouldn't be happy."

"Yes, you would," Keller said.

"No, I wouldn't."

"D, you're crazy. Hang up. I can't talk to you anymore."

When Demetrius was safely off the line, Keller said, "You know, hearing about LeBron getting all that money makes me realize how big all of this is. And also how big it is going to get."

9

Demetrius Walker (#23) before the 2003 Nationals

are were the moments when a subject other than basketball penetrated Keller's world. If you weren't discussing the team or the brightness of Demetrius's future, he tuned you out. If you couldn't listen for hours as he went on about the certitude of the Inland Stars' triumph at Nationals, he'd find someone who would. Given how little he knew about anything else, his obsession seemed at times like a case of savantism. Only when the world revolved around basketball did life make sense; only then was he comfortable and centered.

Only once before had Keller been so singularly fanatical. In the mid-1990s, he believed—like many young men in the Inland Empire—that his car was the ultimate representation of his persona. He drove a lowered forest-green Mitsubishi Eclipse with eighteen-inch chrome rims, and he liked to sit low in the gray seats, sunglasses on, windows rolled down, blaring rap music. Shortly after buying the Mitsubishi, Keller learned of a competition called the California State Sound Off, which was essentially a contest to determine who owned the loudest stereo. Winning this competition became Keller's purpose in life. He ripped apart his Mitsubishi, filling the doors and dashboard and even the floor with Dynamat, an insulator that reduced vibration and prevented road noise from entering the car and stereo sound from exiting. He removed the backseats and squeezed in eight subwoofers and forty-two speakers. Anyone riding in the car had to wear earplugs designed for use at gun ranges, and Keller liked to brag that he could be heard coming a mile and a half away. He worked on the car at least six hours a day for four months and spent more than $25,000 on the stereo alone. That didn't count the cost of replacing the windshield and side windows he blew out while testing it.

As with the Inland Stars years later, Keller's incredible focus paid off. His car finished first in its class at the Sound Off, and the victory awarded him some local cachet, which he parlayed into a business installing people's stereos and alarms. At one point he was netting $4,000 a week, "but then car manufacturers started coming out with those keyless-entry devices, which people thought were an alarm, and the market dried up." Shortly thereafter, he sold the Mitsubishi and became a full-time basketball coach.

With few exceptions, hoop dreams had been Keller's sole preoccupation ever since. Even when he quit coaching after his brief partnership with Barrett, he never stopped thinking about the game. One reason he returned to the sport was that he couldn't get it out of his head. But in early June, a few weeks before the Inland Stars departed for Newport News and the 12-and-Under AAU Nationals, Keller's singular focus was threatened by the news that Violet's obstetrician had scheduled a C-section for the birth of their second child, a girl, for the same week as Nationals. It presented the ultimate test of Keller's priorities: Would he set aside his ambition to tend to his family? Or would his obsession with Demetrius, the team, and roundball riches trump even the birth of a child?

Few people knew about his dilemma until days before the team's departure. John found out while sitting on the couch at Keller's apartment. They were discussing the uniforms and the shoes the boys would wear in Virginia, and then Keller said matter-of-factly that Violet's doctor had advised her to have a C-section.

"The good thing is that you'll know exactly when it's going to happen," John said. "So what day is it?"

"It's for the Tuesday night we're at Nationals."

"So who's going to coach the team?"

"I'm going to coach them. I'm still going."

John assumed he was kidding. "What does Violet think about that?" he said, expecting Keller to laugh at him for taking the bait.

"She's okay with it. She knows that even though I won't be there, she's still my number one priority."

He's trying to impress me, John thought. What greater declaration of one's commitment to the team than to put a tournament ahead of family?

When Tom heard Keller make the same statement, he lectured him sternly. "Joe, this is something you can't get back. Think hard about what you are saying. You are going to miss your daughter's birth—your daughter's birth!—to coach in a tournament."

It wasn't just any tournament, Keller insisted. "No one else can coach the team. If I'm not there, we don't have a chance."

Tom knew better. The Inland Stars would breeze through their three games in pool play. They wouldn't face a real challenge until the second round of bracket play at the earliest, which wasn't until Wednesday. With minimal planning, Keller could witness his daughter's birth Tuesday night, catch a red-eye to Washington, D.C., and be in Newport News for a late-morning tip-off Wednesday. "The team will be fine without you until then," Tom said. "There isn't a parent who thinks you shouldn't be home with Violet. And if the kids don't understand now, they will someday."

Demetrius was the only player Keller told about the C-section, and Demetrius informed none of his teammates. It was a grown-up problem, he believed, which didn't involve him or the others. He did tell Kisha, however, and she rushed to Violet for an explanation.

As Violet described it to Kisha, a victory at Nationals would get them out of that dinky apartment and into Violet's dream home; it would enable them to buy a nicer car and to live more comfortably in every way. Listening to Violet, one would have thought that inside the glass-bowl trophy given to the national champions was the American dream.

"Of course I am mad," Violet told Kisha. "But Joe told me how important it is."

In Kisha's mind, Violet wasn't angry enough. "If I was married to Joe and he left, I would tell him not to come back."

Even so, Kisha didn't believe Keller was capable of missing the birth of his daughter. He would come to his senses, she thought. After all, he had once stopped coaching because Violet had a miscarriage. But on Thursday, July 10, Keller boarded a plane with the rest of the team at Los Angeles International Airport. On the flight, he barely mentioned Violet or the coming baby. All his talk and all his thoughts were focused squarely on basketball.

Late Monday night, on the eve of Violet's C-section, Keller left his room at a Holiday Inn and walked across the hotel's parking lot to a small bar set against a busy thoroughfare. In the many years I had known Keller, he had never been comfortable alone. Even for something as benign as a trip to the grocery store, he dragged along Demetrius. "I like to have my entourage with me," he said. That he intended to have a contemplative drink by himself said something about his state of mind.

Keller ordered a Corona and then sat at the table farthest from the door. It was difficult to know what Keller thought about as he sat sipping his beer. He might have been replaying moments from the Inland Stars' solid start at Nationals. They had won all three of their games in pool play by an average of 20 points and the following day would open elimination play against the Potomac Valley Capital Players, one of the weakest teams left in the field. Demetrius looked unstoppable, and several coaches had approached Keller between games to congratulate him on the praise Demetrius received in The Hoop Scoop. He might also have been looking ahead. If both the Inland Stars and Hoosier Hoops won the following day, they would meet in the Round of 16, fulfilling one of Keller's hopes going into the tournament: to avenge last season's loss to Deuce and his teammates. Most likely, Keller's thoughts were with Violet. She was more than 2,000 miles away, probably alone in their apartment, holding firmly to the idea that her husband's absence at a critical moment in their relationship was best for their future.

Up to that point, Keller's affection for and commitment to his wife could not be questioned. He doted on her, publicly and privately. He didn't just say that he loved her when they were alone; he declared it at times when the most people could hear. "Am I the luckiest guy or what?" he would say. "Violet puts up with all my shit. All she does is love me. She is the best thing that ever happened to me. I mean that; I wouldn't be shit without Violet." She put up with this rocky life of his choosing, believing unequivocally in his master plan. Her tolerance of his mood swings, his outbursts, his incessant talk of basketball, was re-markable. "Violet is like a saint," Carmen said. Without Violet, "Coach Joe would probably forget where he lived," Demetrius added.

Keller met the woman he'd dated before Violet, the one who gave birth to Joey, at Club Metro, a popular Inland Empire nightclub. She was wild, and Keller got custody of Joey for a brief period after she was arrested for drug possession. Violet, by contrast, never dated anyone before Keller, whom she met through her younger brother, a basketball player. She twice turned Keller down for dates before she agreed to go to the movies. "She wouldn't even let me kiss her until we had gone on, like, fifteen dates," Keller said. "I spent, like, two thousand dollars tak-ing her out before I even got a kiss." He proposed to her on Christmas Eve after a few months of dating. He put the box with the ring inside into her stocking, and when she reached in and felt the box, she started to cry before she even took it out. "What are you crying for?" Keller said. "There could be a gum ball in that box."

Keller's intensity, his drive, came mostly from a belief that everyone questioned his ability to succeed. But Violet was not one of those peo-ple. She always had faith in him, even when he told her a basketball tournament was more important than their daughter's birth. As he sat alone in that bar, he had to feel the weight of his betrayal.

That Keller regretted his decision was irrefutable. A few hours before leaving the hotel for the bar, he called Tom and said, "Please help me. I've got to get home. I don't care how much it costs and I don't care if I have to fly with the luggage. Just get me on a plane that gets me back to Violet in time." Tom worked into Monday evening, calling airlines and travel agents, coming up with a single option that was neither cheap (more than $1,500) nor convenient. Keller would have to rent a car, drive to Washington Dulles, and catch a 6:00 a.m. flight that made one stop before landing at LAX around 4:00 p.m. Factoring in potential flight delays and rush-hour traffic along the fifty-nine-mile drive from LAX to Riverside Community Hospital, Keller's chances of making the scheduled 7:00 p.m. C-section were fifty-fifty at best.

"Is there anything else?" Keller asked.

Tom sensed that the cost of the ticket was a problem. "Look, Joe, I'll pay for the ticket. I'll pay for it, and you don't have to pay me back. Call it a baby present. That is how important I think it is for you to be there."

"Hold on," Keller said when Tom asked if he should book the ticket. "I've got to talk to Demetrius first."

It was around 9:00 p.m. when Keller sat down with Demetrius in the hotel room they shared. There were two beds in the room, both covered by a coarse polyester comforter with a flowered print. The shades to the room were drawn, and the only light came from a lamp on the night-stand between the beds. Keller sat on a chair near a little desk in the corner.

"D, I need to know something. I need to know what you'd think if I went home to be with Violet."

"What? You can't. You can't."

Keller did not say anything for a moment. He stared at Demetrius, who was still three months shy of his thirteenth birthday.

"Violet's gonna have the baby tomorrow. I can get there in time if I leave now. I will be back before the quarterfinals."

"But you can't. Who would coach the team?"

"Big Rome and Tom."

"They don't know our team. They're not our coach. If you go, we don't have a chance."

Keller stood up and moved closer to Demetrius. He said softly, "We play the Capital Players tomorrow. They're terrible."

"We can't win without you here."

"Yes, you can."

On this point, Keller was contradicting himself. For years he had professed how superior he was to other coaches, how vital a role he played in the team's success. Demetrius believed him. Now he was supposed to understand that it was all a lie?

Keller moved close to where Demetrius sat on the bed, but

Demetrius looked away and it was evident that they'd reached a stalemate. Keller retrieved his cell phone from the pocket of his shorts and flipped it open to check the time. If he wanted to catch the flight, he needed to leave soon.

"D?"

"If you leave, I won't play," Demetrius said. "I won't play for Coach Rome or Coach Tom. Only you."

Keller put his cell phone back in his pocket and walked toward the door.

Down the hall, Tom waited in his room, ready with his credit card to pay for Keller's ticket home. Keller entered and said, "I'm not going. D needs me." Then he turned around and walked out.

A few hours later, Keller sat in the bar, drinking alone. He repeatedly swept his hand across the table, wiping it clean. At some point it became too much for him to ponder alone. How else to explain what he did next?

John was in his room, in bed, when his phone rang. He saw Keller's number come up and figured he was calling to say he was racing home to be with Violet. But when John answered, making sure to whisper so as to not wake Jordan, Keller said, "Come over to the bar. We need to talk." John put on a shirt and sweatpants and, in the dark, crossed the parking lot, wondering what was so important that Keller needed him in the middle of the night.

As he walked into the bar, John saw Keller before Keller saw him, and in that moment he felt great sympathy for him. Despite their many battles over the years, Keller was in agony, and an urge to console him rushed through John. Yet at the same time he wondered if the pain Keller felt might change him. *Perhaps this will make him treat people a little better,* John thought.

As John sat down, Keller said, "Some big games tomorrow, huh?" He talked about how Hoosier Hoops appeared as strong as last year and how Team Maryland would surely adapt after losing to the Inland Stars in Baltimore. John couldn't believe Keller had gotten him out of bed for this. He hurried through his beer, hoping he could leave when he finished, but then, while talking about a Team Maryland player, Keller abruptly stopped mid-sentence. He fell silent and looked down at the table.

"Joe?"

Keller didn't look up.

"Joe?"

Keller slowly raised his head, and John thought he saw tears in his eyes.

"You know, Violet's having the baby tomorrow," Keller said quietly.

"I know."

"I wish I could have been there, but . . . but . . . the kids would have been let down if I didn't come."

John nodded.

"I was going to fly back, but I talked to D and he begged me to stay. I can't let him down. And we've worked so hard that it would be unfair to the kids and to the parents if I left everyone now. . . . And, you know, Violet didn't even really want me there. She has her sisters and her mom. I'd just be in the way."

There was so much John wanted to say, but he worried what Keller would do if he didn't censor his remarks. *If I say anything negative, he'll hold it against Jordan,* John thought. *He'll teach him another "lesson" like in Baltimore.* Keller wanted John to say he'd made the right choice, that he had no other option but to put the team first. John couldn't do that, but he had to say something.

"Joe, I'm sure Violet will be fine," John finally said. "She has her mom there, the rest of her family. Everything will be okay."

Keller smiled and sat back in his chair. He took a deep breath and said, "So, about tomorrow . . ."

About twenty hours later, at 7:56 p.m. (PST), Violet gave birth to Alyssa Nicole Keller at Riverside Community Hospital. Violet's sister was in the birthing room in place of Keller and was the first to see her. "My gosh, she's chunky!" she shouted. Violet didn't get to see for herself, because a nurse rushed Alyssa to the neonatal intensive-care unit and placed her in an incubator. She weighed eight pounds fourteen ounces, but looked heavier. She was retaining fluid and would have to be monitored for a few days. It was not a serious complication, but it scared Violet. She hadn't gotten to hold her daughter and couldn't go to the NICU to see her through the glass because she was bedridden. For three days after the delivery, Violet's only glimpses of Alyssa came from Polaroids that her sister brought her.

On the night his daughter was born, Keller was across the country, celebrating a 19-point blowout of the Capital Players, which put the Inland Stars in the Round of 16 against Hoosier Hoops. Keller did arrange for flowers to be delivered to Violet's hospital room.

"I think they were lilies, Stargazers," Violet would say later. "I don't remember."

The anticipated rematch with Hoosier Hoops was held in a gym abutted at one end by a raised stage that was hidden by a thick black curtain. With the only locker room occupied, Keller gathered the team for a pregame talk behind the curtain. It was a fitting metaphor, as Keller's cries for vengeance were like something out of Shakespeare. "It's time for revenge!" he yelled to the boys encircling him. "Remember last year? Now's your chance for payback, for revenge!"

To Demetrius he said, "Last time, Deuce kind of kicked your ass, didn't he?"

Demetrius nodded.

"This time he is going to be your bitch, right?"

"I know, Coach, I got you."

Tom looked at each of the boys, trying to gauge their resoluteness, and was struck by the intensity in Demetrius's eyes. Never before had he seen him so keyed up before a game. He hopped in place, unable to stand still, and as Keller talked he went to each of his teammates and slapped him hard on the back or butt. "Let's go. Let's go," he said. When Keller was finished, Demetrius led the team out from behind the curtain, as poised as he'd ever been to put on a show.

The thirty-two minutes of action from that game would be talked about for years by the followers of the team. John, who videotaped it, would watch the tape whenever he wanted to be reminded of how perfect the team, and Demetrius, were capable of playing. Everything that had gone wrong for the Inland Stars in the teams' first meeting was reversed. Terran's presence on the floor meant Van Treese and Bloom, Indiana's skilled frontcourt duo, couldn't double-team Demetrius, and he tormented them inside. Deuce had his hands full guarding Pe'Shon, which enabled Jordan and Andrew to get open shots on the perimeter. When Indiana had the ball, Terran and Xavier matched up well enough with Indiana's big men that Demetrius could act as a sort of freelance defender, blocking shots and helping Pe'Shon and Justin, who took turns smothering Deuce. At the start of the second half, Deuce was so worn down from the big, rangy defenders Keller rolled at him, he looked as if he didn't want to go on.

Demetrius scored 30 points, but his offensive output was not his most impressive feat. It was the totality of the effort he put forth. He contested every shot close to him and chased down loose balls, even ones that were clearly headed out of bounds, diving into the stands after them. He fought so hard for rebounds that he often took them away from teammates. Most important to Keller: No one could watch that game and come away thinking that Demetrius wasn't twice the player Deuce was.

Early in the third quarter, with Inland Stars up 24, Tom and Rome, Sr., began discussing their next opponent, which they expected to be Team Maryland. Sitting at the end of the bench, they talked about resting as many of their stars as possible. There was no sense in expending all the boys' energy in a game that was clearly over when they would have to play again in a few hours.

"Joe, you need to think about getting D out of there, saving him for Maryland," Tom said after walking down the sideline to where Keller stood.

Keller shot him a bewildered stare. "Are you crazy? D is killing out there."

Seated high in the bleachers, John had the same thought. Demetrius was still in the game, still going full bore when the outcome had been decided. At the end of the third quarter, he shut off his video recorder and walked down the stands to the court. He squatted behind the bench and spoke to Tom.

"We need to get D out of there. We need to start thinking about tonight."

"I already tried," Tom said.

"Try again."

This time Rome, Sr., went to Keller and pleaded with him to rest Demetrius. Keller waved him off. He was having too much fun watching Demetrius embarrass Deuce.

At the final buzzer, Demetrius was still on the floor, still competing madly, even though the Inland Stars led 61–31. As John walked onto the court to congratulate him and the boys, Keller grabbed him by the arm and screamed, "Who is the best player in the country now?"

———

Playing two games four hours apart was nothing new to the Inland Stars. They often played three in a single Saturday and then two more on Sunday. The kids were resilient, and Keller had them in great shape. But playing two games in a row at Nationals was different. It was not just physically taxing. Demetrius and the others had been in such a lather to avenge their loss from the previous year that it would be difficult for them to find that level of intensity again only a few hours later.

Coaches often talk about the possibility of a "letdown" after a momentous victory. They guard against it by resting players but also by plotting a larger journey for the team. No one game is considered more important than the one that follows it. Keeping the players' intensity at a constant rate (rather than at a succession of peaks) is also vital. Controlling emotions, especially those of boys so young, can be difficult, but the surest method is to continually downplay the significance of the challenges before them. Keeping them focused on the nuts and bolts of the game prevents them from succumbing to their emotions.

Louis Wilson, the coach of Team Maryland, understood that well from his time as a player at Howard University, as a coach at the high school level in Maryland, and now at the grassroots level. He treated the Round of 16 matchup against the Atlanta Celtics as just another game, and when his team jumped to an early lead, he sent his best players to the bench. Team Maryland won by 32, but the real victory was in advancing to the next round without exhausting the team's best players or allowing them to think their work was finished.

When the two teams arrived at the gym, Team Maryland's players took up space off to a side of the stands. Chad Wilson and a few other players stretched; some dribbled basketballs. The Inland Stars grouped together at one end of the bleachers. Demetrius immediately lay down on a bench and closed his eyes. Rome sat slumped with his back resting against the row of seats behind him, staring motionless toward the court as if he'd been entranced.

From those contrasting images alone, one could have guessed how the game would begin. Team Maryland built leads of 8–2 and then 12–2 and then 16–4, overwhelming the Inland Stars with its energy. It helped that Wilson had come up with a better strategy to contain Demetrius. He asked Murdock to guard him more closely when he didn't have the ball so as to make him work a little harder to get it. When he did receive a pass, other Maryland defenders shaded toward him but they didn't rush to double him. It gave the impression that they were ready to help on defense but didn't leave a man wide open for Demetrius to find with a quick pass. Demetrius drew a second defender to him often, but when he supplied his teammates with a pass that gave them an open look at the basket, they failed to convert. Successive possessions in the second quarter illustrated this. On the first, Demetrius got the ball on the right wing and blew past Murdock, only to find two defenders moving into his path. The closest defender had left Andrew wide open atop the key, and Demetrius bounced him a perfect pass. Andrew caught it and, in one motion, released a 3-pointer that, like so many of his shots, was assumed to be good when it left his hands. But it clacked off the front of the rim, one of six open 3-pointers Andrew missed in the first sixteen minutes. On the following possession, some nifty passing between Terran and Demetrius found Rome clear fourteen feet from the hoop on the baseline. Yet his shot went long, his third miss of the half.

The Inland Stars trailed 32–24 at the intermission, and if it weren't for Pe'Shon's 7 points and solid defense on Wilson, it would have been worse. Trailing by such a large margin was not something with which Keller or any of the boys were familiar. As they exited for the locker room, Demetrius pushed through the door and shouted, "I can't do it all by myself!" Rome shot him a glance. Justin rolled his eyes. Pe'Shon said, "What does that mean?" and walked toward Demetrius. Rome, Sr., said, "Come on, come on," and he put his arm around Pe'Shon and turned him away. Later, several players would remark that it was the first time Demetrius didn't act like a team player.

Keller walked into the locker room and huddled with Tom off to one side.

"Joe, we are not going to win if we keep trying to force the ball in to D in the post. They've got that figured out."

Keller agreed.

"But we need to get the ball in his hands. Let's move him to the point. You've talked all year about making him the point guard—why not do it now?"

It wasn't a bad idea. The Inland Stars' shooters had proved incapable of making Team Maryland pay for shading and doubling Demetrius. With him handling the ball, he would have more opportunities to drive and get fouled, which would open up the game. There were other options: Pe'Shon was playing well, so was Jordan, but Keller didn't have enough confidence in either of them to make them the primary offensive option in such a crucial game. Tom's idea, however, also reeked of desperation. Demetrius was going to make his debut as point guard against the defending national champions? It was akin to moving a wide receiver to quarterback in the middle of the Super Bowl.

Keller mulled over Tom's idea for a minute and then turned to his team. "When we come out in the second half, D is going to run the point. He'll look to drive and get us some easy baskets."

By shifting Demetrius to the point, Keller risked highlighting one of his weaknesses: ballhandling. Demetrius knew this and, as they exited the locker room, he whispered to Keller, "Coach Joe, I don't want to play the point."

"D, you've got to do it."

To start the second half, Demetrius took an inbounds pass from Terran and brought the ball upcourt. His apprehension over his new role was obvious. Rather than burst up the court, as Keller and Tom had envisioned, he gingerly advanced the ball. Team Maryland was sitting back in a zone defense, and as he crossed the half line, he pushed a soft pass in the direction of Rome on the wing. A Team Maryland defender easily stepped in front and stole it and scored. On the next trip, Demetrius looked even less steady. Louis Wilson, like any astute coach, pounced on this. He shouted a few words, and suddenly Chad Wilson and Kendall Marshall ran toward Demetrius. He broke to the left, trying to get around them, but Chad Wilson took advantage of his high dribbling to pluck the ball away and cruise in for yet another uncontested score.

Demetrius didn't chase after him. He turned to the bench and screamed, "I told you I didn't want to play point!"

Keller wheeled to Tom and yelled, "I told you this was a stupid fucking idea!"

Without being told, Pe'Shon returned to the point and tried to calm his teammates. But Team Maryland continued to build on its lead. Midway through the third quarter, Pe'Shon came up with a steal and scored on a driving layup to cut Maryland's lead to 8, and then Keller inexplicably pulled him from the game, inserting Andrew, who had missed all nine of his shots to that point.

Tom and Rome, Sr., tried unsuccessfully to convince Keller to put Xavier in the game and rest Demetrius, even if only for a minute or two.

"Are you crazy?" he yelled. "Man, sit down!"

On the court, Andrew missed more open shots, and Demetrius played hard on offense but lagged on defense because of fatigue. With the exception of Pe'Shon and Jordan, who led the team with 16 points, every one of the Inland Stars had his worst game of the season. They never got closer than 8 points in the second half and lost 57–45.

Athletes carry forever the triumphs from their youth. Anyone who has ever competed in team sports can recall with amazing clarity feats that occurred decades earlier. A fastball launched over the fence in the ninth inning. The touchdown pass that won the game. The last-second shot that miraculously found the net. Ask those same athletes about their failures and their recall is often more precise. The missed free throw. The dropped pass. The swing and miss and shameful walk back to the bench. Often, the richness of detail in those stories surpasses those from their triumphs. As E. M. Forster wrote, a win always seems shallow; it is the loss that is so profound and suggests "nasty infinities."

The Inland Stars would forever remember the loss to Team Maryland. What they would take with them beyond the sting of defeat depended on Keller, on what he said in those indelible minutes when the boys were most distraught. Standing before them in the locker room, Keller, like his players, had tears in his eyes.

"I just wish we would have won," he said, his voice full of regret. "You know, I didn't tell you guys this, but I missed the birth of my little girl to be here." He paused and looked down at his feet. "I really wish we would have won. It would have been much better if we had won."

10

(ROB BOCK)

Justin Hawkins and Andrew Bock

No parent was more distressed after the loss at Nationals than Rob. Almost all the boys performed poorly, but Andrew's struggles stood out. "I've just never seen Andrew play that bad before," Rob said. "I don't know what happened."

Andrew missed twelve shots, including eight from 3-point range, had numerous turnovers, and was incapable of slowing Kendall Marshall. More than anything, his missed 3-pointers in the first half torpedoed the team's chances. Had he made just one or two, it might have forced Team Maryland to abandon the collapsing defense designed to limit Demetrius, freeing him up to score inside. Andrew's misses also drained his teammates' confidence. They were so used to seeing his long shots find the net that, with each miss, the notion that it just wasn't their night sunk in a little more. For the entirety of the game's first sixteen minutes, the boys looked for something to spark them, to help them rise up and seize momentum, but each of Andrew's misses hammered them down a little bit more.

It would have been easy to chalk Andrew's performance up to one of those games when nothing goes right, and Rob would eventually come to that conclusion. But at first his concerns ran deeper. Upon returning to California, he adjusted his work schedule so he could spend more time in the gym working Andrew out, attempting to fix whatever it was that had plagued him against Team Maryland. Keller, in contrast, took Violet, his son Jordan, his new daughter, Alyssa, and Demetrius to Tom's vacation home on the Colorado River. While Rob and Andrew holed up in a gym for at least three hours a day, shooting 3-pointers and working on ballhandling, Keller and Demetrius raced Sea-Doos; at night they ate barbecue, and Keller drank margaritas under starry skies.

When practices resumed at the Rancho Cucamonga Family Sports Center in August, the fruits of Andrew's labor were evident. In one workout I attended, he was the best player on the floor, better even than Demetrius. The release on his shot had become more natural and he could get it off quicker, which made him more effective when guarded closely. He also penetrated with more authority and was less afraid to get his shot blocked or be bounced around by bigger defenders. The boys adopted a word for a shot that looked good upon release: *wet*. It became the adjective of choice to describe Andrew's game at that time. When Andrew cast a 3-pointer, chants of "Wet!" emanated from every corner of the gym. "That boy is just wet right now," Demetrius said. "No one can stop him."

Seeing Andrew return to form calmed Rob, as did the fact that Keller didn't bring in a host of new players in the first few weeks after Nationals. It was usually a tumultuous time as Keller sought to improve the team through new additions. Rob and other parents were pleased with what appeared to be Keller's measured approach to improving the squad. "Maybe Joe finally realizes he's better off working with what he's got," Rome, Sr., said.

But while riding Sea-Doos and sipping margaritas, Keller had plotted the best way to rid the team of several players he saw as superfluous. At the time, the roster consisted of fourteen players, including some who didn't make the trip to Nationals and others who never got off the bench. Keller considered the ideal roster size to be ten kids, and it was easy to see who the favored ten were: Pe'Shon, Andrew, Jordan, Justin, Tommy, and Darius in the backcourt; Rome, Demetrius, Terran, and Xavier in the frontcourt. It appeared Keller needed to trim the roster by only four, but in discussions with me after he returned from Tom's river house, he said he wanted to cut seven or eight boys. "I need a couple extra spots to get some missing pieces," he explained.

If Keller held to that plan, he would need to cut at least a few players who had been major contributors. Rome, Sr., might have interpreted Keller's inaction in the first few weeks of practice as a vote of confidence in the existing players, but it was merely a pause while he figured out how to remove kids while subjecting himself to the least amount of wrath.

There was precedent for how he should have proceeded. Shortly after he found Demetrius and started the Inland Stars, Keller had added a shooting guard named Casey James to the team. Casey was white, which made him unique among the kids Keller took on, but his father, Dennis Dickens, had played briefly for the San Diego Rockets, (which would become the NBA's Houston Rockets), and Keller was intrigued by a good pedigree. Casey's role on the Inland Stars was clearly defined from the start: He camped out at the 3-point line and, when Demetrius or another player got double-teamed, they kicked it out to Casey for the open 3-pointer. At the end of the season, Dennis approached Keller at the team banquet and asked what he thought about Casey playing another year. "I have a couple really good new guys coming in," Keller told him. "The best thing, to me, would be for Casey to play for someone else next season, on a team where he would be the primary scorer. It would help him get confidence in other parts of his game." Dennis didn't like to hear that his son could be replaced so easily, but he appreciated Keller's honesty. Whenever Casey or Dennis saw Keller after that, they exchanged handshakes and hugs.

Keller should have learned a lesson from that experience: Deal with kids and their parents honestly, and a parting can go smoothly. It is never easy to tell a parent that other kids are more talented, but better to be forthright. That's particularly true in the small community of AAU basketball. Casey might get stronger, might develop other aspects of his game. Keller might one day want him back. "A kid you don't like now might grow a few inches and then you'll really like him," Keller said. "You don't want to burn any bridges."

But he did burn bridges. Casey's departure was the last one he handled so diplomatically, Dennis the last parent he treated with respect.

In early September, Keller announced he was splitting the Inland Stars into two teams, the "Black" and "Silver" squads. The best kids would make up the Black (or "A" team), while the others were on the Silver. "If a kid performs well enough on the Silver team, he will move up to the Black team," he explained to parents. "And no kid's spot is safe. If Demetrius isn't playing well, I'll send him down to the Silver team in a second." That was, of course, a load of crap. Keller hoped that some parents wouldn't stand for their kids being demoted and would leave in protest. To increase the probability of discontent, he picked to head the team a young, clueless coach who had been hounding him for a job.

Demetrius, Rome, Andrew, Jordan, Terran, Justin, and a few other notables made up the Black team, while an assortment of recent additions and others such as Tommy, LaBradford Franklin, and Kendall Williams, a talented young guard, were on the Silver. Two players left instantly, and Kendall and LaBradford, who had been on and off the roster for years, depending on Keller's mood, departed a few months later after starring for the Silver team but never getting promoted. Having served its purpose, the Silver team was quietly folded.

For his next move, Keller used a silent veto to kick Xavier off the team. He stopped calling Terrance Mitchell, Xavier's former AAU coach on the Sacramento Raiders, to arrange for Xavier to come to practice or games. As for his promise of shoes and uniforms for Terrance's younger team: "I never got my gear," Terrance said. "Joe did me wrong." When asked why Xavier would be released when the Inland Stars were thin up front, Keller said, "That kid moves like a truck. He's not worth the airfare."

Keller targeted Darius next. Though he considered him a talented player, Keller had tired of his parents' gripes about playing time. A parting seemed mutually beneficial, but Keller still chose deception over honesty. Before a tournament in September, Keller told Darius that he would start at point guard in the opening game but then left him on the bench for that contest and for most of the weekend.

"That was it. I left," Darius said. "I was just tired of all Keller's lies. I wouldn't play for Keller anymore, even if I didn't have a team. Keller doesn't care about anybody but . . . Demetrius."

Keller didn't wish for or orchestrate the next departure. Unbeknownst to anyone, Bill Howard, Pe'Shon's father, had spoken to Louis Wilson, Team Maryland's coach, at Nationals. Wilson told Bill that Pe'shon, not Demetrius, was the Inland Stars' best player. "He has that East Coast toughness," Wilson said, and he hinted that if Pe'Shon played for him, he would be featured more. Emboldened by Wilson's words, Bill called Keller and named his terms: Commit to Pe'Shon as your starting point guard for the season and pay all our travel costs, or we'll leave the Inland Stars for Team Maryland. Keller could have afforded the added expense of getting Bill and Pe'Shon to tournaments, but he wasn't going to let Bill dictate his actions at a time when he was looking to thin the roster. A few months later, Bill moved to Maryland so Pe'Shon could play for a coach "who believed in him."

After Pe'Shon left, the roster seemed thin enough. At the guard spots, Keller had Justin, Jordan, Andrew, and Tommy. In the frontcourt he had Rome, Terran, and Demetrius. He needed to add more size up front and possibly another strong guard, but the rest of the players appeared likely to return for another year. Yet Keller insisted that he needed to make one more cut. He lamented the team's abundance of "slow guards who can shoot." He named Tommy, of course, but he also singled out Andrew.

Judging those two players merely on ability was an easy call: Tommy had to go. During the practices in early August when Andrew shone, Tommy struggled. In one session, Andrew hounded Tommy on defense, making it difficult for him to even get the ball across half-court. Rob attended most of those practices and came away convinced that Andrew would be the Inland Stars' starting point guard once again. Keller, however, seemed to be watching a different set of practices. "Andrew looks slow. He hasn't gotten any faster since he first joined the team." As for Tommy: "I think he's getting better. He's never going to be a big player for us, but he's getting better." When his assessment was questioned, he barked, "Who knows more about basketball, you or me?"

Keller could fall in love with a kid at first glance, and he could lose faith in a player's ability just as quickly. Only six months earlier, at the tournament in Baltimore, Keller and the coach of the Severna Park Green Hornets were watching their teams warm up when the Severna

Park coach pointed to Andrew and said, "That one and Demetrius. That's your bread and butter right there." Keller agreed, calling Andrew his second-best player. But after watching him struggle against Kendall Marshall at Nationals, Keller questioned whether Andrew should even be on the team.

"Can I afford to take up two spots on slow guards?" Keller said. His real dilemma seemed to be: Could he keep a slowish guard on the roster whose dad wasn't lining his pockets? Tom had already promised to increase his support of the team to $30,000 in exchange for a spot for Tommy another season. Pared down, Keller's choice was: Andrew, the better player, or Tommy, his cash cow.

Rob was oblivious to the fragility of his son's position, and for good reason. Had he been told that Keller was considering cutting Andrew in favor of Tommy, he would have laughed. Not only was Andrew better, but Tom and Tommy had been with the team for only a year, whereas Rob and Andrew were among the "core" that Keller often praised. Rob ran practices when Keller couldn't, and Lisa made sure boys without rides arrived at workouts and games on time. In the last year, Rob had taken on even more responsibility, running a team of younger players Keller thought had potential. Rob assumed this bought him some loyalty, and he also presumed that if Keller had doubts about Andrew, he would come to him and discuss them. But Keller wasn't the same person from three years before or even a season earlier. The guy whose straightforward approach had earned the respect of Dennis Dickens and Casey had given way to a person with no allegiances, save the one Darius so shrewdly pointed out—to Demetrius. If he was willing to miss the birth of his daughter to try to win Nationals, why would he feel obligated to a player he no longer deemed vital to the mission?

Still, cutting Andrew would have ramifications. Everyone associated with the team (except perhaps Tom) knew that Andrew was better than Tommy. Rob and Lisa and Andrew were also a link to the team's honest beginnings, when Keller's ambitions were interwoven with genuine concern for the boys and their families. Without them, without what they represented, Keller was just another basketball mercenary, no different from Pat Barrett and all the others.

Keller understood the implications of cutting Andrew, and whenever I asked him about it he said, "I'm not sure what I am going to do." But he *was* sure. He just wasn't sure how to do it. Passing over to the dark side wasn't easy for him, even if he had been toeing the line for a long time.

It was no surprise that Keller ultimately chose the coward's approach. At a tournament in September, he left Andrew on the bench, giving most of his minutes to Tommy. Given his past experiences, he knew that if he offended Andrew strongly enough, Rob would pull him off the team.

Rob didn't realize what Keller was up to at first. He asked John and Rome, Sr., if something had happened during one of the few practices he'd missed. Was Andrew slacking off? Were other players performing better? When the answers came back "no," Rob assumed Keller had used that tournament to placate Tom, who hoped for a greater return on his investment than he'd gotten the previous season. But at a tournament in San Diego the following weekend, Keller left Andrew on the bench again. *Something is up,* Rob thought, and that led to a series of dinner-table talks between Rob and Lisa, after which they concluded that Rob had to confront Keller.

Later that month, Rob cautiously approached Keller after a practice. It was not easy for him; he was demure and hated confrontation. He even cheered softly, never wanting to offend supporters of the opposing team.

"Joe, the past couple tournaments, Andrew hasn't been playing, and I think I need to know: Is Andrew your primary point guard?"

Keller mumbled something about "seeing how things develop" and tried to walk past Rob, but Rob moved in front of him.

"Joe, if you are not going to use Andrew, we are not going to keep him with you. He's too good a player to be sitting."

Keller looked at Rob, looked down at the floor, and just walked away.

Rob and Lisa decided that Keller's actions at the next tournament would decide it. If Andrew played consistent minutes and started at least a few of the games, he would remain on the team. If not, they had no choice but to act. Keller knew Rob was at the threshold, and so he gave him one final push. At a tournament in Lakewood a few days later, not only did Keller sit Andrew for most of the game, he inserted Tommy into the starting lineup. His choice was made: cash over character.

On the drive home from Lakewood, Andrew didn't say much from the backseat as his parents discussed what to do. Lisa wanted to leave immediately; Rob hoped that Keller would change his mind, even though he knew from his years with the team that he rarely did. After several minutes of vacillating, Rob put the question to his son.

"We're thinking about leaving the team," Rob said to Andrew. "What do you think?"

"Fine," Andrew said. He gazed out the window, expressionless.

Rob took a deep breath. It was over, and he needed a few moments to let it settle in. He eventually called Keller's cell phone.

"Joe, that's it. We're leaving," he said.

"Okay," Keller said tersely, which stung Rob. He wanted Keller to at least go through the motions of trying to talk him out of it.

John and Rome, Sr., called Rob after receiving the news. They expressed disbelief and anger, consoling him with lines like: "It's probably the best thing for Andrew." None of them spoke to Keller about it, however. Relief that their child hadn't been dumped exceeded their outrage.

To avoid Andrew having to play against his old teammates, Rob placed him on a grassroots team a grade above the Inland Stars. He remained hurt for a long time, but Rob could never get to the point of hating Keller; that wasn't his nature. "Joe, I guess, just doesn't treat people the same way I was taught to treat people," he said, as if Keller's callousness was a hereditary defect. "Andrew will miss playing with D and Rome and all his friends, but maybe in the long run this will be for the best."

Keller showed regret about Andrew and Rob only once.

A few weeks after they left the team, Keller rode in the passenger seat of a car headed north from San Diego to Fontana. Earlier, Keller's team of mostly sixth- and seventh-graders had played three games against eighth-graders. It was called "playing up," and Keller had begun scheduling more games against older competition to better challenge the boys. In the final, against players already into puberty, Demetrius scored more than 30 points and was the team's only consistent threat during a 6-point loss. He shone mainly because of his speed, beating players to loose balls and on fast breaks. After the game, a man representing a Southern California track club approached Demetrius in the parking lot and handed him his business card. "You should be running track," the man said. "I see you as a sprinter, in the four hundred and maybe the eight hundred. You could be in the Olympics. You're the next Michael Johnson."

"Track," Keller scoffed as we drove away. "There's no money in that."

Keller was so giddy about Demetrius's play that he waved off topics I hoped to discuss on the drive, Andrew's exit chief among them. Whenever I brought it up or mentioned that I'd talked to Pe'Shon or Darius, he changed the subject.

"You know, within six years I am going to be a millionaire," he said at one point, cutting me off as I brought up Rob's hurt feelings.

I ignored him.

"You don't believe me, do you? You don't believe I am going to be a millionaire."

Of course I didn't believe him. But I didn't say so, because Demetrius was lying in the backseat. His size-15 shoes were slammed against one window because his expanding frame, now almost six foot one, didn't fit across the width of a Taurus.

"Demetrius goes to the NBA, that's like $500,000 from his first contract right there," Keller said. "Then when a couple of my other guys—Rome, Terran, Justin—go to college, I'll get some money from that as well, from the schools and from agents, maybe $100,000 each. . . . You see how it all works? I'm going to be a millionaire." Keller pretended to bang his fists against the dashboard. "Admit it," he said. "You're starting to believe."

Keller raised that question with increasing frequency. He meant: Did I believe, as he did, that Demetrius was destined for the NBA. I didn't admit it, but after watching Demetrius play in San Diego I was less skeptical.

I tried again to turn the conversation to Andrew and Rob, but Keller flipped open his cell phone and announced that he was calling Barrett. The charade of the Inland Stars playing under the SCA umbrella had ceased after Barrett failed to come through with money Keller wanted for new uniforms. Keller no longer paid lip service to a partnership but still kept in touch with Barrett, mostly to gloat about Demetrius. "You know what they say: Keep your friends close but your enemies closer," he said as he put the phone to his ear.

While Keller gushed to Barrett, Demetrius and I talked about his life at school, which pleased him greatly. It was as if no one asked him about such banalities.

"Did you ever get into a fight when you were my age?" Demetrius said from the backseat while munching on potato chips. "Guys are always trying to start stuff with me because of who I am." Girls had begun to notice how good he was at basketball, he explained, and other boys were getting jealous. "Oh, they know I am going to play in the NBA someday. They're just hating. I don't want to fight them. I just try to ignore them, but what am I going to do?"

Later, I asked him if he had a girlfriend.

"Oh, George, now, why would you want to know that?"

I told him I was curious.

"Oh, so you're *Curious George!*" he said, and then out came that laugh, with its piercing "Ha!"—and he rolled over in the seat, giggling.

A short time later, while Demetrius slept, I succeeded in turning Keller's attention to Andrew. While discussing the play of the backcourt in San Diego, I mentioned that the team could have used him. "I love Andrew, but he's just too slow," Keller said. He grew quiet and fiddled with his cell phone. "He peaked too soon." He seemed to be anguishing not over having cut Andrew and betraying Rob's trust but over the fact that a player he once hailed as second in ability only to Demetrius had failed to live up to the potential he saw in him. Andrew had let him down, not the other way around.

I wondered: If he could treat Andrew that way, could turn the page on him so quickly, what about Demetrius? If Demetrius stopped growing or hurt his knee, would the player Keller claimed was like a son be cast away as well?

"Joe, what happens if D doesn't make the NBA?" I asked.

Keller shot me a stare as if I had insulted his wife. It was the possibility you dared not speak of. "Now, why would you say that?"

"Well, what if he doesn't?"

Keller thought for a moment and, before he answered, looked to the backseat to make sure Demetrius was still asleep. He was lying on his side, facing the front, and his hands were wrapped together and tucked under his cheek. He looked like a little boy lost in his dreams.

"Well, then all this would have been a waste of time," Keller said. "Demetrius would have been a bad investment."

PART TWO

Starting
to Believe

(MICHAEL J. LEBRECHT II/*SPORTS ILLUSTRATED*)

Sonny Vaccaro

In Fall 2003, Keller drove his Ford Expedition into the Santa Monica Mountains north of Malibu. In the passenger's seat was Wayne Merino, the former coach at Artesia High in Lakewood, who had won three state titles in the 1990s but then lost his job in 1999 after the California Interscholastic Federation determined that foreign players using falsified visas had competed for the school. He had been floating around the youth-basketball scene ever since.

The car approached a manned security gate at the entrance to Mountain View Estates, a lavish neighborhood in Calabasas, a city of less than 30,000 where actor Will Smith, composer James Horner, and other wealthy entertainers lived. Though it is only twenty-two miles from Los Angeles, Calabasas is a world away. Before leaving Fontana, Keller had fretted over what to wear, asking Violet repeatedly if his outfit was appropriate. He had swapped his usual shorts or jeans for tan slacks and a collared shirt.

Once through the security gate, the car wound a mile farther into the mountains before making a left turn onto Collingwood Circle. The houses on this block looked like many in Southern California—stucco, with hints of Spanish architecture—but they were massive. It was a planned community, and the planners had targeted the super-wealthy. Keller parked the car in front of a white house with a wisp of creeping fig bending over the vaulted doorway. He followed Merino up the front walk and took a deep breath as he pressed the bell. The door opened almost immediately, which startled Keller but not as much as what happened next.

"Joe!" Sonny Vaccaro yelled, and then the godfather of grassroots basketball hugged Keller as if he'd known him for years.

Keller would say hard work had put him on Sonny Vaccaro's doorstep, but a series of fortuitous events had helped pave the way. After failing to sign LeBron James to a shoe contract—despite offering more than the $90 million LeBron took from Nike—Reebok hired Vaccaro away from Adidas to, in his words, "establish Reebok as a basketball brand." This was a seismic development in the grassroots world. For a decade, Nike and Adidas had been the only players in the youth game. Now Reebok decided to throw its shoe into the ring, and the hiring of Vaccaro announced the seriousness of its intent.

To build Reebok's profile, Vaccaro needed influential grassroots coaches in key areas of the country. Some Adidas-sponsored coaches would follow him to Reebok, but he would need more. This gave the best coaches leverage to get a sweeter deal from Nike or Adidas or to move to Reebok for more money and gear. Reebok's leap into the market also gave small-time coaches out on the competitive fringe hope that they might finally land a deal.

Given the consistent flow of talent from Southern California, Vaccaro needed to establish a presence there. His roots were in the East, and he would sign up established coaches from there, but Nike and Adidas had a grip on the Southern California market. They also paid their coaches handsomely, so Vaccaro scouted for unaffiliated coaches he could build up.

Keller should not have been under consideration. His players were thought to be too young to be effective marketing tools for the shoe companies. But Vaccaro heard from other coaches that Adidas had its eye on Keller and that the company had considered signing him to a shoe deal to gain access to the young phenoms he controlled. Vaccaro wondered if the Inland Stars wouldn't be a good long-term investment for Reebok. Sponsor them now and then wait for the payoff in a few years when Demetrius reached high school. At the very least, he thought it advantageous to establish a relationship with Keller.

Keller was in his car when he received the call from Merino informing him that Vaccaro wanted to meet. He remained composed on the phone, but once off the line his excitement boiled over. "It's all working out, the big plan," he said. He started to call Violet but then stopped, as he was only a few miles from his apartment. He paused, unsure if he should call someone else before he got home. "This is it. This is it," he said. It was like being summoned to meet his king. "I can't believe it. Sonny. I am meeting with Sonny."

A week later, Keller and Merino stood on Vaccaro's doorstep.

Vaccaro, sixty-five, was wearing a black sweat suit and socks but no shoes. He was shorter than Keller had imagined, maybe five foot six, and had raccoon eyes and gray stubble on his cheeks. He looked like an old Italian mobster enjoying his day off.

Vaccaro's apparent lack of polish was part of his charm. He was a millionaire, one of the most powerful men in basketball, the guy who'd spotted Michael Jordan's potential as a marketing star before anyone else, yet he lacked pretension of any kind. It didn't matter if you were a waiter, a cabby, a sixteen-year-old basketball star, or Nike founder Phil Knight. He treated everyone the same: as if they were the most important and brilliant person. He often forgot names or became confused during the telling of a story, but his wife, Pam, had a sharp mind for details and would jump in, and this further coated him with a sort of grandfatherly innocence.

Vaccaro led Keller and Merino over a large Victorian carpet in the entry, where a round table topped with white orchids centered the room. To the left was a winding staircase that led to the second level, and Keller noticed paintings there and on other walls of the house—one of a lone cypress tree, another of children playing at the beach. "Those were all done by my mother-in-law," Vaccaro said. "She just took up painting a few years ago. She's gotten pretty good, don't you think?" To the right of the entry was a formal living room with shiny couches that looked untouched, but straight ahead was a more informal sitting area with a large television and deep couches. To the right of that was the kitchen, where Vaccaro and Pam spent most of their time. Beyond two picture windows was a giant pool, and beside that were two flowering trees, around which were more than a dozen hummingbirds, drawn to six feeders hanging from branches. Ducks had recently taken up residence in his pool, Vaccaro said, and he loved feeding them. But then Pam called the Humane Society and learned that if they kept at it, the ducks might stop migrating. "Now we shoo them away with a broom or the pool sweep," Vaccaro said.

Pam joined the three men for lunch at a round table in the kitchen. The focus was entirely on Keller, as Vaccaro and Pam wanted to know his story. He talked about how he'd put the team together, how it was "like a family," and how fortunate he had been to find so many talented kids. To support this, Keller cited the recent Hoop Scoop rankings of the top seventh-graders in the country, eight of whom had played for Keller the previous season: Demetrius (1), Pe'Shon (10), Justin (20), Rome (22), Terran (24), Jordan (31), Xavier (37), and Andrew (59). Vaccaro knew Clark Francis's rankings were mostly unsubstantiated hype (how else to explain seven of the top 37 kids all on the same team?), but it proved that people had taken notice of Keller's work.

Keller came across as assured yet grounded, Vaccaro would say later, and also a little naïve. But naïve was good. Vaccaro loved to mentor young coaches and athletes.

After lunch, Vaccaro took Keller to his office upstairs. On the walls were pictures of him with past and present NBA stars—Alonzo Mourning, Tracy McGrady, Kobe Bryant, Charles Barkley—and some of the coaching fraternity's biggest names. In one corner was a chair from the 2000 NCAA Championship game, signed by the University of Florida basketball team. Vaccaro showed Keller one of his prized possessions: a Nike shoe Michael Jordan wore in a game in 1992.

Once back downstairs, they settled into the comfortable couches in the television room.

"I think we can work together," Vaccaro said. "As Wayne probably told you, I am looking for a team in Southern California. So, tell me, how can I help you?"

Keller had prepared for that question. For days after Merino set up the meeting, Keller turned the numbers over in his head. If Vaccaro wanted to talk money, how much should he ask for? He knew what Barrett got in his deals with Nike and then Adidas, but he wasn't as established as Barrett. He concluded that if he asked for too much—say, $100,000—Vaccaro might just show him the door. "Fifty thousand a year to cover expenses," Keller said, and then he listed his product needs, which included hundreds of pairs of shoes and jerseys and other gear.

"It's done," Vaccaro said, so swiftly that it took Keller a few seconds to realize that all his demands had been met.

As Vaccaro showed Keller and Merino out, he mentioned a delay in signing a contract because Reebok didn't officially employ him yet. It would take a few weeks for him to put together a formal offer. Keller barely heard him, as he was in a kind of giddy shock. No more begging for Pat Barrett's scraps. No more having to take on kids just because they had rich parents.

Finally, he had made it.

K eller's landing of a shoe deal would not shake basketball in the way that Vaccaro's move to Reebok did, but it carried great significance. Until Vaccaro met with Keller, no shoe company had explicitly associated itself with the coach of kids so young. There had been teams—such as the SCA squad that played the first incarnation of the Inland Stars at Riverside Community College in 1996—that appeared to be sponsored by Nike or Adidas, but these were cases when a sponsored coach shifted shoes or money he got for his older team to a younger group. Officially, the targets of the sponsorship had been the high-school-age kids.

Keller understood the message this sent, but he was too focused on the financial windfall he stood to land to dwell on it. He began looking at homes in nicer areas of the Inland Empire, and he considered purchasing a new car for Violet. He looked into tournaments the team could attend in areas of the country they hadn't yet visited. Mostly, he reveled in the importance a shoe contract bestowed upon him. No longer would he be known as the dupe who lost Tyson Chandler. He was now a pioneering coach who'd gotten a shoe deal for kids who weren't even in high school.

"That shoe deal, it shows you have credibility," he said. "And the product you get, you can bribe people with. In a way, the product is more important than the money. In this business, with the kids, the product is what matters most."

Eager to fill the boys' closets with new shoes, jerseys, warm-ups, and other Reebok paraphernalia, Keller couldn't wait until Vaccaro signed his contract so he could then sign his. After a month, he was anxious. After two months, he grew agitated. After three months, he left messages for Vaccaro and spoke with Merino, who assured him that Vaccaro was a man of his word and it was just taking time for him to get settled in his new post.

"Something is up," Keller said. "I've been screwed before. I know what it feels like. "

After Vaccaro's hiring by Reebok became official, he learned two things that altered his plan for building Reebok's image among the kids of Southern California. First, the timetable for when Reebok wanted their shoes on the feet of some of America's best young players was sooner rather than later, which flew in the face of his long-term plan of building through the sponsorship of the youthful Inland Stars. Second, Vaccaro realized that the fledging grassroots division at Reebok had signed a sponsorship agreement with a coach in Southern California just before he was hired. That coach had recently been let go by Adidas and, although he did not have any notable players at the time, he was more established than Keller.

His name: Pat Barrett.

Vaccaro didn't particularly want to get into business with Barrett. Former UNLV and Fresno State coach Jerry Tarkanian, a friend of Vaccaro's, once referred to Barrett as the "biggest whore I ever met" for how he tried to profit from one of his players. Vaccaro thought little of Barrett as a person, but he also knew that he could be useful. Also, breaking Barrett's contract would cost Reebok money.

Vaccaro could have sponsored both SCA and the Inland Stars, but as he thought longer about the implications of signing a team of middle school kids to a shoe contract, he decided it was not something he wanted to add to his legacy. He was regularly lampooned for opening the door for the shoe companies, agents, and other profiteers to infiltrate youth basketball, but over time he had found peace with his role. Tennis players, golfers, gymnasts, swimmers—athletes in numerous sports—were courted in the same way Kobe Bryant, Tracy McGrady, and

LeBron James were when they were on the grassroots circuit, and Vaccaro believed those who disparaged basketball stars going pro straight out of high school were hypocritical. "A white tennis player can sign a contract with Nike when she is sixteen and no one says a word, but if a black kid from Compton does it, they say that it is wrong."

Vaccaro liked to take stands, but being the first to sponsor a younger team didn't feel like a stand. It felt like lowering the bar, and he was too old to fight that fight again. It didn't help that, as he called around to further investigate Keller, he heard mixed reviews about his morals. "Look, we are all in it for the money, but from what I am hearing about Joe, he is so driven by it that it is scary," Vaccaro said.

How Keller learned that his Reebok deal was dead would have pleased the kids and parents Keller had discarded over the years. Neither Vaccaro nor Merino called Keller to tell him that Reebok was no longer interested; he was left to assume that from their silence.

At a tournament in early December, Keller stood on the sidelines watching Demetrius during warm-ups. Kids of all ages lined the court to watch Demetrius finish dunk after dunk. His latest slam involved throwing it off the backboard and dunking it with one hand, and it elicited loud cheers from the young boys around the court. "Look at that," Keller said. "Sonny won't work with me. But I know someone is going to put their logo on that kid."

Near the end of 2003, the Inland Stars played in a tournament in the San Fernando Valley. Among those in attendance was Dana Pump, who along with his twin brother, David, ran the Pump N Run teams sponsored by Adidas. Dana and David had learned under Vaccaro when he was at Adidas and then branched out into areas even Vaccaro hadn't tried. They opened a consulting business that universities hired to aid in the search for new coaches and athletic directors, and they partnered with a Southern California ticket broker to help college coaches scalp their Final Four tickets. Most people couldn't tell David and Dana apart but knew it was good to be their friend, as they seemed to know every coach, player, and parent who mattered. The brothers were keenly aware of their importance, enough so to poke fun at it. Around the time Dana Pump was watching the Inland Stars in the San Fernando Valley, some of the biggest names in college coaching received a Christmas present from the Pumps: bobble-head dolls the twins had made of themselves.

After one of the Inland Stars' games, Dana sidled up to Keller and casually mentioned that he had heard about his failed deal with Reebok.

"Yeah, Sonny did me wrong," Keller said.

Dana inquired about some of the Inland Stars, where they were from and how old they were, then suggested that he might be able to help Keller out with some product.

"I'm done taking gear from other coaches," Keller said.

Dana didn't ask, but Keller stated firmly that he planned to keep the team intact through high school. He assumed Dana was angling to inherit Demetrius and some of the other boys when they got older.

Keller didn't know it at the time, but David and Dana Pump's influence at Adidas was on the rise. Vaccaro's successor at Adidas, a thirty-something named Daren Kalish, did not know the grassroots landscape as Vaccaro did, and he relied on the Pumps, who were longtime friends, to guide him. Other AAU coaches, such as Darren Matsubara in Northern California and Jimmy Salmon out of New York/New Jersey, also had his ear. They were part of what became known as the Grassroots Basketball Council, a sort of board of directors who guided Adidas's grassroots vision. It was an unusual setup, as it gave the AAU coaches more power than they'd ever had, something Vaccaro always cautioned against. "They went from having me, little Caesar, running everything and keeping an eye on all the coaches, to having a parliament, with the coaches monitoring themselves," Vaccaro said.

Dana's scouting of the Inland Stars at the tournament in the San Fernando Valley was at least the second time he'd seen them play, and it confirmed what he'd initially thought: Demetrius was a kid Adidas needed to align with.

"Joe, I'm having dinner with Daren Kalish a little later," Dana told Keller. "You should meet him. We should all talk."

A few hours later, Keller sat at a long table at Hal's Bar & Grill in Venice. Among the group were Dana, Kalish, and a few other AAU coaches, including Wallace Prather. Prather was the coach of the Adidas-sponsored Atlanta Celtics, which that year featured Dwight Howard and Josh Smith, both of whom would be picked in the first round of the 2004 NBA draft, with Howard as the number-1 overall selection. Keller was noticeably nervous as he picked at his New York strip steak and sipped a Diet Coke. Kalish, a handsome, light-skinned African American, didn't pay much attention to Keller during dinner because he sat at the opposite end of the table, but Keller got the sense that Dana had already filled him in about Demetrius and the other talented youngsters Keller controlled.

Near the end of the meal, Kalish moved to Keller's end of the table and laid out his philosophy on grassroots programs, which differed from Vaccaro's. "We don't care if Demetrius makes it to the NBA like Sonny does. We just care that we can market him now."

Dana told a story that Keller had passed on to him. On the first day of a recent tournament, Demetrius wore two Adidas shoes from the same line but different in color.

"The next day, all these kids on the other teams were doing the same thing," Keller interjected.

"That's the kind of thing we want," Kalish said. "We want the market on that. We want to be the first ones to do that."

After the dinner, Keller had to make amends with Violet, who had waited in the restaurant's parking lot, along with Jordan and five-month-old Alyssa, for the entirety of the dinner. On the drive back to Fontana, Keller assured her that it had been worth the inconvenience. "Daren wants me to meet him tomorrow at his hotel," he said. "This could be big."

The following morning, Keller met Kalish in a banquet room at the Renaissance Hotel near LAX. Kalish's approach was more formal than Vaccaro's. He said Adidas wanted to sign Keller to a shoe deal but presented it as something of a tryout. They would be the youngest of Adidas's "highlighted teams," but he emphasized that if Keller was caught doing anything illegal, the contract would be terminated. They agreed on a five-year deal in which Keller would make $60,000 in the first year, with his salary increasing by $10,000 in each subsequent year. At the end of the contract, when Demetrius and the other boys would be entering their senior year in high school, Adidas had the right to match any offer Keller received from another shoe company.

"Do whatever you want with the money, but just don't ask for more," Kalish said.

When Kalish asked how much money in product he needed, Keller had no idea how to answer. He knew how it worked—Kalish would give him a product code, and when he ordered something from one of Adidas's many catalogs, the wholesale cost of each item would be deducted from his total—but he didn't know how to quantify it. "I didn't know what to say, so I just took what I thought was the most I would need—fifty thousand dollars—and I doubled it," Keller said. "And Daren didn't even blink. He just said yes to everything."

Kalish said he would send Demetrius a pair of shoes with the team logo on them and said Adidas would like to put the names of Keller's top five players on their shoes. Keller hesitated, as he felt it would make other players jealous.

"Just tell the other kids that the players had it done themselves," Kalish said.

Kalish agreed to reimburse Keller $8,500 he'd earlier spent on uniforms and also to sponsor eight events (tournaments or camps) he staged. To Keller, that was key. He calculated he could make an additional $200,000 for the year by running Adidas-backed events.

Keller's enthusiasm was tempered by his earlier experience with Vaccaro, and he felt more relief than exhilaration. But later that night, Kalish escorted Keller to Pauley Pavilion on UCLA's campus for the Dream Classic, an annual tournament featuring some of the best high school teams in the country. Before they took their seats, Kalish introduced Keller to Danny Ainge, the Boston Celtics' general manager, and Denver Nuggets GM Kiki Vandeweghe. Bill Duffy, a prominent NBA agent, talked to Keller for several minutes. Eventually, Keller and Kalish settled into front-row seats at center court. Keller sat there with a wide smile on his face, hardly believing his own rags-to-riches-to-rags-to-riches story.

Early in the game, during a break in the action, Keller scanned the crowd in search of more basketball luminaries he could tell Violet about later. Glancing to his left, he recognized an older gentleman sitting in the second row of seats behind the basket. He was seated next to his wife, whom Keller also recognized.

"It was Sonny," he said. "I had a better seat than Sonny."

12

(JOE KELLER)

Roberto Nelson

When word of Keller's Adidas deal spread among the grass-roots populace, coaches from around the country called to praise him for being the first to land a shoe contract for kids so young. They asked if he could send them Adidas products and pleaded with him to bring his team to their events. Word leaked that his pact permitted him to give gear to a high school team—presumably the school Demetrius would eventually attend—and several high school coaches placed courting calls. He also heard from more parents like Tom, those willing to pay handsomely for a spot on his team.

"Everyone wants to be my friend," Keller said. "And I've got to admit, I'm feeling pretty cocky and arrogant right now."

On January 21, three UPS trucks stopped at the Citrus Grove Apartments and delivered eighty-four boxes. Every inch of Keller's apartment—save a path from the door to the bathroom—was quickly filled, and Keller and Violet were forced to stack boxes on the stairs outside. The following day, UPS dropped off another fifty boxes.

Keller played Santa Claus, giving each player no fewer than four pairs of basketball shoes—two pairs of the Promodel 2Gs, the A3 Superstar Ultras, and the T-MAC 3s—each pair costing more than $100 retail. He also handed out as many sweatbands, headbands, socks, T-shirts, sweatshirts, practice shorts, and shooting shirts as they wanted, which they stuffed into an Adidas travel bag, sling bag, and backpack. The grassroots executives at Adidas sent special packages for Demetrius, including the first pair of Promodels with the team's logo, then a pair of T-MAC 3.5s, which he got before they were even in stores. Later, when he wanted extra-long black socks, the soccer rep at Adidas procured several pairs for him.

When the team returned to Portland in February for that year's Nike Invitational, grassroots executives for The Swoosh took note of the team's new sponsorship. A man approached Keller and asked for Demetrius's shoe size. A week later, ten pairs of shoes from Michael Jordan's Jumpman line arrived at Keller's house with a note for Demetrius that read: "Best of luck in the future."

Some coaches might have worried that such special treatment would isolate Demetrius from his teammates or cause a rift, but not Keller. "D is the reason we got the shoe deal. Why shouldn't he get more?"

The other boys grumbled about it, but for the most part they understood that it wasn't Justin's defense or Terran's rebounding or Jordan's outside shot that Adidas had invested in, and they were just happy to get the gear they did. Most attended different middle schools, which gave them a limelight all their own when they were away from the team. Each boy walked onto campus wearing a black Adidas sweat suit, a royal-blue Adidas hat tilted high on his head, his books in a black-and-gray Adidas backpack sagging low on his back, and, most importantly, spotless Promodels or T-MACs on his feet, never the same pair as the day before.

When the boys entered a gym en masse, the new gear amplified their ability to intimidate. Wearing identical blue warm-ups, matching shoes (save Demetrius), with sling bags on their backs, they looked like a professional team. When they stripped down to uniforms that cost $250 apiece, opposing players stopped to admire them. Keller also came across as more qualified after he dropped his usual shorts and T-shirts in favor of tan slacks and a blue or black Adidas golf shirt that matched his Adidas running shoes. He insisted that Violet and the kids wear Adidas gear to games as well, even little Alyssa, who favored a tiny hot-pink Adidas sweat suit.

The design of the new uniforms marked a significant shift in Keller's marketing of the team. Gone was the familiar *Inland Stars* script across the front, replaced by *Team Cal* spelled out in jagged lettering. Keller had concluded that the team had outgrown its old name. It was too localized, ill fitting a team with national aspirations. It also had associations with SCA because of Keller's earlier dealings with Barrett. A new name would be clean ground on which Keller could build his own empire, unencumbered by the past. The home uniforms were white with blue lettering, the away jerseys blue with white script. Both sets had the Adidas logo on the left shoulder, and on one leg of the shorts was the new team logo: a basketball with an outline of the state of California inside.

"We're the best team in California, so we should be called Team Cal," Demetrius said. "We don't got just Inland kids, we got kids from L.A. and other places, so it makes sense. Plus, it's just tighter. Team Cal. That's tight."

With the $60,000 in salary Adidas paid him plus Tom's contributions, Keller could have realized some of his ambitions, such as a nicer car or a bigger apartment. To his credit, he earmarked a portion of it to fix the problem he would never admit the team had: his coaching. He used some of the money to hire fifty-four-year-old Mark Soderberg as an assistant coach.

Soderberg's basketball credentials were unimpeachable. He played under Lute Olson at Marina High in Huntington Beach in the 1960s and then for Adolph Rupp at Kentucky. After college, he played in France, Italy, and Switzerland for nine years, then returned to Southern California and was an assistant coach at Marina High, Riverside Community College, and most recently at Mater Dei, the area's most dominant high school program. Beyond his knowledge of the game, Soderberg had no investment other than wanting to see the boys learn and succeed, and he wasn't afraid to tell Keller when his actions threatened those goals.

When he approached Soderberg about the job, Keller told him, "I have this group of kids, and I think we have more talent than anybody, but we've failed at Nationals a couple times. Help me figure out what is going wrong."

After watching four practices, Soderberg concluded that the boys were in fantastic shape, worked hard, and could probably dominate most teams because of their raw ability. "Their athleticism is going to be enough until you meet another athletic team, and then when your athleticism is negated, it will come down to who is more fundamentally sound," he told Keller. "It will come down to what coach can get their five kids on the floor acting as one."

He saw immense room for improvement, particularly on defense. The "gimmicky" defenses Keller ran, such as Fist, "were just a bunch of athletes doing their thing," Soderberg said. "We've got to teach them how to guard man on man, teach them proper positioning on defense."

There were other issues—the boys struggled against some zone defenses and watched Demetrius too much on offense—but Soderberg considered those fixable. He also looked at Keller as a rehabilitation project. "Joe, we've got to separate ourselves from the usual AAU riffraff and mentality," he said. "You're with Adidas now, and you've got to start projecting an image that Adidas would want representing them." It was Soderberg who suggested Keller dress more nicely on the sidelines and who also got him to temper his sideline antics by threatening to videotape him during a game and show him "what a lunatic looks like."

Soderberg looked like a holdover from the 1960s, with a thick brown beard and a red Volkswagen bus. Watching him squeeze his six-foot-ten frame behind the wheel was a constant source of amusement to the boys.

"Coach Mark, you need a newer car," Demetrius told him after one practice as Soderberg slowly packed his legs into the driver's seat.

"Are you kidding? This is a classic," he said, patting the window frame. He tried to explain how popular the car was back in his day, and his long-winded response made him an even more comical figure: a fifty-four-year-old trying to tell a twelve-year-old what was cool.

The players instantly recognized his knowledge of the game, but what appealed to them most was how Soderberg spoke *to* them and not *at* them. Demetrius, for one, had never had a coach who offered measured instruction, who took the time to explain how his teachings would lead to success on the court.

Unbeknownst to Demetrius, he was at the center of an ongoing argument between Keller and Soderberg. Because he had no stake in Demetrius's future, Soderberg wasn't motivated to showcase him. He recognized that he was the best player on the team, but for the team to improve, other boys had to be more involved on offense. The more scoring threats the team possessed, the harder it would be for defenses to key on Demetrius. But it was difficult for Keller to see the bigger picture, and he battled Soderberg on this point.

"It's a bad analogy, but I am trying to wean Joe off of the heroin that is Demetrius," Soderberg said. "He's got to remember, there are other great kids on this team who can also get it done."

On a Saturday afternoon at the Rancho Cucamonga Family Sports Center, Team Cal was preparing for the start of practice when a new boy and his father entered the gym. The boy was about five foot ten, a few inches shorter than Demetrius, and had a medium-high Afro. Keller introduced the new player to the team as "Roberto Nelson from Santa Barbara," but when Roberto stepped onto the court for a drill, Demetrius said, "I've got Puffy."

Neither Keller nor Soderberg had seen Roberto play; he was invited to a practice on the recommendation of a former Team Cal parent, who had seen him hold his own in a tournament in Santa Barbara against Jrue Holiday and Jerime Anderson, two top guards who were a grade older.

Roberto was a quarter Mexican and had lighter skin than most of the boys. He also had a blank look and a quiet demeanor that led Keller to say, "He might be stupid." He was not stupid, but he was uninformed about what he was up against at his first practice, and that ignorance served him well. Most of the players Keller recruited got his attention because of how they played against his squad, so they deferred to Demetrius upon joining the team. Roberto had never played against Demetrius, and as he lined up next to him for the opening drill of practice, his mind-set was: *I'm the best player on the floor. Time to show it.*

Roberto first touched the ball on the left side of the court, and Demetrius stood between him and the basket. Bent at the knees, moving sideways to shadow Roberto's movements, Demetrius looked like a crab. Roberto stood on the tips of his toes, leaning forward in an exaggerated fashion. He walked that way all the time, an awkward dawdle that made him seem uncoordinated. Roberto flashed the ball as if he were going to go up for a shot, and Demetrius moved his weight forward in anticipation. At that moment, Roberto drove past him, getting to the rim so quickly that no other defenders had time to rotate over.

The other players were so taken aback—they had never seen a player abuse Demetrius like that—they looked to Keller for how to react.

"Go again!" Keller shouted, and the boys reset the play.

Roberto got the ball on the left wing again, and Demetrius was more aware now, primed to stop him. Roberto made the same move, but Demetrius didn't fall for it. Roberto still pushed toward the rim, and Demetrius slid with him as if he were attached to Roberto's right hip. Most players would have aborted their drive, but Roberto kept going to the rim. Then, about ten feet from the basket, he moved even closer to Demetrius and used his hip and butt to nudge Demetrius at the same moment he jumped to a stop. Roberto's sneakers screeched as he halted, and in the same motion he rose up for a jump shot. Demetrius tried to stop and contest the shot, but the nudge Roberto had given him prevented him from setting himself. He was flat-footed as Roberto's pull-up jumper found the net.

In subsequent possessions, Roberto scored in a variety of ways, showcasing an offensive arsenal more complete than any of the boys'. He could shoot from mid-range like Rome, was able to slash to the basket like Demetrius, and, if necessary, grind away for points inside à la Terran. He was thick for a wing player, and his explosiveness was not on par with Demetrius's, but as a pure scorer he exceeded him.

At Roberto's second practice, Demetrius walked up to him and announced, "You're not scoring today." He guarded him the entire session, and, true to his word, Demetrius held Roberto without a point. Keller reveled in seeing the two boys square off, and in the workouts that followed, he pitted them against each other at every opportunity. Some practices, Demetrius's superior athleticism would carry the day; in others, Roberto's refinement would win out. At first, these battles seemed to benefit both boys; they were such different talents that they had much to teach each other. Then Keller got in the way. Roberto showed up Demetrius too much for his liking, so he began rigging the contests in Demetrius's favor. He let his star get away with elbows and holds but would call Roberto for the slightest touch. If Roberto complained, Keller made him run a Rambo.

During one session, Demetrius banged into Roberto so forcefully, leading with his elbow, that it sent Roberto flying into the wall underneath the basket.

"And one!" Demetrius shouted as the ball rolled in.

Keller called a foul on Roberto.

"Oh, man, this is bullshit," Roberto yelled, and he jumped to his feet.

"That's right. That's right," Demetrius said tauntingly.

Roberto moved toward him, but Terran and Justin got between them. Roberto turned and walked out of the gym.

Most kids would have quit the team after that, but Roberto continued to show up. On a subconscious level he seemed to understand that being cheated by Keller and Demetrius would make him better in the long run. He also respected Soderberg and liked the other players, who after seeing him play dropped the "Puffy" nickname and called him "Berto."

But Roberto never acquired a taste for Keller. The favoritism he showed Demetrius was part of it, but Roberto also disagreed with almost every instruction Keller offered. Roberto's father, Bruce, had played at Santa Barbara City College and at Cal State Hayward; he then coached Dos Pueblos High, north of Santa Barbara, to the 1995 Southern Sectional title game. Going from his dad to Coach Joe was like being sent back to kindergarten after years in graduate school. "Coach Joe knows just enough to think he knows what he is talking about," Roberto told his dad.

At one practice, Roberto's refusal to follow orders led Keller to make the other boys run. Afterward, Justin pulled Roberto aside and pleaded with him to humor Coach Joe.

"Look, that guy just doesn't know shit," Roberto told him.

"I know. I know. We all know," Justin said. "Don't do what he says for him. Do it for us, for the team."

Roberto could get behind that. He listened to Keller a bit more, but only enough to keep his teammates from having to run.

At a tournament in Las Vegas, in a game against an Arizona team a grade higher than Team Cal, Roberto repeatedly broke out on fast breaks, ignoring Keller's orders to back the ball out and set up the offense, and he charged into a defender on three consecutive possessions. To the unknowing eye, he was out of control, and after the last of his rushes Keller pulled him from the game and lectured him. Roberto looked past Keller as if he weren't even there, knowing that he'd seen the forest while his coach was lost in the trees. The defender he kept charging at was Arizona's best player, a spindly forward with a distinct height advantage, and Roberto's mad rushes to the rim had saddled him with three quick fouls.

As Keller rigged practices against Roberto, as he pulled him from games and yelled at him for no good reason, as Demetrius taunted him, Roberto stared at the road ahead, expressionless. After one brutal practice, during the 133-mile drive back to Santa Barbara, Roberto rubbed his arm where Demetrius had hit him with an elbow and said to his father, "D, man, he's good. But I'm going to be better."

13

(BARBARA MOORE)

Aaron Moore and his mother, Barbara Moore

Your son is going to be in the NBA someday. He's going to make you millions," the coach said, and Barbara Moore reached for a cigarette.

It was a hot late-summer day, and Barbara sweated under a thin blouse. Ovals of flattened chewing gum, dropped by kids exiting the nearby gymnasium, were stuck to the concrete at her feet. The gum—polka dots of blue, green, and red—glistened under the intense sun, adding a hint of color to the drab concrete buildings of the middle school.

"But there are sacrifices you are going to have to make, sacrifices Aaron is going to have to make," the coach continued.

Barbara took a long drag on a Marlboro, then another. She was not so much smoking as rushing the cigarette to an end.

"Aaron will stay with me during the week but can come home on the weekends and stay with you. He won't be far."

Barbara had a long, hooked nose and squinty blue eyes and red hair with big bangs that looked sticky with hairspray. She was an imposing woman, more than six feet tall, but was unsteady listening to the coach.

"You shouldn't worry," he said, wrapping up his pitch. "Aaron will be like a member of my family."

That last word, *family,* rang loudly for Barbara. Hers had not felt much like a family lately. She and Aaron, the middle of her three sons, had been fighting more, loud screaming matches that often ended with Aaron in tears as he bolted out of the house. Micah, her youngest, had a seizure disorder that appeared to be worsening. Barbara was an emotional woman, and her ability to manage life depended entirely on her stability at that moment. When she was not worried about a guy she was dating or the security of her job, she was the most involved parent imaginable. If a dilemma arose regarding Aaron, she took a stand instantly, delivering her verdict in one fiery pronouncement. "No, *my son* will not be doing *that.*" But if she was distracted, the choice lingered in her mind far too long, and Aaron was left to make decisions best suited to a parent. It made her seem alternately a great mother and a very bad one.

It's unclear why Barbara struggled financially, despite a steady job managing the health insurance of students at the University of California at Riverside. Like many Americans, she may have simply spent beyond her means. Joe and some people on the team felt that she partied too much and was quick to trust men who took advantage of her generosity. Her divorce from Micah's father a few years earlier had left her riddled with debt, and paying for the basics—food, rent, electricity—was a constant struggle.

She considered the coach's offer while standing outside the middle school and later while smoking a cigarette in front of her home in Rubidoux. The rented house sat at the end of a dirt road on the side of an east-sloping hill, across from a field where nothing grew, no matter the season. At night, the neighborhood had an almost pastoral feeling, save the noise of cars rushing along nearby Highway 60.

As she smoked, Barbara glanced out across that rocky acre of land that no one bothered to farm. She eventually turned and looked back at her house, with its cracked white paint and faux-stone trim around the garage, and wondered what Aaron was doing at that moment. He could be watching television or playing NBA Live on his PlayStation or wrestling with Micah. He was into his teenage years, but there were moments when he acted like the playful child she affectionately called "Yellow Boy." An African American father and fair-skinned mother had produced a child with skin the color of a "big pencil." The operative word was *big*. Aaron was six feet tall by his eleventh birthday. Near the end of 2002, when he was still only thirteen, he stood six foot five. He played soccer growing up and thus went unnoticed by the area's AAU coaches. But then the father of a boy Aaron knew from school recommended him to the coach, and now the grassroots machine had him in its crosshairs.

How can I send my son to live with a man I barely know? That was the question at the crux of Barbara's dilemma. She discounted the coach's talk of needing Aaron close by to further his development toward an NBA career. Who could possibly say that an eighth-grader was destined for the NBA? The coach promised to secure Aaron a scholarship to a parochial school, and she liked that. He'd attended a private school before they moved to Rubidoux, and his grades and attitude had been exemplary. But he was also doing well at nearby Almeria Middle School. She settled on a concern that had been lingering for a long time: Was Aaron at a point in his life when he needed to be around men? He gravitated toward older boys in the neighborhood, some of whom had done time in jail, and Barbara wondered if time was running out to surround him with positive male role models.

In the past, Barbara's choice of paternal figures for Aaron had produced disastrous results. His father left shortly after he was born, moving out of state and cutting off all contact. She married Micah's father, but then divorced him when Aaron was nine. It wasn't until after the divorce that Barbara learned that the man she'd encouraged Aaron to call "Dad" had been molesting him since he was four years old. She didn't have a clue until Aaron told her about it around his tenth birthday, when he finally was old enough to realize the man's behavior was not normal but immoral.

Barbara often told people she'd just met that Aaron had been sexually abused, and it came across as a ploy to gain sympathy for him and her. It made Aaron feel used and further cracked his delicate psyche.

His nervousness was constant. He bit his fingernails voraciously, moving from finger to finger until there was nothing left to bite.

Given her history choosing father figures for Aaron, Barbara couldn't send Aaron to live with the coach. If she turned down the offer, on the other hand, nothing would change, and somehow she feared that more. Standing outside her house, smoking that cigarette, she slowly talked herself into it. It would be one less mouth to feed. He would be going to a good school. Perhaps he had a future in basketball, and this would help him get there. She wrapped her reasoning up with a tidy bow—"I wanted Aaron to be part of a family"—but her decision was little more than pushing her son's life onto the felt and rolling the dice.

"Call me 'Dad,'" Mark Jefferson said.

It was a few days after Aaron had moved into Jefferson's home in Cypress, and Aaron was helping Jefferson clean the floors of the Warrior Center, a basketball facility in Orange County that he managed.

"That's okay," Aaron said. "I like 'Coach.'"

"No, call me 'Dad,'" he urged. "It's okay. I don't mind."

Jefferson first made that request right after Barbara informed him that Aaron could move the fifty miles to his home in Cypress. At that time and when Jefferson repeated the line later, Aaron nodded but continued to call Jefferson "Coach." Barbara may have seen Jefferson as a father figure for Aaron, but Aaron saw him solely as the means to an end.

When Jefferson said Aaron could one day play in the NBA, Aaron believed him, and he saw the move to Cypress as the first step toward the goal. "I am living in Orange County. It's good for my basketball development," he told friends who asked why he wasn't enrolled at Almeria Middle School anymore. He was parroting one of Jefferson's lines, which he repeated to kids at his new school, Brethren Christian in Huntington Beach.

Jefferson was a portly forty-something African-American with heavy eyes. His home in Buena Park was a brown one-story with a dry lawn and a two-car garage stuffed with so many boxes, old sofas, and other junk that there was not enough room to park a car.

The bedroom Aaron shared with Jeff, one of Jefferson's sons, was not unlike his room in Rubidoux. The walls were covered with posters—one of Shaquille O'Neal and Kobe Bryant together, another of Allen Iverson—and covers of *Slam* magazine. There was a wood bunk bed and Aaron was given the top bunk, which was fine by him.

For the first week, living with Jefferson's family in Buena Park felt like an extended sleepover. Aaron, Jeff, and Jeff's younger brother, Byron, sat on the bunk beds playing with Yu-Gi-Oh! and Pokémon cards they bought at a nearby 7-Eleven with money given to them by Jefferson or his wife. She sometimes cooked chicken or pasta for dinner, or Aaron bought a *carne asada* burrito at a taqueria in a strip mall across the street.

He missed his mother and brother, but the arrangement was bearable. *To make the NBA,* he thought, *I can handle this.* That changed, however, when another player, Keith Wilkes, moved into Jefferson's home so he, too, could attend Brethren Christian. Wilkes's father, Keith, Sr., was an assistant coach on Jefferson's team, and Keith, Jr., was close with Jeff and Byron. That cost Aaron, beginning with his place on the top bunk. "There's a mattress in the garage," Jefferson told him. "Pull that into the room and put it on the floor. You can sleep there."

Aaron didn't tell Barbara about losing his bed, in part because they rarely spoke. He returned to Rubidoux the first weekend after moving to Buena Park, but then Jefferson insisted he stay on weekends to play in tournaments or work for him at the Warrior Center. Aaron thought his mom didn't call because she didn't miss him. Barbara thought Aaron acclimated so seamlessly to Jefferson's family that he didn't need her anymore.

One day, Aaron sat on his mattress leafing through Yu-Gi-Oh! cards, when Byron walked into the bedroom and ordered him to hand them over. After all, *his* father had paid for them. "No, they're mine," Aaron responded, and then he showed his back to Byron. The younger boy casually fetched an aluminum baseball bat from underneath the lowest bunk and struck Aaron in the center of his back.

Sensing that Aaron would tell Barbara about the fight, Jefferson called her first. "You know how boys are," he told her. "His first fight. I guess now he's officially a member of the family."

Jeff, Byron, and Keith, Jr., teamed up on Aaron, and their taunts had a continuous theme: that Aaron was the only boy without a father. "The only reason you are here is so my dad can be your dad," Byron or Jeff would say. "He's *not* your dad."

After a month, Jefferson's older daughter and her son moved in, and Aaron, Keith, Jr., and Jeff lost their room.

"I want you boys to go out into the garage and start cleaning it out," Jefferson said. "Get all that stuff out of there and we'll finish it up and you guys can stay out there."

It took the boys three days to remove the mounds of boxes and other junk. They would get to the bottom of a pile and find bags filled with rancid food and other waste and then fight over who had to clean it up.

Jefferson had the boys drag the bunk bed into the garage. The first two boys home at night slept in one of the beds. The last to arrive—which was almost always Aaron, because of his late workouts at the Warrior Center—slept on a sofa.

Sleeping on a torn and dirty couch in a garage was not an inconvenience Aaron kept from his mother, and she confronted Jefferson during a phone call. "It's a temporary thing," he said. "I am having some people come in a week or so who are going to finish the whole garage, put down a floor and some carpet, and insulate the walls. Then it will be fine."

Aaron was responsible for cleaning the home's only bathroom, which was shared by eight people. One day, he grabbed a bucket and some rags and a bottle of Pine-Sol and faced the task. Standing in the doorway, looking over the mud-caked floor and overflowing garbage, he revolted. He emptied the full bottle of Pine-Sol on the floor and watched it bubble like some sort of witches' brew. Then he dropped the bucket and the rags and left the house. Later, Jefferson's wife berated him, but he refused to clean up the mess, ran out the door, and didn't return until she was gone.

When he wasn't at Jefferson's house, Aaron could be found at the Warrior Center as Jefferson showed him off to coaches and others considering holding events there. "Go out there and shoot around," Jefferson would tell Aaron, who would then run the floor and shoot jumpers while the men watched. Jefferson would boast that Aaron was only thirteen, that he was going to be in the NBA someday, and that the Warrior Center would be known as the place where he got his start.

Jefferson described the setup as ideal. Aaron got to train every day at a top-notch facility, and Brethren Christian was a great school. He also portrayed himself as a concerned guardian: He made sure Aaron took the bus to school every day, did his homework, and he said Aaron had "carte blanche" when it came to food, benefiting from sponsorship deals local restaurants had with the Warrior Center.

Aaron described a vastly different arrangement. After two months at Brethren Christian, he was flunking every class except wood shop, because of repeated absences, he said. On the days he was in school, he was listless and fell asleep at his desk. Teachers who gave him failing marks didn't know that he was barely sleeping at night, that Jefferson would come into the garage often as late as 3 a.m. and wake Aaron and the others. Jefferson would enter through the outer garage door and Aaron would leap from the couch, fearful that Jefferson was driving his car into their makeshift bedroom.

At a time when Aaron's body should have been filling out, he said he lost nearly ten pounds in his first eight weeks in Buena Park. "Mom, when I get home, there really isn't any dinner or anything for me to eat," Aaron told Barbara during a rare phone conversation. She began dropping off snacks for him at the house, but if he wasn't home to receive them, others ate the food before he got home. If Aaron was there, he hid bags of ramen noodles and boxes of Cap'n Crunch and Pop-Tarts under the sofa in the garage.

To make the NBA: That was the justification Aaron whispered to himself, the mantra that held him together. To make the NBA, he would live apart from his mother and brother. To make the NBA, he would go hungry and sleepless. To make the NBA, he would tell no one of his plight, not even about the pain he felt just below his stomach, a hurt so biting he knew it wasn't from a lack of food. Later, a doctor would tell him it was likely caused by anxiety, but at the time he believed it was one of the "sacrifices" Jefferson talked about, the cost of a future in basketball.

Late in 2003, Jefferson's team played in a tournament in Fontana. Before the game against another eighth-grade team, Aaron watched a group of seventh-graders dominate their opponents. Aaron loved their blue and white uniforms and the spotless Adidas Promodels each player wore. Their coach yelled too much, but that didn't really detract from the team's appeal.

Later that afternoon, Aaron scored 38 points and grabbed 27 rebounds to lead Jefferson's team to victory. Though he turned the ball over often and didn't know where to position himself on defense, Aaron's raw skill caught the eye of the coach of the seventh-grade team that had played earlier.

The following Friday, Barbara arrived at the Warrior Center to pick Aaron up and received some startling news. He was now a member of Team Cal.

"But isn't that a seventh-grade team?" Barbara asked.

"Yeah, I'm in the seventh grade now," Aaron said. "Coach Mark pulled me out of school, and Coach Joe has me doing homeschool."

Aaron could see his mother's temper rise. "Coach Mark said he talked to you about it and that everything was cool."

"How could you pull my son out of school without asking me?" Barbara shouted at Jefferson when she found him sitting in his office.

He explained that it was better for Aaron's development to play for Team Cal. He didn't mention that Keller had promised to stage several of his Adidas-backed tournaments at the Warrior Center in exchange for Aaron.

Barbara became more confused than angry. How could Aaron suddenly be in the seventh grade? How did someone set up homeschooling? Who was monitoring his work? She took him home to Rubidoux, giving Jefferson no answer when he asked when they would return.

Aaron had already played one game with Team Cal, and it had been an eye-opening experience. Demetrius and the other players spoke a different language on the court, shouting terms like *back screen, weak-side help,* and *high post.* Aaron also liked the way Keller pushed him instead of merely showing him off as Jefferson had. "You ready to be a horse?" Keller asked him before his first game. Later, when Aaron missed a dunk and came up limping, Keller called him out. "You're not hurt. You're just embarrassed, so you're pretending you're hurt."

Aaron learned that Demetrius—the leader of the team—had no relationship with his father, and he instantly bonded with Roberto, as both were newcomers. Soderberg told him about his playing history and offered to act as Aaron's "personal big-man coach." Demetrius introduced him to older boys who were already talked about as some of the best young players in the area, such as Brandon Jennings and DeMar DeRozan, who were a year older than the Team Cal kids but treated them as peers in a special club.

"Mom, I want to keep playing for Coach Joe," Aaron told Barbara when they were back in Rubidoux. "I don't want to go back to Buena Park anymore. I hate living there. Please don't make me go back. But please let me stay on Team Cal."

Barbara was once again presented with a decision about whether to trust a man she barely knew.

Keller had orchestrated Aaron's removal from Brethren Christian and enrolled him in homeschooling a grade lower, all without consulting Barbara. It was not a first impression that lent itself to unmitigated trust. But Keller invited Barbara and Aaron and Micah to his apartment in Fontana, and he gave them Adidas shoes and clothes, and he laid out how he would supervise Aaron's homeschooling for the next semester. He assured Barbara that either he or Violet would pick Aaron up every day at around 3:00 p.m. for workouts, that she would never be burdened with getting Aaron to Fontana for practice or games. He also said that Aaron could stay with him whenever he wanted and that he would help feed and clothe him. Team Cal was like "a family," Keller said, and he introduced Barbara to Violet and showed off his kids. Later, while attending a Team Cal game, Barbara was moved by how Keller rushed over and picked up little Alyssa right after the final buzzer.

There were contemplative cigarettes smoked in front of her house and a few conversations with Aaron and a few more with Keller, but, Barbara being Barbara, there was never a doubt about the conclusion she would reach.

Joe Keller was exactly the type of man Aaron needed in his life.

14

(CARMEN HAWKINS)

Team Cal at the Gateway Arch in St. Louis in 2004

On an overstuffed sofa in the lobby of a Holiday Inn near the airport in St. Louis, Demetrius and Aaron sat side by side, each with a set of oversize headphones covering his ears.

"This is tight!" Aaron shouted, and he took off his headphones and nudged Demetrius. He removed his own and they traded.

"Oh, that is 'Bone Crusher,'" Demetrius said too loudly. He bobbed his head along with the song for a few seconds and then they switched back.

At the start of the next song, Demetrius said, "Oh, yeeaaaahhhh," and then he poked Aaron with his elbow. They swapped headphones again.

"Usher. That's real," Aaron said.

Outside the hotel, visible from where the boys sat, Keller stood next to a minivan with Soderberg in its driver's seat. Keller leaned in to the passenger window several times but then stepped away in what appeared to be frustration. It went on for so long that it was obvious the men were arguing, although that was nothing new. They sparred during practices and after practices, before games and after games. The point of contention was essentially the same each time: Keller disagreed with the changes Soderberg wanted to make to Team Cal's offense and defense.

Keller was jumpier than usual in St. Louis, because it was Team Cal's first major event after landing the Adidas deal and adding Aaron and Roberto. Team Maryland and Hoosier Hoops weren't in St. Louis, but there were enough quality teams present that Keller fretted about the possibility of a loss. If Team Cal faltered in a tournament less than six months after he'd landed his shoe contract, he and the team would look like a bad investment. When Keller got nervous, he reverted to what had worked for him in the past: Demetrius and Fist. But Soderberg had worked too hard over the past months integrating Aaron and Roberto into the offense and refocusing the boys defensively. "Why would you have me work with the boys on this stuff, Joe, if we aren't going to do it in games?" Soderberg said. "You've got to trust me, Joe."

Keller's anxiety softened upon arriving at the Simon Recreation Center on the St. Louis University campus. He saw Team Cal's first opponent, St. Louis Game Face, and knew instantly they would pose no challenge. "The biggest thing we do is intimidate," a serene Keller said pregame. "We come out and teams look at us and know we are going to rip the rim off."

In a locker room ten minutes before the game, Keller pulled Demetrius aside. "You're the leader. You've got to get them fired up." Demetrius had also seen Game Face when the team arrived, and the look he gave Keller seemed to say: *Really? For them?*

"Are you all going to get hyped or what?" Demetrius said loudly after the coaches left the locker room. "We're the best team in the country. We've got to show it every time out on the court. We have to take this team seriously. We have to . . ." He stopped, looked down, and then started to laugh.

Aaron jumped up and stood next to Demetrius. "Yeah, let's go," he said overzealously, and this made Demetrius laugh even harder.

"Yeah. We gotta do this!" Terran shouted. He never spoke during meetings, and his feigned enthusiasm triggered a wave of laughter that continued as the team exited for the court.

Coupled with Soderberg's direction, Aaron's insertion in the lineup changed the team's core philosophies at both ends of the court. Against Game Face, Team Cal played only man-to-man defense. This would have occurred without Aaron, but his presence smoothed the transition away from Fist. By guarding Game Face's tallest player, Aaron freed Demetrius to mark the opposing wing player and thus stay farther from the basket. His quickness was better utilized there, as he got into the passing lanes and created turnovers. It also allowed him to transition to offense more quickly, using his speed to start counterattacks. He often led the break after an Aaron block or rebound or filled one of the wings as Jordan or Justin pushed the ball.

When Team Cal was on offense, Game Face played zone to try to negate Team Cal's size advantage. In the past, Keller had hindered the boys' efforts to break a zone defense because he insisted that the ball be dumped down to Demetrius, no matter how many players crowded him. The new offense still revolved around Demetrius—Soderberg saw him as the ideal facilitator—but he was being counted on to get his teammates more involved. One play Soderberg drilled was called "high post," and Team Cal relied on it heavily against Game Face's 2-3 zone. Demetrius popped to the free-throw line, between the two defenders atop the zone, where he received a pass from one of the guards. He wheeled toward the basket and then selected from several options. If no one converged on him, he simply shot a 12-foot jump shot. If the post players moved toward him but did so slowly, he drove straight at the hoop. If they stepped to him aggressively, he dropped a pass to Aaron or Roberto down low for an easy score. If the two top guards sandwiched him, he found Jordan or Justin open at the 3-point line. He might have looked short standing next to Aaron, but Demetrius still towered over almost every opposing player, which gave him a clear view of the court. His passing, always an underrated strength, made him the perfect catalyst, and he tore Game Face's zone apart.

Team Cal won 58–40, a victory marked by a rare occurrence: Demetrius was not the team's top scorer. Aaron led the way with 16, followed by Demetrius with 12. But Demetrius had eight assists, the most I had ever seen him tally, and looked just as dominant as in those games when he scored 20 or more.

Against a team from Indianapolis the following day, Demetrius again finished second to Aaron in scoring, but he provided the game's highlight. Late in the first half, Justin got a steal, and as he ran unobstructed toward the basket, he noticed Demetrius trailing him. He turned and nodded at Demetrius, and then he tossed the ball hard off the backboard. Demetrius burst forward, jumped, and in one motion caught the ball with his right hand and slammed it through the hoop. He hung on the rim too long, spinning and landing so that he faced half-court, and the Indianapolis coach hollered at the official to whistle him for a technical foul.

"I've never seen a seventh-grader do that before," the referee said after the game. "He can hang on the rim all he wants."

At times in a 64–36 victory over Team Springfield that evening, Keller behaved like a royal jackass. He got a technical foul for yelling at the officials in the second half with his team up 38, and he reinserted Demetrius late in the game in a failed attempt to execute Red Sea. But he yelled at the boys less and stopped the aimless substituting, and Soderberg's modifications to the offense and defense took hold. Keller also showed compassion for another team for the first time in four years. Leading 40–14, Keller ordered the team into a four-corner offense designed to milk the clock. He earlier agreed with Team Springfield's coach to allow the clock to run during free throws and when the ball went out of bounds, which sped the game to a less humiliating end. Team Cal could have won by 80, but the "new" Joe Keller settled for a 30-point victory.

Aaron's arrival overshadowed two other moves Keller made in the wake of the Adidas deal. He finally convinced Gary Franklin, Sr., to fold the Runnin' Rebels and bring Gary, Jr., over to be Team Cal's point guard. Gary was the pure point the team had been missing since the departures of Andrew and Pe'Shon. Part of the package to get Gary included taking another Runnin' Rebels player, the aptly named Craig Payne. He was a Terran clone with the same wide hips, huge butt, and thick arms. He could be overly aggressive—the hard foul might have been his signature skill—but he was the perfect enforcer to put on the floor when Terran needed a break.

Franklin's decision to join forces with Keller made him feel dirty. But over the previous season, Gary had struggled to acclimate to teammates not as skilled as Terran and Justin. They weren't ready for his no-look passes and couldn't make offensive adjustments fast enough for the Runnin' Rebels to defeat the best teams. "I think I play better with better players," Gary told his father when they discussed joining Keller, "and Team Cal has the best players."

Gary and Craig were significant pieces, but their influence paled in comparison to Aaron's. He was exactly what the team needed, and Keller likened his impact to what Tyson Chandler brought to his team in the 1990s. "Don't tell D I said this, but I think Aaron is more like Tyson than he is," Keller said. He couldn't resist pitting Aaron and Demetrius against each other in practice, but he did not rig these battles like he did when Demetrius squared off with Roberto, and their competition and relationship were healthier as a result. Aaron spent many nights at Keller's apartment and was included on shopping trips to the Ontario Mills mall and other excursions that would have previously included only Demetrius. A few days before the tournament in St. Louis, Keller took Demetrius and Aaron with him to a spa, and the trio got manicures and pedicures.

Demetrius's standing as the team's most touted player remained secure, at least in his own eyes. "Of course he's gonna be taller than me, 'cuz he's a grade older," Demetrius said. After one practice during which Aaron dominated, Demetrius was unfazed: "If I was almost fourteen, I'd be killing people too." For Demetrius, Aaron's age was a soothing excuse. For the team's parents, it was a touchy subject, as it reminded them of the rules Keller bent to make Aaron eligible to play at Nationals.

The AAU's cutoff for determining a player's age group was September 1. A player born before that date was considered a division older than a player born on or after it. The AAU permitted each team three "grade exceptions," players whose birthdays predated the cutoff but who were in the proper grades. Andrew, born August 13, had been the team's only grade exception at the previous year's Nationals, and he was a good case for why the rule existed. He was a slight kid, a late bloomer, and making him play with kids a grade higher simply because of those eighteen days would have been unjust.

Aaron's birthday was October 25, 1989; he was born more than ten months before the September 1, 1990, cutoff. He was nearly a full year older than Demetrius and almost eighteen months older than Roberto and Rome, the team's youngest players. He had also taken classes as an eighth-grader at Brethren Christian. Under the spirit of the rule, Aaron should not have been eligible to compete for Team Cal in what the AAU called the "13:Under/7th Grade" division. But by enrolling him in a homeschooling program as a seventh-grader, Keller instantly made him eligible to compete as a grade exception.

"I actually agree with Joe on this one," John said in St. Louis when asked if he viewed the maneuvering as deceitful. "Other teams have grade exceptions. And Aaron and his mom are happy with him on Team Cal, it's good exposure for him, and they are fine with him repeating the seventh grade. No one is getting hurt."

Except opponents.

In the final of the St. Louis tournament against Game Face, Aaron had four dunks in a 96–54 victory. As coaches and parents lined up to congratulate Keller, he again likened Aaron to Chandler and added, "If I had to bet money right now on who would make the NBA, D or Aaron, I would put my money on Aaron." As he spoke, Aaron and Demetrius were at midcourt, accepting awards for making the all-tournament team. With medals dangling from around their necks, they posed for a picture, each with an arm draped on the other's shoulders. They looked like the closest of allies, the best of friends.

In a meeting room at the Rancho Cucamonga Family Sports Center, a handful of Team Cal parents sat at rectangular tables that had been arranged in rows, like desks in a classroom. Spread out in front of them on the blue laminate tabletops were folders or several papers or note-books, and a few parents hurriedly looked over their documents, re-counting figures or practicing their answers. They were like students cramming for a test.

Keller entered the room, talking on his cell phone, and sat at a table in front, facing the parents. He made them wait a few minutes as he finished talking with Violet, and then he tossed the phone on the table.

"Okay, where are we at with the hotel rooms?" he said.

One parent spoke up, saying that 100 rooms at a Holiday Inn had been blocked, including ten for scouts like Clark Francis. The deposit for the rooms was $4,500. Another parent responded to a question about dorm rooms, saying they had been reserved at a cost of $2,500, and that the gym rental cost an additional $2,500.

"What about programs?"

About $1,000 had been spent already, a parent said, and the printer needed another $100. This led to a discussion about potential sponsors for the program. Keller mentioned that Anheuser-Busch had offered $20,000 for ads in the program and on signs around the gym. "But I called Adidas and they shot that down." The good news, he said, was that EA Sports had agreed to put on a video-game tournament one evening at the players' dorm.

"We're twelve thousand short on what it costs for the merchandise, for the T-shirts and stuff, but I'm hoping Adidas will see the kids we are getting and give us the difference," Keller said. "Let's hope."

That meeting and many others dealt with an innovation of Keller's that he believed would change the structure of grassroots basketball in America. The biggest week of the AAU season was in early July, when Nike, Adidas, and Reebok simultaneously held all-star camps for the best high school players. The competition to get the top players to those camps was fierce, as it was the best barometer of the success of a grassroots division. If more of the top players attended the Reebok ABCD Camp over the Nike Camp and the Adidas Superstar Camp, Vaccaro could claim victory. If Nike had more of the top-50 kids, The Swoosh was the big winner. Keller's idea was to hold a similar national all-star camp for the best sixth-, seventh-, and eighth-graders, which he would call the Adidas Jr. Phenom Camp. It was yet another example of going younger, in the same vein as Vaccaro first sponsoring AAU teams with Adidas or Clark Francis ranking middle school kids. It was hardly revolutionary, yet no one had tried it before, in part because it was difficult to identify the top players. Who really knew who the best sixth-, seventh-, and eighth-graders were? From his travels around the country with Team Cal, Keller could claim that he did.

The ABCD, Nike, and Superstar Camps were invitation-only events, and the shoe companies picked up the cost of travel, hotels, and food for the participants. Keller couldn't fund travel and lodging for 200 kids, and he also viewed the Jr. Phenom Camp as his first big payday. "If it all goes right, I could make a hundred thousand dollars off this event alone," he said. Money would be made off tickets to the event, from the sale of merchandise like T-shirts, shorts, and other gear bearing the Adidas and Jr. Phenom Camp logos, and from advertising in the program and around the gym. Most of the income, however, would come from the $395 entry fee he intended to charge each camper. Would parents pay to send their kids to a camp billing itself as the young kids' equivalent of the ABCD, Nike, or Superstar Camps? In a promotional flyer for the event, Keller made his case:

Jr. Phenom Camp

THE COUNTRY'S ELITE CAMP AND SHOWCASE FOR INCOMING

6th, 7th, 8th grade boy's basketball players

The top 80 Jr. High School Hoopers in each class, more than 200 players in all, will take to the hardwood August 6–8, 2004 at the 1st Annual "adidas" Jr. Phenom Camp. For nearly 20 years, "adidas" has held the Top High School All-Star Camp in the world. The Jr. Phenom Camp will bring this great tradition to the grass roots level, providing a platform for many of the college and NBA players of tomorrow.

This prestigious camp will be held in sunny San Diego, California at one of SoCal's premiere hoop's destinations, Alliant University, home of 6 new wood floors under one roof.

The "adidas" Jr. Phenom Camp is an invitation only camp that offers student athletes a variety of mandatory classes on academics and life skills better preparing young men for success in High School, College and Life. Players must attend class to be eligible to play in each afternoon's session of games.

Top college coaches and elite skill instructors will be in attendance to pass on their words of wisdom. Players will have the opportunity to test their games against other top players in their age group throughout the weekend. The camp will culminate with championship and All-Star games on the final day under the watchful eye of the country's top scouting services.

Joe Keller, Camp Director

Keller knew firsthand never to underestimate parents' hopes that their sons would land college scholarships. He was betting that the opportunity to put their kids under the "watchful eye" of men like Clark Francis (whose hotel room Keller promised to comp) would convince parents to pay the fee. Keller also used Demetrius's standing as the top seventh-grader in the country to sell skeptical parents and coaches: *The number-1 player in the land is going to be there, but your son isn't?*

By mid-May, registrations were pouring in and Keller received more than fifty calls a day from parents hoping to land spots for their children. He hired Violet's younger sister to help with the volume of calls and the paperwork, and the two women worked side by side at desks packed into the small area next to the kitchen in the Kellers' apartment. Keller was the salesman reeling in kids, and Violet and her sister handled the logistics, making certain to get the correct shoe and uniform sizes for each camper, who would receive a pair of Adidas shoes and a uniform emblazoned with the Jr. Phenom logo.

NCAA rules prevented college coaches from attending the Jr. Phenom Camp—none of the participants was old enough to be considered a "recruitable" athlete—but most of the hopeful parents didn't know that. By early June, the camp was essentially sold out, with Keller holding a few spots for top players he hoped to sign up later. From the registration fees alone, he grossed more than $70,000.

When word of Keller's plan reached other coaches and grassroots executives at Nike and Reebok, their reactions varied. Some coaches offered to bring their best kids to the camp if Keller paid them to work the event as counselors. Others worried that the Adidas Jr. Phenom Camp was nothing more than a large tryout, that Keller would use it to poach their best kids for Team Cal. Vaccaro was incredulous. How could Keller and Adidas stoop so low? "It's an all-star camp but he's charging the kids? That's not right. He's exploiting them," Vaccaro said. "But, you know, it will probably work. Enough parents and coaches will think it is important to be there. . . . Still, if there was any doubt Joe is all about money, it is gone now."

Keller was either a genius or the exploiter of children's dreams or both. Daren Kalish at Adidas would render the most important verdict. He summoned Keller to the company's headquarters in Portland to talk more about Adidas's role in the Jr. Phenom Camp, and there was speculation that he was having second thoughts about putting the Adidas name on the event. Keller was not worried.

"No one thought of this before and people are wishing they had, and that is generating a lot of shit talk," he said. "But when Daren hears about all the kids I've got coming to this camp, he is going to do backflips."

15

Joe Keller showing brand loyalty

Before the Southwest Airlines plane left its gate at the Ontario Airport, Keller announced: "This might be the most important day of my life."

Hyperbole was a "Friend of Joe." The greatest win ever, the most devastating loss in history, the best player in the country, the greatest find since Tyson Chandler—so-called pivotal moments arrived so often, it was hard to know when something seminal was actually afoot. Keller's trip to Adidas's headquarters in Portland felt like a potentially transformative moment, like finding Demetrius or landing his shoe deal, but it was hard to know for sure.

Sitting in a window seat in the third row of the plane, Keller nervously rubbed the top of his jeans with his palm as he laid out the stakes. He needed money—there was the $12,000 he was short for the Jr. Phenom Camp—but he went to Portland with more than his hand out. He carried a strategy for how Adidas could redirect its grassroots efforts, which he would convey to Kalish. It was brazen—a coach who had been on the payroll less than a year pitching his boss on a sweeping initiative—but Keller knew that Kalish took cues from the Pumps and other AAU coaches. What did he have to lose by throwing his ideas into the mix?

"It's the master plan. Joe Keller's Master Plan," he said, and then he bounced his left leg excitedly as he laid out the details.

While recruiting kids for the Jr. Phenom Camp, Keller took note of how many of the coaches who controlled the best middle school kids were starving for financing and product. Like him before the Adidas contract, they scraped by, borrowing money or relying on donors like Tom. As he flew to Portland, Keller's mind was on one team in particular: Texas Select out of Dallas. It included two forwards, Roger Franklin and Shawn Williams, whom he considered among the top-20 kids in the nation. In two or three years, when they were in high school, Nike and Reebok and Adidas would clamor to build a relationship with them, and one of those companies would surely offer Texas Select a sponsorship deal. Keller wanted Adidas to make Texas Select an offer now. It wouldn't take much, maybe $5,000 to $10,000 a year and some product, but the payoff could be huge. Combined with the presence of Franklin and Williams at the Adidas Jr. Phenom Camp, the sponsoring of their team now would stamp them as Adidas kids before Nike or Reebok even knew their names.

It was a convincing strategy, all the more pertinent because Adidas had fallen to third among the big-three companies in relevance. Nike remained the powerhouse, sponsoring the most teams, and Reebok's Vaccaro had successfully gone for quality over quantity, securing many of the elite kids like O. J. Mayo, Bill Walker, and Greg Oden. Adidas seemed to have lost its foothold, and Keller, of all people, offered a fix: Stop wasting money and energy courting the current crop of high schoolers, players already beholden to Nike or Vaccaro at Reebok, and go younger in a more ambitious way than just signing Team Cal.

Keller would ask Kalish to expand his role, to let him go out and sign other programs like Team Cal, and, more importantly, to shift the overall direction of Adidas's grassroots initiative. "I don't see how Daren says no," Keller said. "It doesn't cost Adidas much, and he gets all these kids." Plus, Keller had already done the legwork. All Kalish had to do was say the word and he would lock up six of the best teams in the country, raising Adidas's profile with the next generation of stars in one swoop.

Taron Pickett, Keller's day-to-day contact at Adidas, picked him up at the airport in an SUV. Pickett was an athletic African American who, at twenty-seven, still played guard for a traveling team that competed against colleges in preseason exhibition games. Pickett and Keller had bonded during a tournament in Ohio a few weeks earlier, staying out late and drinking. Keller liked that Pickett trusted him enough to talk about his struggles to make ends meet on his paltry Adidas salary. He also liked that Pickett was naïve about the cutthroat world of AAU basketball. "I don't want Taron to ever leave Adidas," Keller said on the flight. "I've got him trained right now. If I call him up and say I need forty pairs of shoes, he'll go, 'Oh, Joe,' and then I'll say, 'Forget about it,' and then he'll go, 'No, no, no, I'll take care of it.' With him, I'm like a little spoiled kid who always gets what he wants."

The Adidas Village in Portland consisted of a series of sleek-looking metal-and-glass buildings on a ten-and-a-half-acre former hospital site. The interior of the building housing the grassroots-basketball division was a mix of spiral staircases, sheet-metal walls, and hanging halogen lamps. When Keller arrived, he went upstairs and greeted Kalish, who suggested they talk after lunch.

Keller went through some Adidas catalogs while sitting next to Pickett's cubicle, and then Pickett led him on a tour of the Adidas campus, showing off the basketball court where employees often played heated games during lunch. After eating at a nearby sandwich shop, Keller and Pickett returned to the grassroots offices, where Keller chatted up the soccer rep who had earlier procured the black socks Demetrius wanted. Late in the afternoon, Kalish finally summoned Keller to a conference room on the second floor.

Kalish was the picture of urban sophistication, dressed in worn-looking jeans but a pressed dress shirt, stylishly untucked, and spotless brown dress shoes. Keller was wearing old Levi's, a blue T-shirt, and running shoes. In front of Keller on the table was a manila folder containing logo designs for the Jr. Phenom Camp, a copy of the flyer he gave to potential sponsors, and other materials. He passed the folder to

Kalish, who slowly reviewed the pages, taking his time with each. He came to the schedule of events for the camp and read some of it aloud, stopping occasionally to make sure he understood each activity.

"This looks good, Joe," Kalish said. "How else can I help?"

"There are a bunch of kids who can't afford plane tickets and the entry fees and all that," he said. "These are top kids who should be at the camp."

This was a half-truth. Keller intended to pay the $395 entry for a few kids, but only a few. But telling Kalish he needed money to get good kids to the camp was better than telling him he needed $12,000 to manufacture Jr. Phenom Camp merchandise (T-shirts, shorts, balls, etc.) that he would resell at a huge markup.

"How many kids invited to the camp can't get there because they can't afford it?" Kalish asked.

"About half in each age group."

"How about if I help you with a couple of the guys?" Kalish said. "Reimburse their expenses."

"I don't like the way that sounds," Keller said. "You're asking me to tell people to pay and then I will try to pay them later. I would prefer you decide on a number you can help with and give me that up front."

"How about fifteen thousand dollars?" Kalish said.

Keller jumped on it, though he acted as if it was not a big deal.

Perhaps wanting to test the knowledge of a coach Adidas was so generously subsidizing, Kalish quizzed Keller on AAU programs from around the country.

"Tell me the names of ten unsigned programs you think I should sign."

Keller listed ten quickly, and Kalish confided that he'd already locked up two off the list. Kalish then named prominent players in various age groups, and Keller knew something about all but a few.

Sensing that Kalish was impressed with him, Keller made his big pitch. "If I get a couple teams in my age group locked, like five or six teams, I will control the market," Keller said. "If I get some of these [coaches] hooked up, they will remember who did it for them. When I need a favor, when I need a top kid to come to an Adidas camp, I can call in that favor."

Keller directed Kalish to a sheet in the folder in front of him. It was a list of the players committed to the Jr. Phenom Camp.

"I can't believe you got all these kids. How did you do it?" Kalish said.

"If I told you how I did it, I wouldn't be valuable to you anymore," Keller said.

"Oh, so that's how it is?"

"Yeah, Daren, it's business."

Kalish laughed, but Keller sensed that he was impressed. He repeated his wish to sign other programs consisting of middle school kids and mentioned that it could help Adidas get in with players before the competition.

"That's interesting," Kalish said. "Let me get back to you on that."

Keller turned the conversation to another topic of great importance to him. It was widely known that some AAU coaches received money from sports agents for steering players to them. When Keller came up with the totals that would make him a millionaire when Demetrius was through with high school, he included money from directing his kids to a specific agent. Recently, an employee of Arn Tellem, the agent who represented Tracy McGrady and Yao Ming, among others, had watched Team Cal play in San Diego, and Keller had also spoken with other agents. Keller asked Kalish if he had an arrangement with a specific agent, and, if not, did he mind if Keller pursued one.

"I don't think it is wrong for you to do that, but for me, ethically, being a part of Adidas, it is not right," Kalish said. "If you want to get kids for agents, that is part of your business. I am not going to be against that."

Enthused by that response, the $15,000, and Kalish's willingness to consider his plan to go after other young teams, Keller was giddy while waiting to board his return flight to the Inland Empire later that night. "I got more money than I needed, and I bet Daren lets me go out and sign other teams," he said. "I might do backflips on the plane."

Keller's blissfulness was short-lived, ending when he arrived at his apartment in Fontana and opened his email.

Dear Team Cal 13u Parents & Players,

Jordan, Shelly, Tanner and I want to wish the boys all the best in Memphis. We hope that you bring the big one home but more importantly we hope the boys will have a positive learning experience.

Joe and I worked together for nearly 4 years. We disagreed on many important people handling, coaching and business issues. In the end our differences of opinion became too great, that is why Jordan and I left.

We will always have great affection for the boys on this team and will continue to pray for their future success.

God Bless,
The Finn Family

From the moment Keller slighted Jordan and John in Baltimore two years earlier, a fantastic blowup between John and Keller seemed inevitable. It was not hard to imagine how the end would come. John would be yelling at Keller, probably about how Keller had showcased Demetrius at the expense of others, and Keller would be cursing at John. Keller would say something insulting about Jordan, perhaps about his struggles to defend quicker guards, and John would reach down and cup Keller's throat and squeeze. Or Keller would react to the criticism John delivered in a condescending tone and throw a punch up toward John's chin, hoping to catch him square and shut him up for good. The boys would be there to see it all, of course, another milestone in their eroding childhood.

Jordan's time with Team Cal ended with no such climax, just an email, sent June 23, 2004—less than a week before Team Cal was leaving for the Nationals in Memphis.

The move didn't come as a shock, but the timing did. Team Cal was one of the favorites to win Nationals after two years of disappointment. Why not put up with Keller for two more weeks and then quit after Nationals?

After receiving the email, Rome, Sr., Carmen, and other befuddled parents called John to extract the *real* reason for the move. "It was Jordan's decision, not mine," John insisted. "I asked him, 'What do you want to do?' And he said, 'Dad, I'm tired of all of it. I don't want to play for Coach Joe anymore.'" No one who had observed John and Jordan over the years believed him. John had yelled at Jordan for not drinking enough water during a time-out. He had switched residences to make it easier for Jordan to play for Keller. Now he was going to let Jordan be the one to decide when to walk away?

John could deny it, but it was *his* decision, rooted in events a month earlier, during the tournament in Columbus, Ohio, that Taron Pickett attended. John was born just outside Columbus, and his mother lived nearby. He had not visited her in two years, and she planned to attend Team Cal's game on Saturday, the second day of the tournament, along with nearly a dozen friends and relatives. Before the team departed, John told Keller that a large contingent from his family would be attending the game that day. He didn't say that he expected Jordan to play major minutes, but he made it clear that this was a special trip for his family. It is doubtful, however, that Keller registered how important the weekend was to the Finns. His thoughts were on Adidas, on enhancing his role with the company. John Finn's mother? How could he worry about her when Pickett was flying to Columbus to see the team for the first time at a major event?

On Friday night, Pickett and Keller headed to P. F. Chang's for dinner. On the drive, Keller asked Pickett a loaded question: "Who was the best player you saw today?" It was a question Keller had asked a hundred people after a hundred of Team Cal's games. The only safe answer was "Demetrius Walker," but Pickett hadn't known Keller long enough to realize that honesty was not a virtue he held in high regard.

"I'd say Brandon Ham," Pickett said, referring to a five-foot-eight guard from Ohio.

"What!" Keller shouted. "Are you crazy? He's not even top fifty in my book."

Pickett made his argument, ticking off Ham's attributes on his fingers. Ham could handle the ball, could penetrate, worked hard on defense, and showed a mid-range jump shot that most young players lacked. Pickett repeated that last compliment, adding, "That is something I haven't seen in Demetrius's game."

"Really?" Keller said over and over. "Really?" His face was white, bleached by disbelief. "Taron, I thought you knew basketball."

"Joe, that's just my opinion. I didn't say he was the best player in the country. I just said that he was the best player I saw today."

As they walked into the restaurant, Keller ended the discussion. "Taron, I understand that that is your opinion, but you are *wrong*!"

The following day, as Jordan's grandmother watched from the sidelines, Keller set out to show Taron just how wrong he was. With 6:40 left in an 88–12 blowout of a team from Cincinnati, Keller reinserted Demetrius into the game, subbing out Jordan. Demetrius immediately commanded the ball on the right side and then penetrated before pulling up for a 15-footer, banking it off the glass and in. It was a perfect mid-range jump shot, and as it went through the net, Keller pointed across the court at Taron.

"Did you just see that?" Pickett said to me. "He had D take that jumper just to show me he had a mid-range game, because of what I said about Brandon Ham last night."

Seated on the opposite side of the court next to his mother, John found no humor in watching Keller run play after play for Demetrius, freeing him for the types of shots Pickett lauded Ham for the previous night. Jordan hardly played in the first half, but John assumed he would be on the court for the entirety of the second, if only because Keller would sit Demetrius, Aaron, and others to save their energy for later games. He also counted on Keller remembering how important the game was to him and his family. But for the last 6:40, Jordan remained on the bench.

John did everything he could to avoid focusing on the game. He chatted with his mother; he called Tanner, his younger son, over and had him sit next to him; he talked briefly with a few of his mother's friends. What he didn't do was look toward the bench, where his son sat with a dour look on his face and where Keller barked out plays for Demetrius, who had already scored 30 points and dunked four times.

At the final buzzer, when the teams met to shake hands and Keller wandered over to where Pickett sat, John stood up in the bleachers and turned his back to the court. The significance of this gesture would emerge later, after he sent the email. He had turned his back, once and for all, on Joe Keller.

After sending the email, John dropped off Jordan's uniforms at Keller's apartment. He claimed he told Keller only "Best of luck at Nationals."

Keller remembered that meeting differently. "John told me, 'You embarrassed me in front of my family.'"

John initially downplayed the malice behind his decision, saying over and over that it had been Jordan's decision, but when pressed he finally said, "Because leaving now will hurt Joe the most."

In subsequent conversations, John sounded at different times like a responsible father, a disillusioned dad obsessed with featuring his son, and a businessman who'd been outsmarted by Joe Keller. The last was a relatively new persona. As Keller's stature rose in the grassroots world, it dawned on John how easily it could have been him that put Team Cal together and landed that Adidas contract. Like Keller after Pat Barrett had fleeced him years earlier, John finally saw the business side of the grassroots game. "I learned a lot from Joe about how it all works," he said.

John hoped Keller would be distraught over losing his best 3-point shooter, but he was unaffected. "John thinks I am going to be screwed without Jordan, but I have one big thing going for me: Shoe Company Money. With that, I can buy a hundred kids as good as Jordan."

But not in time for the Nationals.

Roberto was now the team's only pure shooter, and he rarely got the green light from Keller. Gary and Justin could also shoot, but neither had shown Jordan's ability to make three or more in a row. Still, Keller was unconcerned—and if Coach Joe wasn't worried, why should Demetrius be? "I'm really bummed about Jordan, but he's got a crazy dad, so what can you do? Parents nowadays, they all think their kid should be the number-1 focus."

Demetrius began worrying, however, a few days later. During practice just before the team left for Nationals, Terran fell to the floor after being kneed in the thigh. Instead of icing the injury, as Soderberg instructed, Terran went home and soaked in a hot bath. His thigh swelled so rapidly that he had to be rushed to the hospital, where doctors made a three-inch incision to relieve the inflammation.

When the team departed for Memphis, Terran remained in the hospital, and the confidence built during the victorious runs in St. Louis and Columbus had diminished.

"Before Terran went down, I would have said that we will win Nationals for sure," Keller said. "Now I'm not so sure."

16

(ROBERT BECK/*SPORTS ILLUSTRATED*)

Demetrius Walker

"A m I still the number one player in the nation?" Demetrius asked.

A few minutes before the first game of elimination play of Nationals in Memphis, just before Team Cal took the floor against the Virginia Panthers, Demetrius stood beside the stands at the Nike Center, an athletic complex adjacent to a Nike distribution warehouse southeast of downtown.

"Coach Joe says I'm not number one no more," he said. "If I'm not number one, who is?"

Keller had told Demetrius he lost his ranking after Team Cal's final game of pool play, a victory over the Pueblo County (Colorado) Hornets. The team won its first three games by an average of 28 points, and Soderberg was enthused by their start. The boys were building confidence and continuity, he said, and they were learning not to rely only on Demetrius. Keller, however, could focus only on what he perceived to be a sluggish start by his star. "It is fucking Nationals, and D decides to take a nap."

Demetrius had shown little concern for the Hoop Scoop rankings before, but Keller made it seem as if his future success hinged on maintaining his number 1 ranking. He didn't have access to a computer or a subscription to The Hoop Scoop; he couldn't just sign in and confirm his ranking. Keller's words scared him, and so he asked a few parents if what Coach Joe said about his ranking was true.

"Sometimes he says stuff like that because he thinks that will get me hyped. But I am already hyped. It's Nationals," Demetrius said. "I just wasn't hyped earlier 'cuz we were playing teams that were terrible. If I lost my ranking 'cuz of that, well, that's whack."

The game against the Panthers began like most others, with Aaron controlling the opening tip and Team Cal grabbing an early lead. But the Panthers' coaches had scouted Team Cal during pool play and had a pair of bigger post players bang Aaron and frustrate him with holds and jabs. Lamar Little, a lanky forward, did the same to Demetrius. The moment Demetrius crossed half-court, Little put a hand on his chest, letting him know he was there. As soon as Demetrius received a pass, Little bumped him or grabbed a handful of jersey. It was just enough to make Demetrius uncomfortable, and he repeatedly tossed the ball back out to the guards to reset the offense, hoping to get the ball back in a better spot. Little was shorter but quick, and he jockeyed with Demetrius sufficiently that his drives to the hoop took longer to develop, allowing other defenders to move over and help. Demetrius scored only two baskets in the first half, both on breakaway layups, and it was clear that someone had to pick up the scoring. Aaron was the likeliest candidate, but he picked up two quick fouls and was stymied by the Panthers' physical play.

The Panthers' offensive strategy was simple: Guards Derek Staton and Dominique Palmer pulled up for 3-point shots whenever they touched the ball. Staton buried his first shot from beyond NBA 3-point range, putting the Panthers up 8–7 four minutes into the game. They remained in the lead or within a basket until there were two minutes left in the first period. It was then that Keller sent Roberto to the scorer's table.

Most of the boys bounded into the game, but not Roberto. He strolled onto the court as if he had been woken from a deep sleep. He pointed to Rome to let him know he would be the player coming out and made sure to slap his hand as they crossed paths. Roberto then wiped the bottoms of his shoes and licked the fingers on his right hand. "Play your game, son. You see it," Bruce yelled from the stands. The players rarely acknowledged their parents' remarks from the crowd, but Roberto nodded his head, confirming that he saw what Bruce did: All the attention given to Aaron and Demetrius opened up the Panthers' defense for him.

With Team Cal clinging to a 14–12 lead, Roberto went to work. He stole the ball from Little and scored on a layup to up the lead to 4. He and Justin double-teamed Staton on the Panthers' next possession, leading to a turnover and breakaway layup. When Team Cal had the ball next, Roberto drove on the right and pulled up for a 10-footer to make it 20–13. The Panthers regained some momentum early in the second quarter with two scores, but then Roberto answered with two straight baskets to make it 26–19.

In the second half, a trend emerged: Roberto would push Team Cal to what seemed a comfortable lead—such as 41–26 with a minute left in the third quarter—but then Staton or Palmer would connect from an unimaginable distance, keeping the Panthers in the game. After 3-pointers by Palmer and then Staton cut the lead to 47–41 early in the fourth quarter, Keller picked up a chair and slammed it to the ground, for which he got a technical foul. When a Panther made the free throw, it seemed to swing the momentum, and the Panthers fans stood and clapped. But then Roberto deflected a pass by Palmer on the other end that led to a score and later finished off a miss by Demetrius. A possession later, he knocked down an 18-footer, after which he pointed up to Bruce in the stands, a nod to his teacher.

After that basket, the Panthers' coach reluctantly adjusted his defense, and that opened up the game for Demetrius. After Staton hit a deep 3-pointer with 5:26 left, trimming Team Cal's lead to 53–48, Demetrius provided one of those breathtaking moments that seemed to come at least once a game. As Aaron tossed up a shot, Demetrius swatted Little's hand off him, ducked between him and another player, and then leaped in the air, catching Aaron's shot as it bounced off the rim and slamming it through the hoop in one violent motion.

"My God," another team's coach uttered.

As Demetrius trotted back on defense, he smiled widely, as if even he was surprised by the extent of his gifts. It wasn't the winning shot, but it killed the Panthers' hopes. The game ended 66–59 for Team Cal.

"That number twenty-three is special, but we wrapped him up most of the game," the Panthers' coach, Kevin McHee, said. "The difference was number one [Roberto]. I scouted them during pool play and I didn't even notice him."

It wasn't an oversight. Roberto had missed the games during pool play because he was in summer school back in Santa Barbara. Told that Roberto flew in only the night before, McHee sighed heavily. "He flew in and saved their ass."

The team played only one game in each of the first few days of the tournament, often in the morning. Despite entire afternoons off, the boys saw little of Memphis beyond their hotel and the mall across the street. Before the trip, Carmen had researched landmarks in the area. She had arranged for the team to attend a lecture by a producer at Sun Studio, where Elvis, Jerry Lee Lewis, Carl Perkins, and others had recorded. She also had organized a bus tour that would stop at Graceland, the University of Memphis, and the Rock 'n' Soul Museum. But when the day came for the Sun Studio lecture, Keller said the team was tired and took the boys to a movie instead. On the day of the bus tour, he said the boys needed to "stay focused," which meant remaining in their rooms playing video games. Before the trip, Keller had reluctantly agreed with Carmen that the boys should visit the National Civil Rights Museum, but once there he told her there wasn't any time. "That is something the boys need to see," Carmen said. "That is something every black person should see in their lifetime." Keller didn't budge, and as with the Sun Studio lecture and the bus tour, she took Justin alone.

On Thursday afternoon, Carmen and Justin walked through the museum, taking in exhibits and presentations on Jim Crow laws, Booker T. Washington, *Brown v. Board of Education of Topeka,* and the Montgomery Bus Boycott. At the start of the tour, a video showed how the Civil Rights Movement had prompted human-rights movements in other parts of the world. Clips of speeches by Martin Luther King, Jr., and Malcolm X were spliced with photos and footage, including some of King being arrested. While Justin looked at the screen, Carmen looked at her son. His skinny frame had begun to fill out and he was just under six feet tall. He still wore braces, and wrapped around his left wrist was an assortment of blue and red rubber bands, but she could see the "little man" he was becoming. Another mother might have dreaded Justin's leap into adolescence, but Carmen took pride in it. His grades were good; he looked out for his younger brother; when a group of teachers at Justin's school challenged the kids to a daily basketball game during lunch recess, he organized the team, eventually putting together a group good enough to defeat them.

"Not bad, not bad," she'd say when someone paid her a compliment about Justin. "We're trying." But she was doing more than trying; she was succeeding.

Near the end of the tour, Carmen and Justin peered into Rooms 306 and 307 of what was once the Lorraine Hotel, where Martin Luther King, Jr., was assassinated on April 4, 1968. They saw the wreath that hung on the balcony, the spot where King stood when he was killed. They listened to a replay of the last few lines of King's final speech, delivered in Memphis the day before his murder, and Carmen put her arm around Justin as King's words filled the hall. He didn't pull away, and she kept her arm there during the walk back through the lobby of the museum.

Later, at the hotel, Justin struggled to describe the experience to inquisitive teammates. Over and over he told them, "It was just . . . it was real, you know? It's hard to talk about. It was just real."

Following a 56–44 victory over the Sacramento Jr. Pocket Kings, Team Cal faced the Dallas/Fort Worth NetBurners in the Round of 16. Before the game, Keller looked up at the rapidly filling stands and then motioned to where Demetrius lined up for another dunk during warm-ups. "That's who they're here to see," he said. "The Legend." A few minutes later, the Legend was in a defensive stance, guarding an undersized forward from the NetBurners. Demetrius put a forearm against the player as he ran toward him, and he knew instantly that Team Cal would win. The NetBurners' forward was trembling. "You're a little bitch," Demetrius said to the boy, who responded by running to the other side of the court.

Final score: Team Cal 60, NetBurners 26.

In the lobby of the gym after the game, Keller dialed every number in his cell phone, delivering the news that Team Cal had advanced to the Elite Eight. A parent from another team entered the lobby and said to Rome, Sr., "Well, did you hear? Team Maryland lost." Hoosier Hoops had also been eliminated, the woman said. Team Cal's two rivals, the squads that had knocked them out of the two previous Nationals, were out of the tournament. Keller asked every new visitor to the gym to confirm the news. When he heard it enough times, he said, "We can win this thing. And if we do, I am going to write *John Finn Can Kiss My Ass* on my ass and then go over to his house, knock on the door, and pull my pants down."

Later that night, Keller sat at the bar at a Joe's Crab Shack across from the hotel. He pounded Coronas, ate oysters, and teased the bartender, asking if Soderberg reminded her of Harry from the movie *Harry and the Hendersons.* He wasn't worried about Saturday's quarterfinal opponent, and neither were the players. Hoosier Hoops had been eliminated by American Roundball Corp. (ARC), a Southern California team that the Team Cal kids had defeated so many times they had lost count.

"If we lose tomorrow, I'll kill myself," Keller said between oysters.

His life was spared. Sporting a red, white, and blue headband with the NBA logo on the front, Demetrius looked every bit the future pro as he hammered home three breakaway dunks in a 55–26 victory that put Team Cal into the semifinals.

After that game, Soderberg approached a kid standing near the bleachers; the boy reminded him of Detroit Pistons forward Tayshaun Prince, whom Soderberg had coached briefly at the AAU level. "You've got a body like Tayshaun Prince did at your age," Soderberg told the boy, who looked about twelve. "If you work hard, you could be the next Tayshaun Prince."

The kid gave Soderberg a puzzled look. "I'd rather be the next Demetrius Walker."

At first glance, semifinal opponent Chicago And1 looked no match for Team Cal, except in the wardrobe category. Its two starting guards stood no taller than five feet, and their front line was also small.

But the Chicago boys had style. They wore white uniforms with a burnt-orange trim and white Nike Uptempos with the same orange accent. It was the look the University of Texas basketball team had sported in making it to the Final Four a few months earlier. Several of the players also wore orange headbands, including starting guards D. J. Cooper and Taylor Smith, and each had his hair braided perfectly, with small beads dangling down the back. "That's tight," Rome said of their look as he watched them walk into the gym at Wooddale High School. Their game was equally tight. Cooper and Smith were excellent shooters, as was forward Isaiah Williams, and Chicago's approach would be similar to the Virginia Panthers': hope to make enough 3-pointers to offset Team Cal's size advantage.

Chicago opened in a man-to-man defense, and Aaron destroyed the smaller center. He scored on his first three touches, forcing Chicago to switch to a tight 2-3 zone. The players looked uncomfortable in that defense, but it was the only way they could slow Aaron. In the past, Drew or Jordan would have made Chicago pay for bunching so close to the rim by making 3-pointers. Had Pe'Shon still been around, he almost certainly would have continued to dump the ball in to Aaron, despite the zone. After all, if you lofted the ball high enough, Aaron was the only one who could get it. Keller and Soderberg screamed for this approach, but the perimeter players ignored them and kept jacking up 3-pointers. It was as if they wanted to prove to Chicago—which made five 3-pointers in the first half—that they, too, could bomb away from the outside.

"You guys must be brain-dead," Keller said at halftime. Team Cal was ahead 29–21, but only because of a couple of late Chicago turnovers that led to layups. "I say go inside and you guys shoot threes. We shot eleven threes, and we made one. What the hell are you guys doing?"

Soderberg calmed Keller, then told the team, "Go out there and play our game, and we'll win this thing easily. These guys are not as good as we are making them out to be. And they are not going to keep making those long three-pointers."

But they did.

Late in the third quarter, Cooper and a reserve Chicago guard each made 3-pointers, cutting Team Cal's lead to 35–33. With 4:53 left in the game, Williams tied the score at 39 with yet another from beyond the arc. A steal and a layup by Justin wrestled the lead back, but then Williams hit another deep 3-pointer, this one over Demetrius's outstretched arm. It was the first time Team Cal had trailed since the opening quarter.

Keller sat down and quickly ran his hands over his face. He could scream *Get the ball to Aaron!* over and over, but if no one listened, what did it matter? He stood up tentatively, like a beaten boxer staggering to his feet for the final round. He looked toward the ceiling of the gym, to the lights covered in metal cages, and shouted, "Would someone please, please get the ball to Aaron?"

If you had polled the Team Cal players and coaches, asking them to vote for the player least likely to follow Keller's instructions, Craig Payne would have won in a landslide. The big man Keller had brought over from the Runnin' Rebels with Gary had been a goof since joining the team. If a player's ear got flicked or someone's shorts were pulled to their ankles, Craig was likely the culprit. But Terran's absence forced Keller to play Craig more, and his stomach ached at the thought. "I love Craig. I love his toughness. I love that he won't let anyone intimidate him," Keller said before the team left for Memphis. "But I also want to kill him."

With just under four minutes left in the game, Keller found another reason to love Craig. He received the ball near the free-throw line and, rather than shoot quickly as Team Cal had done most of the game, wheeled toward the basket and dropped a pass inside to Aaron, who scored easily.

"Finally!" Keller shouted, and he punched the air.

After Williams missed on Chicago's next possession, Rome followed Craig's lead. Catching the ball on the wing, he patiently waited for Aaron to front his defender before feeding him the ball. Aaron was fouled instantly and made one of two free throws, putting Team Cal ahead 44–42 with 2:59 left.

A Chicago turnover gave Team Cal the ball again, and when Gary brought the ball upcourt, he saw a pleasing sight: Chicago had gotten out of the zone. He sent the ball to Demetrius, who instantly penetrated to within eight feet and pulled up for a pretty jumper that seemed to hang in the air for days before falling through the net. Demetrius bounced in the air several times as he ran back on defense. "Let's go! Let's go!" he screamed, and his passion lifted his teammates.

Chicago trailed only 46–42, and the 2:10 on the clock was more than enough time to seize back the lead, but the game was over. Demetrius wasn't going to let Team Cal lose. He scored six straight points to finish the game and Team Cal advanced to the finals, 52–44.

Demetrius nodded his head vigorously as he walked off the court, pointing to the small grouping of Team Cal supporters in the stands. Though Aaron finished with more points—19 to 10—Demetrius's strong finish made him the star. Kids ran down the bleachers to slap his hand, and one asked for his headband. Seeing this, Soderberg walked briskly to Aaron. He placed his arm around his shoulder and leaned down so he could be heard over the cheering crowd.

"Aaron, you played a hell of a game. You are the reason we are still alive."

In the locker room, as the players changed out of their game shoes and slipped on sweat suits, Keller cut a speech short for the first time in his life. "Go back to your rooms, ice your knees or do whatever you gotta do for treatment, then get some sleep. Tomorrow's the biggest game of your lives."

17

(GEORGE DOHRMANN)

Rome Draper, Sr., Joe Keller, and Gary Franklin wait to hear if the 2004
National championship will be played.

Walt Harris was not a striking man, yet he carried himself in a distinguished manner. He had a raspy voice with a thick Tennessee drawl, the perfect voice-over for a cigarette commercial, even though he didn't smoke. He also didn't drink or curse or miss church. He had lived in or near Memphis all of his forty-two years, and, prior to 1992, people knew him mostly as an honest real estate agent and a good neighbor.

Harris liked to do favors. He helped people find jobs, loaned money, came to the aid of people he didn't know. His wife liked to tease him about the time he lent his truck to a friend of a friend who said he needed to haul a dresser across town. Harris handed over the keys, even though he didn't know the man's last name. Three days passed before the man returned, yet Harris never reported the truck stolen, nor did he doubt he would get it back.

His kindness could not be mistaken for naïveté. Harris was a smart man, aware of what he called the "wickedness" of the world. But he simply refused to succumb to that wickedness, to believe it ran so deep that he couldn't loan out his car or lend $100 to a friend. His faith in humanity would never be dulled, no matter how many people failed to pay him back, no matter how long before his truck was returned. A favorite line of his was "I believe in goodness." He didn't say it as boldly as Joe Keller said things, but it felt more solid. That certainty, he said, came from the teachings of his father. "No one was more giving than my daddy."

It was no surprise that Harris's introduction to AAU basketball began with a favor. In 1992, his twelve-year-old nephew, Tony Harris, was one of the best young players in Memphis. He was short but quick, and he had such control of the ball that it was like he had it on a string. Tony's father, Walt's brother, wanted his son to play AAU basketball but feared handing him over to a coach he didn't know. He asked Walt if he would coach him, and there was no way Walt was going to say no to family. And so the Bellevue (Tennessee) War Eagles were born.

It surprised no one that Harris was a good coach. He had been a fine high school player while growing up in Bellevue, and he was patient and diligent and threw himself at the task. He didn't have to recruit players; parents brought kids to him. They heard about the honest man whose nephew was a pass-first point guard and beat a path to his door. The War Eagles won an AAU national title in only their second year. In the championship game, Tony and teammates Robert O'Kelley and Cory Bradford led the defeat of a team of 13-year-olds from Southern Cal that featured six-foot-eleven twins Jason and Jarron Collins, who would go on to Stanford and then to the NBA. Two years later, playing in the U–15 division, the War Eagles won a title again, defeating a team from Michigan led by Shane Battier, who became the college player of the year at Duke in 2001.

Tony earned a scholarship to the University of Tennessee. Robert O'Kelley played for Wake Forest. Cory Bradford became a star at Illinois. In the grassroots world, Harris was hot. He coached in Memphis, a boomtown for talented players; he had two AAU titles, and he had just sent three kids to major Division I programs.

Had Joe Keller been in Harris's position, he would have leveraged his success with Tony's team into a shoe deal and then used the money and clout to reload an Under-17 team. But what Harris loved was coaching, not money or power. He enjoyed teaching, seeing a twelve-year-old kid run a play to perfection, something they'd worked on for hours in the heat of the summer in a dingy middle school gym with no air-conditioning. He didn't care if some famous Division I coach sweet-talked him, and he didn't care that other coaches had SUVs nicer than his truck. He cared only about his boys, and that led him to make a decision most grassroots coaches would have called foolish.

"I decided I would start a new team but only take the boys up through Under–Fourteens," Harris said. "After Fourteen-and-Unders, it becomes a business. The shoe companies get involved. The wrong people start trying to get close to the kids. The parents start caring more about what they could get rather than the basketball. Someone else can coach them After-Fourteens, when all the wickedness starts."

With that decision, Harris assured that he would never be an AAU power broker. He stopped having sway over prospects at precisely the moment others saw value in them. To the shoe companies, to the agents, to the college recruiters, he was useless, a fool motivated by—get this—the joy he got from teaching the game to children.

As Team Cal made its way to the finals of the 2004 Nationals, Harris's latest team also claimed victory after victory. He found it difficult to enjoy their success, however, as early in the week of Nationals, his father was admitted to Baptist East Hospital. His father had battled cancer for several years, and Harris knew this was the end. He visited his father between games and sat with him late into the night, often arriving at the gym straight from the hospital. He resisted telling his players, however, not wanting to distract them. But before the War Eagles' final game in pool play, he determined that he couldn't afford to be away from his father, as he could die at any minute. Harris informed his team on Tuesday night when they gathered at his house, which they did before every game, to eat and pray together. "I am sorry, but I need to be with Daddy," he told the boys, and tears streamed down his face.

Calvin Duane, one of Harris's quietest players, got up from the couch and put his hand on his coach's shoulder. "You go be with your daddy. We'll go out there and win this game for you and for him."

And they did, 53–37.

The following morning, Harris's brother called and told him to come to the hospital immediately. Harris made it to Baptist East just in time to see his father take his last breath, to kiss him on the forehead and then on the hand, and to tell him, "Daddy, go be with God now. He is waiting for you." Harris's brother, his mother, his sisters, uncles, and aunts filled the room, and moments after his father passed, Harris felt a rush of heat. "I have to leave, I just have to," he told his mother, and he ran out of the hospital room and down the hall. He left so quickly, ran with such purpose, that his sister would later say, "It was as if he was chasing after Daddy's soul."

Harris climbed into his truck and drove. He didn't know where he was going but led the truck—instinctively, perhaps—to the nearest basketball gym: Ridgeway High School. He entered the gym and went to the far side of the court, where the old wooden bleachers, stripped of varnish and worn down to their original almond stain, nearly reached the ceiling. Harris scurried up the steps, dodging kids and parents watching the game below. He sat on the top bleacher and put his hands to his face and cried. Not the way he wept in front of his team earlier in the week, but loud sobs that would have drawn attention had anyone been seated near him. Harris cried until it became hard to breathe, hard to hold himself up, hard to see the good from the wicked, and then he opened his eyes and looked down at the young boys playing on the court.

"I couldn't say what teams were playing. I couldn't tell you the score or how old they were or even the color of their uniforms," Harris said later. "But watching those boys, just watching them play, something came over me. It has always been in the gym, when I am with the boys, when I have felt the best, where my mind has been clear and free. I don't know what it was, but suddenly I felt free. I watched those kids for maybe half an hour, just watching, and everything felt all right."

He stood up and walked down the bleachers, skirted back across the baseline, and walked out of the gym and got into his car. He might have returned to the hospital, to his family, but instead Harris sped east, in the opposite direction, toward the home of one of his assistant coaches.

"That was where my team was."

———

Two days after his father's death, Harris scouted Team Cal's semifinal victory over Chicago And1. It was the third time he had seen Keller's bunch, and his impression hadn't changed. At the U–11 Nationals in Cocoa Beach in 2002, he concluded, "That team has got more talent than anybody." At the U–12 Nationals in Newport News in 2003, he remarked, "If they put it all together, they are the best team in the country." Watching the semifinal in Memphis with one of his assistants, he said, "They're the most athletic team we have ever faced. And that number twenty-three, I've never seen a kid that good at that age."

Harris considered his options. He did not have a player who could single-handedly keep Demetrius from going to the basket, so the whole team would have to do it. Memphis's best athlete was five-foot-eleven forward Keshun Cowan, and that's where the defense would start. Cowan would guard Demetrius straightaway. The other players, particularly his guards, would be the second line. Whenever Demetrius had the ball, they would be ready to cut off the lanes to the basket. Harris was telling his whole team that their first responsibility was to stop Demetrius, and their second was to keep an eye on everyone else.

It seemed like a classic mistake. Pay too much attention to Demetrius, and the other boys—especially Aaron—would beat you. But Harris recognized how the other players fed off Demetrius's success. When he was scoring, all the boys ran faster and went to the basket harder and played fiercer defense. Harris's plan wasn't simply to stop Demetrius from getting to the basket but to stop him from boosting Team Cal's confidence.

"If we are going to get beat," he said, "someone other than that number twenty-three is going to have to do it."

On the Sunday morning of the finals, a thunderstorm crept toward Memphis. The championship game was scheduled for 1:30 p.m., but three hours before the start time, the storm knocked out the power to the gym. A small glitch, it seemed, but then the starting time came and went and the power remained out. The players lingered outside the gym, in cars with the doors open. Keller, meanwhile, sat in an office, talking to AAU officials who were intent on holding the game at the gym that could seat the most people and in which the largest collection of merchandise was on display, no matter how long it took to get the power turned back on.

Weeks earlier, Keller had booked the team on a 7:00 p.m. return flight, believing that even if they made the finals, that left plenty of time to get to the airport. But as the hours passed, Keller and the parents realized they might need to choose between catching their flight home and playing the game. Staying meant changing flights (at a cost) and another night at the hotel. When Keller presented his dilemma to Bobby Dodd, president of the AAU, he was told he shouldn't have scheduled the flights so early.

Keller found Harris in the parking lot and explained his dilemma. "That's not fair," Harris said, and he suggested that if Team Cal had to leave, it would be only right for the teams to share the title. Dodd, his belt straining to hold his gut inside his tan pants, stepped up on a metal folding table of merchandise and announced that if Team Cal left early, the War Eagles would be crowned champions. He then refused to answer a television reporter's question about why the game hadn't yet been moved to a different site. As Dodd scampered back into the office, Aaron's mom, Barbara, screamed after him, "Run away, then! Run like a roach!"

An hour later, around 4:00 p.m., Dodd emerged again and finally moved the game to a gym with power. But Keller thought it was too late. "What do you want to do?" he asked the parents in the parking lot. Rome, Sr., wanted to stay, no matter the cost. "The boys have worked so hard," he said. Bruce was on the fence; his flight was even earlier than the rest and he couldn't miss it, because he had work the next day. Barbara was so upset with Dodd that she contemplated not letting the boys play just so the AAU wouldn't get the money from the game's gate. The parents were split, so the final say fell to Keller. He looked over at Demetrius, who stood talking to Rome next to one of the cars. He was in uniform but had on a black sweatshirt with the hood over his head. Rome tugged on a rubber band wrapped around his left wrist and swayed to whatever music came from his headphones. Those two boys had been with Keller since the beginning, and they'd heard every speech he'd given about winning the ultimate prize: the glass-bowl trophy given to the national champions.

"Fuck it, we're going to play," Keller abruptly announced. "I may go broke, but we're going to play." Then he screamed at the boys, "Get in the damn car!"

Harris was in his car when a tournament organizer called him with word of the new site. When he heard the AAU official say *Ridgeway High,* he believed it was providence. The final would be played at the gym where, days earlier, he had found peace after his father's death.

The biggest game of the boys' lives started in an odd fashion. Most of the fans that would fill Ridgeway to near its 2,500-seat capacity were still outside when the game started. AAU officials had announced the site change before they had people in place to sell tickets. Fans were held at the door by security until someone showed up to take their five dollars and stamp their hands. Warm-ups were condensed to five hurried minutes, and there was no time for pregame speeches. Harris and Keller sent their teams onto the floor cold, with no final words or instructions, and it showed. The play was sloppy. Aaron scored twice inside, but both scores were put-backs of misses. Leslie McDonald, the War Eagles' center, who was a few inches shorter than Aaron but more explosive, put in two baskets by using his quickness.

Though his team struggled to find a rhythm, Harris was content leading 11–9 at the end of the first quarter. To his coach's eye, it was a smashing start. Team Cal was clearly confused on offense. Demetrius had scored only once, and McDonald had matched Aaron basket for basket. Hard as it may have been for others to see, the game was going just as Harris had mapped it. During the brief intermission, he looked down the court and saw Keller urging Demetrius to attack the basket, and he smiled. Keller was falling right into his trap. "Keep it up. Keep it up," Harris told his players. "No drives to the basket. Cut off the lanes. And everybody rebounds."

As Demetrius walked onto the floor to start the second quarter, he looked up into the stands. By that point, a fan cheering passionately for the War Eagles filled every seat. He then looked behind him, where the stands were also full and all but the cluster of Team Cal parents hoped he'd fail. Closer to the court, Keller shouted after him, "Do your thing, D!" In that moment, who could have blamed Demetrius for wanting to be somewhere else? He didn't ask to be the star, didn't request that an opposing coach like Harris design a defense with the solitary goal of shutting him down, didn't wish for defenders to clutch him and push him and grab him, following orders to do anything to stop him. "Come on, D!" Keller screamed one more time, and with that, Demetrius took a long breath and held it, his cheeks full like a trumpeter's. Then came an exaggerated exhalation as if he were blowing more than air into the gym. And then back to work.

On Team Cal's second possession of the second quarter, Demetrius got the ball on the left wing and did exactly as Keller had instructed. He took a quick step toward the basket, past Cowan, but McDonald and another player rotated over and he had to retreat to the baseline, where he was stranded. He wheeled around, looking to unload the ball, bending backward so much it looked as if he'd fall out of bounds. It seemed certain that he would turn the ball over, but then he spotted Rome. With the ball in two hands atop his head, Demetrius whipped a pass toward him.

Since the arrival of Aaron and Roberto, Rome had become even more of a facilitator, reduced to moving the ball around to get them open shots. But in the biggest game, he broke free. As he caught the ball, he stepped toward the basket, into the hole created when the defense had converged on Demetrius, and after one quick dribble he pulled up for a 14-foot jump shot. It was not his favorite spot—he preferred shooting from the baseline—but it wasn't a bad spot either. As Rome released the ball, Rome, Sr., sitting at the end of the team's bench, inched up from his seat. He was leaning forward, between standing and sitting, when the ball went through the net. For a moment he didn't know how to react. "Rome!" he yelled finally, but his son didn't look at him. He was sprinting back on defense as if it was just another made shot, just another 14-foot drop in the bucket.

After Duane scored quickly for Memphis, Gary brought the ball upcourt and immediately looked for Demetrius on the right. Seeing a horde of defenders cheating that way, Gary faked Demetrius a pass and then flipped the ball to his left. Once again, Rome didn't stop to think, didn't consider that Keller might yell if he missed, might reduce him to tears like he did a year earlier in Baltimore. He caught Gary's pass, stepped forward, and released another high-arcing shot with perfect backspin. "Rome! My boy!" screamed Rome, Sr., as it fell through the basket. Again Little Rome acted nonchalant, acknowledging the pass from Gary with the pointing of a finger, then backpedaling to play defense. On Team Cal's next possession, there was no question where the ball would go. Gary sped upcourt and immediately fed it to Rome. Rome released the ball as quickly as he could. Another 14-footer from the left side, three in a row.

Rome finally reacted, but only for a second. He looked to the bench, to his father, and he shrugged his bony shoulders and smiled. Rome, Sr., yelled, "Keep it up, son! Keep it up!"

Harris could not have foreseen the effect Rome's three makes would have on his teammates. The forgotten Roberto, whom Keller hadn't run a play for since the victory over the Virginia Panthers, scored on consecutive possessions, making a six-foot runner and then a five-foot floater over McDonald's outstretched arm. On defense, Team Cal's intensity led to four consecutive scoreless possessions by the War Eagles. Harris had thought stopping Demetrius would sever Team Cal's supply of confidence. He had not counted on them finding it in Rome.

Team Cal led 21-19 at the half, despite not getting a single basket from Demetrius or Aaron in the second quarter. The players on the bench smothered Rome and Roberto as they ran off the floor toward the locker room. Justin practically knocked Rome over by leaping on his back, and Keller stuck a finger in his chest. "Big-time, Rome. Big-time."

Near the midway point of the third quarter, Demetrius put back a miss by Aaron, tying the score at 29. There was nothing special about the play; he outleaped McDonald to grab the ball and flipped it in before McDonald could reset himself. But as the ball fell through the hoop, a wave of relief swept over Team Cal and its supporters. Demetrius had gone scoreless for more than sixteen minutes. If someone had told Harris or Keller that Demetrius would have only four points after two and a half quarters, both would have predicted that the War Eagles would be winning in a rout. But Team Cal was very much in the game, thanks to Rome and Aaron (six points apiece) and Roberto (five). But they needed Demetrius, and so when he finally ended his drought, the Team Cal parents yelled from the stands. A possession later, when Demetrius scored again on a drive to the basket, it looked as if he was on the verge of one of those magical stretches that always ended with a Team Cal victory. But Harris was too smart to let that happen. He ordered the War Eagles back into the soft-man defense from the first quarter designed to stop Demetrius.

Keller or Soderberg might have called a time-out and reminded the team how Rome had taken advantage of this strategy in the first half, but they seemed to not notice the change. They continually shouted for

Demetrius or Aaron to get the ball when they no longer had the space to operate. After two short jumpers by a guard put the War Eagles up 33–31, all the energy generated by Demetrius's brief scoring spurt evaporated.

Gary Franklin, Sr., sat two seats down from Keller, biting his lip, trying to urge on the boys without giving actual instructions. It had been that way since he and Gary joined Team Cal. He'd leap off his seat, ready to yell something to the players on the court, then catch himself and sit back down. During time-outs, he sought out certain boys and gave them advice. In the first half, he'd told Craig to look for Aaron cutting if he caught the ball low. Like clockwork, Craig got the ball right after he entered the game, saw Aaron cut, and threaded the ball into him for an easy layup. Before the start of the third quarter, he told Gary not to be afraid to go past his defender and right at McDonald. "He'll go for the block. Protect the ball and finish strong, and you will at least get the foul."

Something clicked in Gary as he brought the ball upcourt, his team trailing. As his defender approached, Gary noticed he was leaning toward the right, toward Demetrius's side. So Gary burst past him on the left. He didn't stop until McDonald crashed into him as he threw up a shot that just missed. The referee gave Gary the foul and he netted both free throws, despite loud hoots from the Memphis fans, several of whom banged on drums. After another short jumper put the War Eagles back ahead, Gary repeated the play, blowing past his defender and leaping toward the rim. McDonald reacted so late that Gary was able to finish the layup untouched, which tied the score, 35–35, as the third quarter ended.

"Keep going right at them. Right at them," Gary, Sr., told his son in the break before the final quarter. "Don't look for someone else to score. If you believe you can get your shot, then take it."

When Rome inbounded the ball to Gary to start the final quarter, Gary didn't bother looking in Demetrius's direction. He flew past his defender, got into the lane, and went right at McDonald. He put the ball in his left hand as McDonald came over for the block, and as McDonald lunged for the ball, Gary brought it back inside and scooped it under McDonald's arm, off the backboard, and in, getting fouled in the process.

Keller was more crazed fan than coach at this point. When Gary's shot fell, he thrust his right fist in the air. When Gary made his bonus free throw, Keller turned and looked down the bench at Gary, Sr., his eyes wide, as if to say: *Where did this come from?* Gary, Sr., just nodded, knowing his son had it in him all along.

At the other end of the court, Harris faced a dilemma. Like Rome in the first half, Gary had made the War Eagles pay for focusing on Demetrius. Even as Harris watched McDonald score again to cut Team Cal's lead to 38–37, he knew he was stuck. "Straight man!" he yelled at his team, knowing that by switching defenses again he was inviting Demetrius to drive. "I didn't have a choice," he would say later. "That little guard was killing us."

Because he was such a breathtaking athlete, Demetrius rarely got credit for understanding the nuances of the game. Players of his skill were often so in love with their abilities that they believed they could score no matter the defender or formation. One of the benefits of pitting Team Cal against older teams during the regular season was that Demetrius faced kids bigger and stronger and, at times, coaches more creative at stopping him. During those games, Demetrius had learned— on his own, really—how to probe a defense and catch slight changes in strategy. When Harris called out the shift, his players lined up in a defense that looked no different from the previous one. But Demetrius saw the change and noticed that the players behind his defender were now up tighter on their men—on Gary, Rome, Aaron, and Roberto. When he got the ball along the baseline with 6:51 left, he instantly went on the attack. He drove past Duane, who was so helpless he simply slapped at the ball. The referee called the foul and Demetrius calmly made both free throws, boosting Team Cal's lead to 40–37. After McDonald scored inside, Demetrius got the ball on the right side and slashed to the hoop again, picking up his dribble at the free-throw line, then hopping past Duane and into the key, seemingly changing direction in midair. McDonald helplessly knocked him down before he could even shoot, and Demetrius stepped to the line and sank both free throws to boost Team Cal's lead back to three.

The War Eagles were matching Demetrius's scoring but had to work harder for points. They held the ball for long periods, moving it around the perimeter until McDonald got open or someone found a clear jumper. One of the War Eagles' guards made a 13-footer with 5:04 left, but then Demetrius quickly drove upcourt, penetrated into the lane, and slipped the ball through two players to a wide-open Aaron for a score. Demetrius was dictating play on both ends. On defense, he chased after loose balls and rebounds, snatching a few out of Aaron's hands. On offense, the question was what he would do once he got to the rim: shoot or pass to a wide-open teammate. But just when he was finally in control, Demetrius slipped up. After a War Eagles miss, he got so excited about the possibility of pushing the lead to five that he barreled over Duane on his way to the basket. It was a clear offensive foul, and now both he and Aaron had four fouls, each one whistle away from fouling out.

Moments later, Demetrius got his hand on a pass inside to McDonald and bounced the ball out to Gary, who beat two players downcourt for a layup and a 46–41 edge. On the War Eagles' next possession, however, Demetrius went for the steal again and found himself out of position. Rather than let McDonald have the basket, he gave him a slight push. The gym fell almost silent after the referee blew his whistle. Aaron was close enough to McDonald that it wasn't clear which of Team Cal's two stars was finished for the day. The referee walked to the scorer's table and announced, "The foul is on two-three white," and the War Eagles crowd, numbering almost 2,500, cheered louder with each step Demetrius took toward the sideline. He plopped down next to Rome, Sr., and put his hands to his face, his long fingers stretching well up his forehead. He started to cry, and Rome, Sr., rubbed his back. "Don't worry, D, your teammates will get it done."

McDonald made one of two free throws, cutting Team Cal's lead to 46–42 with 2:42 left, and the crowd rose, urging the War Eagles to get a stop on defense. Barbara, Carmen, and the rest of Team Cal's parents climbed down from the bleachers and snaked to the far end of the court. They would watch the finish from there. Win or lose, they could reach their sons the minute the game ended.

Gary brought the ball up and slowed the game down. The War Eagles were in a tight man-to-man defense, and Gary might have been able to drive again, but he smartly held the ball, milking the clock, waiting until two minutes remained before feeding the ball to Rome on the left. Rome held the ball, waiting as Roberto fought through defenders from across the key, cutting along the baseline until he got free in the corner, where Rome passed him the ball. McDonald moved out to guard him, and Roberto stood with his left foot forward, sizing him up. McDonald was expecting him to drive to the right, into the middle of the court and away from the baseline, and he shaded that way. Roberto gave a head fake and, when McDonald stepped toward him, Roberto put the ball on the floor and slithered around him, going along the baseline. It wasn't an explosive move, more like a sly trick. Another defender rotated over as Roberto pushed past McDonald into the key, and Roberto jumped to a stop and pumped as if he were going to shoot. When that defender jumped, he calmly ducked under his reach and rolled the ball up and in, a cheeky little shot that you'd expect to see in a game of H-O-R-S-E but not in the finals of Nationals.

The War Eagles panicked on their next possession. A guard forced a pass that Roberto deflected, which ended up in Justin's hands for a breakaway layup. It put Team Cal up 50–42 with only 1:12 left, and the crowd fell silent and a few fans moved toward the exits. The War Eagles tried to get back into the game by fouling, but Gary made four free throws in the final minute.

When the final buzzer sounded, the Team Cal players, coaches, and parents streamed onto the court. They met Justin, Rome, Gary, Aaron, and Roberto after a few steps and they mashed into a group hug, with Keller in the middle. On the outer ring were the parents, including Rome, Sr., and Gary, Sr., who embraced every parent or kid who came within reach. Carmen finally found Justin, and he hugged her and lifted her off the ground for a moment, which made her blush. Aaron and Demetrius embraced, and as they broke free, Aaron put his hand out. Demetrius took it, and then he pulled Aaron close and they hugged again.

Keller made his way to midcourt, to an AAU official who was setting up a table to present the crystal-bowl trophy to Team Cal. He grabbed the trophy before the presentation even started and held it in the air with his right hand. He then turned toward the section of War Eagles fans and thrust the trophy in that direction. He abruptly turned around, as if an alarm had gone off in his head, and pushed the trophy into Demetrius's arms.

"What the hell are you all doing?" he yelled at the team. "Get in the cars! We've got to get to the airport!" Keller looked at his watch. It was six-thirty. He caught Violet's eye and mouthed, "Get to the car," and then he ran out of the gym.

As Team Cal loaded into cars and sped toward the airport, Harris pulled his team around him in a quiet locker room. Some of the boys were crying, and as Harris began to speak, Calvin Duane said, "Coach, we let you down. I'm sorry. We wanted to win this one for you."

"No, no, you didn't let me down," he said. "You boys helped me get through one of the toughest weeks of my life. Thank you for that. Thank you. I love all you boys." Then he led them in a prayer.

Between sorting out tickets and returning rental cars, it was improbable that Team Cal would catch its flight. The parents had checked bags and retrieved boarding passes earlier in the day, but there were so many people to keep track of that most of the group were still hustling through the security line more than fifteen minutes after their scheduled departure time. Yet it was such a large party that Northwest Airlines held the plane, and they made their flight.

Once the plane was airborne, Tom gave a flight attendant $200 and told her to give the parents and coaches whatever they wanted to drink.

"I don't believe it. I don't believe it," Justin said over and over as his mom sipped white wine. It was the first time he'd seen her drink alcohol.

Gary, Sr., and Gary reviewed Gary's drives to the basket in the second half. Rome, Sr., and Rome talked about his release on those three big baskets early in the game.

Demetrius was in a chair next to Keller, the glass-bowl trophy in his lap. He was the quietest boy on the plane, the one most ready for the celebration to stop, for the lights to dim, wanting most of all to put on his headphones and let the music bring him sleep. But Keller wouldn't allow it, not yet. He grabbed a flight attendant and explained why the team had been so late. She took the news to the cockpit, as Keller had hoped she would, and a few minutes later one of the pilots made an announcement. "Ladies and gentlemen, we've got some very special guests on board with us tonight: Team Cal. They just won the Thirteen-and-Under national championship. Congratulations."

As the rest of the passengers applauded, Keller urged Demetrius and the other players to stand. One by one they rose—Demetrius was the last to his feet—and then Keller stood, and he and Demetrius and the rest of Team Cal took a bow.

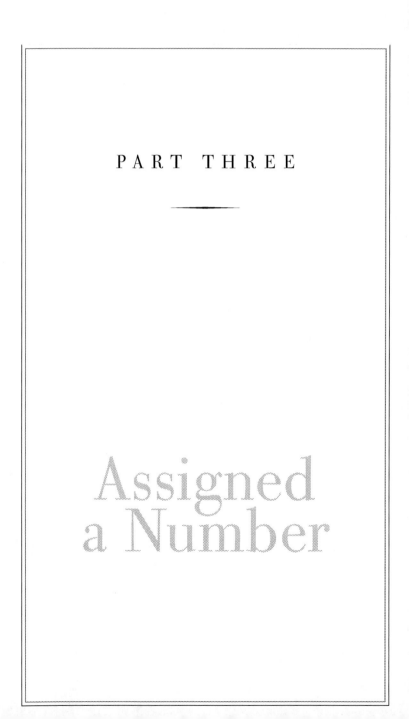

PART THREE

Assigned
a Number

(ROBERT BECK/*SPORTS ILLUSTRATED*)

Demetrius Walker posing in 2005

I n the fall of 2004, Karl Taro Greenfeld, a writer for *Sports Illustrated,*
called Keller. He had seen Demetrius's name atop the Hoop Scoop
rankings of eighth-graders, he said, and wanted to do a story on
the young phenom. Keller had long courted media attention for his
star, but an article in *Sports Illustrated* was beyond his wildest dreams.
In his business of promoting Demetrius and himself, *Sports Illustrated*
was the perfect vehicle. If the magazine called Demetrius the best
player in the country, that news would reach nearly 3.5 million sub-
scribers in every corner of the United States. Demetrius had helped
Team Cal win Nationals, and Clark Francis had ranked him number 1
in his age group for two years, but there remained some skepticism

about his ability. The Hoop Scoop's dubious rankings alone would not convince rival coaches and players, especially those in hotbeds like New York City or Houston who had never seen Demetrius play. If *Sports Illustrated* tabbed him the next big thing, however, his potential would be gospel, and the brushfire of hype Keller had stoked for years would rage.

Putting Demetrius in *Sports Illustrated* had a downside. Every good player who lined up against him would look to inflate his own profile by diminishing Demetrius's, and the coaches of those players would rip him publicly and privately because it was in their interests to do so. Otherworldly acts would be expected each time he took the floor, an immense burden for a boy so young. If he had a bad game or missed a dunk, fans would shake their heads and say, "That kid's the best player in the country?" This had already happened on a smaller scale. In a tournament shortly after Francis ranked Demetrius number 1, two boys stayed in the gym after their game to watch Demetrius face a squad from Utah. As the referee tossed the ball upward for the opening tip, Demetrius hesitated—he hadn't expected the referee to throw the ball at that moment—and he was late getting off the ground. The center for Utah reached the ball first, which prompted one of the young observers to remark, "Man, you *can't* lose the tip if you're the number one player in the country!"

Keller foresaw this consequence and wavered on whether to go forward with the article. It would do wonders for Keller's profile, particularly with Adidas; it would announce his importance in the same way that the Adidas contract did, only more publicly. Team Cal and the Jr. Phenom Camp, his two brands, would be in the spotlight, which could lead to more sponsors and money. But Demetrius could get a big head and stop working hard, thinking he had already made it; he could be humiliated by opponents gunning for him and fear later challenges; he could be derailed by the rush of people looking to attach themselves to a rising star or by the "haters" jealous of his success. Appearing in *Sports Illustrated* would not help Demetrius get a college scholarship or make the pros. There was no potential gain to him other than the one he keenly noted to Keller: "A lot of girls will hear about me being in that article."

Sports Illustrated had previously highlighted three basketball phenoms. In 1994, the magazine put Felipe López of New York on the cover before his first college season. In that same year, a writer profiled sixteen-year-old Schea Cotton of Santa Ana Mater Dei, calling him the kind of player who could bring college coaches "job security; bring them a better job and a more lucrative sneaker deal; bring them to the Final Four." In 2002, the magazine put LeBron James on the cover and coined his nickname: "The Chosen One." James was a high school junior at the time, and the article announced his arrival as a future superstar. It opened the floodgates to more features in *Sports Illustrated* and other publications, and ESPN televised some of his high school games. *Sports Illustrated* helped make him a global brand before he was drafted into the NBA, and it boosted his appeal to Nike and Gatorade, who signed him to lucrative sponsorship deals after he declared for the draft the following year. López was entering college when the magazine profiled him, and although he enjoyed a solid college career at St. John's and a brief stint in the NBA, he was widely viewed as having never lived up to the potential of a *Sports Illustrated* cover boy. The same was said of Cotton, who was a sophomore in high school when he appeared on the cover. He eventually played two seasons at Alabama but never stuck in the NBA.

The failings of Cotton and López were blamed partly on the spotlight that found them at too young an age. They crumbled under the scrutiny, people said. Cotton was one of Barrett's protégés, and Keller knew well his struggles dealing with the pressure. "Being in *Sports Illustrated* changed my life. I lived in a fishbowl from there on out," Cotton said. "Not only was I a marked man by the opposition, but as far as the public was concerned, I was always being scrutinized. The biggest thing was, nothing was ever good enough. I'd have a game where I'd score twenty points, and people would say I should have scored more. I'd have a game that, because of injury or whatever, I would play so-so, and the critics would lay into me. . . . It forced me to grow up faster than a teenager should, because I was a national figure at fifteen or sixteen years old. . . . Pat tried to prep me for it, but it was never talked about that we wouldn't do [the article]. It was good exposure for him, for the program. It would bring notoriety to him, and that would bring more talent."

Keller had no choice but to involve Kisha in his deliberations—Greenfeld would surely want to talk with her—and her instinct was to turn the article down. "I don't know if I am ready for all this," she said.

"All the attention. I don't know if I can handle it. . . . And little D, every-one is going to be coming after him. It's like putting a big target on his back."

The decision was ultimately Keller's to make, and his concern moved from what the article might do to Demetrius to what it could expose about him. He had recently held Demetrius—and Terran—back a year in school; they would repeat the eighth grade, which would put them in the same class as Rome, Roberto, Justin, and the others. Both boys were young for their grade, and holding players back in school was common. But Keller enrolled Demetrius and Terran in the same home-schooling program in which he had placed Aaron, and then he did nothing to assure that they did any work. Demetrius and Terran slept in late at Demetrius's home, played video games until the afternoon, and then went to practice or the mall. Neither Kisha nor Keller nor any other adult supervised them, and their repeat of eighth grade amounted to a yearlong summer break.

Keller also worried that Greenfeld would focus on any number of criticisms common in articles written about young basketball players, such as their exploitation by coaches and the shoe companies. During phone conversations with Kalish and Pickett at Adidas, Keller weighed the pros and cons of an article and ultimately concluded that even if Greenfeld focused on the negatives—if, for example, he took Keller and Adidas to task for going after middle school kids—the boost it would give to the profiles of Demetrius, Keller, and the Jr. Phenom Camp was worth it. "All of that stuff has been written before, so no one is going to care," Keller said. "To get me and D in *Sports Illustrated,* and if the article talks about the Jr. Phenom Camp, it will be worth it."

Greenfeld reported the article over several days and it was published January 24, 2005. The grassroots grapevine would say that Demetrius was on the cover, and technically he was. The cover photo was of New England Patriots linebacker Tedy Bruschi, but on a small banner on the bottom right corner there was a picture of Demetrius dribbling a ball and the headline:

MEET DEMETRIUS WALKER.
He's 14 years old.
You're going to
hear from him.

Inside, the article carried the headline:

The Fast Track
The next LeBron? Some say 14-year-old Demetrius Walker is on the express to the NBA. Others say he's traveling too quickly, too soon

It began:

"You see?" Kisha Houston storms across the Rialto High basketball court, waving a blue, filigreed document—her son's birth certificate. "You see? Demetrius Walker is 14 years old. Say that. Write that. Tell them D is 14. Stop all this about his being 16, 17, people lying, saying we held him back. He's the right age."

She holds the document up for inspection. "That's his birthday right there," she says. And sure enough, Demetrius Walker, or D, the best eighth-grade basketball player in the country, is only 14 years old. But that man out there on the court, 6'3", 175 pounds, built more like an NFL tailback than a junior high school point guard and with enough game to be running the point for a Division I program—how can he be 14? It doesn't seem possible, but deal with it: This kid is 14 going on LeBron. I shouldn't be writing this. You shouldn't be reading it.

The larger points raised in the article were far from original but worth considering: Should we be focusing attention on kids so young? What damage does it do to kids to tab them for stardom in their prepubescent years? Greenfeld quoted Houston Rockets star Tracy McGrady, who went straight from high school to the NBA, as saying: "Fourteen? That's too fast. That means you don't even get a chance to be a teenager. At least I got to be a teenager for a while. Now they're gonna take that away too?"

But the article spent as much time praising Demetrius as it did scrutinizing those who would steal a fourteen-year-old's youth, glowingly describing one of his drives from the basket and quoting Keller comparing him to Tyson Chandler and Clark Francis saying, "If he grows, it'll be scary; if he doesn't, he can still make a lot of money at this game."

The people touting Demetrius as a future NBA star were the same characters—Keller and Francis—but the forum had changed. Appearing in the hallowed pages of *Sports Illustrated,* their remarks came across more like facts than propaganda. Keller also told Greenfeld that Team Cal hadn't lost in two and a half years, 160 straight games, that Demetrius was homeschooled by a tutor, and that Keller checked to make sure he did his homework. He said he had Demetrius on a special diet and vitamins and that Soderberg had been with Team Cal for five years, among other embellishments. Keller was most pleased with the section on his expectations for Demetrius, in which he said: "As long as he graduates from high school, I don't care if he becomes a ballerina." He also loved the ending:

> "I know how this looks," says Keller as he backs the truck out of the driveway. "I know you are going to say that what is going on here is weird. People are going to say it looks bad, like I'm manipulating this kid. Like I'm trying to take advantage. But I'm not going to get a thing out of this. My only hope is that maybe, one day, when Demetrius is in the NBA, he can come back and sponsor my team. We'll call it the Demetrius Walker All-Stars. If he wants to do that, great. If not, that's fine. I'm doing everything that's right for the kid, and right now, what he wants, what I want, what his mom wants—we all want the same thing, and that's for Demetrius to succeed and grow and graduate and do all those things he is supposed to do."
>
> How could that be bad for him?

"Of course that is all bullshit," Keller said when I called him on his comments. "If Demetrius quit basketball, I'd kill him and myself. But it looks good, me saying that shit." Keller's only criticism was that Greenfeld described him as having a potbelly. "Other than that, that article couldn't have been better if I wrote it myself."

The article was not a puff piece; it raised legitimate questions about how young basketball talent was cultivated and, specifically, whether Keller and Adidas would do more harm than good to young Demetrius. But smart yet subtle criticism of the grassroots machine had as much impact as spitting into the ocean. Only the broadest strokes of Greenfeld's analysis would spread: Demetrius was special; he was the next LeBron; and Keller was an emerging basketball titan.

The main photo accompanying the feature was of Demetrius holding a basketball while standing on the train tracks that ran through Fontana. To Keller, the photo illustrated how Demetrius was going places; he was on the fast track to the NBA. A cynic might have viewed the photo's symbolism differently. Keller had put Demetrius in danger's path. The weight of expectations rushed toward him like a train, threatening to flatten him.

The grassroots division at Adidas was overjoyed with the article. The coach and player they had invested in had been written about glowingly, and the launch of the Adidas Jr. Phenom Camp was presented as a pioneering endeavor in the push to identify kids at a younger age.

The camp had been held at Alliant University in San Diego a few months before Greenfeld contacted Keller, and by all accounts Keller accomplished his primary objectives. He proved to Kalish that he could deliver the top eleven- to fourteen-year-old players in the country to an Adidas event, and he made a boatload of money. An estimated 10,000 spectators paid either $25 for a two-day pass or $10 to get into the event for a single day. Violet sold 400 programs at $15 or $10 apiece (the price was lowered the second day). They sold 800 T-shirts at $10 a pop and uncounted drinks and food at concession stands. Advertising from the program and related marketing brought in another $20,000, and the players' parents or Adidas footed the $395 registration fee for 225 kids. Housing and feeding the kids, renting the gym, and paying coaches to work the event cut into Keller's profit, but he exceeded his goal of $100,000.

"Guess where I am right now?" he said a week after the camp. "Driving out of a dealership with Violet's new SUV. Paid, like, fifty thousand in cash. Life is good."

He talked about creating a Jr. Phenom Camp for girls, also to be sponsored by Adidas, the following summer and of improvements he would make to the boys' camp. "It's going to be even bigger next year. I'm getting calls already from people who want to come. It's going to be huge. Just the advertising from the program alone, I think I can get up to forty thousand dollars. I wouldn't be surprised if I make double what I did this year."

Kalish was so impressed by the camp that he gave Keller the title of Director of Youth Grassroots Programs, a two-year extension on his contract, and a raise that brought his annual salary to $70,000. Kalish also signed off on Keller's proposal to sign other young teams to shoe contracts before Nike or Reebok learned of them. He was given $15,000 per team, but if he could sign them for less—say, $10,000 or $12,000— he could pocket the difference. He traveled the country with a figurative bagful of money and then, after the *Sports Illustrated* article, with as much clout as any coach in youth basketball.

Vaccaro learned of Keller's new role and title nearly a year to the day after he had reneged on their deal. "Between having me at Reebok and Nike, with all the money they have, Adidas is shut out with the top high school players right now," he said. "You look at the high school teams in Southern California that Adidas had this year, and none of them won a single tournament. Across the country, it is the same. They don't have any of the top players. That is why Joe might be the single most important person Adidas has right now. He has the best players in that age group. In a way, everything they are trying to do depends on him, on his ability to keep his players and get others from around the country. Joe Keller is all Adidas has right now."

Demetrius cut out the *Sports Illustrated* article and taped it to a wall in his room, placing it next to a recruiting letter from Duke. On a Sunday evening a few days after the article hit newsstands, Demetrius sat on his bed, his back against the wall. The article was above his head, and he kept looking up at it, as if to make sure it was real.

"A lot of people are going to be watching me now 'cuz of this, huh?" He meant watching him in a good way, noticing his talent. But then, after a few seconds, the smile left his face; he seemed to realize the downside. He picked up a basketball and spun it on his finger.

"It's cool. I can handle it."

19

(TODD BIGELOW)

Aaron Moore outside the circle of Team Cal friends

Mom, why does Coach Joe have to lie?"

Aaron sat at a table in a Mexican restaurant not far from his home. He waited until Barbara was well into her steak tacos before asking the question.

"You knew going in to this team that Joe was going to favor Demetrius and that he wasn't going to tell the truth all the time," Barbara said.

"Mom, what kind of excuse is that? He lied to me."

"But you know from when you started in all this crap—"

"Mom, Mom, you try to pacify—is that the right word, *pacify*? You try to pacify the situation and make it okay that Coach lied. You make excuses for him. It's not okay that he lied."

Keller had told Aaron (and all the boys) that the *Sports Illustrated* article would focus on Team Cal's victory at Nationals and not Demetrius alone. The more perceptive kids, such as Rome and Justin, quickly saw through the fib. Greenfeld never interviewed them, and the photographer shadowed only Demetrius. They had long ago accepted supporting roles in the Demetrius show, and they had also grown so accustomed to Keller's lies that they barely registered anymore. Aaron, on the other hand, was different. His happiness hinged entirely on his standing with Keller. If Coach Joe praised him or worked him out individually or took him shopping for a new pair of shoes, he returned home overjoyed. If Keller ripped him in practice or declined to let him tag along on some errand, Aaron ran to his room the minute he got home and didn't emerge for hours.

Keller was Aaron's ally only when it suited Keller. He would promise to pick Aaron up for a one-on-one workout and then wouldn't show. When Aaron would call him, Keller would rattle off an excuse like "I called to see if you still wanted to go, but no one answered." Aaron initially believed him—he always did—but then he searched the caller ID on his home phone and didn't see Keller's number. Later, when Aaron learned Keller had worked out Demetrius instead, Barbara had to spend hours calming him. Aaron also kept track of the gifts Keller gave Demetrius. If Demetrius showed up at practice wearing the newest Tracy McGrady shoe or the latest Kevin Garnett model, Aaron seethed.

Keller did not recognize that Aaron's happiness peaked or plunged because of him, and he was equally oblivious to his role in forming a rift between Aaron and Demetrius.

In practices in the months after Nationals, Keller pitted Demetrius and Aaron against each other more and more. He let them foul and hack each other, stopping the action only when it looked as if they'd come to blows. If Aaron had a good practice, Keller would be sure to tell Demetrius how impressed he was. When Demetrius starred, Keller would shake his head at Aaron and ask if he liked being mediocre. Keller justified this as needing to push the boys, but he went beyond pushing. When they were alone in the gym at the Rancho Cucamonga Family Sports Center, Keller would tell Aaron, "While you're working out, D is at home playing video games. That's why you're going to the NBA and D will end up at some junior college." When Aaron lifted weights at a gym in Fontana, Keller would stand over him during bench presses and yell, "One more and D will never be better than you." Demetrius ignored Keller's tricks, but Aaron didn't see them as devices.

After reading the *Sports Illustrated* article, Aaron couldn't let Keller's deceit pass, couldn't brush it aside, the way Justin and Rome did, as Coach Joe being Coach Joe. He looked to his mother to help him make sense of it, but Barbara was in no position to give counsel. Keller helped pay the rent and utility bills on her home, and he regularly handed her wads of twenties. Aaron knew that Keller occasionally gave his mother money, but he didn't know the extent to which she depended on him.

"You are right. The lying is not okay," Barbara said at the Mexican restaurant. They had stopped eating. The table that separated them was painted the bright colors of the Mexican flag, and Aaron leaned intently across it, his long neck straining over his plate toward his mom. "But you know that with this situation, that is what to expect. If you want to be on this team, you have to expect—"

"Mom, can I talk, please?"

"Go ahead."

"I don't mind the publicity and hype Demetrius gets. Regardless of the situation, whether it was an article about D or an article about me and the team, I would have gone to practice and played just as hard. I would have done the same things I always do. I'm just upset because Coach lied."

Barbara paused, and she might have been reviewing her quandary. Should she do what was best for her son, which was to get him away from this two-faced coach, or do what was easiest for her, which was to keep Keller's money coming?

"But that is what he is going to do. If you are going to play on his team, you know two things. One, he is going to put Demetrius first and foremost, and second, not everything that comes out of his mouth is the truth."

"But, Mom, the ratio is eighty percent to twenty percent, with eighty percent being the lies."

Barbara didn't respond. She was done defending Keller's indefensible acts.

Keller's lie about the focus of the *Sports Illustrated* article came at a time when Aaron was more fragile than usual. After Nationals, Tommy had invited Aaron to his family's vacation home on the Colorado River. Aaron did not know it when he agreed to go, but Tom, Sr., had decided

Tommy would not be returning to Team Cal. He had asked Keller what it would cost to reserve a roster spot for Tommy for another twelve months, and Keller answered, "Fifty thousand dollars." Tom had forked out more than $40,000 over the previous year, yet Tommy hardly played the last half of the schedule and not at all in the final three games at Nationals. He was done opening his wallet to Keller for so little return on his investment.

Tom hooked up with another father whose son had played briefly on Team Cal, and they discussed creating a squad of their own. It was worth doing, they determined, if they could assemble enough talent to compete with Team Cal. Keller had already picked through the best eighth-graders in Southern California, so the best approach was to steal one of Keller's kids, weakening Team Cal and strengthening their roster at the same time.

"You should hear what Joe says about you behind your back," Tom told Aaron once he had him at the river house. "He calls you soft and weak and a baby. He said that you don't have the talent to make it."

For three days, Tom and the other father repeated every putdown Keller made about his sensitive center. They didn't need to embellish; Keller savaged every player except Demetrius.

"I hate Coach," Aaron told Barbara when he returned from the river. He repeated everything Tom and the other father told him. "I don't want to play for Coach Joe anymore."

At that time and again the day after their conversation at the Mexican restaurant, Barbara let Aaron know whose side she was on.

"If you leave Joe, you're not going to play for anyone," she told him. "It's Joe or nothing."

When Aaron first joined Team Cal, he was one of the most popular boys. Before Keller held him back in school, he spent several months in the eighth grade, and that made him the envy of his younger teammates. But after a few months, the other boys made excuses not to room with him on the road and stopped inviting him to the movies or trips to the Ontario Mills mall. "He's always talking stuff, you know, putting people down," said Rome, who by the start of 2005 was one of the few boys still inviting Aaron to sleep over. "He wasn't like that before, but he's been doing it a lot lately, and no one wants to hang out with him."

During a tournament the previous spring, Aaron and Terran got into an argument in a hotel room that would have led to punches had hotel security not heard yelling and interceded. Following that incident, Demetrius severed relations with Aaron, avoiding him outside of practices and games. "Now I just try to not talk to him at all," he said.

In the wake of the article in *Sports Illustrated,* Demetrius began to divide people into two groups: those he felt showed him the proper amount of respect and those, like Aaron, who did not. It was eerily similar to Keller's "Friends of Joe" and "Enemies of Joe" approach. When Demetrius met other top thirteen- and fourteen-year-olds at the Jr. Phenom Camp, some became fast friends. Those included Dexter Strickland (ranked number 9 by The Hoop Scoop) in New Jersey and Leshon Edwards (number 3) in Maryland. "With Dexter and Leshon, it's, like, I know you are real and I respect your game," Demetrius said. "Everyone among the best guys I respect, except Aaron. That's because he doesn't respect me."

Aaron's disrespect, Demetrius said, manifested itself in comments such as "You're not all you're hyped up to be" or "You're the same player you were a year ago." Aaron claimed Demetrius insulted him as much or more, but the other boys backed Demetrius, and Aaron became the team's pariah. During downtime on road trips, when the players were dropped off at a mall and Demetrius led the pack from store to store, Aaron would linger far behind or walk with an adult chaperoning. If he was spotted with a teammate, it was usually Roberto, whose relationship with Demetrius had been poisoned by Keller, or Rome, who was too compassionate to treat anyone as an outcast.

The rift between Demetrius and Aaron wasn't noticeable on the court unless you looked closely. In one game, Aaron leaned into a huddle during a time-out and put his arms around Demetrius and another player, and Demetrius shrank at his touch. "I wanted to turn and say to him, 'Get your hands off me,'" Demetrius said afterward. "But I can't do that, because we're a team and I can't bring that onto the court."

Any chance of repairing their relationship ended early in 2005 outside the Ontario Mills mall. Demetrius had called Rome to ask him to go to a movie, and because Aaron was already with Rome, he got invited too. After the movie they cruised the mall, then ended up outside, waiting for Rome's mom to pick them up. Aaron claimed Demetrius dogged him about his basketball skills in front of a group of kids, including some older girls. Demetrius said the opposite was true: Aaron clowned him. The boys would have come to blows had Rome not come between them.

When Rome talked about the incident days later, the smile that was forever present on his face disappeared. "It was real bad," he said. "Real, real bad. And it was Aaron who started it."

Keller never envisioned the Jr. Phenom Camp as a recruiting tool for Team Cal, but once all 225 kids were in the same gym, he couldn't help but put together a wish list. At the top was Roger Franklin, the nimble forward from Texas Select. Keller envisioned inserting the six-foot-four Roger alongside Aaron and Terran on Team Cal's front line and moving Demetrius to shooting guard. Shortly after the camp, Keller traveled to Duncanville, Texas, and sat down with Roger and his parents in the living room of their home.

"Your son can be in the NBA in five years," he told them.

Roger's father recently had surgery to remove a brain tumor and had trouble speaking. He had also lost partial use of one leg, which dragged behind him as he walked. Roger's mother did most of the talking, and she questioned Keller's claims that he was a close friend of Texas Tech coach Bobby Knight and could guarantee Roger would get a score of at least 1200 on his SATs if he moved to California. Keller left Duncanville without a commitment, but he eventually convinced Roger's mother to send her son to California for what was termed a "trial period." Roger's grandfather lived in Los Angeles; if anything went wrong, Roger was only a little more than an hour away from family. If Roger didn't like it, Keller promised he would put him on a plane back to Texas.

A mere two days after Roger arrived in Fontana, Keller complained about having to house him. "The kid is a handful," he said. "He's driving me crazy. He's crying all the time."

Violet was more sympathetic. "He's just real homesick. This is the first time he's been away from his family."

Roger's father flew to the Inland Empire for a weeklong visit, but it helped little; Roger cried even harder in the days after he left. Keller theorized that if he put Roger in a house with another player, he might stop pining for his parents back in Duncanville. It was a premise with merit, but Keller's choice of host family astounded everyone.

"Aaron and Barbara?" Soderberg said when told of Keller's decision. He was no longer an assistant coach for Team Cal, but he kept in touch with Aaron. "Those two have enough of their own issues. They don't need any more to deal with."

Roger's first tournament with the team was at Rialto High. The early games were against mediocre foes, but in the quarterfinals, against a team of kids already in high school, Roger made two 3-pointers during a second-half run, including one deep shot from the right side over two defenders. His long arms also made him a force as a rebounder and a defender.

"Is Roger real or what?" Keller said after the game. "It's like I said: Not only does he look like Chris Webber, but he plays like him too." Keller also gushed over G. J. Vilarino, a point guard he added to the team whose family had just moved from Dallas to Phoenix. Gary had fractured his arm playing football and would be out for months, necessitating the addition of another point guard. G.J. was a different player than Gary, more of a smooth shooter and facilitator than a dribble-drive scorer, but he had played with a team in Texas a grade older and was unflappable. To get him, Keller promised G.J.'s father, Gerry, that he would secure G.J. an invitation to the Adidas Superstar Camp the following summer, a rare honor for a player not yet in high school. Keller also paid a $1,000 "finder's fee" to the coach in Dallas who made the introduction.

As Keller fawned over Roger and G.J., Aaron stood a few feet away, hearing every word, biting his fingernails. "Coach Joe, did you see me block that kid's shot in the first half?" he said at one point, but Keller pretended not to hear him.

In the semifinals, Team Cal faced a team of varsity players from high schools throughout the Inland Empire. It included a six-foot-eleven center who weighed more than 320 pounds and would eventually earn a scholarship to UC Riverside.

"Coach, he *drove* to the game," Terran said after seeing the big teenager walk in from the parking lot.

Aaron drew the task of guarding him, and despite giving up five inches and more than 140 pounds, he played one of his best games. He banged with him inside, rendering him useless on the offensive end, and Team Cal pulled away for a 55–39 victory.

Keller said nothing about Aaron's play afterward, and he again praised the newcomers in front of him. At one point he called Roger "the missing piece," which a year earlier he had said about Aaron.

With two hours to kill before the tournament final, Aaron, Demetrius, Roger, and the rest of Team Cal loitered outside the gym. A few of the boys sat on a metal railing near the steel doors. Others leaned against a cement wall that had been painted white. Rome and Terran took turns dribbling a ball Rome had brought out of the gym.

As they often did during downtime, the boys teased one another. Terran was usually the butt of their jokes. They taunted him about dunks he missed or about how much he sweated. A big kid and a big target, he rarely teased back. But Demetrius had been teasing Aaron more lately (about the light color of his skin, his gangly gait), and Terran, overjoyed at not being singled out, would play Ed McMahon, laughing loudly at Demetrius's taunts.

Aaron made certain he would not be singled out this time. He started making fun of Roger's Texas accent and his physical features. "They gotta do liposuction on your forehead, your head's so big, nigger," Aaron said. Roger didn't react, so Aaron turned to topics beyond the good-natured taunts of young boys.

"Nigger, all you do all day is cry. You sit around the house and cry, cry like a bitch."

No one had ever talked to Roger that way before. He didn't know whether to hit Aaron or retreat into the gym and to his grandfather, who had driven from Los Angeles and was inside, talking to Rome, Sr.

"You don't like being here, so why don't you go home?" Aaron said. "Go home instead of sitting around my house and crying all day like a little bitch."

As he spoke, Aaron paced a few feet in front of Roger, like a stand-up comic during a show. Roger remained in one place, rocking forward and back, his right foot in front of his left. Aaron never looked directly at Roger as he spoke. He looked over him or down at the concrete. But Roger's eyes never left Aaron.

"Maybe I *will* leave, then. I *will* leave," he said.

At one point Roger remarked how fat Aaron's dog was, but he was not used to tearing another kid down.

Demetrius stood off the side, enjoying the exchange too much. Rome wanted to do something, but instead he walked a few yards away from the other boys. He climbed on a railing and watched from there, shaking his head as Aaron's insults got more personal. "This is just wrong," he whispered. "Why does it have to be like this?"

As the posturing dragged on for more than ten minutes, Demetrius grew bored and walked in to the gym, Terran at his heels. Roger then showed how much he had learned in his short time with Team Cal.

"I am no Terran," he shouted, breaking a long silence. "I am not just going to stand here and take it. Come over here and hit me, then, Aaron. Do something."

Aaron was stuck. He didn't want to fight Roger, and he didn't want to continue insulting him. But he had come too far to stop. He either had to fight Roger or insult him so strongly that Roger walked away. If Aaron retreated, it would mean he'd backed down, that he was a punk.

"What about your dad?" Aaron yelled. "He be all retarded and shit, walkin' all funny." Aaron then mimicked Roger's father, walking with his right leg trailing behind him as if it were deadweight. "Your dad's a fuckin' retard."

Roger, still rocking forward and back, didn't immediately respond. Both boys were on the verge of tears, but it was more noticeable on Roger. His huge brown eyes gave him away. Aaron did not know that Roger's father had almost died a few months earlier, how he had collapsed in the family's living room. He did not know that Roger had begged his mom to let him pray over his father before he was taken to the hospital, believing that if he didn't, his father was certain to die.

After a long silence, Roger said in a voice cracking with emotion, "I love my daddy." He then wiped his nose and his eyes with the back of his arm. "I just thank God every day that he is still walking this earth."

Then he walked past Aaron and into the gym.

Rome was the only other player who stayed until the argument's end. There was no sidekick, no Terran, to congratulate Aaron or make him feel his comments were justified. There was no parent around to explain that the uneasy feeling Aaron had in his stomach was the loss of his virtue.

Roger found his grandfather standing on the baseline of one of the courts. They spoke for a minute and then approached Keller, who was just hearing about the dispute from Terran.

"I'm taking Roger home," his grandfather said. "I'm not going to have him around boys like this."

Keller knew from the hurt he saw in Roger's eyes that there was no point in trying to change their minds. He walked Roger and his grand-father to their car. Neither Aaron nor Demetrius bothered to say good-bye. Only Rome followed them to the door, yelling after them, "Yo, Roger, we cool?" He then flashed Roger two fingers, the peace sign. Roger, looking back as his grandfather led him away, nodded and gave a half smile. He was cool with Rome, but he was going back to Dun-canville.

"Fucking Aaron, that's about three thousand dollars wasted," Keller said later. In addition to the airline tickets Keller paid for, he had given $1,000 each to two Dallas-area coaches, more finder's fees.

When Keller asked Aaron why he'd done it, Aaron lied and said that Roger had insulted his mother. Barbara said Aaron's actions were "a de-fense mechanism." Aaron was driving Roger away before Roger could abandon him.

Keller was presented with another theory a week later, while he dined with other coaches at a T.G.I. Friday's following a day of games. Roger's name came up, and the coaches consoled Keller for losing a kid with such potential. "Fucking Aaron," Keller began, and he provided a short version of what occurred. When he finished, I asked if he had con-sidered that Aaron lashed out at Roger because he was worried about his place in Keller's heart. Roger was a new boy Keller favored, and that threatened Aaron.

Keller sighed and put his hand to his forehead. He leaned back in his chair and looked upward, still holding his head as if he were checking for a fever. It was rare for Keller to acknowledge a mess he'd created. Sit-ting at a table covered in a red-and-white-checkered cloth, with a half-empty Corona in front of him, he seemed poised to finally admit the responsibilities he inherited when he courted a fatherly image with the boys. But just as he was about to speak, a young coach at the table blurted out, "Hey, Joe, that's good. You want them seeing you that way, like a father."

Keller gave a half smile and reached for his Corona and let the topic pass.

20

(CHIP HOOPER)

Darren Matsubara

arren Matsubara entered the gym at Asbury Park Middle School, wearing a black velour sweat suit and spotless white Adidas running shoes, and carrying a black leather man purse. He looked out of place among the working-class parents finding their seats in the wooden stands. His black hair was slicked back à la Pat Riley, and he wore an oversized gold watch. California chic had come to the blue-collar New Jersey shore.

"Mats," as he was widely known, was one of Adidas's most powerful coaches. His AAU outfit, the Elite Basketball Organization (EBO), was based in Fresno, although he was in the process of moving it to Las Vegas. NBA players Carlos Boozer, Robert Swift, and DeShawn Stevenson were alumni, and in 2005 his prized prospects included Robin and Brook Lopez, seven-foot twins headed to Stanford.

As he walked briskly across the floor, Mats pulled a tin of Altoids from his pocket. "It's not a question of how many mints he goes through in a day but how many tins," Teron Pickett said as he watched Mats walk toward him. When he finished retrieving a mint, Mats snapped the lid closed quickly and stylishly, the way an experienced smoker might snap shut a Zippo. Mats was one of the few prominent AAU coaches who played well the role of a hustler; even when he lied, he came across as trustworthy. Once, after giving me a long-winded response to a question about AAU coaches and agents, Mats sensed that I didn't believe him and said, "Come on, you thought I was going to tell you the truth?"

Mats had played college basketball at Cal State Northridge and still regularly scrimmaged against his players, even at the age of thirty-eight. His teams were among the best-coached, and he was known for turning away kids he considered undisciplined. When recruiting a player, Mats often sprang a test on them: He pretended to get lost while driving. "I want to see which kids just sit there and do nothing and which kids jump in and try to figure out where we are and how we can get where we need to go," Mats said. "What they do under those circumstances tells me what kind of player they are going to be."

In 2002, Mats was one of four AAU coaches named in a lawsuit filed in California by an associate of agent Dan Fegan, who represented NBA stars such as Gilbert Arenas, Shawn Marion, and Jason Richardson. In a deposition, the associate talked of payments to grassroots coaches, which he said Fegan labeled "brown-bag payments": an unspecified amount of cash sent in a FedEx envelope. Mats was also rumored to have received money from the agency SFX and its founder, Arn Tellum, as reciprocity for helping secure Boozer and Stevenson as clients.

Mats's connection to sports agents was why Keller had sought him out after signing his Adidas deal. He was looking for a mentor, someone within the Adidas family to offer guidance, and Mats came across as less threatening than the Pumps. By 2005, Mats was a regular at Team Cal's games, which prompted speculation among the parents that he would look to poach the best Team Cal kids for EBO. "With Mats, you know there is an angle," Carmen said. "Joe better figure out what it is."

Mats's reason for traveling to New Jersey was twofold. He wanted to see Demetrius and Team Cal play Team Next from New York, which featured six-foot-three guard Lance Stephenson of Brooklyn. Stephenson was the best eighth-grader in New York City, and he had recently been elevated to the spot just below Demetrius in The Hoop Scoop's rankings. In basketball, as in rap music, there was a running debate about which coast turned out the best talent. East Coast coaches swore their players were tougher and more equipped to jump to college or the NBA because they constantly played against older competition on the playgrounds and in AAU events. West Coasters complained that their kids were slighted only because they didn't grow up playing in Rucker Park in Harlem or the West 4th Street courts in Greenwich Village known as "the Cage."

The drumbeat for Demetrius and Stephenson to duel—and prove which coast had the next superstar—had sounded loudly for more than a year. Keller had invited Team Next to a tournament in California the previous season, and Stephenson's coach had confirmed with Keller the week of the event. But Team Next never arrived in Los Angeles. A year later, Keller took the fight to Stephenson's turf, entering his team in the Martin Luther King Classic in Asbury Park.

Mats also traveled to New Jersey to investigate a concern that had been discussed at length during a recent meeting at Adidas's offices in Portland that included Kalish and several of the company's AAU coaches. "Is Joe the guy to take these kids into high school? That is the question everyone was asking," Mats said. "It's a difficult transition for some kids. They go from dominating in middle school to struggling against older kids, stronger kids, kids just as talented as them. [Adidas] is worried about whether Joe can help the kids go through that. But I told them at the meeting, 'I got this one.' I'm going to look after Joe, put a safety net under him."

The safety net included a radical suggestion that Mats presented to Keller just before the team left for New Jersey: He told him to disband Team Cal after the summer and let Demetrius, Rome, Aaron, Roberto, and maybe others play for EBO. That would put some of Adidas's best young talent with a coach more qualified to develop them as players and one more experienced at keeping poachers from other shoe companies away. It would also free Keller to focus on the Jr. Phenom Camp, which Adidas's coaches across the country now saw as a potential feeder system for their teams. Mats wasn't willing to go down and court grade school and middle school prospects, but he saw how it could help Adidas's teams if Keller continued to do so.

"Joe, it's important to have the grassroots program, but I am going to create something else for you," Mats told Keller. "It's called 'Project Seed.' There is the grassroots, but below grassroots is the Seed. That's where you are. You are going to be a man of the Seed. We are going to have each division set up and there is going to be continuity, a flow. You be the Seed. You be in that space. You be where it starts."

Keller would need to give up coaching, but as the ruler of the Jr. Phenom Camp he would wield substantial power in the industry. He would be the guru parents consulted and AAU and college coaches came to for information on the youngest kids.

"Joe, you are going to have the influence because you're before the grassroots," Mats told him. "Kids are going to ask, 'Joe, where should I go, this camp or this camp?' You can advise kids, and you'll be someone everyone courts."

Keller slowly took to the idea. He referred to himself as "the Seed" in an email to Mats and then came up with a plan to franchise the Jr. Phenom Camp. He would sell the rights to regional Jr. Phenom Camps to other AAU coaches, and the best players from those camps would earn a trip to the national Jr. Phenom Camp in San Diego every August.

"I love it," Mats told Keller, but he reminded him that it wouldn't work if Keller tried to steal the kids who attended his camp, as he did with Roger Franklin. "You need to be bigger than that, and that means not having a team. You want to be the next Sonny. Well, you can be. You can be the Sonny of grade-school kids. But you've got to remember: Sonny has never coached a team in his life. His thing is bigger than coaching, bigger than a team."

At Asbury Park Middle School on Friday, Keller's focus was on getting Team Cal through to the finals, to the showdown with Lance Stephenson. They routed their first opponent, the C. J. Hawks, 92–24. The Hawks had once been a New Jersey power, producing NBA players Rodrick Rhodes and Luther Wright, but since the founding of the Tim Thomas Playaz, the Hawks had fallen on hard times. Thomas was one of several NBA players who funded AAU programs, and he sometimes attended their games, which contributed to the feeling among kids that the jump from grassroots to the NBA was a short one.

In their second game on Friday night, Team Cal defeated an undersized local team called the Hurricanes coached by Dan Calandrillo, who played at Seton Hall and was the Big East Conference Player of the Year in 1982. Before the tournament, when he saw the draw, Calandrillo called an old friend: UCLA coach Ben Howland. "He knew all about them and told me all the things Number Twenty-three could do," Calandrillo said. Despite the tip, the Hurricanes lost 113–47, with Aaron scoring 27 and Demetrius 26.

On Saturday, Team Cal met the Lloyd Daniels Rebels from New Jersey. In the five years since I'd interviewed Kenny Brunner, his teammate with that ABA team, former New York playground legend Lloyd "Swee'Pea" Daniels, had retired from basketball and remade himself as an AAU coach. A former drug addict who once was shot three times in the chest and who sparked an NCAA investigation at UNLV—despite never playing a game there—because of his ties to a man twice convicted for sports bribery, Daniels was now guiding the basketball youth of the Garden State.

Daniels was six foot seven, his New York accent heavy, his voice hoarse. I never thought a coach could be more demonstrative on the sidelines than Keller was, but Daniels topped him. When his team opened in a full-court press, he pulled his sweatpants up above his knees to make it easier for him to crouch and then got into a defensive stance like his players. He was wearing a bright red-and-blue sweat suit from the 2004 NBA All-Star game, and he was such a massive man that his sliding up and down the sideline detracted from the game. He also carried a white towel at all times. It served the practical purpose of soaking up the sweat running down from his bald head, but he also waved it when he got excited.

It often seemed as if Keller forgot that there was a crowd watching him; how else could an adult act as he did? Daniels, on the other hand, was well aware that he was onstage and used it to his advantage. If the referee made a dubious call against one of his players, Daniels didn't yell at him; he turned and raised his hands to the crowd and shouted, "Did you see that?" When his cheering section expressed the proper level of outrage, he turned back to the game and, after getting the referee's attention, pointed into the crowd, as if to say, *See? Even they think you made a mistake.* This was another difference between East Coast and West Coast basketball: Keller worked the refs; Daniels worked the crowd.

As a basketball tactician, Daniels was superior to Keller in every way.

"Look at all the coaches I've had—Tark, Larry Brown, John Calipari. Some of what they know had to rub off," he said. Daniels made that remark while at dinner with Keller the night before the game, after Keller predicted that Team Cal would win by 50 and Demetrius and Aaron would combine for at least 10 dunks. Daniels said his boys would lose by less than 20. He had scouted Team Cal the day before against the Hurricanes; he told Keller, "I know how to play you."

"It doesn't matter," Keller scoffed, and although they didn't wager any money, their reputations were on the line.

Daniels put four good 3-point shooters on the floor to start the game. This prevented Keller from sitting back in a zone, and it also made the bigger lineup he favored—with Aaron, Craig, and Terran along the front line—a defensive liability. In the opening minutes, the players guarded by Craig and Terran made open 3-pointers because Craig and Terran were too slow to get out and contest the shots. By the time Keller recognized the problem, the Rebels led 16–12.

Team Cal didn't have trouble scoring—the Rebels had no player over six foot one—but Daniels kept finding mismatches, and he slowed the game down. Team Cal led 35–26 at halftime, but given the talent Daniels had to work with, he had gotten the best of Keller. He bounded off toward the locker room waving his towel in the air.

Demetrius made three consecutive pull-up jumpers, all from around 16 feet, to open the second half. On each shot he was well guarded, but his ability to elevate and get a clear look at the basket made the difference. Team Cal's lead moved comfortably into double digits, but Daniels didn't stop coaching and kept switching defenses, preventing Keller from blowing the game open. Instead of the 50-point victory and 10 dunks Keller had predicted, Team Cal won 75–60, and the closest Demetrius or Aaron came to a dunk was in the final minute when a tired Demetrius tried one and missed.

"Joe, Joe, Joe, come on, you got to admit it. You got to admit it," Daniels said as he trailed Keller out the gym doors. Keller would admit nothing—not that he'd been outcoached, not even that Daniels knew the game. "Joe, Joe, Joe. Come on, man. Joe, Joe, Joe . . ."

Daniels joined Pickett, Mats, and others for dinner that night, and he again tried to get Keller to acknowledge that, at the least, Daniels coached his team well. Daniels reminded the group that at the previous year's Nationals, before he became coach, the same group of kids didn't get out of pool play. Now they had lost to the defending champs by only 15.

"I don't have to admit anything," Keller said.

Daniels's nervous energy made it seem as if he pounded seven espressos an hour. As he pushed Keller for a concession, he stood with a foot propped on a chair. A poinsettia that hung from the ceiling kept hitting his head, but he didn't seem to notice. "Look, I am saying you are real. Joe, you are real," Daniels said. "Demetrius, oh, my God, he is real. But Aaron, oh, my God, he is Tim Duncan, dawg. I'm saying he's Tim Duncan, dawg. He's real, but you got to admit, Joe, you got to admit it, my team, they gave you a run."

"Joe, you've got to admit, he had a good scheme," Pickett interjected.

"Those refs were terrible," Keller said. He looked up at Daniels. "You don't have a single kid I would want on my team."

Lloyd drew back, incredulous. "Come on, dawg."

The ring of Keller's phone interrupted the conversation. "Saved by the phone, Joe," Daniels said, "saved by the phone."

On Sunday around noon, the boys were dropped off at a mall, where they ate lunch at the food court and went to see the movie *Coach Carter*. Afterward, they tooled around the shops, stopping in every store that sold basketball shoes or athletic apparel.

Justin walked behind the pack with Aaron, his hands stuffed into his black Team Cal hoodie. Usually one of the most social players, he was quiet and distant, and when I asked him what was wrong, he said, "Everything. I am ready to be done with all of this."

Two incidents from earlier in the weekend had upset him, he explained. In the hallway before the game against the Hurricanes, Keller spoke with Dexter Strickland, the player two spots below Demetrius in the Hoop Scoop rankings. His team was not in the tournament, but he had come to watch Demetrius. "Why don't you come out and play with us in Portland next month?" Keller asked him. "I'll pay for your plane ticket and everything."

"We win Nationals with this team, and all Joe does is go and recruit these players we don't need," Justin said at the mall. If Strickland joined Team Cal, Justin's playing time would be cut, but that wasn't what bothered him. Over the past three years his minutes had gone up and down, fluctuating with Keller's whims, and he had never complained before. "I guess I thought that at some point Joe would get it, see how lucky he is. He's never going to, is he?"

Justin was also affected by something that happened the previous night. While Keller drank Coronas, Justin, Aaron, and Blake O'Donnell, a white guard Keller occasionally used as a roster filler, ate at a restaurant near the hotel. Aaron teased Blake about not playing in that day's games, and Blake suddenly ran out of the restaurant. Justin sprinted after him and found him crying behind the building. It had recently snowed, and both boys had left their jackets inside. Blake paced back and forth in the cold, repeatedly bringing his hands to his mouth to warm them.

"I am the laughingstock of the team," he told Justin. "I work harder than anybody, but I never get to play."

In practice, Keller often drew attention to Blake's effort and criticized others for not working as hard. He held him up as an example but never gave him meaningful minutes. In that moment, Justin realized how unfair Keller had been. After talking Blake back into the restaurant, Justin called Keller—it was his call that saved Keller from Daniels's prods—and he said, "If you don't play Blake tomorrow I will turn in my jersey."

Keller's response: "Fine. Turn in your jersey."

Keller convened a team meeting when he returned to the hotel a few hours later. He said that Blake understood that he wouldn't be playing much in the tournament and that he was fine with it. Blake nodded in agreement, as if he had a choice.

"I'm not the only person who feels like Blake is being treated wrong," Justin said. It was unusual for a player to speak so directly, particularly in a team meeting. "We all think that he should be getting more playing time than what he's getting."

"That's not your decision," Keller said. "That's my decision."

"Well, we just feel that he's on the team for a reason. And if he's just here to sit on the bench, that is wrong, 'cuz he could go anywhere and play. You brought him on the team, and we feel like you are doing him wrong."

"Look, I'll play him some more. Does that make you happy?"

"Well, that's all we were asking for."

It was not surprising that Justin was the first player to stand up to

Keller. But doing so would come at a price. "I know he will hold it against me, but I don't care," Justin said at the mall. "My mom taught me that when I see something that is wrong to do something about it. . . . You know, this whole thing, being here for this tournament, that's wrong too. We're here so D can play against Lance. But why is that important? Why aren't we playing Team Maryland or the War Eagles or another team we'll face at Nationals? Coach Joe just wants D to play Lance so he can hype him. But D doesn't need any more hype."

Sonny Vaccaro traveled to the East Coast a few days before Team Cal landed in New Jersey, and the purpose of his trip was to discuss the issue Justin raised at the mall: the wisdom of hyping an eighth-grader. The parents of Lance Stephenson were concerned about the rising interest in their son. More and more people compared him to Stephon Marbury, Sebastian Telfair, and other former New York phenoms. They didn't know how to manage the attention or the expectations.

Early in their conversation at the Vaccaros' hotel room in Manhattan, the proposed matchup against Demetrius at the Martin Luther King Classic was brought up. "Nothing good can come out of this," Vaccaro told the family. "You are a great player. The spotlight is going to come. Playing this game is like manufacturing attention, and there is no point in that. At some point in time the world will see you. Don't rush it."

Stephenson wanted to play Demetrius and, one can imagine, would have liked to be featured in *Sports Illustrated* and ranked number 1 by The Hoop Scoop. "But right now none of that matters," Vaccaro insisted. He then told a story: In July 2001, at his ABCD Camp in Teaneck, New Jersey, the number-1 ranked senior in the country was six-foot-six Lenny Cooke, who was also from Brooklyn. He had been the camp's MVP as a junior in 2000 and was one of the most hyped athletes to emerge from the city's boroughs. His spot atop the 2002 NBA draft seemed preordained. Also at camp that summer was a junior named LeBron James, a kid from Akron few people knew about. When their two teams met, Cooke was expected to dominate, but James scored 23 points, held Cooke to 9, and made a 3-pointer at the buzzer to give his team the victory. That one game began James's rise to the top of basketball, and as Vaccaro saw it, it was the beginning of the end for Lenny

Cooke. In a New York minute, he was declared a bust. After he went un-selected in the 2002 draft, he faded into obscurity.

"People can judge you on one game," Vaccaro told Stephenson. "You don't want that game to come when you are in eighth grade."

Team Next pulled out of the tournament not long after Vaccaro left New York, but Keller did not get the news until Sunday, after Team Cal advanced to the finals of the tournament. He learned that Team Cal's opponent would be the lightly regarded Reebok Raiders. Keller's analy-sis: "Lance is scared."

On one level, the news put Keller at ease; Lance backing out of the game was equal to a victory for Demetrius in his eyes. But he had prom-ised the boys a challenge and had promised Mats and Pickett and oth-ers they would see a show. Dominating the Reebok Raiders in the final was not what he had in a mind. Like a movie producer scrambling after a star who has pulled out of the production, Keller needed to find a headlining opponent fast. He called the organizer of the Martin Luther King Classic and informed him that Team Cal would forfeit the final. There was no point in beating up on the hapless Raiders, he said. With help from Pickett, he organized a game with a 15-and-Under team, the Boston Saintz, for the following afternoon. The Saintz had won the AAU title the year before as fourteen-year-olds, and forwards Nasir Robinson and Gabriel Fumudoh were considered future college players.

"This will probably be the best team we have played in our lives," Keller said.

He had no idea.

A few hours after Keller told the organizer of the Martin Luther King Classic that he didn't consider the Reebok Raiders a suitable op-ponent, news of that slight reached the ears of Tyreke Evans. A six-foot-four guard from Philadelphia, Evans was the top-rated freshman in America. He was also a member of the Reebok Raiders' Under–17 team, and he was upset that Team Cal had refused to play his program's younger team. "That's not how we do things on the East Coast," he said. When Evans found out that Team Cal would be playing the Boston Saintz instead, he contacted their coach and asked if could join his team for that one game. He wanted to teach Team Cal, its coach, and its star player, Demetrius Walker, a lesson.

————

As Team Cal walked from the parking lot to the gym at Shore Christian Academy in Allenwood, Demetrius rubbed his shoulders through his sweatshirt. "Man, I need to get drafted by the Lakers so I don't have to play somewhere cold like this." He was buoyed by Stephenson's decision to pull out of their duel. In the car on the way to the prep school, he said: "If I was Lance, I wouldn't want to play me either. I'm killing people right now."

Keller was equally pleased with himself—until he entered the gym lobby through the glass doors and saw Daniels standing near a concession table, eating a hot dog. "Joe, Joe, Joe," Daniels said with his mouth full. Keller walked past him briskly.

Keller had been told Evans might make a cameo for the Saintz, but Evans wasn't in the gym as Team Cal went through warm-ups or when Keller tabbed Roberto, Aaron, G.J., Terran, and Rome to start the game. Demetrius would not start, Keller explained, because his back was bothering him. Demetrius showed no signs of an injury pregame and had said nothing about it on the car ride to the gym. Most likely, Keller withheld Demetrius from the starting lineup to maximize the drama. Most of the 150 or so fans had come to see him, and they would wonder why he wasn't starting. When Demetrius entered the game—a grand arrival all his own—they would sit up in their seats in anticipation.

Evans arrived at the gym two minutes after the start. As he strolled down the baseline carrying a box of Reeboks under his arm, all eyes turned to him. People stopped following the action on the floor; instead they watched Evans lace his shoes and eyed Keller for a sign that he was ready to unleash Demetrius. The Saintz had jumped out to a 9-0 lead, but that was preamble. The show wouldn't begin until the team's respective stars took the stage.

When Mats saw Evans enter the gym, he said incredulously, "Who is advising this kid? What does he have to gain playing down against Demetrius? If he dominates, well, he was supposed to, because he is older. But if Demetrius outplays him, he looks bad."

It was similar to the advice Vaccaro had given the Stephensons.

"Whoever is handling that kid is leaving money on the court," Mats continued. "He is a nice-looking kid, with no tattoos. He can be Tracy McGrady. He's got to make Demetrius come up to play him, not the other way around. Make Demetrius play up against [his Under-17 team]. If you are him, you don't even acknowledge Demetrius."

Demetrius entered the game at the 16:28 mark. (The teams played two twenty-minute halves, high school rules.) Evans waited another two minutes more before approaching the scorer's table. Everyone in the crowd expected them to square off immediately, but the first time Evans got the ball, he found Team Cal in a 2-3 zone. The Saintz had already made four consecutive 3-pointers, and Keller should have gotten out of the zone long ago, but he stayed in it, with Demetrius down low. Evans didn't stretch or touch a basketball before checking in, yet he casually netted a 3-pointer from the right side to up the Saintz' lead to 19-7. He looked to Keller as if to say, *I'll do that all day if you don't switch defenses.*

Keller ignored the challenge. He kept Team Cal in the zone, and the Saintz continued to bomb away from outside. Robinson made five 3-pointers in the first half, Evans connected on all three of his attempts, yet Keller refused to switch to man-to-man. It made sense to start the game in a zone, to negate the Saintz' size advantage and experience, but as the Saintz lead grew to 30 and beyond, Keller's refusal to get out of it came across as an attempt to shield Demetrius from Evans.

On offense, when Demetrius got the ball on the wing with Evans guarding him, he instantly sent the ball back to G.J. at the point. He acted like a facilitator, like Rome or Justin, and not the star. He played so passively that it threw off his teammates. Aaron scored a few times inside, and G.J. smartly got into the lane and was fouled on back-to-back possessions, but the offense had revolved around Demetrius for so long that when he refused to engage Evans, it stalled.

Robinson's final trey of the first half put the score at 53-17 with 3:14 left, and Keller—having endured shouts from the crowd, repeated looks for Evans, and pleas from his players on the bench—finally pulled Team Cal out of the zone. Evans immediately demanded the ball and, after more than ten minutes courting a matchup with California's best, he got the ball on the right wing with Demetrius between him and the basket.

Evans dribbled in place as Demetrius crouched low, his left hand raised and pushed toward Evans's face. Demetrius overplayed Evans slightly, urging him to go to his right. Evans had to decide between going where Demetrius anticipated him going, trusting that his speed would get him by, or tricking Demetrius by faking in that direction and then cutting back to the left. Pulling up for a 3-pointer was also an option, but a jump shot could be perceived as a concession that he couldn't get past Demetrius.

Evans elected to test Demetrius's quickness, and he broke to the right, exploding forward in a blur. Demetrius somehow got in front of him, forcing Evans to change directions. He cut left, but as he dribbled the ball across his body, Demetrius knocked it loose with his left hand. It fell between them, and Demetrius dove to the ground and wrapped his arms around it at the same time that Evans grabbed it. The referee whistled a jump ball, and the possession arrow favored Team Cal.

"That's right!" Demetrius shouted as Terran helped him up.

G.J. was fouled shooting a 3-pointer eight seconds later, and he made two of three free throws. It started a 10–0 Team Cal run that cut the deficit to 53–27. During a free-throw attempt by Aaron with thirty seconds left in the half, Demetrius walked over to the bench and shouted at his teammates, "This ain't over! Get ready! The second half is going to be a war!"

On the final possession before the intermission, Evans and Demetrius dueled once again. Evans got the ball atop the key with Demetrius on him. He dribbled casually, letting the clock tick down, while Demetrius stayed low in his stance and crept closer and closer, a sign of the confidence he'd gained from their first showdown. With 0:05 showing on the scoreboard clock, Evans leaned forward and crossed the ball from his right hand to his left and then back again. He showed Demetrius enough of the ball that Demetrius reached for it, at which point Evans spun to his right, around Demetrius, and then powered into the lane and rose up and over Aaron for a spectacular layup.

At halftime, Keller delivered a speech unlike any the boys had heard from him before. "The second half is a brand-new half. Forget the score," he began. Team Cal had put so many teams in that position over the years, playing only for pride in the second stanza, and it felt odd to have the tables turned. The players' mood was good despite knowing that they couldn't win the game. By any count, Demetrius had stopped Evans once and been beaten by him once. A draw. He hadn't tested Evans on offense, and that would have to change, but his reputation remained intact, as did those of the other boys.

As Mats settled in a seat above Team Cal's bench, he said, "We're going to learn a lot about Demetrius this half." Mats didn't care how many points Demetrius scored: He wanted to see him compete against

Evans, to court the type of one-on-one situations that ended the first half. "The game is over. The score doesn't matter. So this is when Demetrius needs to go out there and demand the ball and say, 'I'm going to show what I can do against one of the best players in the country.' That's the attitude you want to see."

The Saintz had the ball to start, and as Evans brought the ball into Team Cal's half, he didn't see Demetrius across from him. Instead, he spotted G.J. and Justin atop the 2-3 zone. Across the gym, Daniels shouted, "Why, Joe, why? Let them play, dawg!" and Mats sighed. Making matters worse: On Team Cal's first offensive series, Demetrius retreated to the low block, a friendly place in part because Evans passed him off to one of the Saintz' interior defenders.

"Look at that," Mats said. "Demetrius is struggling, so where does he go? Down to the block. See, when he was younger, that is where he would get all his points. He was taller than everybody else, could jump higher; he could score at will down there. But he's not taller than everybody anymore, and let's face it, he's not going to be six eight or six ten. He's a guard, and Joe needs to start preparing him to play on the perimeter."

Mats shook his head as Demetrius had a shot blocked by a Saintz forward. "These boys need to start getting prepared for what they are going to face a year or two from now. Demetrius, Aaron, all of them—they need someone to put them in a position where they are learning what is best for their future."

Team Cal finally came out of the zone with twelve minutes left, but it was Justin, not Demetrius, who stepped up to Evans. On the Saintz' possession, Evans dribbled over to where Demetrius stood guarding another player. He had that player screen Justin in a way that would usually force a switch on defense. But when Justin called for the switch, Demetrius stayed with his man. Evans looked at Demetrius and shook his head. Then he drove at Justin, who managed to force him into an awkward shot that he missed.

Realizing Demetrius wasn't going to engage him, Evans left the game and gathered his gear and walked up into the stands. Mats hurried over to him. "For business reasons, this didn't make sense," he said, and he explained his logic while Evans listened attentively.

Even with Evans out of the game, Demetrius only tried to score down low, and he managed only a single basket in the second half as

Team Cal lost 87–47. Evans scored 32 points to Demetrius's 9, and although there were only two instances, both in the first half, when they went head to head, a consensus was reached quickly by those in attendance, one that would spread on message boards and in articles on recruiting websites: The East Coast kid had come to play, while the West Coast phenom shied away.

Keller was full of excuses after the game: Evans and the Saintz were a year older; Team Cal was tired from the three games played earlier in the weekend; Demetrius's back was bothering him; he stayed in the zone because it wasn't fair to pit Demetrius against Evans when he wasn't 100 percent healthy.

On the drive to the airport, Demetrius blamed Keller for being "too negative" and Aaron for being "too soft" and said, "I'm not going to win a game by myself against kids who are already in high school."

What would people say about his matchup with Evans?

"Nothing. He's a grade older. It's not like we are going to see him at Nationals. This game, it's not even like it really counts."

21

(JOE KELLER)

Team Cal's stars: Aaron Moore, Demetrius Walker,
and Roberto Nelson in 2005

Everywhere Demetrius went, the question followed him, as constant as the recruiting letters that arrived daily in his mailbox: "Where are you going to high school?"

Dexter Strickland asked him in New Jersey. "I don't know. Maybe Oak Hill [Academy, in Virginia]," he responded. One of his neighbors raised the question while Demetrius stood in front of his house. "I think Fontana [High]. I'm not sure." Asked one Tuesday afternoon in February when his teammates were in school, he said, "I don't know, but I'd like to know. Ask Coach Joe."

Eight months from beginning his freshman year, Demetrius, like any kid, thought often about the leap from middle school to high school. He was excited, anxious, curious. But unlike most kids his age, he didn't know where that leap would take him. His future was wrapped up in what Keller called "My High School Master Plan," but like most of Keller's plans, it was subject to change without warning and had already been through several drafts.

When Keller first formed the team, he spoke of his intent to send several of his players to the same high school in the Inland Empire. The "core" of Demetrius, Rome, Andrew, and Jordan would enroll together, all start as freshmen, and win multiple CIF Southern Section championships and a state title or two. When Andrew and Jordan left the team, Keller plugged in Terran and Justin and eventually Aaron. "It will be like the Fab Five of high school classes," Keller said.

Keller promised the kids to several local high school coaches over the years, usually in exchange for free use of their gyms. It didn't cost the high school coaches anything, and catering to the needs of AAU coaches had become part of the job. Behind some of the most successful programs in Southern California (and across the country) was a grassroots coach. Pat Barrett was an assistant under Gary McKnight at Mater Dei when SCA's first star, Tom Lewis, enrolled there. In 2005, one of the elite players being guided by both men was forward Taylor King, a top-25 recruit. At another famed private school across the country, St. Anthony's in New Jersey, coach Bobby Hurley, Sr., benefited from a pipeline of kids from the Playaz, the state's premier AAU program, run by Adidas coach Jimmy Salmon.

As Demetrius received more fanfare, Keller altered the High School Master Plan. "I'm going to move my family to Virginia in a few years," he said one afternoon in April 2003, a few days after Carmelo Anthony led Syracuse to a national championship in his one college season. Anthony had attended Oak Hill Academy in Mouth of Wilson, Virginia, the nation's premier prep school and the alma mater of more than a dozen NBA players. "D's going to Oak Hill, and I'll have to move there to keep an eye on him." But the success of the Jr. Phenom Camp scuttled that plan, as Keller needed to live near the camp's base in Southern California. He couldn't become the Sonny Vaccaro of middle schoolers babysitting Demetrius in Virginia.

For a brief time, Keller considered sending Demetrius to one of the top programs in Los Angeles or Orange County, where he would face the best competition. Mater Dei's connection to Barrett ruled that school out, but public-school powers such as Westchester, Compton Dominguez, Fairfax, and Taft were options. Those schools had open enrollment, meaning any student could attend as a freshman regardless of whether or not they lived in that school district, and they also made exceptions for star athletes. They routinely fielded teams with five or more kids who lived outside their boundaries, many of them directed there by an AAU coach. Sending Demetrius to one of those schools, however, would mean surrendering some control over him. The coaches there would demand a power-sharing agreement: Keller could continue to be Demetrius's surrogate coach and train him during the spring and summer, but during the high school season he would not call the shots. Complicating matters was the fact that those schools had their own sponsorship arrangements, and Adidas would not want one of its prized prospects at a Nike or Reebok school.

In New Jersey, before Mats addressed what high school he thought Keller should pick for Demetrius, he asked, "Are we talking about what school is best for the agenda or for the objective?"

The objective was: make Demetrius a better basketball player. To achieve that, he needed a high school coach with a history of preparing kids to play in college and the NBA, and also one who would monitor his academics. The objective, however, often takes a backseat to the agenda, Mats explained. Keller's ideal school included a coach who would give him unfettered access to the program, where Demetrius would be the best player on the team the minute he walked on campus, and where he would be featured in a manner befitting the top-ranked player his age in America. Adidas would sponsor Demetrius's high school team, so it needed to be a good flag-bearer, too, winning big tournaments and doing well in the playoffs. "If Joe is thinking about exposure for Demetrius when he chooses a school for him, or about Adidas, he is putting him at risk," Mats pointed out. "Often, all exposure does is expose a kid."

The perfect school for Demetrius, Mats believed, was right in his backyard: Etiwanda High, on the border of Fontana and Rancho Cucamonga. Coach Dave Kleckner had led teams to the Southern Section finals four times, and in 2005—when the "High School Master Plan" was on everyone's mind—he sent Darren Collison to UCLA and Jeff Pendergraph to Arizona State. His abilities as a tactician were unassailable; UCLA's Ben Howland praised how his players were ready to play defense in college, and Etiwanda had one of the best academic reputations among the schools in and around Fontana.

"That's a proven program with good players, so Demetrius wouldn't be forced to do it all by himself," Mats said. "No freshman dominates against high school juniors and seniors, and people forget that one reason these kids look so good in the spring and summer is because their teammates [on the AAU teams] are so good. Also, don't remove him from his safety net. He lives close by. He's got his mom, his friends; that is a good thing. It will make the times when he struggles easier to overcome."

But Kleckner didn't fit with Keller's agenda. He favored upperclassmen; even Collison didn't make varsity as a freshman. Etiwanda already received shoes through Collison's coaches at the Inland Empire Basketball Program (IEBP), an Adidas-sponsored team, but he wasn't beholden to them. Once, when the IEBP coaches complained about the lack of gym time he afforded them and threatened to stop giving shoes to the Etiwanda team, Kleckner said, "Fine. We don't need them."

A coach who couldn't be bought or influenced, who felt no player was bigger than the program, and who wouldn't build his team around a freshman—that was Keller's nightmare. "No way I would send D there," he said. "Anybody who sends their kid to Etiwanda needs to have their brain checked."

That would include, evidently, John Finn, who filled out transfer papers for Jordan (he lived outside the Etiwanda district) at the earliest allowable date. Not long after, he ran into Keller at a tournament and told him Jordan would be playing for Kleckner. "That's a huge mistake," Keller said. "Jordan won't even make varsity as a freshman."

Later, John said, "Hearing Joe say what a bad move it was, that convinced me it was absolutely the right move."

In the first three months after Tom Reasin took over as principal of Fontana High in April of 2003, he expelled seventy students. Another 110 were ousted by the end of his first year, and that was just the froth of troublemakers roaming the halls of the 4,000-student school. Two months before Reasin arrived, a schoolwide protest of a change in the lunch schedule led to nine students being arrested, including one for spitting in a police officer's face. A brawl between Latino and black students had taken place a few days before, a somewhat common occurrence at the tightly packed school, which was built in 1952 to accommodate 1,800 kids. The unruly students included members of the school's athletic teams. In 2001, a melee had broken out during a soccer game between Fontana and Rialto High. Two years earlier, a Fontana football player punched an opposing assistant coach after Fontana lost a playoff game.

The disciplinary problems were compounded by the school's poor academics. Fontana—known as FoHi throughout the Inland Empire—qualified as what one Harvard Civil Rights Project termed a "dropout factory" and finished below the state average in tests for reading, math, and English comprehension. During one three-year period, the percentage of tenth-graders considered proficient in mathematics went from 14 percent to 10 percent to 8 percent.

After moving into his office in the FoHi's concrete-walled main building, Reasin looked up the grades and disciplinary files for the varsity basketball players and was stunned by what he found: In one year they had accumulated seventy "referrals"—instances when a teacher or administrator flagged them for improper behavior—and several should have been ruled academically ineligible to play. Teachers later told him that the varsity coach pressured them to give his players passing grades.

Reasin fired the coach and chose Corey Hogue, the coach at nearby Pacific High, as his replacement, saying at the time: "[Corey's] very concerned with the ethical part of coaching and character-building, as well as developing high esteem in the athletes."

Hogue was tall and thin, with brown hair and an easygoing manner. While at Pacific, he'd let Keller use the school's gym free of charge in the hopes of landing Team Cal's phenoms. He was not naïve, but it was easy to see why Keller mistook him for an innocent. He was calm and a good listener and inherently trusting, hints of his small-town roots as the son of a high school basketball coach in Lubbock, Texas.

After Hogue was hired at FoHi, Keller became a regular at the school. He charmed Reasin, and the two went out to dinner regularly and talked on the phone every few days. Keller told him of the big crowds that would one day come to see Demetrius in high school, and that FoHi was in the running to land him. Keller was not merely laying the groundwork for a power play. He liked Reasin, and in a sign of their burgeoning friendship he hired him to do the marketing for the first Jr. Phenom Camp.

In the young stars of Team Cal, Reasin saw a chance to return FoHi to the glory days of the 1980s, when the football program was a national power and kids felt pride in their school. The football team averaged at least ten victories a season during the mid- to late 1980s and won section titles in 1987 and 1989. That success energized the school and a community still recovering from the closing of the Kaiser Steel plant in 1983. Fontana could have become a western version of Rust Belt relics like Aliquippa, Pennsylvania, as more than half of its residents took paychecks from the mill, but the city's population jumped from 35,000 to 70,000 between 1980 and 1987 as a development boom lured Los Angelenos to the area. Talented athletes who would have played for Dorsey, Crenshaw, Inglewood, and other inner-city schools ended up at FoHi, and the football team became the centerpiece of the community in a manner most often seen in small towns in Texas, Ohio, and Pennsylvania.

To keep up with the influx of new residents, the Fontana Unified School District opened A. B. Miller in 1991 and Kaiser High in 1998. This signaled the end of FoHi's football dynasty, as the new schools diluted the talent pool.

By the time Reasin arrived in 2003, the football program was a lost cause. The basketball team, on the other hand, had the potential to be a source of self-respect for the kids and the community. It had happened before, in 1996, when six-foot-six guard Corey Benjamin, a top-10 recruit nationally, led the school to a section title before heading off to Oregon State and, later, the Chicago Bulls. "The basketball team can be the foundation to get that Steelers pride back," Reasin said. "If you add Demetrius and Aaron and others kids who are great athletes but also good students, that sends a strong message to the rest of the student body."

Hogue's first team finished 20–9 and lost in the Southern Section quarterfinals to Long Beach Poly. By any measure it was a successful season, but a few weeks after the final game, Reasin informed Hogue that he "didn't like the direction the program was headed" and stripped him of the coaching job.

There were various explanations for why Hogue was let go after a single winning season. The public line was that Hogue "resigned to explore other opportunities." Keller said Hogue's "conduct" toward other teachers led to his dismissal, which Keller knew because Reasin had consulted with him before the firing. Hogue believed that Reasin was doing Keller's bidding, that they had another coach in mind for when Demetrius got to high school. "If my conduct was the problem, why was I allowed to continue teaching until the end of the school year? Why did I then get asked to teach summer school?"

A few months later, the High School Master Plan took a turn that bolstered Hogue's suspicions: Mark Soderberg became the new basketball coach at FoHi.

Soderberg always looked on his stint coaching Team Cal as short-term, as if he were a veteran political consultant brought in for the final push that wins a campaign. Playing the calm sage to Keller's bombastic neophyte was no dream job, and so after Nationals he thought he would move on, perhaps to a career outside basketball. Then, late in the summer, Keller called: "What about the job at FoHi?"

Soderberg was initially resistant. The school was forty miles from his home in Lake Elsinore. He did not have a teaching credential and would be considered a full-time substitute, which paid only $100 a day. Even with a coaching stipend, he would make less than $20,000. "It was by the grace of my wife that I took the job," he explained. "She said, 'You like coaching these kids, Demetrius and Aaron and the rest of them, so forget about the money.'"

Soderberg's hiring was an indelible revision to the plan. Keller couldn't back out of sending Demetrius to FoHi after persuading Soderberg to take the position. Gang problems, overcrowded classrooms, poor academics—none of it mattered. Demetrius was going to FoHi. The question became: Which of his Team Cal teammates would join him?

When the team traveled to Portland in February, talk about who would attend FoHi dominated the downtime between games. The speculation continued in the months after, and from day to day it was hard to keep up with the rumors: Rachel was moving to Fontana after Keller lined up a job for her and promised to help pay her rent; Bruce would become one of Soderberg's assistant coaches, move to the Inland Empire, and enroll Roberto at FoHi; Barbara was moving into the Fontana district, the only holdup being the percentage of her rent Keller would pay to make it happen; Rome, Sr., wasn't sure about FoHi for Little Rome, but his mom, Sharon, had overruled him, and he would continue as Demetrius's running mate through high school.

When questioned about their intentions, most of the parents didn't have an answer. They liked the idea of keeping the team together, but FoHi's gangs, racial makeup (it was 80 percent Hispanic), and poor academics troubled them. For Carmen, Bruce, and Rachel, committing to FoHi meant either moving to the Inland Empire or a grueling commute for their sons each morning.

Carmen finally ended the conjecture surrounding Justin: She phoned Keller after the Portland tournament to inform him that Justin was leaving Team Cal immediately and would enroll at Woodland Hills Taft.

"I don't care about hotels and trips and shoes and all that stuff; I care about how you treat the kids," she told Keller. "Justin has wanted to leave for a while. He is tired of all the lies and the put-downs."

Justin called Demetrius and explained his decision, and he got Kisha's cell-phone number for his mom. (Keller refused to give it to other parents, most of all Carmen.)

"I just want you to know that us leaving has nothing to do with D. We left because of issues we had with Joe," Carmen told Kisha. "Every time someone leaves the team, Joe dogs them and tells people they left because they were jealous of Demetrius. He tries to build up animosity with D and with you. But we care about D and wish him the best."

Justin's departure shook up the High School Master Plan in a way that Keller couldn't have imagined. Carmen's opinion was respected, and when she told other parents, "No way would I send my son to FoHi," they began questioning the wisdom in sending their sons there as well. Her choice also opened the door for other parents to defy Keller; there was safety in not being the first to go against his wishes.

Rachel quickly enrolled Terran at Taft High as well. Justin and Carmen helped push her to that choice, but the school was unquestionably a better fit. It was only a few miles from Terran's home in Chatsworth, stronger academically, and more racially balanced. The basketball team had several young guards but few big men, and Terran would play a more prominent role there than he ever had on Team Cal.

"Terran is from over near Taft, and when he walks onto campus it is like when I go over to Fontana. People are talking about him, and he likes that," Demetrius said. "And Taft has a good football program and sends all these guys to USC. Terran is a beast on the football field, and if he decides his future is in football, it is smarter for him to be over there."

Keller tried to convince Bruce to move to the Inland Empire and coach under Soderberg, but Bruce said he would move only for a job as a head coach—plus, Roberto didn't want to go to high school with Demetrius. Bruce took a position as an assistant coach at Santa Barbara High and announced his intention to enroll Roberto there.

The High School Master Plan wasn't coming together as Keller anticipated, but he didn't panic. He still had Demetrius, Aaron, and Rome, a core with which Soderberg could build a great team. He also claimed to be in the process of importing two French kids, a seven-foot-one center from Africa, and a super-secret player that he would only say was from somewhere in the Midwest.

In February, Barbara and Kisha filled out enrollment papers for Aaron and Demetrius at FoHi. Keller anticipated Rome, Sr., doing the same for Little Rome, but Rome, Sr., had been talking with John Finn about Etiwanda and, looking closer at that school, concluded it was a better fit. Sharon lived in the Etiwanda district, and Rome's friends from middle school were headed there.

As with Justin, Terran, and Roberto, Demetrius didn't blame Rome for wanting to go elsewhere. "Rome has been taking a beating for five years, doing the dirty work for me, and for high school he wants to do his own thing," Demetrius said. "I don't blame him. I would do the same thing if I were him. . . . Coach has made all these promises: 'Oh, you're going to win state your sophomore, junior, and senior years. Oh, we'll have kids from France and Nebraska or Michigan or somewhere. Oh, we'll have Terran and Rome and everyone.' Well, they're not coming, and why would they come here to go to a sorry school? Coach has made all these promises, and he doesn't live up to them."

Demetrius recalled the original plan: he, Andrew, Jordan, and Rome attending the same school. "Coach Joe messed up so many friendships. You know how nice it would be to go to high school with those guys? That's how it should have been. But Coach Joe screwed those guys, and so now it's just me and Aaron. And I'd say there is only a little chance that Aaron goes to FoHi. His mom doesn't want to mess up her relationship with Coach Joe. She might send him to FoHi to keep Coach Joe taking care of her. But Coach Joe might just screw that up as well, and then it will be just me up there."

Asked why he didn't investigate going to another school, Demetrius said, "I talk to my mom about it, but we beat around the bush about it and then nothing ever happens. I guess I gotta hope that Coach Joe can live up to all his promises. Hopefully, he's got, you know, some sort of plan to make it all right."

22

(TODD BIGELOW)

Demetrius Walker taunting after a dunk

Somewhere around Barstow, as the rental car crossed the desert between the Inland Empire and Las Vegas on a hazy spring morning, the old Joe Keller returned.

He had sulked in the front seat for the first hour of the drive, barely speaking to Demetrius and Terran in the backseat. Other than to comment on how good the team looked in new black Adidas sweat suits, Keller showed no enthusiasm, not even for the trip to Sin City, one of his favorite haunts. Uncomfortable at the thought of a weekend around the parents who'd spoiled his high school plan, uncertain how the team would do in the Las Vegas Easter Classic against players a year older, and troubled by the decision facing him on whether or not to keep coaching Team Cal, he brooded.

Then "Lovers & Friends" by Lil Jon & the East Side Boyz came on the radio. Demetrius and Terran simultaneously screamed "OOOHHHH!" and danced in their seats to the opening groove. Keller slowly nodded his head with the beat, then a little more, and at the opening line he sang loudly in a surprisingly soulful voice: "'Baby, how ya doin'? Hope that 'cha fine, wanna know what you got in mind.'"

Keller knew every word to the song from his hours of chauffeuring Demetrius and Aaron. He knew as much about hip-hop music as most teenagers. "Lovers & Friends" featured three singers—Usher, Lil Jon, and Ludacris—and after Keller took Usher's opening verse, Terran sang along with Ludacris and then Demetrius with Lil Jon. They stuck with their roles, often harmonizing behind one another or shouting a single word. By the final verse, the song flowed as if they'd practiced for months. Keller and Terran chanted *shawty* while Demetrius belted out Lil Jon's lines:

> *I's been know you fo' a long time (shawty),*
> *But fuckin' never crossed my mind (shawty),*
> *But tonight, I seen sumthin' in ya (shawty)*

When the song ended, Keller and the boys slapped hands. "That was live," Demetrius said. "I wish we could do that again." It was like the scene in the movie *Almost Famous,* when the band sings Elton John's "Tiny Dancer" on their bus and in the process forgets about their squabbles. Boyish and without pretension, the grand schemes forgotten for a moment, Keller was their friend, and five years of shared history connected them. But the tenderness of that scene also underscored how seldom that side of him had been displayed in the last few months. He was conflicted, torn between continuing to guide the boys and relinquishing control of the team and Demetrius to focus on his business ventures. Two additions to the team for the Las Vegas Easter Classic personified this conflict. Vondrae Tostenson, a six-foot-two guard Keller had moved to Fontana from Omaha, Nebraska, after weeks of dealing, would make his debut with the team. He was the mystery player from the Midwest who Keller had spoken of earlier and was a potential teammate for Demetrius at FoHi. The tournament would also be the first for Dave Taylor, a former assistant of Air Force, who ran camps for Adidas. Taylor would sit second chair to Keller during the Las Vegas Easter Classic. If Keller and, to a lesser extent, the boys were comfortable with him, he'd take over as Team Cal's head coach.

Keller's uncertain future, Justin's departure, the feud between Demetrius and Aaron, Keller's resentment over the decision by parents not to send their kids to FoHi—all of this lingered over the team like the smog that perpetually blanketed the Inland Empire. But as the car crested the last of the Spring Mountains and with Las Vegas spread out before them, it seemed less likely that those issues would tear the team apart.

Keller realized that my digital recorder had caught their rendition of "Lovers & Friends," and he played back the recording over and over, teasing Terran for being the voice that cracked and Demetrius for singing too high.

"Coach, you're so dumb," Demetrius said, and with that Keller unbuckled his seat belt and climbed into the backseat, pinching Demetrius's leg with one hand while fighting off Terran with the other.

"Stop! Stop! Stop!" Demetrius shouted through laughter, but no one wanted him to stop.

On Wednesday afternoon, Team Cal routed their opening-game foe. The game was uneventful save for Taylor's observation afterward, which he conveyed to the team at a meeting at their off-Strip hotel: "I'd swear, after watching you guys, you must hate basketball." The players were seated before him on the floor of Keller's room. "I mean, damn, no one on this team cheers for each other, no one slaps hands or slaps the floor on defense. There is no enthusiasm. I mean, damn, you guys play like you hate playing and like you aren't friends."

It was an astute comment. After winning Nationals, the boys found it harder to get enthused for games. The goal Keller set before them since the team's inception—to win Nationals—had been reached, and it was difficult to attach a new purpose to their effort. Keller talked of defending their title—when he was around—but his lack of passion for that aim was obvious. And, because they rarely practiced together, there were fewer shared experiences between tournaments. They showed up at a gym after a week or two of not seeing one another, played a couple of games, then left. They were more like a group of independent contractors than teammates.

Taylor's comment about the lack of camaraderie on the team was also on the mark. The boys were not all friends, not anymore. Aaron and Demetrius hated each other. Roberto and Demetrius hung out separately whenever possible. G.J. was not close with any of them, having been on the team such a short time and living in Arizona, and now the same was true for Vondrae. Justin's departure also damaged solidarity because, like Rome, he could bridge the divides.

Keller insisted that Demetrius and Aaron could hate each other off the court but get along between the lines. One could have nothing to do with the other. "You don't have to be friends to be teammates," he claimed. But they were teenagers, not college or professional players, and they didn't have total control over their emotions.

This was on display a few hours after Taylor's speech at the hotel. The boys roamed the Adventuredome, an indoor theme park at Circus Circus, where they met up with Aaron's girlfriend, who had traveled to Las Vegas with her mother to watch him play. Keller forbade anyone but family to be at away tournaments, but who was going to tell?

Demetrius slipped away from the group and called his mother on his cell phone. Aaron had brought a girl to Las Vegas, he told her, and it wasn't fair. He knew she would call Keller; in fact, he counted on it.

Keller was at a P. F. Chang's with G.J.'s parents when he received Kisha's call. He had been jovial, drinking a Chinese beer and joking with Gerry about his younger son and his future with Team Cal, but then he answered the phone and his mood visibly changed. His face turned red as Kisha informed him of Aaron's violation of team rules.

"I'll handle it, Kisha," he said just before hanging up. "No, I will. I'll take care of it."

Keller called Aaron on his cell phone and ordered him to meet him at the front of Circus Circus in fifteen minutes. He picked Aaron up and ordered the other boys to meet in Demetrius's room back at the hotel.

"The thing is, guys, at the end of the day, we all have little woodies that are hard," Keller said, when he had the attention of the entire team at the hotel. He was leaning against a wall that separated the sitting area from a kitchenette. "I know D has a girlfriend. I know Terran is talking to some girl. I know Aaron has a girlfriend, and I know Rome had a girlfriend three months ago. Guys, I don't mind that. I'd rather you tell me you have a girlfriend than that you have a boyfriend. But at the end of the day, don't screw with our time and what our goals are.... Don't fuck my shit up."

After fifteen more minutes of distributing wisdom along those lines, Keller turned to the dispute between Aaron and Demetrius. He had never addressed it directly with the team.

"D, you as the leader—I am going to put you on the spot. I want us to quash all this bullshit. We need to end all this. I am not dumb. I know Aaron and Demetrius have been bumping heads for the last year. I don't want Aaron and D not to get along. Look, I am not asking D and Aaron to play hopscotch together. I *am* asking that when you are around each other, you don't talk trash about each other. You gotta cut that out, because it affects the way you play on the court.... I want you guys to stick together. I want no more of this little group stuff. It's all over. You may not like each other, but you have to get along because you are going to spend more time together than with anyone but your family. This is your second family.... D, come up here. Talk about team. What does that mean to you?"

Demetrius got up from the floor and stood next to Keller. He didn't want to be there; it was a while before he spoke. "I don't like people who talk trash all the time. There are people on this team who talk a lot of trash. A *lot* of trash. A lot of us are like brothers. Some of us aren't.... Okay, I don't like Aaron. I'll be flat-out honest. I don't like Aaron. He talks too much trash. But as Coach says, we gotta be a team. It doesn't matter what I think about Aaron. Everybody else on this team, you are like brothers to me. I will always be there for you."

Keller wanted Demetrius to lead the team to the high road, for Aaron and Demetrius to shake hands and move on. But there were no hugs or handshakes. Demetrius did nothing more than make clear what everyone already knew: He hated Aaron. When Demetrius was done, he never looked toward Aaron, who sat on the arm of a sofa near the window, biting a fingernail.

Keller called Aaron to the front next and told him to apologize to the team. He announced that he was taking away his cell phone and that he was on "probation."

In his room later, Aaron sat slouched on a blue couch and asked, "Why did D get to go up there and say all that? What good did that do? Coach just let him go up there and trash me in front of everybody." When no answer was offered, he picked at a loose thread on the couch for a moment, then went back to biting his fingernails.

Thursday afternoon, the boys took the court against Texas Show-time. Team Cal struggled before Roberto's strong second half led to a 57–49 victory. The bench was chaotic. Keller screamed at the players and was particularly hard on Vondrae; his honeymoon with the team, if he ever had one, was over. Keller's antics harkened back to his wild sideline behavior in Team Cal's early years. He was once again the crazed coach who, at the tournament in Maryland in 2002, was handed a note by a mother from another team that read: "You belong at the National Zoo."

He even criticized Demetrius. After Demetrius threw an errant pass intended for Roberto, Keller shouted, "D, what the hell are you doing?" Demetrius felt that Roberto could have received the pass if he had kept running upcourt, and he yelled back, "Roberto needs to keep moving!" He then turned away and shook his head so demonstratively that no one in the gym could have missed it. Demetrius had returned Keller's fire before but always during a time-out or break in the action, never when a gym full of people could see and hear him.

Taylor spent most of the game pulling players aside after Keller berated them. To Rome, he said, "Keep your head up. You're playing hard. But remember to keep your hands up on defense and cut off the baseline better." To Aaron, he said, "Joe's telling you to rebound better, but what he means is you need to do a better job boxing out. Find your man and get into him and then look for the ball."

Demetrius played poorly, which made his outburst at Keller all the more noticeable. It looked as if he was blaming his teammates, which in a sense he was. "When someone else is feeling it, I make sure to get them the ball. If G.J. is knocking down threes, I make sure he gets the ball. When Rome is knocking down mid-ranges, I make sure he gets it right there," Demetrius said to Terran as they rode back to the hotel after the game. "But when I am feeling it, no one gets me the ball. It's like I am always looking out for everybody else, but when Demetrius is feeling it, no one gives him the ball. . . . People are coming to the gym to see me play, and I can't be struggling like I did today. People are expecting more from Demetrius Walker."

It was the first time I had heard Demetrius talk about himself in the third person, and it demonstrated the attitude change parents and teammates had whispered about since the *Sports Illustrated* article.

Taylor's earlier observation that the team played like a divided bunch echoed as the players branched off that night, finding dinner at different places close to the hotel. While Demetrius and Rome went to Taco Bell, Vondrae, Aaron, and Roberto went to Wingstop, where Vondrae and Aaron each ordered twenty chicken wings and then bet on who could eat them all.

As they sat gnawing on wings, the boys talked of Vondrae's move to California, which came after Keller made numerous promises to Vondrae's uncle, his legal guardian. Roberto said he doubted Vondrae would put up with Keller for long, that he'd be back in Nebraska before the end of the summer. He then made a bolder prediction: "I'd bet this team ain't together by Nationals. I'm just saying, the way things are going, people fighting and Coach doing his own thing, I bet we don't even got a team by then."

Mats walked into the gym moments after Demetrius took a pass from G.J. in for a layup in a Friday afternoon game against the Arizona Stars. He didn't look at the action on the floor but rather at the parents in the stands. He looked for the ones ready to move their sons to another team. "The vultures are circling," Mats said at halftime. Earlier, he had warned Keller that Pat Barrett likely had his eyes on Aaron. "Joe, what you have created with Aaron and Barbara, Pat is going to steal that. Pat is going to up the ante. The way you have it set up with the mom, you are going to get outbid at some point. Pat is good at finding the weak and putting them under his spell. Pat likes the soft, sensitive guys. Aaron is all Pat Barrett. He is all Pat Barrett."

Keller doubted him but was also too distracted to worry about it. Since before New Jersey, when Mats discussed the idea of him becoming the middle school grassroots guru, he had been building on the idea to franchise the Jr. Phenom Camp. He put together a packet for prospective buyers for what he called a "regional" Jr. Phenom Camp and required those who read it to sign a confidentiality agreement, because he worried that Reebok or Nike would steal his idea. He gave the packet to coaches he knew across the country, and by the Las Vegas Easter Classic he said he had fifty regional camps sold or about to be sold.

The purchaser of a regional Jr. Phenom Camp franchise paid Keller $15,000 up front. That included $10,000 a year for the mandatory two-year commitment and a required $5,000 for Jr. Phenom gear—T-shirts, headbands, shorts, hats, and other merchandise—to be sold at the event. (The merchandise cost Keller $2,500 to manufacture.) Every player attending a regional camp received an official Jr. Phenom Camp reversible jersey, which Keller sold to the franchise buyer at a cost of $40, a markup of $17. Keller also sold insurance, asking $200 per camp. He paid only $1,500 total for coverage of all the camps, with an additional $25 for every camper he added to the policy.

The prospectus Keller handed out to buyers estimated that with a minimum of 200 attendees and with all merchandise sold, the operator of a regional Jr. Phenom Camp would net $50,500 a year. A more staggering sum was the one that popped up on Keller's calculator when he sat down to tabulate his expected profits:

Franchise Fees:	$10,000 × 50	= $500,000
Merchandise:	$2,500 × 50	= $125,000
Jerseys:	$17 × 200 × 50	= $170,000
Insurance:	$175 × 50	= $ 8,750
TOTAL:		**$803,750**

That total did not include Keller's profits from the national Jr. Phenom Camp, which in its inaugural year netted nearly $100,000. It did not include profits from the girls' Jr. Phenom Camp, debuting in August. It did not include income from sponsors of those camps or the regional camps. It also took into account only fifty regional camps sold, with 200 kids per camp. Keller believed he would have more than 100 camps sold by June and that many camps would involve 300 or more kids. "When it's all said and done, I'm going to make four million dollars," Keller said. "Mark my words, Joe Keller is making four million this year." He was not rubbing his hands together as he spoke, but his glee was obvious.

Mats understood the money involved, which is why he traveled to Las Vegas. He came to urge Keller to hand the boys over to Taylor for the rest of the season and to begin telling some kids that they would be graduating to Mats's EBO program. After New Jersey, Mats thought that Keller would inform a few of the kids, and he arranged for Demetrius, Rome, Aaron, and G.J. to receive a pair of the shoes that his EBO team wore. Keller delivered the shoes but didn't say where they

came from. When Mats approached Gerry to say he was excited to have
G.J. playing for him in the future, Gerry ignored him and warned Keller
that Mats was moving in on his kids. "I feel like I walked into an am-
bush," Mats said.

Watching Team Cal defeat the Arizona Stars 60–47, Mats took note
of how Keller did more yelling than coaching, how Demetrius and
Roberto refused to pass to each other, and how parents in the stands
grumbled about it all.

"I hope this works out with D.T. coaching the team the rest of this
season," Mats said. "Because if it doesn't, I don't know if Joe is going to
be able to keep the team together much longer."

In defeating the Arizona Stars on Friday afternoon, Team Cal looked
considerably better than the disjointed, careless team from a day earlier. Players heeded Taylor's call to behave more like friends and teammates. They cheered one another on and slapped hands after they made
baskets. But Taylor wasn't focused on the positives as he pushed open
the glass doors of the community center and walked briskly to my car.

"That's it. Joe and I are going to get into it," he said. "Wait until Joe
gets in this car. We're going to have it out."

Taylor's blond hair fit his California roots, as did the large white
sunglasses always perched atop his head, even at night. He had a rotating collection of more than 100 throwback jerseys, including prizes like
Pete Maravich's Louisiana State jersey and Jerry West's from West Virginia. He came across as calm but forceful, and his voice was like a can-
non's boom. Words shot out in quick bursts. Spit flew. Like Keller, he
had mastered the art of profanity. His particular skill was merging two
curse words to form a profane original such as *pussybitch*.

Taylor had been set off by an incident during the second half. He
was encouraging Demetrius and the other players to push the ball upcourt against the slower Arizona Stars' players. But his instruction
came at the moment Roberto took the ball one-on-four and forced a
shot that missed badly. Taylor was leaning down in front of Aaron, explaining defensive positioning, when Keller shrieked at him: "You don't
know what the hell you are talking about!" It took all of Taylor's
willpower not to run up the sideline and grab Keller by the throat.

When Keller climbed into the car, taking the seat directly behind
Taylor, he said, "D.T., I thought we played pretty well, don't you think?"

"I don't know. Look, Joe, we gotta talk," Taylor said. His voice was always raised, but it was now louder than usual.

Keller began to say something.

"No, no, listen."

Keller tried again to break in.

"No, let me say what I gotta say without you fucking interrupting. Then you can say all your bullshit you gotta say."

Taylor talked quickly, in shouts, and he repeatedly wheeled around in the passenger's seat, trying to look at Keller as he spoke.

"You don't fucking treat your coaches that way. I am not some fucking punk-ass bitch who never coached before. I've coached longer than you and at a higher level than you. You do not disrespect me or anyone on the bench."

Keller again tried to interrupt.

"Let me finish! Let me finish! Talk about a sensitive guy; let me say what I gotta say. . . . All I said was 'Push it.' And then we turn the ball over and you have a heart attack and start yelling at everyone. I didn't say, 'Jam it down their throats and shoot it one-on-four.' All I said was 'Push it up the floor.' If your guys are not smart enough to know that doesn't mean go one-on-four, well, then, I apologize for that. But you were wrong for what you did, because it sends a bad message to the kids."

Taylor was breathing hard and pausing often, but Keller stopped trying to defend himself. He just stared out a window as Taylor punctuated almost every sentence with "God damn, Joe!

"If you had ever been an assistant coach, you'd know not to treat guys like that," Taylor continued. "I'll be damned if I'm going to let you treat me like that, let you chew me out like I don't know what the fuck I am doing. Show me some fucking respect on the bench."

Taylor moved on to the way Keller treated the players.

"Joe, you can't be swinging your arms, screaming, 'What the fucking, fucking fuck, fuck.' God damn, Joe, you are better than that. A kid plays hard but he misses a layup, and you yell, 'Fucking Aaron, fucking get him out of there. Fucking fuck, fuck, fuck.' You are acting like a goddamn idiot. A goddamn idiot. The fans are looking at it. The refs are looking at it. And it just don't look good. You cleaned up your look, you are looking nice, but you are yelling at me, yelling at the players, yelling at the refs. You are out of control!

"Today the kids finally got to feel good. They are running off the court. They are playing hard. They are slapping hands. They are helping each other on defense. They are all getting in the huddle. But then there is their leader, bitching like we are not a team. No wonder these kids freak out so much. God damn, Joe.

"How do you not have a grease board? How are you not diagramming things for them in every huddle? How do you not tape these games and then show them what they are doing? Give them a chance, Joe. Coach them. Don't take them out after every mistake. Don't yell at them after everything. Coach them, Joe, coach them."

Few people had ever spoken to Keller this way. Fewer still weren't banished instantly from Team Cal. When Taylor was done, when the car fell silent save a low bass line coming from a Snoop Dogg CD Demetrius had left in the player, Keller said nothing. He just looked out the window at the Las Vegas skyline.

In the tournament final on Friday night, Team Cal faced Houston Hoops at the recreational center on UNLV's campus. The Hoops were one of the better Under–15 programs in the nation and were affiliated with Nike. Coaches from both shoe companies filled the gym in anticipation of a showdown between two teams with high profiles.

After two days of playing before small crowds, the stage suddenly got bigger, a fact not missed by Demetrius. During warm-ups, he wore a weighted black vest that looked as if it was bulletproof. He had heard that some NBA players wore them pregame so they would feel lighter and bouncier. He jumped rope with it on while his teammates ran layup lines. He also was the only player with his jersey untucked, and he wore black shoes while the rest of Team Cal wore the royal-blue Adidas that Keller handed out on the first day of the tournament.

Early in the game, Keller heeded Taylor's criticisms. He didn't yell at the boys, and he even encouraged them when shots didn't fall. When Vondrae missed a jumper from the left side with eight minutes left in the first half, he looked to the bench in anticipation of being scolded or pulled. Keller started to say something but turned away from the court and retained his composure. When he looked back at Vondrae, he clapped his hands violently and forced out a positive line: "That's . . . all right . . . Vondrae. . . . Keep . . . pushing . . . it."

Houston Hoops went on an 8–0 run with about five minutes left in the half, turning a 2-point Team Cal lead into a 26–20 deficit. The Hoops were bigger and stronger and in much better shape. They got out on the break and took advantage when Keller's players were too tired to get back on defense. When Team Cal had the ball, the Hoops didn't let Demetrius penetrate and doubled Aaron in the post. Only G.J. understood how to attack their matchup zone, but when he got into the lane and looked for cutting teammates, no one had moved into the open space he created.

With two minutes left in the half and the Hoops' lead growing, the cork popped on the anger bottled inside Keller.

"What the hell are you doing?" he yelled at Aaron as he walked off the court during a time-out. Aaron anticipated the bashing and before getting to the bench tried to defend himself.

"D shot before we could run the play."

"No, he didn't. Shut the hell up."

Aaron ripped off his headband and threw it under the bench. "Fuuuuuck!" he yelled, and then he sat down and covered his face with his hands.

Taylor sat down next to him and put his hand on his knee. He looked up at Keller, who was thrashing the other players. "You know who is watching?" Keller screamed. "You guys are playing like a bunch of limp dicks!"

Houston Hoops pulled away further in the second half and won 67–53. It was not unexpected. Like the Boston Saintz in New Jersey, they were older, and the objective wasn't so much to win the game as to give the boys a taste of what they would face as they got older. Demetrius scored 13 points, but only 3 in the final twenty minutes. Late in the game, he took over ballhandling duties from G.J. but just dribbled atop Houston's zone, as if running out the clock.

"The thing I have always loved about Demetrius was the way he competed," said Mats, who watched the game from the stands with Pickett. "But tonight he stopped competing." He pointed to a corner of the gym, where Keller and Taylor had gathered the team. "Look at that. Joe and D.T. are talking, but he's not listening to them. He's tuning them out. He's tuning everyone out."

23

(DAVE TAYLOR)

Dave Taylor (in Lakers jersey)

n advance of the Adidas Superstar Camp in the first week of July, someone within the company's grassroots division—possibly Kalish or Pickett—compiled a list of seventeen players from the 220 attending the four-day event outside Atlanta. All of the players invited were among the best in the country, but these seventeen were special. They were termed "Highlight Athletes," and Adidas considered them the elite of the elite. They would be pushed to media outlets and photographed the most and, in the competition between the shoe companies to control the best kids, those seventeen would be used as proof that Adidas held its own with Nike and Reebok.

Most AAU coaches, regardless of their shoe-company affiliation, believed Vaccaro's Reebok ABCD Camp had the most talent of the three, with Adidas's camp second and Nike's a distant third. The number-1 rising senior, Greg Oden, and the top-ranked junior-to-be, O. J. Mayo, were at the ABCD, making it seem as if the other camps got the leftovers. But Adidas had made huge strides in its second year without Vaccaro, and the Highlight Athletes represented that progress.

The seventeen players were divided into two groups. The "Priority B" athletes included seven-footers Brook and Robin Lopez, Mats's Stanford-bound twins; Javaris Crittenton, who was headed to Georgia Tech; and a number of other players who either had or would commit to top college programs, including Erving Walker (Florida), James Keefe (UCLA), Wayne Ellington (North Carolina), and Nolan Smith (Duke). Also among the second tier of Highlight Athletes was Michael Beasley, who in three years would be the number-2 pick in the NBA draft by the Miami Heat, one of four Priority B players who would be in the league within three years.

The six "Priority A" athletes, those considered the phenoms of the phenoms, were Eric Gordon (Indiana), Darryl "D. J." Augustin (Texas), Thaddeus Young (Georgia Tech), and B. J. Mullens (Ohio State)—all future NBA players—as well as Korie Lucious (Michigan State). The sixth Priority A, the last of the players Adidas considered its most precious, was fourteen-year-old Demetrius Walker.

It was a resounding statement about Adidas's expectations for Demetrius and also the company's investment in his future. His ability, in the company's view, was on par with some of the most polished and talented players in the country, some of whom were three or four years older. He was not only expected to hang with the other kids at the camp but to outshine them and then to perform as well as or better than the sixteen other Highlight Athletes. Such expectations were outsized, even for "the next LeBron," which some grassroots coaches had begun calling Demetrius (often facetiously) after the *Sports Illustrated* article. Even if he was "fourteen going on LeBron," LeBron's breakout moment at a summer camp—against Lenny Cooke at ABCD—had not come until before his junior year.

Adidas ratcheted up the stakes in what was already a defining week for Demetrius and Keller. Adidas's grassroots brass as well as its top coaches would be at the camp, as would more than 100 college coaches. For most, it would be their first opportunity to see Demetrius play and judge whether the hype was warranted. For Keller, the performance of Demetrius and, to a lesser degree, Aaron and G.J. would validate or put into question Adidas's decision to tie the future of its grassroots division to him and the Jr. Phenom Camp. Grassroots coaches could be a catty bunch, and many arrived in Atlanta full of skepticism about Demetrius and Keller. They doubted Demetrius was as good as advertised, and most hoped he'd fall flat, as that would diminish Keller's star. The older players would be gunning for Demetrius. It had taken some until their junior or senior years to get invited to the Superstar Camp, and they wouldn't take lightly that Demetrius was there straight out of middle school. As Vaccaro said when told that Adidas had invited Demetrius: "They've turned that kid into the hunted."

In contrast, almost nothing was expected of G.J. and Aaron, who were at the camp only as favors to Keller. As a smallish pass-first point guard, G.J. possessed a game ill suited for the all-star camp format. Games were short—forty-four minutes of running clock—and players dominated the ball in the hopes of impressing the college coaches. G.J.'s unselfishness would work against him. Aaron was too slight to play inside against power forwards like Beasley and Young, so he would have to transition to a new position, small forward. On Team Cal, Aaron was never permitted to drive to the basket or shoot from the outside, the offensive skills most often associated with a small forward. When Keller told him about the position switch on the flight to Atlanta, he felt like an actor told of a new role moments before the opening curtain. "I'm going to get killed," he said.

Games were staged on one of four tightly drawn courts in a warehouselike building at the Suwanee (Georgia) Sports Academy. The complex was cordoned off so coaches were kept separate from the players, to whom they could not speak, per NCAA rules. On one side of the rectangular building, the college coaches sat in metal folding chairs that ran along the baselines of all four courts. On the other side were the players, their AAU coaches, and a spattering of spectators.

Superstar campers were divided into twenty-two teams of ten that were named after Adidas-sponsored colleges like UCLA, Indiana, and Louisville. Each team played at least one game a day, from Tuesday through Friday. The Superstar Camp, as well as the Nike and Reebok versions, mixed in just enough skill sessions and lectures to give the illusion that the camp was more than just a series of games. But the games were the main attraction. College coaches watched them, as did scouting-service types like Clark Francis, who used the camps to determine a player's ranking heading into the school year.

Adidas didn't strive for balance when dividing the athletes into teams; it stacked certain squads so as to create exciting matchups. How else to explain the Louisville team, which included Ellington, Augustin, and Keefe? Or Virginia Tech, which had Beasley, Nolan Smith, and Russell Westbrook (UCLA)? Demetrius's team included six-foot-eight Quincy Pondexter from California and seven-footer Hamady N'diaye from Florida. It was a good but not a great team, and much of the backcourt scoring would fall to Demetrius, easily the most heralded of the guards. Aaron's team looked stronger, if only because the six-foot-eleven Mullens was at center. G.J.'s team might have been the most talent-rich, but with trigger-happy guards Calvin Haynes III from California and Crittenton among the backcourt rotation, G.J. would be lucky to touch the ball. "Aaron's team is by far the best," Keller said when sizing up his players' prospects. "And D's team is the worst in camp."

As Demetrius walked into the gym on the first day of games, his eyes were drawn immediately to the far wall, where gigantic photos of Adidas-sponsored NBA stars Tim Duncan and Kevin Garnett stretched from the floor to the ceiling. They were reminders of where a starring turn at the Superstar could take him. Later, NBA players Josh Smith and Carlos Boozer wandered in to watch some of the action.

Despite his youth, Demetrius carried himself like the best player in the gym. He made small adjustments to his attire to assure that he stood out. Campers were given a yellow headband with the Superstar Camp logo. Demetrius, however, wore a white Adidas headband he'd brought from home. He also ignored the short white socks given to players, opting instead for his trademark long black soccer socks with three white stripes. His demeanor was different as well; he exuded a sense of entitlement. Before his opening game, he was the last of his team's starters to leave the bench for the floor, idling behind for seemingly no other reason than to ensure that his entrance would not be overshadowed. As the players greeted one another with hand slaps or a bump of knuckles, he stood near his team's free-throw line, waiting for the opposition to come to him. He would say later that he was so nervous his stomach hurt, but if it was anxiety, it came across as arrogance.

Keller stood next to the bleachers, never sitting during Demetrius's first game. Like all the AAU coaches hovering over the four courts, he prayed for a good showing by his players. At the end of the camp, Kalish and others would pick the twenty-four best seniors-to-be and the twenty-four best underclassmen (any player not going into his senior year) to participate in two all-star games. Coaches used the number of all-stars they had as a measure of their worth, and the selection process was heavily politicized. From the moment coaches landed at the Atlanta airport, they lobbied anyone with a say in the selection process. Having a kid ranked high by a scouting service helped, so the coaches schmoozed the likes of Francis as well. Highlight Athletes were expected to make one of the all-star games and would be given the benefit of the doubt during deliberations. Demetrius had to play only reasonably well, and the forces of the grassroots division would do the rest.

In his first game, Demetrius lined up at shooting guard and was matched up with six-foot-five Matt Bouldin from Colorado, who would eventually play at Gonzaga. Bouldin was not the athlete Demetrius was, but he could handle the ball deftly, enabling him to rotate between either guard spot, and the form on his outside shot was like something out of an instructional video. He had obviously spent hours and hours polishing the small aspects of his game. The first time Bouldin got the ball on the wing, he gave Demetrius a jab step, testing his quickness. Bouldin recognized that he wasn't going to blow by Demetrius, so he calmly set him up. He teased that he was going to drive until Demetrius leaned back, bracing for his move. With Demetrius on his heels, Bouldin stepped back, creating just enough space to launch his picture-perfect shot.

Watching Bouldin drain a long 3-pointer in his face early in the game angered Demetrius. The minute he touched the ball on offense, he tried to drive, but Bouldin used his strength to usher Demetrius wide of the key. Demetrius retreated to outside the 3-point line on the right side and dribbled there, looking for another seam to the hoop. Bouldin shadowed him perfectly, never falling for his head fakes or reaching for the ball. Frustrated, Demetrius stepped back and launched a desperation 3-point shot that barely grazed the front of the rim.

It was hard not to draw some conclusions from that one exchange: Demetrius didn't know how to play on the perimeter. Ballhandling, outside shooting, defending against penetration—these were not skills Keller had instilled in him. Other than a few workouts just before they left for Atlanta, when Keller had him shoot nothing but 3-pointers, Demetrius had not been schooled in any of the skills he needed to succeed against a guard like Bouldin. The matchup with Tyreke Evans in New Jersey six months earlier had highlighted Demetrius's deficiencies, but nothing had been done since then to fix them. He was the same player he had been that day, except now Keller couldn't protect him with a zone defense.

After a game in which he scored only 6 points, all on transition layups, Demetrius said his ankle bothered him. Following his 4-point effort in a game that evening, he said it was his knee. He also blamed "selfish" teammates and even his height. "Imagine if I was six foot eight: I'd be killin'." None of it explained his struggles. Demetrius simply didn't know how to play against kids as big or as athletic as he was. Yes, he was the youngest player on the court and could be forgiven for not shining against the older players, but he was also one of the rawest.

Contrasted with Demetrius's early struggles, Aaron's performance on the first day was a revelation. He scored in double figures in both games, collecting most of his points on 3-pointers from the corners, shots he was never allowed to attempt with Team Cal. When teams collapsed to the middle to stop the talented Mullens, B. J. kicked the ball out to Aaron for open jumpers. Aaron was not a seasoned outside shooter, but he had decent form and, like anyone, was capable of a hot streak. Back at the camp hotel that night, some AAU coaches wondered if Keller had miscast Aaron all along. He possessed good size and length for a small forward and, if the first day was any indication, a decent perimeter game. In short, his stock skyrocketed.

Against their wishes, Demetrius and Aaron were assigned to the same room at the camp hotel. As midnight approached on Tuesday night, Aaron couldn't sleep; he was too excited over his play from earlier in the day. He watched ESPN and took calls from his mom and others who wanted to hear about his performance. "I was wet. I was killin'," he told them. He bragged about the players on his team, mainly Mullens. "He is real. I mean real. But he is nice too. No attitude." The last comment was a dig at his roommate, who endured every word while wrapped up in a green comforter. Demetrius talked to his mom and his uncle, and his remarks were delivered in a somber voice. "It was terrible," he said, more grumbling than talking. "In the first game, I think I touched the ball only twelve times. I think some of my teammates are like, 'You're young, you'll have other camps, but this is my last shot.' So they don't pass nothing." He started to criticize the coach of his team, saying, "My coach is, man—" but then he stopped himself. "Look, man, the only time I touched the ball was when I ran the point in the second game. But if I passed the ball like a point guard should, I never got it back. It was horrible."

The long gym at the Suwanee Sports Academy was filled with AAU coaches, Adidas employees, college coaches, scouting-service writers, and 220 players. There were very few parents and almost no kids who weren't competing. Thus it was a surprise when, on Wednesday morning, Justin Hawkins paid five dollars admission and walked into the gym.

He was in Atlanta visiting his father and had talked him into driving to Suwanee so he could watch the games. Several of Justin's future Taft High teammates were at the camp, and he wanted to see how they and his former Team Cal teammates fared. While watching the first set of games Wednesday, he pounded his right fist into his left palm as he said over and over, "Man, I wish I was out there." If a player he knew asked him why he wasn't in uniform, he told them he hadn't gotten the necessary paperwork in on time. The truth was that he lacked a sponsor. The Taft High coaches backed their older kids, and rightfully so, as they were closer to graduating and needed the camp to enhance their chances of landing scholarships. Keller had been given three spots, for Demetrius, Aaron, and G.J. There wasn't room for Justin, not that Keller would have extended an invite even if he could have. Part of Justin's penance for leaving Team Cal and not going to FoHi was to watch the most important event of the summer from the sidelines.

The first to see Justin was Roger Franklin, the sensitive kid driven back to Duncanville, Texas, by Aaron's cruel comments about his father. Justin and Roger hugged, and Justin admired the uniform Roger and all the campers wore. It included shorts and a reversible jersey in UCLA colors. Each camper wore a pair of white shoes, the newest Adidas Ultras.

Roger told Justin that he was having fun despite struggling on the court. "They have me playing the three, but I am really a four or a five," he said in his Texas accent. "But I don't care. I am just here trying to have fun." As he spoke, he had his thumbs tucked under the straps of the sling bag given to every camper. "This is something I can learn from and then try to get better."

Justin asked how Demetrius and Aaron looked, and Roger lowered his voice. "I walked past Demetrius last night in the hall at the hotel. I said hello and tried to talk to him, but he just nodded and kept right on walking."

As for Aaron, Roger conceded: "Aaron got a lot better. He looks good."

Just then Aaron bounded down the baseline to the corner where Justin and Roger stood. Finding success on the first day had transformed Aaron into a sociable camper. Before the morning session, he buzzed around the different courts. He joked with Mullens and another teammate near one court, then walked out of his way to ask a guard about his injured leg. On the way back to where Mullens stood, he got sidetracked by another group of players he'd met at the hotel. He slapped a ball away from one and started a game of keep-away. He eventually bounced over to where Roger and Justin stood, and he immediately hugged Roger as if they'd never had harsh words.

"Did you see? They got me ranked among the top twenty guys in the camp," Aaron said. The Hoop Scoop had posted rankings of the players in the camp on its website, listing the top overall, by position, and the top seniors and underclassmen. After the first day, Aaron was ranked as the eighteenth-best player out of the 220 at the camp.

"Where is D ranked?" Justin asked.

"He's not," Aaron said, with a little too much enthusiasm. He then pointed to the court farthest from the door, one left unoccupied so players could practice before games. Demetrius was alone at one end, shooting 3-pointers. He kept missing, and after chasing down one rebound, he quickly heaved up another shot as if he were trying to get all the bad shots out of his system.

"I don't think Demetrius will talk to me about it, but if he asked me, I would tell him that he shouldn't worry about how many points he scores and just be thankful that we get to be here," Roger said. "Think of all the players that didn't get invited."

Justin nodded, keeping to himself that he was one of those players.

———

Demetrius and Aaron played simultaneously on adjoining courts Wednesday afternoon, and Keller positioned himself on the top row of the aluminum bleachers between the courts. From that perch, he could spin around and watch either game. Just before tip-off, Keller stopped Dave Taylor, who was one of the camp coordinators, and said, "Watch how much pull I have. Demetrius will be playing the point this game. I got it done." He had spoken to the coach of Demetrius's team about how little Demetrius touched the ball on the first day, he said, and he threatened to get Kalish involved.

Taylor waited until the start of Demetrius's game and, upon seeing him open as his team's point guard, said, "Way to go, Joe. You're important. Now let's see if D knows how to play the point."

In a development sure to boost Demetrius's confidence, Roger drew the assignment of guarding him. He was the same age and height, but he was slower than Demetrius. He was also as uncomfortable playing defense twenty feet away from the basket as Demetrius was trying to score from that distance. There might have been no player in the gym less prepared to defend Demetrius. Yet Demetrius inexplicably shrank from the challenge. The first three times up the court, he passed the ball off rather than charge at Roger. On his team's fourth possession, seven-footer N'diaye stepped out and screened Roger, but instead of coming off the screen and driving strong to the basket, Demetrius ran off the screen, bounced to the right, and fired a 3-pointer that missed badly. A few minutes later, he chased down a long rebound and blew past others for a transition layup, but that was the lone highlight in his six minutes on the court.

"He's playing like he's afraid," Taylor said, "like he'd rather not shoot than miss or have his shot blocked."

Spinning around to Aaron's game, Keller saw him make a 3-pointer from the right corner, then, a possession later, sprint free on the break and, after blowing the layup, hustle to collect his miss and put it in. Keller didn't react positively to Aaron's strong play; it annoyed him. Aaron remained on the court, but Keller spun back around when Demetrius reentered his game. He saw Roger make a 3-pointer over Demetrius, who was late finding him in the left corner. Demetrius's attempt at atonement was a wild, ill-advised jump shot that he let fly while drifting to his left, and it never reached the rim. Keller quickly spun back to Aaron, but he was exiting the game, so he reluctantly turned to the unraveling of his prodigy.

When Demetrius converted two layups late in the second half, Keller broke a long spell of silence. "That's six points. He needs to get to ten to have any shot at the all-star game." Demetrius didn't score again, however, leaving the game, like the two before it, marked by an array of turnovers and wild shots.

Keller stared out onto the court at the end of Demetrius's game. He'd missed Aaron's finish, which included another 3-pointer from the right baseline, then a blocked shot with his team ahead by 3 and only seconds remaining. Aaron's final line of 9 points, 5 rebounds, 2 assists, and 1 block was not overwhelming, but it was impressive for a freshman-to-be. He affirmed that he could play his new position well and that he was willing to contribute in small ways to help his team win.

Keller briefly congratulated Aaron, then set out to repair Demetrius's psyche. He had long preferred tough love to babying him, but with Demetrius's struggles continuing into a second day, Keller took a different approach.

"D, listen. Are you good? Yes, you are. Are you playing good right now? No. It's because you are trying too hard. If I gave you a million dollars to make one free throw, would you make it? No, because you'd try *too* hard to make it. You are putting too much pressure on yourself. Relax and just play." They were standing along the baseline of one court. "Do you hear me? Just relax. It's just a game. Play like it's just a game."

For five years Keller had hammered home the idea that every game was life-or-death; Demetrius's future was on the line whenever he stepped onto the court. Now, in the midst of his worst experience as a player to date, when he could see the college coaches watching and he felt as if his future was indeed at stake, he was supposed to treat basketball as if it was just a game.

Demetrius reached down to pick up his bag, and Keller put his hand on Demetrius's neck and squeezed. "It's gonna be okay, D," he said.

"I gotta go," Demetrius said, and he walked slowly down the length of the gym and out the back exit. Just before getting on the bus, he pulled the hood of his sweatshirt over his head, as if to hide his face from the other players waiting to be taken back to the hotel.

————

Keller's signature player, the kid who'd made him, was struggling, but that didn't stop Keller from pushing his business interests. Nights at the camp were reserved for networking and deal-making, and Keller thrived in that environment. One night, he sat at a table at a T.G.I. Friday's across from the hotel with an AAU coach from Atlanta and an assistant coach at a small private college in the area. He was close to a deal with the AAU coach on a Jr. Phenom Camp franchise (one of five he would sell that week), and he showed him pictures of the trailers he brought to transport equipment to and from the Jr. Phenom Camp. He talked of the money the coach would make from operating a camp, stopping only to sip his cosmopolitan or down a watermelon shooter or order another round for the table. When Mats entered the restaurant, Keller yelled across at him, ridiculing the matching golf shirts all the EBO coaches wore. When UCLA coach Ben Howland walked past the table, Keller stopped him and asked if he'd speak at the Jr. Phenom Camp. Howland said he was taking his family to Hawaii that weekend, "but had I known about it sooner I would have rescheduled the trip." He discouraged Keller from having Lute Olson speak at the camp, because Arizona was a Nike-sponsored school. "Hey, Nike isn't doing us any favors," Howland said.

Keller loved talking shop with a big-name coach like Howland, but he loved making money more, and his most important meeting of the week occurred Wednesday in a conference room at the hotel. Keller met with the head of girls' grassroots basketball for Adidas to discuss the inaugural girls' Jr. Phenom Camp. Keller asked White for $50,000 in product for the camp and $35,000 to cover expenses. Keller sensed that the amount of product would not be a problem, but the Adidas rep balked at the $35,000. Keller smoothed him over with small talk and, when he thought the rep had warmed a little, he turned the discussion back to the expense of operating the camp. The rep said he would be willing to give Keller $25,000, but Keller had to agree to kick $10,000 back to him, an under-the-table payoff that Adidas would never know about. "But that will fuck me up on my taxes," Keller remarked. The rep said that he could cover the tax hit with his profits from the camp, and in the end Keller agreed to the deal, as he was still coming out ahead.

"I'm out here getting shit done," Keller said gleefully after the meeting, forgetting for a moment that his star player was not.

When Keller and Gerry arrived at the complex for the morning games, they grabbed chairs along the baseline of Court #4. The teams warmed up before the 10:30 a.m. scheduled start, but Keller barely glanced at the players. He and Gerry were looking at the event program, sizing up the players on the team Demetrius would face and also G.J.'s opponent in his game an hour later. More than five minutes passed before Keller looked up from the program and, after scanning the floor, said, "Where's D?"

He stood up and craned his neck from side to side, looking around at the players, who were huddled near their respective benches getting last-minute instructions from their coaches. He thought Demetrius might be lying on the ground behind the bench, stretching.

"Is he in the bathroom?" Keller asked. As the game started, he walked over to the bathroom, went in, and then quickly came out. He looked toward Gerry and held his hands up. He next called Demetrius's cell phone but got not answer. He tracked down Aaron, who was sitting with Mullens, watching another game.

"Where is D?"

"Isn't he playing right now?"

"No, he's not with his team. Did he get up with you this morning?"

"When our alarm went off around eight a.m., he got up. I saw him get up. I brushed my teeth and got dressed and left, and I figured D was coming down too."

"Jesus Christ, Aaron! You couldn't have made sure he left on time? If he misses a game, he can't make the all-star game."

Keller found Taylor standing between two courts with his arms folded. They discussed the ramifications of Demetrius's absence, and Taylor mentioned that Demetrius might have also missed a session of one-on-one drills a day earlier. Taylor had heard that from another player, but he could not confirm it because no one tracked attendance. It was assumed that a player wouldn't miss a workout, because it was such an honor to be invited to the camp.

Keller went back to Aaron and asked about the one-on-one workout.

"I don't know if D was there or not. I can't say," he said. "I didn't see him there, but that doesn't mean he wasn't there."

Eventually, Demetrius called Keller's cell phone and claimed that he had overslept.

"D, how can you oversleep? Do you know what this means?" Keller shouted into his phone.

Keller scurried back and forth between Kalish, Pickett, and Taylor. They discussed kicking Demetrius out of the camp and putting him on an earlier flight home, which Taylor said would teach a valuable lesson about responsibility. They settled on a penalty they knew would resonate with Demetrius. *SLAM* magazine had scheduled a photo shoot for that afternoon, featuring the top players at the camp. In part because of the *Sports Illustrated* article, Demetrius had been asked to pose. Not only would he now miss the shoot, Aaron would go in his place. "You always say I give D stuff. Well, I take it away as quick as I give it," Keller told Aaron.

Taylor delivered the news to Demetrius outside a ballroom at the hotel and scolded him in the same way he had Keller in the car in Las Vegas. When told his penalty, Demetrius began to cry. "No, no, no," he said, and he pleaded with Taylor to reconsider.

"No, you deserve this," Taylor said.

Demetrius was alone in his room when Aaron stepped in front of a camera in a ballroom that *SLAM* magazine used for the photo shoot. He was given a spongy basketball a little smaller than a tennis ball and was told to put it near his face and squeeze it in his fist, as if crushing it. The photographer and his assistant kept asking Aaron to look meaner. "Try to make a face like you are crazy," they said. But Aaron couldn't do it. The kid who had always felt second to Demetrius suddenly had the spotlight all to himself. He couldn't act mad. Heck, he couldn't stop smiling.

After Demetrius struggled in his Thursday-night game, Keller mentioned his knee injury and said something about his back, but no amount of shadowing could hide his blemishes. To be fair, his team had no chance against a group that featured Gordon and Duke-bound Gerald Henderson. His team went down so quickly that Taylor had the scoreboard operator turn a 54–21 deficit into a 54–41 margin so as not to embarrass Demetrius's team. When Demetrius said after the game, "My teammates aren't even helping me get my own shot," he was right. But he also played without passion on defense and sat slumped in a chair when he wasn't on the court. He followed that with another lackluster showing in his only game on Friday morning. It got so bad that Keller turned away from the action several times. He couldn't bear to watch.

"Jesus Christ," Keller said. "D picks this week to play like he's got his thumb up his ass."

Taylor sat in on the final round of all-star deliberations. G.J.'s name never came up, he said, and when Kalish asked the coach of Aaron's team who from his squad deserved to make the all-star game, he didn't mention Aaron. Demetrius's name was floated at one point, but the loud lobbying for other players drowned it out. There were eight freshmen-to-be in the camp—Demetrius, Aaron, G.J., Roger, Derrick Favors, Noel Johnson, Shawn Williams, and Zheng Zhun, who played for a team of international kids called the Global All-Stars. None of them was picked for the all-star game, and rightfully so. Some had played well in spots, but none shone all four days. Yet, at the end of the meeting, someone from Adidas (Taylor did not remember who) remarked that they should be careful not to insult these young players, as that might lead them to switch to Nike or Reebok. "We've got these great kids going into the ninth grade. We need to keep them happy so they will come back next year," he said. That spawned an idea both brilliant and ludicrous. Why not hold a game for the freshmen-to-be before the underclassmen's all-star game? That there were only eight kids that age in camp didn't seem to matter, as someone suggested they could fill out the rosters with two older kids.

Keller learned of the arrangement on Friday afternoon, and at first he tried to act disappointed, but only because Gerry was so against the game. "What's the point?" Gerry said. "It's better if the boys leave knowing they have to work harder if they want to make the all-star game next year." Keller pretended to agree, but he also liked that Adidas had created a game to keep him and his players happy. It proved that he was important and also offered Demetrius a chance at redemption. Put on the court with kids his age—two who he played with regularly— Demetrius was bound to shine.

Most fans were still finding seats in the stands at the Northview High gym when the game announcer introduced the starting lineups for what was billed as the Junior Superstar Showcase Game. G.J.

and Aaron were on the white team; Demetrius and Roger headlined the blue team. On the stands opposite the benches, two dozen college coaches (including Duke's Mike Krzyzewski and Georgia Tech's Paul Hewitt) waited, having arrived early enough for the scheduled all-star games to witness the impromptu freshman version. Only twelve minutes were put on the clock, which kept running even when the ball went out of bounds. In all, they would play the equivalent of seven minutes of basketball, making it seem as if organizers were rushing the game to its end.

The game announcer attempted to get the crowd to stand up for the start, but most people remained seated as Aaron hustled down the wing and was rewarded with a pass he finished for the game's first basket. Two possessions later, Aaron executed a drop step and up-and-under move to make the score 6–2. Back at his more familiar center position, Aaron was as dominant as ever.

Aaron's two quick baskets woke Demetrius. He scored on a fast break, then a possession later was fouled while swooping in for a layup along the right baseline. It was an impressive move, his leaping ability and body control on display, and he drew confidence from it. After Aaron broke free for a dunk, Demetrius answered with a 3-pointer, the first he'd made the entire week. Two minutes later, Demetrius missed a 3-point try, but he atoned by collecting a steal on defense that led to a breakaway layup.

It was a glorified game of pickup, wide-open with minimal defense, and that fit Demetrius's strengths. He could get out and run and finish in transition, and none of the other players was as developed athletically as he was. But it was boring to watch. By the time Demetrius scored on a late layup for a game-high 10 points, few people in the stands were paying attention. When Roger dunked at the buzzer to give the blue team a 44–29 victory, there was only a smattering of applause. The game announcer tried to elicit more cheers, but the fans ignored him, and the players left the floor quickly, as if they were embarrassed.

"It was . . . okay," G.J. said when Gerry asked him about the experience. "It wasn't really a game."

For Keller, it was a delight. "MVP. Demetrius was the MVP!" he shouted. He repeated the line several times, as if saying it enough would make it true. Told that no MVP award would be given, Keller adapted. "If they gave out an MVP, Demetrius would have won it."

He strutted over to a far wall of the gym where Taylor was seated alone.

"Team Cal representing," he boasted, and Taylor shook his head.

"Like everyone else, I wasn't watching, Joe. That game was bullshit. No one cared."

No one but Keller. Matched up with players his age, Demetrius scored more points and looked more athletic than the others, Keller pointed out. Taylor reminded him that it was a ragtag game with no defense, that three of Demetrius's scores came on uncontested layups, but Keller wouldn't hear of it. He felt vindicated, even more so later that night when he spoke to Kalish outside the hotel. "Demetrius is still the future," Kalish said.

Keller and Adidas could keep the hype rolling.

24

The next generation at the Jr. Phenom Camp

When the phone rang, Aaron was at the kitchen table of the house his mother had recently rented on the western border of Fontana. He had returned home after playing basketball at the park, cooked himself some macaroni and cheese, and reached for the phone just before taking the first bite.

"Is Aaron home?"

"This is Aaron; who's this?"

"It's Tyson Chandler."

"Man, you didn't really just say it was Tyson Chandler. Come on, who is this, really?"

"Aaron, it's really Tyson Chandler. I got your number from Coach Otis."

"No way!" Aaron said.

"How you doing? I'm out here for a wedding and wanted to give you a call."

"Why would you want to call me?"

"About going to Dominguez."

The coaches at Compton Dominguez High had first noticed Aaron earlier in the summer, in a showcase event run by the Pumps that included some of Southern California's best high school players. The following day, Victor Clark, who acted as something of an unofficial assistant to head coach Russell Otis and also had ties to Barrett, called Aaron's home. "Coach Otis would really like to meet you," he said.

It was before the Superstar Camp, and Aaron remained loyal to Keller. He immediately called him to tell of Dominguez's advances, but Keller did not answer his home phone or his cell. The following morning, Aaron called Keller again, and he continued to call him almost every hour from 8:00 a.m. until 2:00 p.m. Keller practically slept with his cell phone; Aaron knew that if he didn't answer it meant you weren't important enough at that moment. "I wanted to go meet Coach Otis, but I wasn't going to if he told me not to," Aaron said later. "But then he never answered his phone. That made me mad."

Aaron and Barbara met Otis at an Applebee's in Corona the following afternoon. Otis had a bushy mustache and spoke in a higher pitch than you would expect from a tall black man. He was in his early forties and wearing gear from Reebok (the company that sponsored Dominguez that year), and his manner, when contrasted with Keller's eagerness, was almost stately. He acknowledged Dominguez's shortcomings in a serious tone—an academic reputation worse than even FoHi, gang infestation, its distance from Aaron's home—but he mostly talked about Chandler, how he had also hailed from the Inland Empire, and how Dominguez had been his springboard to the NBA.

Near the end of lunch, Otis asked Barbara to allow Aaron to play a few games with the Dominguez varsity players in an exhibition tournament in Orange County. Consider it a trial, he said, to see if Aaron was comfortable with the team and his coaching style.

Had Keller still been intimately involved in Aaron's life, he would have told him that Otis was unlikely to make him a featured player on the Dominguez team, particularly with star point guard Brandon Jennings there. At the "trial," he might get to shoot as much as he wanted, but during the season Otis would play him in the post and use him primarily as a defender and rebounder. At most, he'd be a role player. Soderberg, on the other hand, cared about him and would make sure he got the minutes and shots he needed at FoHi. But Keller was busy with his camps. He hadn't held a practice in more than a month, and many players, even Demetrius, complained about being unable to reach him. Keller was divorcing himself from the team, even if he wasn't ready to admit it.

The following week, Aaron suited up for Dominguez in a tournament at Whittier College. He started all three games and played four different positions, every spot but center; he even ran the point for a quarter. Otis's offense, at least for that tournament, was freewheeling. He encouraged everyone to attack the basket. The only time Otis criticized Aaron was to tell him that he passed *too* much.

"Mom, I was doing all this stuff that Coach Joe never lets me do," Aaron told Barbara afterward. "I was shooting threes; they were running the offense through me. And Coach O, he's calmer. He doesn't yell at you for unnecessary things. As long as you're playing hard, he won't say nothing."

Two days after the tournament, Otis asked to meet with Barbara again to discuss enrolling Aaron at Dominguez, but she refused. It was Keller who'd paid the $2,000 security deposit on their Fontana house and who gave her $1,000 a month toward the rent, she reminded Aaron, and that meant he was going to FoHi. A week later, when Aaron left for the Superstar Camp, he was resigned to a future tied to Demetrius.

After returning from Atlanta, convinced more than ever that he was a superior player to Demetrius, Aaron looked into getting a job that would pay $1,000 a month, enough to cover the rent lost if he didn't go to FoHi. "I have nothing against FoHi or anything, but the main reason I don't want to go is, I don't want to be part of the, like, the Demetrius Walker era. I want to be part of my own era," he explained. He concluded that he couldn't work enough hours to make that much and still go to school and play basketball, but he hoped that some compromise with his mom could be reached. The Dominguez coaches kept in touch, and Otis also arranged for a guest membership for Aaron at a nearby fitness center, so he could work out on his own. "I am thankful for Dominguez," Barbara said. "If not for them, my kid would be sitting around, doing nothing."

Still, she was not going to give up Keller's money.

A few days later, Tyson Chandler called.

"I'm not going to tell you what to do, but I will say that Dominguez was a great place for me," Chandler said. "It is nationally known and a great place to play, because Coach Otis makes it fun."

Aaron mentioned that his mom and Keller were pushing FoHi.

"You can go to Fontana and get twenty to twenty-five [points] a game, but people will say you don't play anybody," Chandler said. "The most important thing is playing with and against good players and having fun. That is what's going to make your career, competing and having fun."

Aaron explained that Keller paid some of his rent and how that influenced his mom. Chandler said it was possible that he or someone else affiliated with Dominguez could match that deal. Aaron should talk to Coach Otis about it.

"I was in the same situation as you once. I know what it is like," Chandler said at the end of the conversation. "If you ever need to talk, give me a call."

When Keller finally got word that Dominguez was after Aaron, he sent Soderberg to see him. Soderberg spent three hours explaining to Barbara why FoHi was a better fit, but Keller didn't communicate with Barbara or Aaron directly.

In late July, Keller was in San Diego preparing for the Jr. Phenom Camp when Barbara sent him a text message. He had forgotten to send August's rent money. Keller responded that she'd have to drive to San Diego to retrieve the check, as he was busy setting up for the camp. She couldn't miss work, however, so she continued to text him over the next few days, trying to set up a meeting closer to Fontana. She could stall her landlord for a few days, she said, but not too long. Keller promised several times to call with a place and time when they could meet, but he never did.

"Do you think Coach Otis will give you the money?" Barbara asked Aaron.

"Maybe, if he knew I was going to Dominguez."

"Call him," Barbara said. "Whoever pays the rent is who you are going to play for."

Within a few hours, Otis dropped off $1,000 in cash. He told Barbara that if Aaron ended up attending FoHi, she could pay him back when she was able.

Later, Barbara negotiated with Otis to match Keller's contribution—$1,000 a month—in exchange for Aaron enrolling at Dominguez, and she got $2,000 from him to repay Keller's security deposit. "Aaron's going to Dominguez," Barbara said when the deal was done. "Joe dropped the ball."

He likely dropped it on purpose.

"I am so happy to be done with Barbara," Keller said. "Aaron, he's a good kid, but I feel sorry for him, because his mom will just use him and use him. Going to Dominguez with Otis, that's the worst possible thing for Aaron."

Playing for a winning program and an experienced coach like Otis, getting out from under Demetrius's shadow and Keller's apathetic guidance, netting $1,000 for rent—these were all good reasons for Barbara to choose Dominguez. But there was one giant reason why she should never have considered it, and this was what Keller meant when he said there was no place worse for Aaron.

Five years earlier, one of Otis's former players, a seventeen-year-old identified in court papers as John Doe, accused him of sexual assault. Otis was tried on four charges, including sodomy and oral copulation, and during the trial another former Dominguez player testified that Otis had molested him as well. No charges were filed in that case, as the alleged acts had occurred in the 1980s.

The trial divided Compton. Some felt Doe was a gold digger. (His family filed a civil suit against the Compton school district.). Others believed Otis used his power as coach of a nationally recognized basketball program to molest young boys. Otis was ultimately acquitted and later returned to coaching Dominguez, but that did little to close the divide. The parents of some top players ruled out Dominguez, believing that Otis had benefited from a friendly jury and the difficulty in proving sexual-assault cases. Others felt that their hometown hero, a Dominguez graduate who built a program that instilled great pride in the community, had been wrongly accused and vindicated in a court of law.

Barbara fell somewhere in the middle, as that was the position that fit her needs. She was aware of the accusations against Otis, and they troubled her, but not enough for her to pass up $1,000 a month. Asked if she was worried about sending Aaron to play for a man accused of the very crimes he had been the victim of as a young boy, she said, "I told

Coach Otis, 'I don't have blind faith in you.' I will keep my eye on things." But how vigilant could she be from fifty-five miles away? Worse still, some days Aaron would have to ride to and from school with Otis, who lived in nearby Corona.

"I don't like how Coach Otis got in trouble for that stuff," Aaron said. "I heard it was bad, what they said he did. He got off. I know that. But people get off all the time for stuff they really did. I don't know. It makes me think about what kind of person he might be. Like I thought Coach Joe was this great guy. But then you play with him for a while and you learn he has this other side. You learn that he's not a good person."

If there was a player best positioned to see the totality of the tumult that had befallen Team Cal, it was Gary Franklin, Jr. He had been away from the team for most of the last twelve months rehabilitating the broken arm he suffered the previous fall. His recollection of the team, his memory of the players and Keller, was imprinted during the halcyon days at Nationals in Memphis, when ten selfless boys worked together for a common goal.

At the Ontario airport on the final day of July, Gary saw a team that only faintly resembled that bunch. Enlisted by Keller to fill Justin's spot on the roster for the 14-and-Under Nationals in Lake Buena Vista, Florida, Gary entered the airport and saw the division before hearing about it. Demetrius sat alone off to one side, headphones on, a hoodie covering his head. Roberto and Aaron sat together as far away from Demetrius as they could and still be in the same gate area. Rome was seated near his father, Terran sat by himself, and the others were spread out as well. If the boys hadn't been dressed in identical Adidas gear, you wouldn't have assumed they were traveling together.

Waiting with the team to board the flight was like watching a familiar movie with the sound turned off. Carmen was not blabbing into her Bluetooth; Terran wasn't snickering at Demetrius's jokes; Justin wasn't explaining where his mom planned to take him sightseeing; and the most noticeable absence of all: no Keller. Preparations for the Jr. Phenom Camp would cause him to miss pool play.

After landing in Orlando, half the players went to one condo and half to another. The condos Keller had reserved were several miles from each other, which had the effect of splitting the team in two. It made it impossible to organize team breakfasts and dinners. Other than for games, the entire squad never gathered in one place.

But even when they were together, they were not a team.

Demetrius sat away from the rest of the players at the gym, and if Aaron or Roberto or Gary or another teammate tried to engage him, he usually reached for his Sidekick and started typing. "Who is he texting?" Roberto asked before one game. He and the rest of the team stretched while Demetrius pecked away on his Sidekick. "What's so important he's gotta say it *right now*?" Demetrius continued his ritual of warming up separately from the team, in his weighted vest, jumping rope while his teammates shot. Fans approached him and he smiled as he signed autographs, but when one of his teammates got near him, he turned away.

Gary thought back to Demetrius's behavior when he joined the team two years earlier. He had assumed he wouldn't like Demetrius, that his ego would be massive, but Demetrius was welcoming, and he called Gary often to make sure he wasn't frustrated by Keller's ranting. As Demetrius's star ascended, as The Hoop Scoop began touting the brightness of his prospects, Gary saw no change. A week after the publication of the *Sports Illustrated* article, Gary called Demetrius to congratulate him. "Wassup, Mr. *Sports Illustrated*," he said.

Demetrius was embarrassed. "Come on, man, be quiet about that. We're a team."

Gary saw him differently now. He told his father: "You look at D now and you just know in his head he's thinking, *Man, I'm the shit.*"

In pool play, Team Cal slogged to victories over the PG Ballers 74–46 and the Bay State Magic Elite 63–50, and narrowly defeated the Little Mizzou Tigers 52–49. Conditioned by Keller to jump on teams at the start, to "take their hearts out," the team rebelled in his absence. They played with little energy, switching from lackluster to driven only late in the game when provoked by the possibility of a defeat. In elimination play, Team Cal would eventually face a team too good for such an approach, and Gary, Sr., and Rome, Sr., the two acting coaches, knew this. Yet they were incapable of jump-starting the team, mostly because they couldn't get through to Demetrius. He averaged less than 10 points over the first three games, as he refused to assert himself. As in Las Vegas against Houston Hoops, he dribbled aimlessly on the perimeter or quickly gave the ball up to teammates, his only contribution on offense the occasional long jumper.

The day before the elimination rounds, as a few of the boys walked to Disney's Wide World of Sports Complex, Gary caught up to Demetrius.

"D, what's wrong, man? You aren't into this, are you?"

"I just don't want to play," he said.

"For real? Why?"

"My knee's been bothering me, and I should be resting it. I talked to my mom, and she said I shouldn't be playing at all. She's actually mad at me 'cuz I'm out here."

Gary didn't believe him. If his knee hurt, why was he jumping rope before games with that stupid vest on? Why did he throw down dunks in warm-ups? It didn't help his case that all the boys were banged up to some degree. Gary's broken left arm hadn't healed completely, and he dribbled exclusively with his right hand. Rome had braces on both his ankles, and Aaron had rolled his right ankle as well. Roberto had twisted his back in a fall and had to ice it between games.

"I wanted to be mad at D, but you know who I was really mad at? Coach Joe," Gary said later. "He was always giving D excuses just in case he didn't play good. 'Oh, D's sick,' or 'D's knee is hurting.' Coach Joe let D think it was okay to do that."

And only Coach Joe could reach him now. Only Keller could fly in and convince Demetrius to reembrace his teammates. Only he could inspire the boys, get them to play with the enthusiasm they displayed the year before in winning the title. He had said he would fly in after pool play, but then he called and said he would be a day late. The next day, he repeated that line.

Team Cal drew ARC, from Southern California, in the Round of 64. They defeated that familiar foe 52–39, although in the past a win by less than 30 would have been a disappointment. The boys returned to the condos, expecting Keller to arrive at any moment. They woke up the next morning anticipating that, like Santa Claus, he'd simply appear and deliver the new shoes he had promised them. He never arrived, however, and at one point he called Demetrius and claimed to have missed his flight. As for the new shoes he had promised them: "I swear I sent them," he told Demetrius. "I bet they got there but someone stole them."

Keller had confided in a few people before the tournament, admitting that he wouldn't be joining the team in Florida because he was too busy. He also predicted they would lose well short of the finals. They hadn't practiced together; Demetrius was out of shape; off-the-court squabbles bled onto the court. "I don't need to be there to see them get killed," he said.

It was a fitting way for Keller to finally step out of the boys' lives. He lied to them, had no faith in their abilities, and pointed out their short-comings with nary a mention of his role in their emergence.

In the Round of 32, Team Cal faced the Georgia Hurricanes, a good team that had brought a huge crowd to Florida. When Team Cal arrived at Disney's Sports Complex, they were jeered as they entered the gym. Most of the fans targeted Demetrius. If he missed a shot during warm-ups, chants of "Overrated!" cascaded down to the floor. "You ain't that good!" people yelled. As Demetrius stretched under one basket, Gary, Sr., walked up to him and helped him stretch his arms behind his back. "I could feel his pulse, and it was just pounding," Gary, Sr., said later. "The pressure on Demetrius, man, it was intense."

The Georgia Hurricanes featured several long and athletic forwards, players similar in size to Demetrius, Rome, and Roberto, too mobile for Terran and Craig to guard. Team Cal could have used another rangy athlete, someone like Vondrae, but his absence was another example of Keller letting the team down. Vondrae's uncle had asked for $1,000 a month (the amount Vondrae told him Aaron received) to move to Fontana from Nebraska. Keller declined, and he put Vondrae on a plane back to Omaha before Nationals, just as Roberto had predicted.

The Hurricanes jumped to a 6-point lead, then 8, then 10. They were not more skillful, they just worked harder, fighting for rebounds, hustling after loose balls, playing good help defense. Early in the game, Demetrius caught the ball on the right baseline and drove hard to the basket. All the attributes that made him special—his speed, body control, and leaping ability—were exhibited, but as he lifted the ball to the rim, a Hurricanes forward slid over and blocked it. It wasn't a clean block, but it was enough for the ball to fall short, eliciting loud hoots from the crowd.

Demetrius stuck to the perimeter after that, moving the ball and leaving Aaron to battle the Hurricanes' frontcourt. In the second half, with Team Cal trailing by 12, Demetrius asked out of the game, claiming his knee hurt. Gary, Rome, Aaron, and Roberto were on the court when he subbed himself out, and they couldn't believe it. The game was not over; they could still battle back. Yet Demetrius waved the white flag. When the game ended with Rome missing a shot at the buzzer that would have won it, the boys talked not of that miss and the hard-luck nature of their 58–57 defeat but of Demetrius.

"He's supposed to be all this shit, the best player in the country and all that, but he didn't help us at all. He quit on us," Roberto said to Gary back at their condo. "Coach Joe and him, they both quit on us."

The team qualified to play in the third-round losers' bracket, the winner of which would finish in sixth place, but many of the boys didn't want to play another game.

"Can't we just forfeit?" Demetrius said. "It doesn't matter, so why play?"

Late that night, a handful of boys sat together talking in one of the condos. Their anger at Keller and Demetrius had dissipated, and they reminisced about their years together, remembering not only the great victories and the national title but also silly little moments, like the crazy coach in Portland who threw his watch into the stands. They recalled the run at Nationals the year before. "Remember when Roberto got off the plane and just tore it up against the Virginia Panthers?" Aaron said. As the memories flowed, they realized that the team would certainly die after this tournament. The players would go to different high schools and eventually land on different grassroots teams. The plan to keep the team together from the beginning of their grassroots experience to the end was dead.

Kids are usually too busy looking toward the future to notice the last few seconds of their childhood. In less than two months, they would be high school freshmen. The pressures and responsibilities would multiple quickly. Core courses, qualifying SAT scores, official visits, unofficial visits, verbal commitments, letters of intent—it would all happen fast. Their basketball innocence had probably died years earlier when Joe Keller cut a deal to brand them with Adidas's three stripes, but sitting in that condo in Florida, the boys decided to seize one last moment of purity.

"Fuck it. Let's just go out there tomorrow and play as hard as we can," Aaron said.

"So what if the best we can do is sixth place?" Gary said. "Let's get sixth place, then. Let's go out as high as we can."

Roberto seized Keller's familiar rallying cry and made it his own. "Let's just play our hearts out. Everything we got."

The following morning, Team Cal defeated the South Florida Heat 70–67. The margin of victory would have been greater had Demetrius given maximum effort and if Aaron, who dominated in the first half, had not reinjured his ankle early in the second. Regardless, it was Team Cal's best game of the tournament. They cheered one another on, played hard on defense, and shared the ball on offense.

They played the Suffolk Blazers next, a very beatable team. Aaron entered the gym on crutches, his ankle swollen to the size of an orange, but he still demanded to play, and Gary, Sr., relented, even though Aaron could barely run up and down the court. He was not the only boy hurting. Gary's arm was killing him, and Roberto's back flared up, as did one of Rome's ankles. But if Aaron was going to keep playing, there was no way they would sit out.

With the game tied and about five minutes remaining, Aaron rolled his ankle again. He was fighting for a rebound and came down on a defender's foot and fell to the ground. As Aaron limped to the bench, he pleaded with Gary, Sr., to let him stay in the game. "Sorry, Aaron, we can't risk doing permanent damage to that ankle," he responded.

Aaron sat down next to Demetrius, who had taken himself out of the game much earlier, citing his injured knee. Demetrius barely watched the game. If he could have gotten away with it, he would have typed on his Sidekick from the bench.

"D, man, we need you in there," Aaron said.

Demetrius looked away.

Aaron watched Gary miss a jumper from the right side, which led to a fast break that gave Suffolk a four-point lead. The game was slipping away. Aaron got up gingerly, balancing on one foot, and stood over Demetrius.

"Man, D, we need you out there! What is wrong with you? The team needs you!"

"Man, this ain't no team." Demetrius didn't stand up, and he didn't match Aaron's anger.

"You're wrong, D. It *is* a team. It's *your* team."

Suffolk scored again, pushing its lead to 52–46, which would be the final score.

"I ain't going out there," Demetrius said. "It ain't worth it for me. It ain't worth me injuring my knee some more. I got a career to worry about it."

"A career?"

"Yeah, I can't be worrying about this. I've got to think about my future."

25

(MARK SODERBERG)

Mark Soderberg (wearing glasses) *coaching Fontana High in New York in 2005 while Demetrius watches in street clothes*

ad Demetrius matriculated to Fontana High a decade earlier, the classroom in which he sat for intro Spanish would not have existed. It was a "relocatable" classroom, brought in to ease an enrollment crunch that had swelled FoHi's numbers so much that it was the fifteenth-largest high school in the United States. Meant as a temporary fix, these boxy prefabricated structures were now a permanent part of the campus, as they were at schools across the state. They went by many names—portables, modulars, trailers—but at FoHi they were known as the "bungalows."

Demetrius's left foot was propped on the desk in front of him, the only empty seat among the forty metal-and-plastic desks in the room.

He wore a royal-blue dress shirt with French cuffs that was two sizes too big and hung untucked over jeans so baggy, he had to hold them at the waist when he walked. His jeans were rolled at the bottoms, just enough to show off his spotless blue-and-white Vans high-tops. He ironed his shirt and jeans before he'd left home that morning, a ritual that Kisha teased him about. He ironed everything—T-shirts, sweatshirts, even his underwear. He also took great care to make sure his attire matched perfectly. It was not by accident that the blue on his shirt matched the blue rubber bracelet on his right wrist.

The teacher, Mr. Marchese, ran through the various holidays, saying each in Spanish and having the class repeat them. Upon reaching Veteran's Day, he asked, "Does anyone have any relatives who fought in a war?" A young girl, the only other African American in the class, raised her hand. "My grandma was in the Watts riots," she said.

"Oh, my God, that is dumb," Demetrius said quietly. He covered his mouth with his hand.

The teacher moved on to *Día de los Muertos* and *Día de Todos los Santos,* and that spurred a discussion on who got to go to hell and who went to heaven. It hijacked the class for the next thirty minutes.

"This class is *so* boring," Demetrius said.

He was never called on, and at one point a short Latino boy wearing a white undershirt and jeans pointed to Demetrius and asked Mr. Marchese, "How come you never call on *him*? He just sits in the back and says nothing."

"No, I don't," Demetrius said.

"Yes, you do."

"No. If I didn't do nothing, then how would I have an A in this class?"

That exchange continued to bother Demetrius after class ended. "I wish I could have punched that kid, but you gotta be careful around here," he said. He stood in line to buy lunch from one of several windows divided by metal railings, which resembled the betting windows at a horse track. "Things are crazy around here, and you gotta be careful. That kid, who knows who he's got watching his back? He could have brothers, he could be in, like, a little gang; you just never know."

He bought a slice of pepperoni pizza and a Powerade and walked to the center of campus, to an open quad where students congregated. He passed a thin Latino girl talking with other girls in a small circle. She stepped away from the group, into Demetrius's path, and smiled. "Hi, D," she said. Demetrius gave her a half smile and walked around her.

"Did you see that? That girl is into me. She's in one of my classes. But I've got to be careful with her, 'cuz she's Mexican. I could get in trouble just talking to her. She might say she doesn't have a boyfriend, but you know she does. Or there is some guy that likes her or used to go out with her, and if he sees me talking to her, he and some of his friends might try to fuck me up. So I don't even talk to Mexican girls."

In the center quad, students sat at cement tables or on patches of brown grass, eating their lunches and socializing. Demetrius walked across the quad and then up a few steps to the front of the science building. About thirty kids, the only African Americans in sight, congregated there, and Demetrius greeted most of them with a hug or slap of hands. A girl with big silver hoop earrings and her hair in a bushy bun atop her head approached Demetrius, and he teased her about the size of her earrings, which prompted a dirty look.

"See, you are always mad-dogging me," he said, meaning she gave him cross looks.

"I do not."

"You do. You got the sweetest voice, but you're always mad-dogging me."

She stormed away in fake protest, making sure to look back at Demetrius and smile.

Demetrius sat between two boys and ate his slice of pizza while looking out over the quad. The homogeneousness of the student body was striking; everywhere you looked were clusters of Latino students. Asked if this was what he expected when he enrolled at FoHi, he said flatly, "No." He expected to be the BMOC, the Big Man on Campus, he said, but instead he was a Black Man on Campus. "I knew there were a lot of Mexicans but not like this. Man, I'm, like, the minority here. How often does a black guy say that?"

The problem, as he would describe it later, was not only that the school was 80 percent Latino but that "Mexicans don't care about basketball." The high school experience he envisioned included hordes of girls chasing after him, boys anxious to be his friend, and teachers willing to doing whatever was necessary to keep him happy. But the boys didn't care that he was a basketball prodigy, and he couldn't talk to most of the girls because of fear that he would get jumped. His teachers, like Ms. Chavez for biology, seemed to go harder on him because he was a basketball player, perhaps to prove that times had changed.

That evening, FoHi would play Eisenhower High, its second home game of the season, but you wouldn't have known from surveying the students or the grounds. Players did not wear jerseys or lettermen's jackets. There were no cheerleaders wearing the school's crimson and white, no banners promoting the game. Principal Tom Reasin hoped to restore "Steelers Pride" through the success of the basketball program, but six months into Demetrius's high school career there was no noticeable progress.

The team had not done its part, losing five consecutive games to start the season. They won their home opener over Colton High but were a paltry 3–7 going into that night's game. They were a motley group—Demetrius and eight players who would have had trouble making the junior varsity at some schools. Keller had failed to come through on his promise to surround Demetrius with good players, running off Aaron and Vondrae and losing Terran, Rome, and the others. He did manage to import a six-foot-six kid from France, but "Frenchy," as Keller called him, couldn't play on the varsity team because of CIF rules. "Even if he could play, he wouldn't help," Demetrius said. "He's terrible."

Demetrius was not blameless. The *Riverside Press-Enterprise* had covered FoHi's season opener as if it were the sports equivalent of Neil Armstrong's moon landing. The lengthy article, titled INAUSPICIOUS DEBUT FOR FONTANA FRESHMAN, included a picture of Demetrius sitting on the bench with his hands covering his face. He scored only 7 points in a 62–33 loss to Ocean View High from Huntington Beach, making only three of fourteen shots. "Nothing was falling for me today, but every player is going to have those games," Demetrius told the newspaper. "Even Michael Jordan had bad games, and if the 'The Great One' can have bad games, then I can have one too." But the bad games outnumbered the good. Demetrius scored more than 20 points in only two of his first ten high school games, rarely resembling the player who once dominated on the grassroots scene. The obvious change in his game was the position he played. He was now a guard, forced to handle the ball more and shoot jump shots and guard smaller, quicker players. His unfamiliarity with that role hindered him, even against mediocre competition. The more striking difference, however, was in his demeanor. He often played afraid—the criticism Dave Taylor had first voiced at the Superstar Camp—as if he was more worried about protecting his reputation than enhancing it.

All across the country, talented young players were facing the same challenge as Demetrius, adjusting to a new position while also playing against older kids. Dexter Strickland in New Jersey, with whom Demetrius kept in contact, and Leslie McDonald, the center for the Bellevue War Eagles, realized they wouldn't be tall enough to play forward or center in college. They were both in the process of changing their game, and while it was frustrating, the fruits of their labor would pay off later. In a few years, Strickland would be one of the top five point guards in the nation; McDonald, a top-10 shooting guard. They would both sign with North Carolina.

Demetrius's future hung on him making the same transition, but he appeared averse to change, or at least to the labor that came along with it. Over and over, Mark Soderberg reacted to something Demetrius did or didn't do by stating: "D . . . I just don't understand him." He didn't heed requests to eat healthier; he showed up late to practice or didn't stay after to work extra; he refused to lift weights, because his uncle said it would hurt his jump shot. Soderberg was not a taskmaster, and his approach was the opposite of Keller's. He made himself available to Demetrius but didn't call to make sure he would attend a voluntary workout or pick him up and drag him to practice. "If D needs me, all he has to do is ask, but I'm not going to hold his hand," he said.

Soderberg complained to Keller about Demetrius's ways, but Coach Joe was too busy or disinterested to intercede. He kept only a finger in Demetrius's life, probably out of guilt and perhaps because he had yet to find the best way to cut him off completely. Keller's competitiveness resurfaced from time to time, such as after Demetrius's poor showing at Nationals. The Hoop Scoop dropped Demetrius from number 1 in the class of 2009 all the way to number 29. "No way Demetrius is not at least in the top ten," Keller said. "He's gonna prove a lot of people wrong. I'm gonna get him fixed, and then look out." But he rarely followed up on his promises to "fix" Demetrius. He was simply too busy expanding the Jr. Phenom brand, coming up with new camps and moneymaking ventures. He also bought a nearly 4,000-square-foot home in Moreno Valley, a thirty-minute drive from Fontana. The distance kept him from helping Demetrius, as did his focus on his new abode. He filled it with flat-screen televisions and was in the process of having the kitchen remodeled and a pool installed in the backyard. "When it is all done, my house is going to look like something you would see on MTV's *Cribs*," Keller boasted.

Demetrius noticed Keller pulling away, but Keller called just enough and mailed him enough shoes that Demetrius thought his absence was temporary.

"I've been with Coach for . . . for forever, basically. All through my basketball career he's been there for me, helping me through everything," Demetrius said. "Now he's not around as much, but I know he will be there for me when I need him."

The game between Fontana and Eisenhower was the first of Demetrius's high school games that Keller attended. He was one of only 150 people in the Fontana gym, and that included the ten-member cheer squad for Eisenhower and the twelve cheerleaders for the home side. It was a far cry from the overflow crowds Keller had told Tom Reasin to expect. The Fontana cheerleaders had made signs, painted in the school colors, for each player. Demetrius's was the most prominent, and the cheerleaders, most of whom were black, paid him special attention. One girl, wearing blue overalls over her cheer outfit, yelled at Demetrius just before the tip: "Show us your game, D!"

Eisenhower carried the same 3–7 record as Fontana and was undersized, with no one capable of guarding Demetrius; he should have dominated. But he missed his first four shots, including two long 3-pointers, and then he disengaged. He seemed most intent on letting the crowd know that he disapproved of his teammates. After one committed a turnover, he looked up into the stands at Keller and rolled his eyes. When one of FoHi's guards failed to hit him with a pass when he was open in the left corner, he walked back on defense, his bottom lip covering his top as he shook his head. There were so few people in the gym, and he was so demonstrative, that it was impossible not to notice him showing up his teammates.

Demetrius scored only 2 points in a first quarter that ended 13–13. In the second he didn't score at all, and FoHi trailed 26–23 at the intermission. He picked up his fourth foul one minute into the second half and sat for the rest of the third quarter. As his teammates fought back to take the lead, 27–26, he didn't cheer them on or even pay attention to their efforts. Soderberg called a time-out with 5:54 remaining in the third, and Demetrius stayed seated at the end of the bench as Soderberg addressed the team in a huddle on the court. Demetrius remained seated again when Soderberg later called a time-out to slow a run that had put Eisenhower ahead 33–28.

Rome, Sr., who arrived just before halftime, saw Demetrius fail to join his teammates in the huddle and said, "If I was his coach I'd tell him, 'Go ahead and take off your shoes. You ain't going back in with that kind of attitude.'"

FoHi went on a 16–5 run to seize the lead 44–38, with Demetrius on the bench. The players moved the ball better and played better team defense without him. They were short on talent, but Soderberg had coached them well. As the fourth quarter started, Soderberg reinserted Demetrius, and he scored two quick baskets. He then committed a needless reaching foul with 3:42 left, fouling out with 6 points. His teammates held on for a 70–54 victory.

"I knew it would be bad. Sod told me they weren't any good. But I had no idea they would be *this* bad," Keller said after the game. "Next season, D will have some horses around him. I promise. I've already got some things in the works."

Keller did not attend Demetrius's next three games as the Steelers lost to Redlands and Yucaipa and then defeated Colton to reach 6–9. He reemerged before the biggest game of the season: a matchup with Lincoln High of Brooklyn at Iona College in New Rochelle, New York. The game was part of the Basketball City Shootout, a showcase event organized by Jared Rice, an attorney and former player at New Rochelle High. Showcases were becoming more common as promoters tapped into the public's obsession with seeing future college and NBA players in action. They were marketed not as games between top teams but duels between highly ranked stars, more like boxing matches than basketball games. One showcase in Cincinnati, featuring Oak Hill Academy and a local school, North College Hill, drew a crowd of 16,202 to U.S. Bank Arena with the promise of a showdown between Oak Hill's Michael Beasley and O. J. Mayo. The year before, the ESPN networks televised nine showcase games, and regional networks televised games as well. The shoe companies' involvement with some events added a whiff of controversy, as did the backgrounds of some of the organizers. Rodney Guillory, who was a well-known middleman for sports agents, organized the Reebok Rise or Fall Challenge in Los Angeles and got Mayo and North College Hill to participate. Guillory would later come under NCAA scrutiny for giving Mayo cash and other gifts at the behest of a sports agent while Mayo was at USC. Rice, the attorney behind the Basketball City Shootout, later expanded his practice to include athlete representation, which made the event look, in hindsight, like one big recruiting effort.

Several elite players went head to head in the Basketball City Shootout, including Kevin Love (who would eventually attend UCLA) versus Justin Burrell (St. John's), and Darrell Arthur (Kansas) against Curtis Kelly (UConn). Those matchups were eclipsed, however, by the hype surrounding Fontana versus Lincoln. In flyers promoting the event, the game was billed as a showdown between Demetrius, the number-1 player in the class of 2009, and the player just below him in the rankings, Lance Stephenson. After two years of dancing, finally, the top-ranked players in the class of 2009 would meet. Or so Rice, the promoter, thought when he agreed to pay the airfare, hotel, and other expenses for the FoHi players and coaches.

Demetrius flew with the team to New York, but he sat on the bench in jeans and a jacket adorned with the logos of all the NBA teams. He claimed he had an injured hamstring and watched as Stephenson scored 16 points on 8-for-10 shooting in only twenty-one minutes, and Lincoln routed the Steelers 71–42.

"I wanted to play against him," Stephenson told reporters after the game. "I heard he is really good."

Three days later, Soderberg became convinced that the injury was a fake, an excuse devised by Demetrius and endorsed by Keller. On the day of a game against Redlands East Valley, Demetrius said that he was good to go, that his hamstring felt fine. "D, don't you think all those people back in New York will be watching to see when you come back?" Soderberg told him. "You can't just come back that quick. They will think you were scared to play." Demetrius agreed to sit out one more game; he made his return two days later against Rialto. Soderberg brought this up with Keller, who admitted that he had advised Demetrius not to play because being outclassed by Stephenson would have been harmful to his reputation.

Fontana finished 8–15 and missed the CIF playoffs. It was a humbling season for Demetrius, who did not make first-team all–Citrus Belt League, and his poor attitude and work ethic suggested darker days ahead. But then Keller announced that he'd hired someone to transform Demetrius, the perfect tutor to get him back on track.

"If anyone can fix D, it's him," Keller said.

In the near decade since he starred for SCA and Pat Barrett, Schea Cotton had played at Long Beach City College and the University of Alabama and professionally in Europe and South America. The closest he would get to the NBA career that had once seemed his destiny were short stints with the summer-league teams of the Orlando Magic, the Los Angeles Clippers, and the Golden State Warriors. Yet who better to counsel Demetrius than another grassroots phenom who had also been prematurely hyped in the pages of *Sports Illustrated*? Who more qualified to guide his transition to a new position than a player who started high school as a burly forward but became an all–Southeastern Conference shooting guard with the Crimson Tide?

"If he questions me, I can say, 'Okay, let's roll the ball out. Let me show you.' I can still play, can still show him how things are done," said Cotton. "I can also relate to Demetrius beyond basketball. The stuff he is going through, it is what I went through at an early age."

Twice a week, Cotton arrived at FoHi after Demetrius's sixth-period class and they went into the gym, which they usually had to themselves. Cotton dressed to play, in shorts and a tight T-shirt, and Demetrius noticed his considerable biceps. He was in fantastic shape, around 230 pounds, and still harbored hopes that an NBA team would call.

"D, don't read the articles. Don't pay attention to the rankings," Cotton told him one day as they stretched. "All they do is stagnate your growth. Just worry about getting better, and all the rest will take care of itself."

Being closer to Demetrius's age than Soderberg and Keller were, Cotton framed instructions in a more relatable way. In one drill, Cotton had Demetrius run around without the ball, moving from one side of the court to the other, often down the baseline. Demetrius then sprinted to the wing, coming around a chair Cotton had set on the court, where he received a pass and either shot or drove to the hoop.

"You know how Rip Hamilton runs around and around and then comes off a screen and hits a shot?" Cotton said, referring to the Detroit Pistons' shooting guard. "That is what this is teaching you."

It shocked Cotton how out of shape Demetrius was so soon after his high school season, but he was encouraged by his willingness to learn. "When Coach Joe used to show how to come off a screen, he would tell me to pump-fake, then take a power dribble to the side and pull up," Demetrius said. "Now I'm noticing that when I take that power dribble to the side, kids are getting faster, so they can recover. So Schea tells me to just shoot or cut the angle and go right at the basket."

Demetrius shot free throws after every drill so he'd get used to shooting them when tired, and they worked on his ballhandling for the majority of one practice a week. They also played one-on-one every day. "He's a beast, and we are just banging," Demetrius said. "I'm learning how to handle it when players hold me and bump me and how to shoot over a bigger opponent."

After two months of working with Cotton, Demetrius's shot and ballhandling were noticeably better. He had a long way to go, but he now understood the work he needed to do. "I'm in such a good situation now," he said. "I know why I struggled last summer and that I didn't play my best in high school. [But] I feel like this is going to be my comeback summer."

Keller paid Cotton $150 per session. That came out to about $75 an hour, not counting the time it took Cotton to drive from Orange County to Fontana. Given how much Keller gained from leveraging Demetrius's talent, it was a pittance. But in the early spring, when asked how his workouts with Demetrius were progressing, Cotton said, "I'm not doing that anymore. Joe stopped paying me. I don't know if he thought it was too much or what, but he just decided he didn't want to pay me anymore. I wasn't going to do it for free."

Keller claimed Cotton asked him for a raise. "He wanted too much money."

Demetrius never learned why Cotton stopped working him out. As with Keilon and Olujimi years earlier, Cotton was just suddenly out of his life, and for a time Demetrius wondered if he had done something to piss him off. "Man, people are always leaving me these days," he said.

It didn't stop with Cotton.

"I resigned," Mark Soderberg announced at the end of the school year. "It just wasn't the job I signed up for. If all the kids Joe said were going to be there had come, or if Demetrius was still a hardworking kid who wanted to learn, well, then I would have kept at it. But it just wasn't the job for me anymore."

26

(ROBERTO NELSON)

Roberto Nelson and Bruce Nelson during a visit to Ohio State

Bruce Nelson stood just off the court in a gym on the campus of the University of California at Santa Barbara. It was late in the summer, a few weeks before the start of Roberto's freshman year, and Roberto was playing in an exhibition tournament with the Santa Barbara High varsity team. A man approached Bruce and introduced himself, although no introduction was necessary. Pete Carroll coached the University of Southern California football team, which had won the national championship the season before.

"Are you his dad?" Carroll said, and he pointed toward Roberto. Carroll had been in the stands a day earlier when Roberto scored more than 30 points against Peninsula High, which counted Carroll's son among its players.

"Yeah, that's my boy," Bruce answered.

"How old is he?"

"He's just fourteen."

Carroll's jaw dropped. "Really? Fourteen? I've never seen a kid that young who was so poised and who could play like that."

"What's amazing," Bruce said, adopting a chattier tone, "is that he's a better football player than he is a basketball player."

"What position?"

"Quarterback."

"Did you say quarterback?"

"Yeah. Roberto's a quarterback. And he's a better quarterback than he is a basketball player."

Carroll thought for a moment. "What school does he go to, again?"

"Santa Barbara High."

Carroll paused, as if making a mental note, and then he shook Bruce's hand and complimented him one last time on Roberto's abilities.

That chance meeting was the first link in a chain of unlikely events, but its immediate effect was to brighten Bruce's mood, which was no small occurrence. Bruce had large, sad eyes that suited his disposition most days. He was six foot four but walked hunched over and with his head down, as if burdened by the weight of life. He lived in one of the most pristine beach cities in America, a place where, on average, the sun shined 285 days of the year. Yet by looking at him you'd have guessed it rained above his head every day.

Bruce's playing and coaching career had not gone as he'd planned, and that fact was the seed of his discontent. A high school star in Columbus, Ohio, he was recruited by Jerry Tarkanian, then the coach at Cal State Long Beach (now Long Beach State), and told to spend a year at Santa Barbara City College before transferring to play for the 49ers. But then Tarkanian left for UNLV, and Bruce ended up playing for a lesser program. He found his calling as coach of the boys' team at Dos Pueblos High and led that school to the section finals in the 1995–96 season, only his second as coach. Then an influential coach at a rival school in the same district pushed Dos Pueblos to enforce a previously ignored regulation that mandated that every coach be a full-time teacher. Bruce did not have a teaching credential, and losing that job decimated him. His life spiraled downward from there, and a short time later he split with Roberto's mother. She moved to Hesperia, a desert between the Inland Empire and Las Vegas, and Bruce rented a two-bedroom apartment on Santa Barbara's west side, where he and Roberto lived like two bachelors: dirty dishes in the sink, a pair of basketball shoes on the kitchen table, unopened mail piled up near the front door.

Bruce could have worked to get his teaching credential and would certainly have gotten another coaching job at one of the local high schools. But he wallowed in his misfortune, blaming others rather than taking the steps needed to remedy his situation. He hated his night job as a rehabilitation assistant at a facility for the mentally disabled, carrying patients to the bathroom and cleaning up after them; he hated that the best coaching position he could get was as an assistant at Santa Barbara High, earning a measly $3,000 a year; he hated that, while everyone acknowledged his stout basketball mind, no one would make him a head coach again. Waves of sorrow rolled over him, and there were days it seemed Bruce would sink into it and never surface.

Roberto kept him afloat. "He is the only thing that keeps my heart beating," Bruce said.

It was not only Roberto's prospects as an athlete, not only that people like Pete Carroll praised his ability: It was that Roberto never allowed life's obstacles to deter him. Roberto never saw gloom, only possibility.

"Dad, I want to play golf," he announced one day during his freshman year. He had never played the game, and Bruce didn't have money to get him a nice set of clubs. Bruce warned him that he might feel out of place, a black teenager on the golf courses of Santa Barbara with his secondhand sticks. "Who cares?" he said. "I want to play." He would show up at a course, his shorts hanging down to his calves, not another African American in sight, and stroll into the pro shop as if he'd been playing there for years. He got so good so quickly that he eventually made the varsity golf team and got his handicap down to eight.

Great players just know they are good, and Roberto had that, but his confidence came across as selective blindness, not arrogance. He never accepted the notion that someone could be better than he was or that he might fail. And when he did lose, the defeat didn't stick with him as long as it did with other kids. It wasn't that he didn't care; he just knew there would always be another game to play. He was the only one of the

Team Cal kids to play three sports in high school (basketball, golf, and, eventually, football).

Roberto's approach to life was so different from his father's that he would have been forgiven for rebelling. Instead, he pulled Bruce closer, reversing the normal roles of a father and his son. Roberto encouraged Bruce, talking about the brightness of their future, how Bruce would move to wherever he went to college and then, if they were lucky, an NBA city after that. "Just the Two of Us," a Will Smith remake of the Bill Withers song, was the tune Roberto chose to play whenever his dad called his cell phone. "That's how it is, you know, just me and my dad," Roberto explained. "Like the song says, 'We can make it if we try.'"

Roberto was the only member of Team Cal to star in his first year of high school. The *Los Angeles Times* wrote about the 21 points he scored, including 17 in the second half, and thirteen rebounds, in a playoff victory over Anaheim Loara. He scored 32 against Ventura High, which would eventually win a section title. Roberto's teammates were a step up from what surrounded Demetrius at FoHi, but not a big step, and he helped improve the Dons from 13–17 the year before he got there to 18–10. Cal-Hi Sports, the state's best canvasser of prep athletics, named him the state's Freshman of the Year.

Coaches often drop the cliché that a player "makes those around him better." Identifying the qualities that form that ability can be difficult. Being a strong passer with good vision helps, but there are also intangibles much harder to quantify. Watching Roberto play for Santa Barbara High, you recognized that some kids were just born knowing how to dissect the game to their benefit and to the benefit of those around them. In the years ahead, some of the best players in Southern California, including Renardo Sidney and DeMar DeRozan, would ask Roberto to play on their grassroots teams, and, as in the case of Sidney, their high school teams as well. This was because the whole game just flowed better when you were teamed with Roberto.

That might have been what Pete Carroll noticed when he watched Roberto play against his son's team. Bruce can't say for certain. They did not speak again, nor does he know precisely what Carroll did with the information that Roberto was a star quarterback. Bruce couldn't help but think of Carroll, however, when less than a week after their encounter he received the first of several calls from parents and alumni affiliated with St. Bonaventure High in Ventura. St. Bonaventure was a football power; the year before, it had won its fifth section title in six years. More importantly, USC frequently recruited the school's players and had recently landed two recruiters from there. These parents said they had heard about Roberto's exploits as a Pop Warner player and called Bruce into the fall and winter, through Roberto's first basketball season, posing the same question over and over: What would it take to get Roberto to transfer to St. Bonaventure for his sophomore year?

In February, Bruce received a call from Jon Mack, the school's athletic director and longtime football coach. He asked the same question as the parents had: What would it take to get Roberto? During that conversation and later, when Bruce visited with Mack at the school, he provided an answer. "I'm a basketball coach, and the only reason I would pull Roberto out of Santa Barbara would be because I got a job as a head coach at another school." It just so happened, Mack told him, that the St. Bonaventure job was opening up. They discussed what Bruce would need to build a successful basketball program, including the number of scholarships he would have at his disposal. Feeling confident that a deal could be struck, Mack showed Bruce a schedule of the football team's off-season workouts, and they examined how many practices, if any, Roberto would have to miss while playing in AAU tournaments. Mack said the school would pay for Roberto to attend a summer camp run by former New York Jets quarterback Ken O'Brien. He didn't mention that Pete Carroll and O'Brien were friendly (Carroll had been O'Brien's offensive coordinator with the Jets) or that O'Brien had once coached at USC.

Mack gave Bruce until the end of April to make a decision. A week before that deadline, as Bruce braced to tell Roberto that he would be transferring to St. Bonaventure, he got a call from Jeff Lavender, the basketball coach at Santa Barbara High. He had heard about the overture from St. Bonaventure, he said, and was willing to do whatever was necessary to keep Roberto at Santa Barbara High.

"Well, you basically have to let us have the program," Bruce told him. "You can still be part of the program—we don't want to run you away. I don't want that perception out there. But I would want more control of the program. We gotta get a style of offense in here that suits the way Roberto plays. Your style doesn't fit him. Plus, I want my son to learn how to play man-to-man defense. You're playing zone."

Lavender responded: "I'll do whatever you need."

The next day, Santa Barbara High fired its football coach. "When I heard that, I realized Roberto and I were in the middle of something, that things were happening that I didn't know about," Bruce said. No one ever told him that the football coach was fired to entice Roberto to stay, but "everyone knew that the coach was one reason Roberto and I decided he wouldn't play football as a freshman."

The following Monday, Bruce informed Mack that he and Roberto were staying put.

"It was just so crazy, the whole thing," Bruce said. "But I kept most of it from Roberto. I'd be dealing with this mess and he'd be out on the golf course."

Like all the boys of Team Cal, Roberto was a grassroots free agent, available to join any team now that the dream of keeping the boys together under Keller had died. St. Bonaventure's courtship ended about the time his recruitment by the top AAU teams in Southern California came to a head.

The highest level of grassroots basketball was Under-17. When kids talked about playing for SCA or EBO or Pump N Run, they meant the Under-17 teams of those programs. It was not unique for a freshman like Roberto to play for an Under-17 team—that is what most of the elite young prospects did—but it wasn't always the wisest move. Was a prospect better served playing Under-15 or Under-16, giving his body another year to develop? Would he get the minutes he needed on an Under-17 team stacked with older players? Mats and the Pumps and other coaches who had seen Roberto play with Team Cal knew he was good, but now, like Pete Carroll, their jaws dropped when they witnessed his composure and skill. Whereas they might have once seen Roberto as a nice addition to their U-17 teams, he was now a player they could build around, and he became the most coveted young player in Southern California.

Nike and Adidas were Roberto's primary suitors. (Intermediates for Pat Barrett called Bruce, pushing SCA and Reebok, but he never got into the running.) Nike waged a steady campaign, led by Don Crenshaw, Nike's manager of high school basketball, and Mike Lewis, the coach of The Swoosh's top team in the area, California Hoops. Crenshaw began sending Nike gear to Roberto's apartment early in his freshman season. Over a six-month period, he shipped him twenty pairs of shoes, three sweat suits, and an untold number of socks, T-shirts, headbands, and hats. Roberto gave the hats to his dad, who quickly compiled an impressive collection. Sometimes the gear would arrive unsolicited; other times, Roberto would see a pair of shoes he liked—perhaps the newest from Michael Jordan's Jumpman line, or the new Kobe Bryant shoe—and either he or Bruce would call Crenshaw and ask him to ship a pair to Santa Barbara. In his role as Roberto's personal shoe valet, Crenshaw never failed to come through.

Adidas's push came care of the Pumps. One or both of the brothers attended a few of Roberto's high school games and called regularly. One weekend day, they picked Roberto up and took him to the Adidas outlet store near Ventura and bought him twelve pairs of shoes. They later gifted him with a black leather jacket with the logos of all the NBA teams on it, which retailed for nearly $1,000. They also promised to pay the airfare and lodging for Bruce and Roberto's mother so they could attend every tournament.

On January 22, Bruce, Roberto, and eight of his high school teammates attended a game between the Los Angeles Clippers and the Golden State Warriors at the Staples Center. Their tickets came care of the Pumps, and they were no ordinary seats. "We had a whole luxury box to ourselves," Roberto said. That impressed Bruce, as did the Pumps' promise that Jim Harrick, the former coach at UCLA, Rhode Island, and Georgia, would be Roberto's coach. "It's got to be a good thing to have a coach like that working with Roberto," Bruce said. That was debatable. Harrick had been fired from Georgia after the uncovering of multiple NCAA violations, including academic fraud. Rhode Island and UCLA also ran afoul of the NCAA under his watch, and he left the college game branded as one of the sport's biggest cheats. No amount of wrongdoing, however, could disqualify him from coaching at the grassroots level.

The Pumps organized back-to-back practices at Loyola Marymount over one weekend, which included about two dozen players they were considering. Roberto played the first day but told Bruce afterward that he didn't want to return for day 2. "Too many guards," he told his dad. The Pumps had a number of backcourt players, including Larry Drew, Jr., and the son of NBA coach Mike Dunleavy.

It appeared Nike and California Hoops would win by default, but before making a decision, Bruce asked a friend to set up a meeting with Sonny Vaccaro.

As with Joe Keller more than two years earlier, the reception Bruce received upon arriving at Vaccaro's home in Calabasas overwhelmed him. "I'm just honored that you would have me in your home," he said several times as Vaccaro and Pam showed him around. They took him outside to see the pool and the hummingbirds, and then they sat down in the kitchen for pasta with Italian sausage.

Bruce referred to Vaccaro as "Mr. Vaccaro," even though they were not that far apart in age and even after Vaccaro asked him repeatedly to call him "Sonny." Sonny knew some of the players Bruce grew up with in Columbus, and they also talked about Connie Hawkins, the former ABA and NBA star. Vaccaro had met him when he played for the Pittsburgh Pipers of the ABA; Bruce was introduced to Hawkins after he was traded to the Lakers late in his career.

Vaccaro asked Bruce about his ex-wife and then about Roberto, but not about Roberto's basketball skills. How was he as a student? What athletes did he admire? What were his interests other than basketball? Bruce looked embarrassed telling Vaccaro that Roberto had recently joined his high school's golf team.

"Oh, my goodness, that is wonderful. Pammy, did you hear that? Young Roberto plays golf. How wonderful for him!"

After lunch, they moved upstairs to Vaccaro's office and sat side by side on a leather couch underneath the window. Behind Vaccaro's desk was a portrait of former Pittsburgh Pirates outfielder Roberto Clemente.

"That's my favorite athlete," Vaccaro said after Bruce asked him about the picture.

"Mine too," Bruce said. "That is who I named my son after."

Bruce struggled to formulate his questions on how to best steer Roberto's career. He lumped several issues together: choosing a team, staying at Santa Barbara High versus moving to a more heralded school close to L.A., and the need for Roberto to play at one of the big shoe-company camps that summer. Vaccaro let him ramble on, then put his hand on his arm and said, "Okay, let's look at this one at a time. Let's start with the camps, because everyone knows that is my thing. I'll say this up front: Roberto's in my camp right now. I've never seen him play, but from what I've heard and now meeting you, he has a spot in the ABCD Camp if he wants to go and if you decide that is the best thing for him. And, I think, if he is ready, he should go to one of the camps—

if not mine, then the Nike Camp or the Adidas [Superstar] Camp. . . . What he has to do, and it may not be this year but at some point, he has to make a name for himself at one of the camps. That's where . . . see, there, it's like a bonfire at the camp: You're good and then all of a sudden you get the attention, and that's where it'll explode. It's not the same as at these tournaments everyone plays in. There are some tournaments—Bob Gibbons's tournament or the Vegas tournaments—where everyone goes and he will be seen by everyone, but most of these events, even if he goes to twenty a summer, they just don't matter, because everybody's not there.

"But I want to stress that going to one of these camps . . . he shouldn't do it unless he is ready. Maybe he is ready now. That is what I hear, but if he isn't, there is nothing wrong with letting him grow some more. What happens at these big camps and these big tournaments is that Roberto gets assigned a number. I know he already has a number from Clark Francis and these other people, but he goes there and they are going to all put a new number on him, and we gotta make sure he is ready to handle that number. It's not important that he gets a high [ranking] now. That's not important. What is important is that he can handle whatever [ranking] they give him. Look at that poor kid he used to play with, what's his name . . . Demetrius, right? The worst thing that ever happened is that Demetrius was [ranked] number one. That poor kid, people are going to see him as a failure the rest of his life. That doesn't mean he won't go to college, won't have a good career, might still play in the NBA. That doesn't mean that at all. But he is carrying this burden, and it will get to a point, if it hasn't already, where he won't be able to look his peers in the face anymore."

Bruce mentioned that Nike and Don Crenshaw were pushing California Hoops and that they were leaning toward that team.

"Okay, now you are in Sonny territory. This is great. From what you told me earlier, your son has friends up in Santa Barbara he likes to be with and, you said, he likes to play golf and might play football too. Well, let him be with his friends! Let him play golf! Let him play football! Nothing is going to happen for him playing AAU ball with the Pumps or this Nike team, California whatever Hoops. Nothing matters this year when he is, what, only a freshman? The only reason to do it would be to get Ben [Howland] and coaches like that interested, and we already know they are interested. After this summer, Roberto has two more years of this. Plenty of time. What you don't want to do is break him. You don't want to put him in a situation where he is unhappy, where he's not playing or whatever. That makes it tedious, hard, and he could stop loving the game the way he does now."

Vaccaro acknowledged that his advice ran contrary to his mission with Reebok. He should have pushed Bruce to have Roberto play for SCA or another Reebok team. "[But] I'm not going to lie to you," Vaccaro said. "Hey, I invented the whole damn thing, and I am telling you that your son doesn't need it right now."

Bruce told of St. Bonaventure's advances and how he regularly received calls from parents or coaches at Westchester, Mater Dei, and other schools. It was enticing to put Roberto on a team with a chance to win a state and section title. "If Roberto doesn't win enough games in high school, could that hurt him?"

"He could lose twenty games a year in high school and it won't matter," Vaccaro said. "And he could win three state titles and that wouldn't matter either. There is no need for him to go to one of those schools. And, thank God for Roberto, you don't live in Westchester or Compton. So, maybe that means you don't get in the *L.A. Times* every week. So what? You live in this beautiful place and Roberto can just grow there, away from all this shit."

By the conclusion of their three-hour meeting, Bruce was nodding enthusiastically at every word. As Vaccaro led Bruce downstairs, he made him promise to return in a few weeks with Roberto.

After giving Bruce a hug and watching Pam do the same, Vaccaro said, "I bet one of the things that makes your son a good player is he doesn't care what other people say about him."

"That's true," Bruce said.

"Well, then, you need to be more like your son. Just be a good father, stay involved, and don't worry about what other people think."

Back in Santa Barbara later that night, Bruce and Roberto came to a decision: Roberto would play for Mike Lewis and California Hoops, but only in events of his choosing. If at any point he wished to play for the Pumps or Barrett or another team, he would do it, regardless of how Don Crenshaw or anyone at Nike felt about it.

Throughout the spring, players, parents, and coaches asked Roberto what AAU team he had chosen, and his response was always "No one."

"No, I mean, are you playing for a Nike team or an Adidas team or a Reebok team?" they would say, as if Roberto were confused.

"Not Nike or Adidas or Reebok," he would answer. "I play for me."

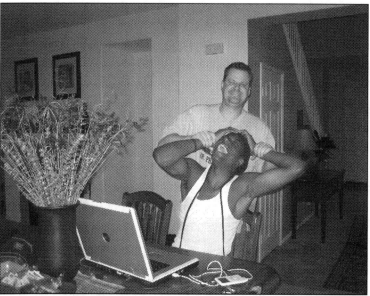

(GEORGE DOHRMANN)

Joe Keller and Demetrius Walker in 2006

e's hiding in the bathroom, Joe," Dave Taylor said into his cell phone. "Did you hear me? He's hiding in the fucking bathroom, in a stall."

On the other end of the line, Keller sighed.

Taylor looked around. A few yards from where he stood in the gym at the Suwannee Sports Academy were more than 100 of the best young basketball players in the country, and he didn't want them to overhear his remarks. He wasn't shouting, but his statements were firm. He had been around Keller long enough to know that he didn't respond to subtleties.

"Do you understand what I am saying, Joe? He's in the bathroom. Right now. Hiding."

Keller was across the country, in his home in Moreno Valley, but the distance did not lessen the gravity of the situation. Demetrius Walker, the prodigy *Sports Illustrated* had labeled the next LeBron, the young soul Keller often bragged was "like my son," was hiding in a bathroom on the third day of the 2006 Adidas Superstar Camp, the most important event of his grassroots season. College recruiters lined the walls of the gym, and many had circled Demetrius's name in their programs, anxious to see if he'd improved from the previous summer. Now, with his future hanging in the air like a ball on the rim, he cowered in a bathroom stall.

"I don't know if he can ever come back from this, Joe," Taylor said into his phone. "Do you understand, Joe? Do you hear what I am saying? This is it for him. This is it! It's the bottom. Demetrius has hit the fucking bottom."

The bottom came during a July week of overcast days, the air thick with the promise of rain and a wisp of southern wind. It reminded me of the week of Nationals in Memphis, when on the last day a storm knocked out the power and it looked as if the finals against the War Eagles would never be played. That day ended with Demetrius asleep on the plane, the glass-bowl trophy in his lap, Keller next to him sipping a beer and reveling in how far they had come together.

Joe and D.

Their partnership had taken them to wondrous heights, but in Memphis greater achievements seemed certain. There was Keller, his shoe deal in place but his Jr. Phenom Camp riches yet to come, his financial fate still moored to his young star. And there was D, the number-1 player in the country, as hard a worker as any of the boys, fearless and full of himself in that way that great athletes have to be.

There had always been something worrisome about their bond—a coach who'd been no father to his own son, Joey, leaping into that role for one of his players—and a happy ending was never preordained. But the broader strokes of Demetrius's failure couldn't have been predicted. It came so soon—two months before he turned sixteen—and Keller was so utterly absent, so unwilling to do anything but let their partnership dissolve. Even in the grassroots game, where tragedies outnumbered successes, this one was epic.

In the months leading up to the Superstar Camp, Demetrius sensed that his great undressing was afoot. "I really don't want to go," he said.

"[But] I know Adidas wants me there, so I guess I just gotta suck it up and play. But, you know, I haven't been playing a lot lately. "

Roberto, Justin, Andrew, Jordan, and the other Team Cal kids played a packed schedule with their new grassroots teams in the spring and early summer when Demetrius had played only sparingly, and once again Keller was to blame. Keller realized his contract with Adidas stipulated that he operate a grassroots team and enter it into the top tournaments. He created a shell of a team and hired Dave Taylor to coach it. Taylor lived in Sacramento and naturally recruited players from that area and held practices there, few of which Demetrius attended. Keller also operated the team with an eye on keeping costs down; he entered it into the minimum number of events.

If you saw Demetrius walking the street, he appeared as fit as ever. He was sinewy and his biceps were bigger, as he'd recently begun lifting weights. But inactivity had left him in such poor shape that he got fatigued early in games, making it impossible to sustain solid play. He would make a few stellar plays in a game's opening minutes but then grab at his shorts or put his hands on his knees during stoppages. That was the signal that his energy was gone, and he would do nothing of consequence the rest of the game.

Contrasted with the year before, when Keller considered the Superstar Camp the ultimate judgment on himself and his star player, his disinterest in even attending the event bespoke the change in his goals. His financial interests were no longer tied to Demetrius, and thus he couldn't be bothered to get him physically ready for the challenge.

Demetrius was not without friends at the Superstar Camp. Rome and Rome, Sr., were there, G.J. and Gerry as well. Dave Taylor also kept an eye on him. Compared to a year earlier, however, when Keller had watched his every move, Demetrius felt alone. On Wednesday, when the players learned what teams they were on and scrimmaged together, he looked around the gym at the many coaches—Mats, the Pumps, Jimmy Salmon—and said, "Everybody's got somebody here but me. It's like I got nobody in my corner anymore."

In his two games on Thursday, Demetrius attempted a total of twelve shots. Most players were so eager to get the attention of the college coaches that they gunned without even thinking. Demetrius acted as if shooting was a risk he couldn't afford.

"He's hiding on the court," Taylor said. "He's not doing anything that will draw attention to his game."

Taylor gave him a brief pep talk on Thursday night, during which Demetrius made a statement that alarmed him. "You know, D.T., I don't know if I want to do this anymore," he said.

"What do you mean?"

"This camp. I don't know that I want to come back next year. I just don't see the point anymore."

There was no guarantee that there would be a Superstar Camp the following summer. Adidas's purchase of Reebok eleven months earlier had shaken up the grassroots landscape, and the joint company talked of reconfiguring how they went after elite players. The camp model, where hundreds of kids were invited to one place, was inefficient.

"Don't worry about next year, worry about right now," Taylor told Demetrius. "People are wanting to see if you've improved from last time you were here, and you need to show them that you've gotten better."

The next morning was key, Taylor knew, as the coaches would watch the individual drills closely; they were better gauges of a player's abilities as a ballhandler, shooter, and defender than the games. Already a coach from Xavier had mentioned to Taylor that he was eager to scout Demetrius.

On Friday morning, just before the start of the day's first drill, Taylor scanned the gym. His gaze moved from one hopeful basketball player to the next as they stood two-deep around one side of a court, dressed in identical black-and-orange uniforms. Across the court were the college coaches they hoped to impress—Ben Howland, Bill Self, Bruce Pearl—so many that they almost outnumbered the players. In a few minutes, the instructor running the drill would yell out the names of two players, and they would be the first to be judged. Being called out first could be a blessing or a curse. Everyone remembered the opening duel, and it set the tone for the rest of the session.

Taylor had arranged for Armon Johnson, a guard he knew from Sacramento, to be one of the first two players selected. Taylor was awarding him prime placement to show his abilities, and now he had to decide who to match him against. Taylor's eyes moved down the sideline, finding some of the best talent in the country—Eric Gordon, Nolan Smith, Jerime Anderson—before finally stopping on a six-foot-three kid so eager to get under way that he jumped in place. Lance

Stephenson's presence at the Superstar Camp was one of the most anticipated developments of the summer. He was a Reebok kid, one of Sonny's boys, but at the last minute he switched from the ABCD Camp to the Superstar. (Vaccaro claimed that Adidas cut a sponsorship deal with his AAU coach and high school that exceeded $100,000.) It was a major get for Adidas, and Stephenson arrived with a camera crew in tow, as his every move was being filmed for a documentary. The full wattage of the New York spotlight had found him, but it hadn't changed the way he played, at least not yet. In a game the previous day, Stephenson picked up a loose ball and broke down the court, and the fans rose in anticipation of a thunderous dunk. But Oscar Bellfield, Justin's teammate on Taft, caught up with Stephenson and blocked his shot from behind, sending it out of bounds. The players, fans, and even a few of the college coaches hooted in delight. It was the most talked-about play of the day. What Taylor thought of as he considered pairing Stephenson with Armon was how Stephenson had reacted after being embarrassed. He immediately demanded the ball and used a screen to isolate Bellfield. He faked as if he were going to drive on him but then shot a 3-pointer over him. As the ball fell through the net, Stephenson got into Bellfield's face, jarring at him, and then he checked Bellfield with his shoulder as he ran back on defense. His instinct after being showed up was to go right back at Bellfield, to erase a humiliating moment with a spectacular play of his own.

Taylor saw a probing look in Stephenson's eyes, as if he were searching the gym for the next challenger to his throne. *It's tempting*, Taylor thought. If Armon showed him up, that would get the attention of the coaches. But then a better choice came to mind.

Demetrius.

Pitting him against Armon could boost Demetrius's stock and his confidence. They were about the same height and weight, and although Armon was a better shooter, Demetrius was more explosive and a little stronger. Most significantly, Demetrius had played with Armon. He knew his game, his strengths. He couldn't possibly fear a challenge from Armon.

Taylor looked around the gym for Demetrius. He knew he was there; he had noticed him when he got off the bus, because Demetrius wore different shoes—blue Promodels—from the rest of the campers. That had annoyed Taylor at the time, but it would now make Demetrius easier to find.

Taylor moved his focus to the players' feet, hunting for those blue shoes. He was still searching minutes later when the coach leading the drill called out Armon and then, after getting no indication from Taylor of who else to pick, selected a player at random.

Where the fuck is Demetrius? Taylor thought. There was no way for him to go back to the hotel, and the trainer's table was visible from where he stood. If he wasn't at one of those two places, that left only one possibility.

Taylor strode across the gym and pushed open the door to the bathroom, stopping just inside. No one was at the sink or at the urinals, and it looked as if all the stalls were empty. Then something caught Taylor's eye, something in the second-to-last stall. He took a step closer and leaned down, and then he saw them: the blue shoes. The accessory Demetrius had chosen to stand out had given him away.

Taylor quickly left the bathroom and sat in a chair near the door, positioned so Demetrius couldn't rejoin the group of players without passing him. He looked at the time on his cell phone. There were fifty minutes left in the two-hour session of individual drills, and he guessed Demetrius had been in there since the start.

The minutes passed and Taylor assumed Demetrius would emerge only after the final drill was complete, when he could blend in with the rest of the campers as if he'd never been gone and catch the bus back to the hotel. At the thought of this, Taylor dialed Keller's number.

Prior to the start of the camp, Keller predicted that Demetrius would feign injury or sickness to avoid competing. On Friday morning, when Taylor called Keller while sitting outside the bathroom waiting for Demetrius, Keller reminded him of his earlier comments.

"So you were right, Joe. So what now?"

Keller didn't say anything.

"Joe, kids like Demetrius are why people say all these bad things about AAU basketball. What has happened to him makes everyone look bad. He shouldn't even be here. He's afraid to compete."

Keller remained silent.

Demetrius emerged forty-five minutes later, just as the individual drills were breaking up, as players headed to the exit and the waiting buses. Had Taylor not been sitting there, Demetrius would have joined the rest of the campers, and his absence might have gone unnoticed.

"You been in there the whole time?" Taylor said.

"Yeah, my stomach is messed up, D.T." Demetrius put his hand to his belly.

Taylor led him to the bus and told him to get some rest back at the hotel.

"He's quitting, Joe," Taylor told Keller in a later phone call. "He's not even a sophomore in high school and he's giving up."

Keller offered another "I told you so" and called Demetrius "soft" and "weak."

"That's not good enough, Joe. Tell me what you are going to do about it. Saying D is fucked-up is not enough. You are responsible for him. Don't just tell me how fucked-up he is, tell me how you are going to fix him."

Taylor pushed hard enough that Keller made hollow-sounding pledges. *I promise I am going to take D back under my belt. I'm going to refocus him and get him back on track. I promise you that,* he wrote in one text message. *I love that kid like my own son.*

The final game Demetrius played at the Superstar Camp came Friday afternoon. There were games scheduled for Friday night and another round Saturday, but he would skip those, citing a stomach illness. The final impression he would make would come against Rome's team, and at the start he walked to the center of the court and playfully stuck a finger in Rome's chest and said, "I got this guy."

"I thought he would go right at me," Rome would say later. "He knows he can get by me."

He did drive past Rome on a few possessions, but he refused to continue toward the rim. He either dished to a teammate or pulled the ball out to the perimeter. He attempted only three shots, missing all of them, and allowed Rome to score 13 points, mostly on little pull-up jumpers and hustle play that took advantage of Demetrius's poor conditioning.

"It's sad seeing Demetrius play without any intensity," Rome, Sr., said before the game was even over. "It's like he is a different person."

Added Gerry: "It used to be that when Demetrius was playing, you almost didn't notice anyone else. Now you hardly notice *him.*"

The college coaches at the camp didn't expect Demetrius or any of the young players to exhibit a completely refined game. When scouting kids entering their sophomore year in high school, they looked only for small signs that a prospect could make the jump to the next level. A little burst of speed, an athletic finish on a drive to the rim, or a signature skill, such as G.J.'s passing or Justin's defense, was all they needed to see in order for their interest in that player to continue. The mental side of it was also important. Lance Stephenson's competitiveness, even if it made a mess of games as he attempted crazy shot after crazy shot, was something the coaches wanted to see from Demetrius. They didn't expect him to dominate as he had as a middle schooler, but they wanted to see him try.

Demetrius gave them nothing. Even worse, he planted a poisonous seed in their minds: *Was Demetrius afraid to compete?* There was no room for fear in big-time basketball. A coach could teach a player to be a better ball handler or shooter or defender, but he couldn't teach courage. Even if Demetrius was indeed sick—the college coaches did not know that he was faking—they wanted to see him fight through it. Even if he got his shot blocked five times in a row, they wanted him to attack the rim again. That was what Lance Stephenson did.

The recruiters talked to Taylor, and he knew the extent of the damage Demetrius had done. They questioned his basketball ability and his mental toughness. Most said flatly that they weren't interested in him.

"I don't know if he is a [Division I] prospect anymore," Taylor said. "Maybe some low-major like Loyola Marymount or Long Beach [State] might get interested, but no big programs."

On Saturday afternoon, Phil Bryant, the director of the camp, gave a closing address. He stood at the center of the middle court, the players in a circle around him. Demetrius was on the outer edge of that circle and paid no attention to Bryant as he read off the names of the campers who had been selected for one of the two all-star games.

"Will D come back from this? That is the question," Taylor said. He stood with his arms folded a few yards outside the circle, looking out over the hopeful kids. "He can. There is time. But if you are asking me if I think he will, well . . ."

His voice trailed off as Bryant ended his talk by telling the players: "Whoever it is who is responsible for you being here, say thank you." He then urged the players to give a round of applause to their AAU coaches. Demetrius's head shot up as the players around him applauded, and he clapped lightly three times, a nearly silent salute to the man responsible for his state.

nce Demetrius was back in California, Keller didn't begin working
him out again as he had promised. He barely spoke to him, and
when they did communicate, it was usually through text messages.

One of the few phone conversations they had came after the start of
school, in September, when Demetrius heard that The Hoop Scoop had
dropped him to number 215 in its rankings of prospects in the class of
2009. There was something fishy about Demetrius's placement. More
than a dozen players who'd once played for Keller were ranked ahead of
him, including Craig Payne, even though he had recently decided to
focus on football, believing that was his best chance at a college scholarship.

"How could they have me so low?" Demetrius asked Keller. "That's
bull."

"I told Clark to drop you that far," Keller confessed.

"Why would you do that?"

"I feel like you aren't working as hard as you can and that I need to
motivate you."

"You think that by embarrassing me that is going to motivate me?"

"I don't know what else to do. You've already got everything you
want—shoes and stuff—so there is nothing I can give you to motivate
you."

"That is bull. You are trashing my name. That's like the biggest slap
in the face ever. People are seeing that ranking and laughing at me."

That conversation triggered weeks of introspection as Demetrius focused on how Keller treated him in the present rather than what he had
done for him in the past. Meeting the bottom brought Demetrius clarity, most of all about Keller.

"You know, me and my mom have started talking a lot lately about
Coach Joe, and, I mean, I start thinking to myself, like, is it 'cuz of me
that Coach Joe is now living like he is? It eats me up sometimes, because
I don't really know the whole truth, but if it wasn't for me, if I had
joined another team, would Coach Joe be rich like he is now? Would his
name be as big as it is? My mom says that what Coach Joe has probably
has a lot to do with me, and I think she is right. 'Cuz, see, it went like
this: Adidas wanted a younger kid coming up that's gonna be good,
that's gonna be marketable. So whatever they had to do to get a kid like
that, they were going to do. And at the time Coach Joe had me. Which
means he got paid for it, for me. He got the Adidas shoe contract, with

the Adidas money, and everything else, and now he's got everything he wants and it's, like, you know, I'm down here and he has no time for me."

He felt betrayed, used, suddenly aware that the man who often claimed to love him like a son had only exploited him to get rich. Over the next several weeks, Demetrius composed a letter to Keller on his Sidekick. During class or alone in his room, he pecked out the words with his thumbs, and he labored to get across how he felt. He was still coming to terms with his feelings, and it was natural that the finished email centered less on how Keller made him feel and more on what Demetrius felt he was owed.

> I don't understand how you say I'm like your son, but you aren't there for me anymore. You came out of retirement and you found me and I made you who you are. If it wasn't for me being good you would have nothing. You got money from me being successful. You bought a house and Violet a car and you got wood floors all through your house and a big pool and what do I have?
>
> How come when I ask for shoes you take so long to get them for me or you don't get them at all? How come when I ask you for a ride or to come take me to work out you say you are going to come but then I just sit here and wait and you never show?

It was not a "Dear John" email. At no point did he express a desire to sever all ties with Coach Joe. There was anger behind his words but also fear. He had hit bottom, and he was scared. Keller had to know that even though Demetrius wrote of what he was owed, what he really coveted was for Coach Joe to be part of his life again. Yet Keller focused on the anger, on Demetrius's veiled demands to be compensated.

"When he started talking about the money I owed him, I knew that was it," Keller would say later. As he would do with anyone staking a claim to his hard-earned fortune, Keller cut Demetrius out of his life.

It's a shame we can't continue our relationship. I guess we have to go our separate ways, Keller wrote in response to Demetrius's email.

Demetrius replied immediately: *I don't want that.*

Keller wrote: *I wish we could solve all our issues but I guess we will have to go our separate ways.*

Demetrius reached out to Keller a few times after that—when he was looking for a new grassroots team, when he was deciding whether to stay at FoHi, after he and his mom got into a fight. He sent Keller text messages, and sometimes Keller responded, but most often he did not. Eventually Demetrius stopped trying, and Keller was out of his life forever.

"Man, I'm not gonna lie, it does hurt. I mean, I looked at stuff like . . . like he was my pops, you know. I didn't have a pops and he was like my pops and, you know, okay, I'll just say it: I loved him like he was my pops."

Early in 2007, I traveled to Moreno Valley to say goodbye to Joe Keller.

We would still keep in contact, of course, and I gave updates on Demetrius and his other former players even after he stopped asking for them, but his journey was over. He had gone from a punch line, the guy who lost Tyson Chandler, to one of the most important figures in basketball, the Sonny of middle schoolers. The ending he had long sought had arrived, and he didn't see the advantage in letting me remain inside his world. Phone calls had begun to go unanswered, messages unreturned. When I did reach him, he was annoyed by my inquiries.

Keller greeted me at the door of his home with a hug and asked that I not tease him about the weight he'd gained. He was pleased to be able to show off his house and led me from room to room. The kitchen had been completely redone, with dark cabinets, stainless-steel appliances, and an extra refrigerator with a glass front, full of the Gatorades and soft drinks Keller preferred. New wood floors covered the kitchen, den, and dining and living rooms. The house looked as if it had recently undergone a makeover. There was an overabundance of candles, vases, lamps, and pillows, and ornate place settings were arranged perfectly in front of every seat at the dining table.

The most obvious sign of Keller's prosperity was his backyard. His bean-shaped pool had a waterfall along the far side that was so large you had to raise your voice to be heard over the rush of water. There was a circular spa attached to the pool and a thatched-roof cabana nearby. "My pool's better than Sonny's, don't you think?" Keller said as we took seats at a tall bar table. "Sonny's house is probably still nicer than mine, but my pool is better."

Keller knew I wanted to talk about Demetrius, and he tried to avoid it by rattling off the projects he had in the works, including the purchase of a sports bar, the renovation of the guest bathroom, and the redecorating of his downstairs office. "I also think I am going to buy the house next door," he said. "That's right, Joe Keller is not done buying houses. We are going to buy the one next door and then another one at the end [of the cul-de-sac]. Violet's sister is going to move into one and her parents into the other one. I told them, 'Just keep it as an investment.' All they have to do is pay the taxes on it, which is like three thousand a year."

Business had never been better, he said. He was starting another camp, Phenom Elite, which he said would resemble Sonny's ABCD Camp, and he had recently partnered with former NBA player Antonio Davis. They'd visited with Adidas officials in Portland a few months earlier, and Keller claimed that the three-day summit had changed his perspective on developing young phenoms.

"I'm telling you, we're going to change basketball. Kids now, they think everything should just be given to them. And then when they don't make it, they don't know anything and aren't educated about how to live. We are going to change that by doing all this educational stuff at our camps. We are going to have these assessments for kids, and we are going to have educational stuff for the parents. We're going to do more of that stuff than the basketball stuff. . . . You know what, I know what you are going to say, and I'm at fault for a lot of it because I didn't do it the right way. But Antonio and me, we are going to end that. It took Antonio and me getting together and figuring things out for me to see what is best for kids."

Without being provoked, Keller brought up Demetrius, although he put him at a distance. He was just one of those kids who didn't learn how to manage life.

"D's gotta make some choices in life. I don't think he knows what he is going to do, and, see, that is what I am talking about. That is the problem. Everyone did everything for him. Everyone makes excuses for him. . . . Kisha, she doesn't help. She sent me a letter the other day. She was saying, 'It's your fault,' or some shit like that. Everything she talks about is so negative. . . . She wrote, 'I never thought you were the kind of person that was gonna just leave. Why would you leave him? Why wouldn't you be there for him every minute of his life?' I didn't respond, but I was thinking, *Lady, you want me to forget my whole family for you and your son?* And the thing is, all the money I used to spend on the team, on D and Aaron and all the kids, I now spend on *my* family. And Violet's so much happier, and Jordan and Alyssa are happier, and *I'm* happier.

"With D—and I know what you are going to say: There are some things that I could help him with, like finding a new school and a new [AAU] team—I *could* help him, but, fuck it, you know, with Kisha involved now, and her attitude, fuck it, I'm done. I'm not going to hold his hand anymore. People holding his hand was what fucked him up in the first place."

Keller's attitude reminded me of something playwright Arthur Miller once said about one of his characters, a patriarch named, coincidentally, Joe Keller. Miller described the Joe Keller in *All My Sons* as having "a crazy quilt of motivations and contradictions in his head." The real-life Keller had his own crazy quilt, among several similarities between him and Miller's character. The fictitious Joe Keller was a self-made businessman who, despite no education, rose to great heights, driven by the desire to provide for his family and achieve the American Dream. But in his greed, he knowingly shipped airplane parts that were defective, resulting in the deaths of several pilots, including his son. He lied about his culpability, letting his partner take the blame.

The salient difference between the two Joe Kellers was in the endings to their stories. The structure of *All My Sons* was intended "to bring a man into the direct path of the consequences he wrought," Miller said. At the end of the play, Keller kills himself offstage, proving the existence of social justice.

The grassroots-basketball society was not a just one, and the real Joe Keller would never face the consequences of what he wrought. His camps would remain full; parents would still dial his number, hoping to land a spot for their children; his business would expand to the point that he estimated he could sell it for $10 million. The American Dream was alive and well in his Moreno Valley home, and the demise of Demetrius would never threaten that.

Before leaving Moreno Valley, I asked Keller for some photos of the team that he had promised me. We went into his office and he searched for a long time, going through a file cabinet and a dozen boxes piled up in his closet. He got frustrated and repeatedly called out to Violet to help him. She shouted directions, but he still couldn't find his "Team Cal box." She finally came into the room and helped him locate an un-labeled medium-sized brown box at the very bottom of the closet. Keller pulled out programs and pictures and a manila folder that contained the birth certificates of the players. He had once needed them to prove that his amazing collection of phenoms were indeed as young as he said. He tossed them to me unceremoniously and asked that I return them to the players or their parents.

As I prepared to leave, a pile of pictures and birth certificates in my arms, I noticed the glass-bowl trophy given to the team at the 2004 Na-tionals. It occupied an inconspicuous spot in his office, atop a file cabi-net in the corner. Keller had begun purchasing signed sports memorabilia that he intended to place around the room, and it was easy to imagine the trophy from Nationals getting supplanted by a bat signed by Derek Jeter or a football helmet autographed by Terrell Owens. In time, it would likely find its way into that box at the bottom of the closet, shoved in with what few memories he had yet to purge.

I pointed to the trophy and asked Keller what he planned to do with it.

"What do you mean?"

Would it still have a place in his office after the remodel? If not, did he want me to take it, to give it to Demetrius or Rome or Aaron? They would surely display it proudly; nothing they had accomplished had meant more.

"Hell no!" Keller said. "Are you crazy? I'm not giving it to *them*. That is mine. I earned that."

A few weeks later, Kisha found Demetrius alone in his room, sitting on his bed. After his struggles during his freshman season and at the Adidas Superstar Camp, *ESPN The Magazine* wrote a brief story about him titled "Didn't you used to be?" The *Riverside Press-Enterprise* wrote its own obituary of his career, quoting Clark Francis as saying: "The question is, how bad does Demetrius want it? I don't think he has the burning desire to be great." Demetrius didn't tack those articles to the wall above his bed, where the *Sports Illustrated* article labeling him the "next LeBron" still hung, along with other clippings from his glory days.

Kisha sat next to him and, after a moment, Demetrius looked at her and asked, "Mom, am I going to end up like Schea Cotton?" Without pause, she jumped into a lengthy explanation for why that would not be his fate, how he wouldn't be just another touted young player who never lived up to the hype. But Demetrius had succinctly stated what was now the great question. Whereas the debate had once been how good he could be—whether he was the next LeBron James or just a future NBA player—it was now where he would rank on the list of the greatest flops.

The grassroots machine rarely allowed for a player's ending to be rewritten; it was easier to just shift focus to the next junior phenom. So when you mentioned Demetrius's name to prominent AAU coaches like Mats or the Pumps, they spoke as if the case on him was closed, his career dead. "It's sad how he ended up," one of the Pumps said at a tournament in Arizona.

It never occurred to them that a sixteen-year-old might rediscover that "burning desire"—that a great success story might start at the bottom.

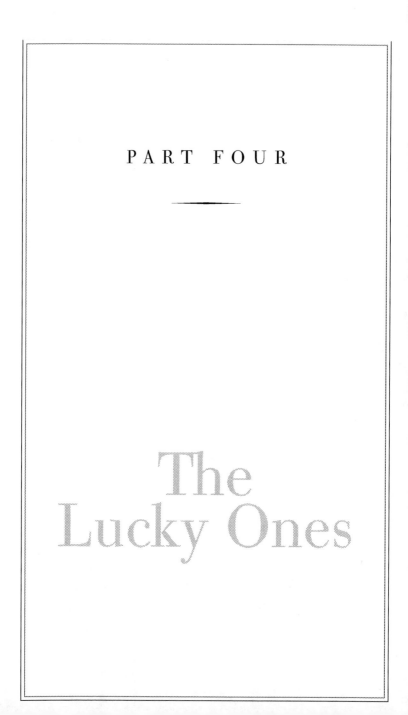

PART FOUR

The
Lucky Ones

28

(NICK KOZA)

Aaron Moore playing for Dominguez High in 2007

About the time the grassroots world anointed Demetrius one of its biggest flops, he received a phone call from Aaron Moore.

They had not spoken in almost a year, since Aaron chastised Demetrius for refusing to play hurt in Team Cal's final game, and time had not dulled their enmity, at least not on Demetrius's end.

"Why you calling me?" Demetrius said after Aaron identified himself.

"I thought maybe it would be cool to talk," Aaron said. There was a tinge of wanting in his voice, and that confused Demetrius.

"Why would I want to talk to someone who keeps starting rumors about me? I hear all the time how you're talking shit about me."

"Whatever, nigger, you are hardly on my mind," Aaron said, now on the defensive.

"If I'm hardly on your mind, why you calling me?"

"I was talking to a friend and he said I should call you and see what's up."

"I got nothing to talk to you about."

"All right, then, nigger."

"All right."

That exchange troubled Demetrius for days. Why had Aaron thought it was okay to call him? What did he *really* want to talk about? He regretted not letting Aaron say a little more, to discover what he was after. Demetrius eventually concluded that Aaron had probably called to gloat, and that wouldn't have been out of character. Aaron continued to compare himself to Demetrius long after they stopped being teammates. Hearing about Demetrius's struggles as a freshman and at the Superstar Camp pleased him. He also obsessed over the rankings, and seeing Demetrius fall into the 200s validated the point he'd long argued: Demetrius was all hype.

But Aaron didn't call to revel in Demetrius's failings. After a year of high school and a summer of grassroots basketball, much of the talk about former Team Cal players was on Demetrius's flameout, and rightly so. His failing got the attention of the youth-basketball populace in a way rarely seen before. But Aaron was also one of the nation's elite young players, and his basketball future was in peril as well. Like Demetrius, he struggled adjusting to high school basketball. Russell Otis, Dominguez's coach, positioned him primarily at center or power forward, where his slight build and lack of strength left him overmatched against good teams. Aaron wanted to play small forward, and at six foot seven he had the height and raw skills to play that position in college and maybe the NBA, but Otis stuck him in the interior, and he resented that. By season's end, he'd played less than ten minutes a game, and frustration over his role permeated everything. He feuded with teammates—who considered him moody and cocky for a freshman averaging 8 points a game—and his grades plummeted.

Playing for H Squad, a Los Angeles–based grassroots team, in the spring and summer had been equally discouraging. Aaron was the last man off the bench, and he sulked and missed more tournaments than he attended. Adidas thought he would attend the Superstar Camp again, but Teron Pickett was unable to reach him in the run-up to the event. Like Demetrius, he fell in the rankings, landing at number 45 according to Hoop Scoop, four spots below Rome.

There were any number of potential dangers that could derail the dreams of the Team Cal kids, many of them the social challenges confronted by any teenage boy growing up in Southern California, such as girls, gangs, and drugs. Like all teenagers, their ability to pilot this stage of life depended greatly on the support they got from their families. The players who made the smoothest transition to high school were Justin, Jordan, Roberto, and Andrew, and the common thread between them was obvious: at least one supportive and involved parent. Demetrius and Aaron hated to be linked, but it was impossible not to note the most relevant parallel in their declines: the role or lack thereof played by their mothers.

Kisha's faults, when set next to Barbara's, were minor. She had entrusted the wrong man with her son and had been a bystander for too many of Demetrius's salad days. There was no discounting that. But she also came through when she was most needed. As Keller stepped out of their lives for good, she picked up the phone and called schools (Taft, Westchester, Etiwanda), trying to find a better setting for Demetrius. She waited too long for anything to happen before his sophomore year—he would have to endure another season at FoHi—but she reengaged in a way that comforted her son. In his weaker moments, when Demetrius longed for Keller and sent him text messages, she cautioned him: "Little D, remember what he did to you? How he abandoned you? I will not let him hurt you again." Kisha wasn't going to make anyone's list of the world's best mothers, but when Demetrius hit bottom, she did her best to pick him up.

Barbara, in contrast, deteriorated as a parental figure at the moment Aaron needed her most. If her only fault had been absenteeism (of which there was plenty), Aaron could have managed. But she put him in harm's way, especially when it suited her needs.

As a basketball prospect, Aaron was better positioned than Demetrius. He regularly heard from Pacific-10 Conference schools, Washington most of all. Assistant coach Cameron Dollar attempted to get him to make a verbal commitment to that school. "When do you want to set up the press conference to announce it?" Dollar asked. Another Washington assistant sent Aaron twenty-seven text messages in a single day, mostly chatter about his recovery from a sprained ankle. Aaron had the one attribute no amount of time on the bench could diminish: height. Even ten minutes of action was enough for the college scouts to project him to the next level. But with Barbara in the picture, it was not hard to imagine Aaron missing out on a college career.

In January of his freshman year, Aaron announced in a phone call: "I'm not going back to Dominguez. It's because of Coach Otis. What people say about him, the rumors about him messing with boys, it's true."

How did he know?

"Because he tried it with me."

His retelling of what allegedly occurred mirrored in some ways the claims made by the former Dominguez player six years earlier, which had led to the felony charges that Otis beat in court. Like that boy, Aaron had no proof beyond his word. Otis's improper behavior occurred mostly during car trips to and from the Inland Empire, he said, when it was only the two of them.

On one such drive, in September, Otis made the first of many suggestive comments, posing his words in a way that could have been perceived as harmless. "What would you do if Pat Barrett said, 'I'll give you a thousand dollars to let me touch you?'" Otis asked Aaron on the drive.

"I don't want another man touching on me like that," Aaron said, and Otis dropped it.

He made similar comments on later trips, and Aaron, while disturbed, brushed them off. "He hadn't done nothing to me, really, and I just thought I could deal with it."

Before Thanksgiving, Otis moved beyond suggestions during a car ride from Dominguez back to the Inland Empire. As Aaron slipped into the backseat (he often slept there during the long drive), Otis said, "You're not getting chauffeured. Get in the front." Aaron did as he was told and quickly fell asleep, but he woke later when he felt Otis's hand in his crotch.

"What are you doing?" Aaron shouted.

"Oh, you didn't like that?" Otis responded.

"No!"

"Why don't you touch mine and see if you like it."

"No, I'm good."

"Oh, I'll get you a Sidekick if you let me touch you."

"No, I'm good."

On a drive a few days later, Otis produced a Sidekick. "Let me touch you and I'll give it to you."

"No," Aaron said again.

This went on for a week, Aaron said, but he told no one. "It was the middle of the season and I didn't know if I could transfer out, so I didn't say anything." He wondered if Otis made advances toward other players and if he was giving them money like the $1,000 he got each month.

"Would you let me see it?" Otis asked him during one drive.

"What do you mean, would I let you see it?"

"You should let me look at it. How much money would it take?"

"Give me two thousand dollars a week."

Otis laughed.

He continued to proposition Aaron, and Aaron continued to decline his advances. On one drive, when Otis was more persistent than usual, Aaron snapped at him.

"You're a fucking fag."

"I'm not gay," Otis said.

"But you like penises."

"Yeah."

"You're a fag."

Aaron finally told Barbara about Otis's improper behavior in December, just before Dominguez went to a tournament in Florida. She sent him to the tournament anyway, telling Aaron she didn't want Otis to know that she knew what he'd done. When Aaron returned, and while on Christmas break, he pleaded with Barbara to let him transfer to a new school immediately.

"You need to stand up to Coach O and talk to him," she responded.

"Why do I need to talk to him?"

"You need to put him on the books about what he's doing."

Barbara dialed Otis's number, but Aaron refused to speak to him on the phone. "You want to be a punk and not stand up to him?" Barbara said.

"What is it standing up to?"

"You guys need to clear the air."

"What air is there to clear?"

Aaron felt Barbara was being too "buddy-buddy" with Otis. He asked her why she wasn't outraged.

"Because I'm trying to get him to help me out this month," she responded.

In later conversations, Barbara attempted to convince Aaron that he had to go back to Dominguez for reasons other than the $1,000. He couldn't transfer without first getting a grade check from his teachers, she said, because the Dominguez coaches might change his grades when they learned he was leaving. "Why can't we just do the grade check over the phone or by mail?" Aaron asked, and there was no reason they could not. Next, Barbara promised to buy Aaron a car when she got her income-tax-return check, enabling him to drive himself to and from Dominguez. "But that means I gotta ride with Coach O until March or April," he said.

Barbara explored placing Aaron at FoHi or moving him in with Bruce and Roberto in Santa Barbara. Mats talked of founding a prep school in Las Vegas, and she looked into that as well. None of the coaches in question—not Soderberg, not Bruce, not Mats—promised to match Dominguez's $1,000 contribution, and so Barbara reiterated that returning to Dominguez was Aaron's only option.

"I shouldn't have said anything," Aaron said. "It's worse now because my mom knows, and she's telling everybody, and Coach Otis knows that I told her. And I still gotta go back."

It was possible that Aaron concocted the allegations to get out of returning to Dominguez for another reason. He wasn't happy, as a player or socially, and saying Otis had acted improperly might have appeared the surest way to facilitate a transfer. "It happened," Aaron said sternly when this possibility was raised. He made similar definitive statements when grilled later.

In late January, Aaron returned to Dominguez for the remainder of the school year. By the spring, he looked frailer, his skin lighter and his eyes dark. In the summer, Barbara informed him that he would be going back to Dominguez for his sophomore year as well.

"If I could choose I would move to Santa Barbara, live with Bruce and Roberto, and go to Santa Barbara High. Bruce, man, he will give you the shirt off his back. I know he really cares about me. And Roberto and me are like brothers. I wanna move there, too, because it's the furthest away. I just want to get away from all this. [But] whatever my mom says, I gotta do. I gotta do what she says whether I like it or not."

During Aaron's sophomore year, Barbara moved the family four times. If you stopped by a home they had been in only a month before, you would find a mailbox full of old catalogs and nothing but garbage inside, as if they had left in a hurry. Barbara and Aaron's cell- and home-phone numbers were often disconnected or changed, as she failed to pay a bill or he lost a phone. For all of Aaron's sophomore year, chronicling his life was nearly impossible. Some Dominguez games he would play, others he would inexplicably miss. "He might have dropped out of school," the parent of a Dominguez player said before one game he missed. In the spring, he would appear at some showcase tournament where Justin or Roberto was playing, and they would get his new cell- or home-phone number and keep in contact with him for a week or two, but then the number would get disconnected and he was back in the wind.

The only person he contacted with any regularity was Roberto. Weeks would pass and no one would hear from Aaron, then Roberto would be sitting in class, his cell phone would vibrate, and it would be a number he didn't recognize from the 909 or 951 area code.

"BER-TO!" Aaron would shout.

He would promise to come to Santa Barbara for a visit and offer a vague explanation for what he had been doing the past weeks. "Shit, it's crazy, Berto, you're not going to believe it. But I am still ballin'. You won't believe my handle right now. No one can stay in front of me. I be killin' people."

Roberto never dug too deep, and that was probably why Aaron chose him. He could remind himself that he had a friend and then drift back into the tumult.

The correlation between a stable home environment and emotional stability in children has been so thoroughly examined over the last fifty years that psychologists, a group prone to placing qualifications, rarely dispute it. When handicapping who—Demetrius or Aaron—was more likely to rebound from his rocky start in high school and achieve his hoop dreams, Demetrius had a decided edge: Kisha. For all her faults, she provided her son a safe haven. Demetrius had clothes and food and a home. Living in the same place for nearly a decade anchored him, contributing to a psychological firmness. He had hidden in a bathroom at the Superstar Camp, and he doubted his abilities for the first time, but one got the sense that he could recover.

A child can overcome a lot of adversity, even an unsettled home life, but it usually requires a responsive and warm parent. Barbara was not that. A psychologist needed to know only the number of times Aaron moved and how Barbara handled the Russell Otis problem to predict his behavior during his sophomore year: feelings of insecurity, a tendency to get into trouble, inability to regulate aggression, difficulty representing himself as being worthy of love and respect, self-medicating with drugs or alcohol. All of the above applied to Aaron after Barbara forced him to return to Dominguez, and it only got worse.

In the spring of 2007, Barbara called the police on Aaron for the first time, after he and his older brother (who lived on and off with them) got into a fight. "My mom and I were arguing and I was trying to leave the house, and my brother pushed me and so I hit him, and that is how it started," Aaron said. As the fighting ceased, he repeatedly yelled at his mother, "I don't want to be here no more!" He meant he didn't want to live with her anymore, but Barbara told police that Aaron had threatened to kill himself.

He spent the next seven days at Canyon Ridge Hospital in Chino. "That doctor there, man, he was trying to say I had all these diseases and stuff, like bipolar and manic–depressive." He was given medication upon his release but refused to take it. "There ain't nothing wrong with me." He went to his girlfriend's house, avoided Barbara, and also stopped going to school, even after Barbara transferred him from Dominguez to Riverside Poly.

The *Riverside Press-Enterprise* wrote of Aaron's transfer to Poly after the CIF granted him a hardship waiver, making him eligible to play immediately. (Barbara claimed in her filing with the CIF that the death of Aaron's grandfather and her diagnosis with emphysema necessitated a transfer.) In the article, Barbara was quoted as saying: "It's been a very traumatic year for our family, and [Aaron] wanted to be closer to me."

In reality, Aaron wanted nothing to do with his mother. He stayed at his girlfriend's house or with friends and he began experimenting with marijuana, which Barbara soon learned about. After one shouting match over the phone, Aaron said, "Just leave me alone." It was something every teenager probably says to a parent at one time or another, the anthem of teenage angst, but Barbara responded by calling the police and telling them that Aaron had threatened suicide again. Officers found him a few days later at his girlfriend's house, pinned him to the floor, and handcuffed him in front of her.

Per police procedure, Aaron was placed on a seventy-two-hour hold and examined by a psychologist. "We don't think you need to be hospitalized," Aaron says the doctor told him. "Is there somewhere [other than Barbara's] where you can go?" He said he could stay with his grandmother or Bruce and Roberto in Santa Barbara. But Barbara refused to sign off on his release (Aaron was not yet eighteen), and so he was transferred to Loma Linda University Medical Center for a ten-day stint. Much of that time, he shared a room with a boy who had been hospitalized for cutting his dog's ear off.

Aaron didn't surface again until late in the summer. He appeared at a tournament on a team made up of Dominguez players. While Aaron was hospitalized at Loma Linda, Barbara had reenrolled him at Dominguez, no doubt hoping the $1,000 payments from Otis would resume when she did. "I didn't have any say in it. She just went up there and signed me up without even asking me." He was also living with his mother full-time again. "I'm just trying to make the best of it, you know, stay out of her way."

When Aaron was at Canyon Ridge and Loma Linda, Barbara was unreachable or didn't return phone calls. She showed up at the tournament and, when asked why she had Aaron hospitalized, she said: "I had to give my son to God. I had to put him in God's hands. As his mother, that was all I could do to save him." She said nothing more, as she said she needed to focus on watching her "baby" play basketball.

Over time, Aaron came to adopt a rosier disposition than his plight dictated. Times were tough, he'd admit, but then he would offer some new outlook on life that he swore was going to enable him to overcome his troubles.

"Do you know what an epiphany is?" he said one day. "I had one. I just want to play basketball now and have fun and experience my life. The one thing I can influence is how hard I play. So now I know that's just what I have to do, no matter what goes on at home: just play as hard as I can. Then one day I can just bail and get out of my mom's life for good."

Immediately after each conversation, there was hope that Aaron might survive until college, when he would be free from Barbara. But then there would be another fight—like the time Barbara kicked him out of the house for weeks without even letting him pack any clothes. He was also flunking classes because of repeated absences and missing practices and games for unknown reasons. Two years of high school remained, and that was too much time. Aaron needed to "get out for good" now. He couldn't take any more obstacles.

And then one evening, Aaron called Roberto and delivered the news.

"My girlfriend's pregnant," he said. He was neither happy nor despondent. It was just what life brought. "She's gonna have the baby, and I guess I'm going to help take care of it. . . . My mom says she will help me."

29

(GEORGE DOHRMANN)

Ryan Smith

I f there was one aspect of Demetrius's game that personified the vastness of the work he needed to do yet also represented hope that a recovery was possible, it was his jump shot.

The jump shot appears to be a straightforward endeavor: A player leaps in the air and releases the ball. Yet few aspects of the game are more technical. It is like a golf swing in that it requires a series of interconnected movements done properly to achieve the desired result. One book, *The Perfect Jump Shot* by Scott Jaimet, breaks down the shot into twenty-two separate steps, beginning with (1) controlled stop and ending with (22) balanced landing with feet in open position. Where Lakers coach Phil Jackson saw similarities between basketball and jazz,

Jaimet, who achieved a perfect score on the math portion of the SAT as a teenager, saw a wondrous combination of physics and mathematics, deserving of 174 pages of analysis, including a section in which he compares the Lilliputians' method of tying down Gulliver in *Gulliver's Travels* to a basketball player who shoots from "an unbalanced position with multiple flaws."

Two tenets of the jump shot as deconstructed by Jaimet that were particularly relevant to Demetrius were covered in sections of his book titled "Release" and "Drift." Demetrius's most visible flaw was in his release. It differed on almost every shot. Late in games, he would not shoot until he began his descent, which gave the impression that he forgot to let go of the ball and hurried to get rid of it before he landed. Other times, he shot on the way up, as if he couldn't wait to let it go. This inconsistency was probably an instance in which his physical blessings acted as a curse. A young player with tremendous leaping ability often tries to jump as high as he can on every shot. But how high a player can leap changes over the course of a game; his legs will have more spring in the first quarter, for example, than in the fourth. "A great release has the ball leaving your hand at the peak of your jump with your body in full extension," Jaimet writes. "If the top of the jump passes before the release, the energy of the legs is wasted. If the body is falling while the arm is trying to throw the ball forward, there will be major opposing forces, and the brain won't have a clue how hard to shoot."

Demetrius also tended to jump in a manner that forced his body to drift backward in the air five or ten degrees, making every shot a "fadeaway" jumper. This was not uncommon with kids his age, and the NBA was probably to blame. Demetrius emulated the superstars he saw on television, and they commonly attempted shots slightly off plumb because of the influence of defenders. But they never chose to make a shot more difficult than it had to be, which Demetrius did by fading away from the basket even when no defender was nearby. "When the vertical alignment is off, it starts a chain of events," Jaimet writes. "The jump acts as a multiplier of the original imbalance. The higher the jump, the greater the drift. That is why great jumpers are often not great shooters."

Demetrius had good wrist snap, and from start to finish he got the ball in the air quickly (what a coach would call "release time"). He always put the proper amount of backspin on the ball, and his follow-through was excellent. Also working in his favor was the small number of outside shots he'd attempted over his career. One benefit of Keller not working with him on his outside shot was that he hadn't gotten comfortable with unsound mechanics. Some young players have relied on a shot with flaws for so long that changing their form is next to impossible. Demetrius's bad habits weren't ingrained. He was winging it, and in some ways that made him a more malleable pupil. As a college coach noted after watching Demetrius at the Superstar Camp: "There's nothing wrong with his form that a little coaching and five thousand shots won't fix."

Ryan Smith learned to shoot on a portable hoop he and his three brothers dragged into the street in the cul-de-sac where they lived in San Dimas. The base was a tire filled with cement, and the backboard was dented from the many times they'd dropped it during setup. "We were pretty poor, and basketball was one of those things we could do that didn't cost anything," Smith said.

At six foot three, Smith was the shortest of the brothers, and discovered at a young age that basketball offers one salvation to those not born with great height or quickness: "If you can shoot, you can play."

While at San Dimas High, Smith often spent three or four hours a day shooting nothing but 3-pointers. He admired the school's coach, Gary Prestesater, who had also been a great shooter as a young player. (Prestesater scored 62 points for Azusa [California] College, later known as Azusa Pacific University, in a 1964 game against Western Baptist Bible College of El Cerrito, California, for which he made *Sports Illustrated*'s "Faces in the Crowd.") It was an ideal pairing, the onetime marksman passing his knowledge down to a kid cut from the same cloth. Smith started on the varsity team for three years, was named all–Valley Vista League for two years, and was the league's most valuable player his senior season. He played for Prestesater's alma mater, Azusa Pacific, for two seasons before transferring to the University of Sioux Falls, where he played a semester before injuring his wrist and returning home.

Smith credits Prestesater for turning him into a great player and for helping forge a direction for his life after college. Their relationship seems antiquated today, given how grassroots coaches have usurped high school coaches as the molders of young players, and to hear Smith talk about Prestesater is to be reminded of what basketball was like before the shoe companies got involved and the stakes got so high. Keller gave Demetrius more than fifty pairs of basketball shoes during their years together; Prestesater bought Smith a single pair. "His parents got a divorce and they were having a hard time, and I would have helped out any of my players in that situation," Prestesater said. That single gesture moved Smith. "I grew up believing that was how a coach should treat his kids."

In the summer of 2006, Smith was hired to teach special education and coach basketball at Fontana High. Like anyone who followed high school basketball in the Inland Empire, he knew that the school's talent was down, and he also had heard about Demetrius. The kid was raw, not a basketball player, people said. He had a bad attitude, didn't work hard in practice, and often showed up his teammates, which Smith considered a cardinal sin. Smith decided to reserve judgment on his work ethic and attitude—he didn't know how Demetrius's relationship with Soderberg might have contributed to the problem—but in his first meeting with Demetrius, he delivered a frank assessment of his skills.

"Demetrius, you've got all this hype but not the game to back it up," said Smith, who had seen Demetrius play once as a freshman and also watched tape of him. "You've got all this athletic ability. You're probably the most athletic player I've ever seen in high school, but you don't know what to do with it. You're a post player in a guard's body."

"I know, Coach," Demetrius said, and then he mumbled about that being the reason he had fallen in the rankings.

"Who cares about your ranking?" Smith said. "You've got to create a whole new game, and that isn't going to be easy. You're going to struggle a lot, and so you're probably going to fall in the rankings some more. . . . I can help you. I've got an overall plan how we can make you into a guard. But if you are going to be a problem, you should just go to some other school right now. I'll sign whatever I need to sign and you can go somewhere else."

Smith was one of the youngest teachers at the school, and his manner of speaking and style of dress made him seem even younger. He was rarely spotted without a baseball cap on his head, which he wore turned backward. Even when he didn't wear a cap, he looked as if he'd just taken one off. His wavy brown hair was permanently matted down, turning up only in the back along a line where the cap ended. When he dressed for school, he often wore a polo shirt from the King City golf course untucked over long shorts and low-top Vans, looking like a skateboarder who had reluctantly entered adulthood.

Smith talked to his players as he would his friends or his brothers. He never spoke down to them, and he loved to tease. One day, as Demetrius talked to a girl seated in the bleachers of the football stadium, Smith walked past him and said in a serious tone, "Demetrius, don't you have a girlfriend?" Before Demetrius could answer in the negative, Smith walked away, shaking his head. "You know, if you ask out every girl in school, one is bound to say yes," he said on another day, after spotting him socializing with a girl in the main quad. "I mean it. Someone will go out with you eventually. Keep trying."

It was hard not to like Smith. Still, Demetrius kept his distance for the first few weeks. It wasn't that he disagreed with Smith's evaluation of his shortcomings; he just had a newfound skepticism about coaches in general. He was trying to figure out Smith's angle. "I never had a coach who didn't want something from me," he said.

Smith opened the FoHi gym on weekend mornings, and he invited his players to come. He brought along his brothers and a few friends so they would always have enough for a full game. One Saturday, Demetrius showed up and for the first few minutes just watched as Smith, his brothers, and a few students played a lively game. Smith made every 3-pointer he attempted, and Demetrius was impressed. *Coach Smith can ball,* he thought. He entered the game, joining the team opposite Smith. On one possession he caught the ball on the wing and then drove past his defender, anticipating an easy dunk in this glorified pickup game. Smith left his man on the opposite side of the court and slid between Demetrius and the basket. As Demetrius rose up, Smith jumped, too, even though he had no chance of blocking his shot. He then brought his right arm down on Demetrius's shoulder so hard that it knocked him to the ground before he could even release the ball. Demetrius landed on his butt with a thud and then fell onto his back as the gym went silent. It was the hardest foul of the day, and the impact it had on the other students was obvious: Their new coach had hammered the team's best player to the ground.

Demetrius stayed on the floor for a moment, staring up at Smith in disbelief. "What are you looking at?" Smith said, standing over him. "There's no easy layups here. Get up and play."

Demetrius told Kisha about the play later that night, and she carped about Smith being a coach who would risk injury to his best player. Demetrius eventually judged his actions differently. Being treated as special was what had gotten him to this point—ranked number 215 in his class. Smith was going to make him work for everything he got, and Demetrius knew deep down that was what he needed.

Smith left a standing invitation at their first meeting to work with Demetrius individually after school and on weekends if he wanted. All Demetrius had to do was ask politely, show up on time, and follow Smith's instructions to the letter. At the first of these workouts, Smith told Demetrius: "Look, my job is to win, but it is also to make you into the best player you can be. To do that, we've got to turn you into a guard. And to do that, we first have to get you comfortable shooting from the outside."

On that first day, Smith ordered Demetrius to put all the balls on a rack and move the rack off the court. He then walked him through a series of drills focusing on Demetrius's balance and footwork. He had him jog along the 3-point line and then quickly stop and jump as if he were taking a shot. "Your feet! Your feet!" Smith yelled, and then he stopped the drill and demonstrated the proper way to square your body to the basket before jumping. "Jump straight up. You should land in the exact same spot you took off from," he said. For all the high-level basketball Demetrius had played, his footwork was atrocious—another indictment of Keller and the grassroots system—but Smith was glad not to have to undo the work of others. "Demetrius, you are a blank slate," he said. "We are starting from scratch."

Five days a week for almost three months, Smith helped Demetrius find a jump shot from the feet up. Some weekend mornings, Kisha would come to the gym and sit on a chair along the baseline, counting out Demetrius's makes and misses. Smith and his pupil played a shooting game at the end of each workout that Smith and his brothers had devised, called "100," pitting the teacher against his student. Demetrius arrived at the gym each day anxious to get to the end and take on his new coach, hoping it would be the day he finally beat him. "Today's the day. You're going down, Coach," Demetrius would say, and Smith would smile and nod. "Sure, sure. Just like last time."

Smith pestered Demetrius in a passive-aggressive way about taking better care of his body. Demetrius would send him a text message like *What time is practice?* and Smith would respond: *You should be eating more vegetables* or: *You need to stretch more before workouts.* His responses would have nothing to do with the question asked, and to Demetrius there was nothing funnier in the world. Smith also passed along sayings that Prestesater had once used on him. "You don't take a shot in a game unless you've tried it a thousand times in practice," he chimed.

Smith came to conclude that what he'd heard about Demetrius upon taking the FoHi job—he was lazy, a prima donna, a bad teammate—were interpretations by people who didn't know Demetrius and what he'd been through. "No one has ever taken him and said, 'Here is the right way to do it. Here is what you've got to do to get better,'" Smith said. "There is all this pressure put on him; people expect him to be great, but no one has showed him how to get there. He knows he is falling behind, and that scares him. Demetrius's problem isn't that he has a big ego. It's that he's scared."

FoHi's opening game of the season came in the San Dimas Tournament in early December. FoHi drew Etiwanda in the opener—a stout challenge for any team, let alone one transitioning to a new coach and system. The task was made easier by the absence of Jordan and Rome from Etiwanda's lineup. Jordan was sidelined by a stress fracture in his foot, which would heal completely in a few weeks. Rome's absence was more problematic. He had been ruled ineligible for the first semester after accumulating a 1.3 GPA, including three Fs, during his freshman year. He and his parents didn't want to discuss the cause of his academic slide, but the former Team Cal players who still spoke with Rome were unanimous in their view of what had happened. "He's gotten into smoking weed," Demetrius said. Added Justin: "The people I talk to say he is smoking like a couple times a day." Jordan Finn—his classmate, teammate, and friend since they were ten—stopped hanging out with Rome outside of the physical education class they had called "Basketball," which was essentially a period at the end of the day when the team worked out. Jordan didn't speak about why he disassociated himself from his longtime friend—not even with his parents—but his actions sent a clear message: Rome was headed in a direction he would not follow.

Sharon, Rome's mom, treated his drug use and apathy at school as a phase, as if it would pass quickly, and she was unable to differentiate between the gentle boy Rome had been and the teenage slacker he'd become. "That's my baby, I just can't," she said when I asked her before the game if Rome had been grounded or otherwise punished for his sorry grades. Rome, Sr., had gotten more involved as of late, she said, and was picking Rome up from school each afternoon. But his involvement varied from month to month, leaving Little Rome with one parent who couldn't bring herself to discipline him and another who did so only when it fit his schedule.

Rome, Sr., had a saying: "Twenty years from now, this will all be chaff in the wind." It was adopted from Scripture (Psalm 35:5), and he used it to avoid confrontation. In the early days of Team Cal, when John Finn would try to mobilize parents to confront Keller, Rome, Sr., would wave him off with that line or another, like: "It just ain't that important compared to an eternal perspective." Rome, Sr., took a similar stance when John attempted to elucidate the seriousness of Rome's predicament. College coaches would find out that Rome had been ruled ineligible, and some schools would rule him out for that reason alone. UCLA had shown interest in Rome during his freshman season, but that school and others would look at his grades and question his discipline and commitment. Like Aaron, he had slipped behind in credits, which meant he would have to retake old classes while also passing new ones to have any chance of being eligible as a college freshman. There was still time, but he had to get back on track immediately and lose no more ground the rest of the way.

Once, when John asked Rome, Sr., about punishing Rome more sternly, he answered, "I don't want to be too hard on my son, because I want to have a relationship with him later in life." Rome, Sr., hadn't been close with his father, and John understood his concern, but it was too convenient an excuse. The logical move, as John saw it, was for Rome to move in with Rome, Sr., and his wife, Debra. Only then could Rome, Sr., properly monitor his son's whereabouts and his commitment to his schoolwork. "But I don't think Big Rome wants to disrupt the nice life he has now," John said.

Before the start of the game between FoHi and Etiwanda, Rome climbed to the top row of the bleachers with a video camera, where he would film the game for the coaches. He wore a plaid ski cap so low that it covered the tops of his bloodshot eyes. He was disconnected from the game and from his teammates, and he was no longer the gentle and gregarious soul who Keller had once used to gauge the trustworthiness of new recruits to Team Cal. He wasn't dying to be out there on the court. In fact, he acted as if he'd rather be doing something else. It wasn't hard to guess what that was, and where it would lead him.

Shortly after Rome started the video camera and began recording the action, Demetrius came off a screen, caught the ball near the 3-point line on the right side, and used a head fake to get his defender off balance. He then drove past him, scored on a layup while being fouled, and converted the free throw to give FoHi a 3–2 lead. A few possessions later, he repeated the action, but when his defender didn't fall for the head fake, he rose up and made a 16-foot jump shot.

John Finn had not seen Demetrius play in two years, and that made him a good assessor of any progress Demetrius had made. "I can tell you right now, he's gotten a lot better," he said, watching as Demetrius assisted on two scores to put FoHi up 10–8. "The form on his shot, the way he is attacking the defense without going into the post—those are things I've never seen from him before."

With the score tied early in the second quarter, FoHi executed an inbounds pass for a score, using the lure of Demetrius getting the ball on a cut to the basket to free another player for an open layup. It was a noteworthy development because it required a level of execution the team lacked the year before. In all facets, FoHi played more like a team than it had under Mark Soderberg. The players showed more enthusiasm on defense and were more synchronized on the offensive end. The team's personnel was largely unaltered—it was Demetrius and a bunch of junior-varsity athletes—but the kids played above their talent level. Soderberg might have possessed as much basketball knowledge as Ryan Smith, but he never had a fully committed Demetrius, and with Demetrius buying into Smith's leadership, there was no disconnect between the teacher and his student.

The lead changed seven times in the first half, with Etiwanda scoring off its defense and FoHi relying on Demetrius to create shots for himself and others. Occasionally, he went to the low block and scored on a post move, but it was a strategic move, not an act of desperation. He recognized that a smaller player was on him, and he chose the option best suited to exploit that mismatch. In this way, he played like Roberto: analyzing, then attacking.

Etiwanda's forte was its man-to-man defense, and it was a testament to the havoc Demetrius caused that Coach Dave Kleckner switched to a matchup zone in the second quarter. He put a man on Demetrius and then a 2-2 zone behind him to guard the basket against Demetrius penetrating. Upon seeing this, Demetrius got the ball atop the key and made a long 3-pointer as his defender—nicknamed "Spider" for his long arms—underestimated the range on his jump shot. Spider adjusted, playing farther out on Demetrius, and so his options were limited. Spider wasn't going to give Demetrius an open shot on the outside, and four players were in his way when he drove. He began feeding his teammates, finding them open for short jumpers and on cuts to the basket, but they missed open shots and flubbed his passes and Etiwanda pulled ahead, taking a 31–21 lead at halftime.

In the middle of the third quarter, Demetrius rebounded a miss by an Etiwanda guard and quickly looked upcourt, seeing one of his teammates open ahead of the retreating defenders. On instinct, he whipped a pass toward him, throwing it hard and high, something he had done for years with Team Cal. Andrew or Justin or Jordan would break out after a miss, and he would find them with a long pass that would end with an uncontested layup. The FoHi player was a skinny Mexican kid, and as the ball rushed toward him he looked like a Little League catcher standing in the path of a Roger Clemens fastball. The ball bounced off his hands and went out of bounds. It was a key play in the game. Etiwanda led only 33–30, and Demetrius had fought hard to get FoHi back into the game. He had scored 6 straight points, two baskets coming on long jump shots, and then assisted on a teammate's 3-pointer. If his skinny teammate had caught the ball and converted the layup, FoHi would have trailed by a single point. Instead, Etiwanda's Marcus Barrow made a 3-pointer on the next possession to push the lead to 6, killing the momentum Demetrius had worked so hard to seize.

After his teammate flubbed that pass, Demetrius spun around and put his hands over his face. Compared to how demonstrative he had been when showing up his teammates the season before, his reaction was muted. But not enough for Ryan Smith. He immediately pulled Demetrius from the game and grabbed him by the jersey as he passed him on his way to the bench.

"First, don't *ever* do that again. *Ever.* Leaders don't embarrass their teammates like that. Second, that turnover was your fault."

"What?" Demetrius shouted, loud enough for people seated behind the bench to hear. "That pass hit him in the hands."

"Look, you know he can't catch. You know it. You've seen it in practice. So why would you throw him a pass like that? Part of being a guard and being a leader is knowing what your teammates can and can't do. You know he can't catch, but you threw him the ball anyway. How does that help him become a better player? How does that help us?"

Demetrius nodded. "You're right. That's my bad, Coach, my bad."

Smith sent him back to the scorer's table and, as Demetrius reentered the game, he ran over to the skinny player, slapped him on the butt, and then pointed to his own chest and said, "That was my bad. I'm sorry."

Demetrius single-handedly kept FoHi in the game the rest of the way, but his teammates missed too many shots, and Etitwanda won 54–47. Demetrius hurried over to his teammates and slapped each of their hands at the end of the game, then he got in the front of the line to congratulate the Etiwanda players and coaches.

His play had been far from flawless. His jump shot deteriorated by the fourth quarter as his release point began to vary, and although he finished with 25 points, he had eight turnovers. Smith had yet to focus his tutoring on Demetrius's ballhandling, and it remained atrocious for a player of his stature. Still, it was hard not to be encouraged by that first game and those that followed it during his sophomore season, which unfolded in much the same way.

As John said while leaving the gym, "Maybe there is hope for Demetrius after all."

30

(DAVID CRANE)

David and Dana Pump

(KATIE ANDERSON)

Keith Howard (right, seated)
and Julius Patterson

A few days after the end of Demetrius's sophomore season, Ryan Smith began mapping an off-season program for him. FoHi finished the season 16–13, doubling its win total from the previous season, and Demetrius had gotten better with each game. He was named all-Citrus Belt League and all-area by the *Riverside Press-Enterprise,* and he scored 51 points against Redlands East Valley, the highest point total by a player in the Inland Empire that year. His average of 31 points per game was also tops in the area. Judging the season as a whole, he had made great progress, but there were times when the breadth of work he had left to do was apparent. Smith's plan included more work on

Demetrius's jump shot, but most of the emphasis would be on improving his ballhandling. To excel in college, Demetrius would have to play point guard, Smith believed. It was also his only hope of reaching the NBA; at six foot three he was probably too short to be a shooting guard.

Smith gave Demetrius a few weeks off and then approached him about reviving the one-on-one sessions that had been so fruitful the previous fall. But Demetrius told him the grassroots season would begin soon. "Going to tournaments all over the country isn't going to help you," Smith responded. "What you need is to spend every hour in the gym, working on individual skills. I don't think you should play grassroots basketball at all."

Demetrius may have shown people in the Inland Empire that he was no longer the regressing prospect from the summer before, but news of his exploits never made it down Interstate 10 to Los Angeles and beyond. His ranking remained in the 200s, which he felt was the result of the limited "exposure" he got playing for FoHi. The grassroots season was his chance to show the world that he'd revived his prospects.

"You need to be worrying about your game, not what other people think," Smith implored.

It wasn't easy for Demetrius to devalue what Keller and the rest of the grassroots machine had impressed upon him. His ranking. The hype. Perception. It still mattered to him, and so, against Smith's wishes, he intended to play the circuit, putting his future in the hands of a grassroots coach once again.

During Demetrius's sophomore season, Julius Patterson and Keith Howard, the coaches of the Inland Empire Basketball Club (IEBP), periodically attended his games. They often came to watch him compete against one of their players; other nights, they just wandered into the gym to see some basketball. They lived in or near Fontana, and it was common to see them in the area's high school gyms.

IEBP occupied a unique spot in the pecking order of grassroots programs in Southern California. If SCA and Pump N Run were USC and UCLA, IEBP was San Diego State or Pepperdine. "We're like a mid-major," Howard admitted, "but we know that and we've come to own that." The kids who played for IEBP usually ended up at the University of San Francisco or Wyoming or another college outside the major con-

ferences. There were exceptions—Darren Collison played for IEBP before going to UCLA—but Howard and Patterson rarely had a player
ranked among the top 150 in the country.

Patterson—like Howard, a Los Angeles native—played at UC Santa
Cruz and contemplated getting into grassroots coaching for many
years before he partnered with Howard in 1998. One of the first tournaments he attended was in Houston, where he watched one of the nation's best players, six-foot-eight George Williams from nearby Elskin
High. It occurred to him that the Inland Empire rarely produced players that big and agile. At a meeting with Sonny Vaccaro later, Patterson
remarked on this, to which Vaccaro responded: "Well, Julius, if you
don't have them, then you need to get into the gym and make them."
That became IEBP's mission statement. It was the program that
churned out modest diamonds from the Inland Empire's lumps of
coal.

Patterson and Howard were colleagues of Barrett and the Pumps,
but they had more in common with Walt Harris of the Bellevue War Eagles and Gary Franklin, Sr. They held jobs outside coaching—Howard
was the coach of the girls' basketball team at Los Osos High; Patterson
worked for Toyota—and you never heard rumors of them chasing the
power and money that tempted other coaches. They didn't push for
more influence within Adidas or get tied up with agents or attempt to
broker kids to specific colleges in exchange for "donations" to their programs. "They keep themselves clean," Vaccaro said. "And when you are
operating [in Southern California], that is not easy to do." Perhaps they
would have gone down that road if they controlled more top-150 kids,
but even operators like Mats admitted, somewhat reluctantly, that Patterson and Howard weren't the same breed of shark.

No grassroots program in the country felt the impact of Joe Keller's
rise to power more than IEBP. Had Keller not gotten back into basketball, the Team Cal kids living in and around Fontana, including Rome
and Demetrius, would likely have matriculated to play for Howard and
Patterson. "But even more than taking that class of kids, what Joe did
is, he changed the marketplace," Howard said. "Julius and I are telling
kids that through hard work and perseverance you can win the battle at
the end and get a scholarship. Joe was telling them when they are in the
fifth or sixth grade that they are going to be in the NBA. He took Pat
Barrett's model and brought it to the younger levels."

After the emergence of the Jr. Phenom Camp, Howard and Patterson saw another change. "Before Joe's camp, there was not an event for people like Clark Francis to come to and rank the Southern California kids. Joe gave the recruiting guys an opportunity to put a number on the young kids out here." While recruiting one high school freshman, Patterson was told by the player's father that he expected compensation should his son join IEBP, because he was "ranked" by The Hoop Scoop after one of Keller's camps.

"Joe changed everything, and now he's kind of out of the game and we've got to deal with it," Howard said. "He's got his camps now and he has, some people would say, legitimized himself. He's got this product that people think they need. But the way I look at it is like this: Joe is just a capitalist. He was in it all along for the money, and I guess that is a very American thing. His story is a very American story. But Julius and I, we're not like Joe."

An unwillingness to employ more-aggressive tactics cost Howard and Patterson some great players. In 2006–07, they pursued Kendall Williams, the guard that Keller had used sparingly in the early years of the Inland Stars. Kendall had grown to six foot four and become one of the best players in the class of 2010, a grade below Demetrius. He attended a camp at the University of Florida after his freshman season, and Billy Donovan offered him a scholarship on the spot. Offers from Duke and UCLA followed, and soon Kendall, once cast down to the lowly "Silver" version of Keller's team, had every top school in America pursuing him. He had long dreamed of playing for the Bruins, so early in his sophomore year he verbally committed to play for Ben Howland. At the time, Demetrius wasn't being contacted by any big-time schools.

IEBP seemed a shoo-in to land Kendall. It was the grassroots team that practiced closest to his home, and he attended Los Osos High, where Howard coached. Kendall's parents had also hired Howard to run individual workouts for Kendall on Sundays during his freshman season. If they considered him qualified enough to work Kendall out individually, surely he and Patterson would get the nod. But Kendall's sudden rise to a national prospect brought other suitors. After UCLA showed interest, so did the Pumps, and before Howard and Patterson even knew IEBP was out of the running, Kendall was on Pump N Run. Howard later asked Kendall's mother for an explanation, and she said that the family felt obligated to go with the Pumps because "UCLA [recruits] play for them."

College coaches often form an alliance with a grassroots coach.

Howland's friendship with the Pumps, however, went beyond the common hobnobbing. When he was a young coach at Northern Arizona and UC Santa Barbara, Howland befriended the Pumps and would sometimes stay at their home when visiting the area. Howland's hiring by UCLA (an Adidas-sponsored school) was a great victory for the twins—one of their own, running the program that John Wooden built. His arrival in Westwood coincided with the Pumps' rise at Adidas, when Vaccaro left and they became the de facto heads of the company's grassroots initiative. Howland would rebuild UCLA into an elite program at the same time the Pumps created a national brand of AAU teams, with "Pump" squads popping up in Salt Lake City, Kansas City, Memphis, Tucson, even Puerto Rico. Their partnership became the most symbiotic of any formed between a college coach and a grassroots program.

At the core of their alliance were the players both sides wanted, talented kids like Kendall Williams. The Pumps used their connection to Howland to get the best players, and the UCLA coaches encouraged kids to play for the Pumps. If a California prospect verbally committed to UCLA early in his high school career, it was a good bet that he would end up on Pump N Run Elite, the best of the three teams the twins fielded in Southern California, and rival college coaches grumbled that the team was a holding pen for the Bruins. At one point during Kendall's time on Pump N Run Elite, the team could have fielded a starting five who had committed to play for Howland. This was unprecedented. The Atlanta Celtics never boasted a starting five of Georgia Tech recruits. The Michigan Mustangs didn't have five future Michigan or Michigan State players in their lineup. Pump N Run Elite was essentially UCLA's farm team.

For Patterson and Howard, the loss of Kendall was maddening. The Pumps were part of the same (Adidas) family. Kendall would have been tied to the company regardless of whether he chose IEBP or the Pumps, and Howard and Patterson were unquestionably the best fit. When one of the Pump brothers showed up at a Los Osos High game, he had to ask Howard the name of Kendall's mother, and this was after Kendall had played a summer with Pump N Run Elite. "But what are you going to do?" Howard said. "That's the system."

Instead of Kendall in IEBP's backcourt, Howard and Patterson would have to get by with the type of overachievers they'd long molded into small-time college prospects, Andrew Bock among them. Andrew was skinnier than most players his age, and he had to rely on his smarts. He was not as bad an athlete as Keller had made him out to be, but he wasn't the kind of physical specimen the major college programs sought. Barrett or the Pumps would have seen no use for such a player, but Howard and Patterson saw a kid who, with a little work, could land a scholarship.

During his freshman season, Andrew practiced every Sunday with Patterson or Howard. In the spring, IEBP practiced another two days a week. In the summer, IEBP alumni like Collison, Sean Marshall (Boston College), and Anthony Goods (Stanford) returned to the Inland Empire, and Andrew worked out with them every day.

IEBP played half as many tournaments in the spring and summer (seven or eight) as SCA, Pump N Run Elite, and EBO. A player would not get as much "exposure" playing for Howard and Patterson, and that was by design. They focused on developing better basketball players, not crisscrossing the country attending events. This philosophy perfectly suited the needs of a player like Andrew, and after watching Demetrius play several times during his sophomore season, Howard and Patterson felt IEBP was the perfect fit for him as well. "I would love the opportunity to work with Demetrius," Patterson said. "I think with the way we run our program, we could make him better in a hurry."

Patterson would not go begging. He felt Demetrius needed IEBP more than the program needed him. He let it be known that he and Howard were open to working with Demetrius and pointed out that Demetrius's uncle, Jordan Walker, had once played for IEBP.

"I heard from my uncle that those coaches are good and they are not going to do me like Coach Joe, but I need to be on a program with a higher profile," Demetrius said one day in March. A few days later, he went to his first workout with his new team and its coach:

Pat Barrett.

When Roberto saw him, emotions dulled by the two-plus years since he last stepped on a court with Demetrius came rushing back.

He entered the gym at a Houston-area high school with his teammates on California Hoops and noticed Demetrius off to the side, wearing the familiar red and black of SCA. To that point, Roberto had expressed mostly indifference to Demetrius's plight since they parted. Told that Demetrius had struggled during his freshman season or that he hid in a bathroom at the Superstar Camp, Roberto shrugged. "Man, I don't really care what D's doing." Roberto was also not one to attach exterior motivation to a sporting contest. If a coach drummed up a fire-and-brimstone speech about earning "respect," he was more likely to roll his eyes than go firing out of the locker room. But he spotted Demetrius before an elimination game of the Kingwood Classic, watched him stretch off to the side of the court while wearing those same high black soccer socks and a different model shoe from his teammates', and resentment bubbled to the surface. Roberto's thoughts returned to the humiliations he'd been served as a younger player, the practices when he and Demetrius went toe to toe and Keller rigged the contents against him. "What's *your* ranking?" Demetrius would say often during those battles, and what could Roberto say to that? Back then there was no doubting Demetrius's status, his importance, and Keller and Demetrius let Roberto know every chance they got that he was not as special.

But, oh, how things had changed.

Roberto was ranked in the top 25, getting calls almost every week from coaches like Ohio State's Thad Matta, who lobbied him to come to Columbus for an unofficial visit on the weekend of the Ohio State–Michigan football game. Florida's Donovan told Bruce: "Your son is a pro," the highest of compliments. Demetrius, in contrast, had fallen off the grid. He told people that Memphis and Villanova wanted him, but the truth was that no big-name recruiters called or sent him text messages or pleaded with him to make an unofficial visit. He was the less special one now, and Roberto gave in to the urge to show the nearly 1,000 people in the gym just how ordinary Demetrius had become.

Payback, motherfucker, Roberto thought, and while his vehemence was directed at Demetrius, Keller was in his thoughts as well. If he humiliated Coach Joe's boy, surely word would get back to Keller.

"I'm guarding Demetrius," Roberto told his coach as warm-ups ended. He repeated that statement to his teammates, knowing a few might try to make a name for themselves by undressing the onetime *Sports Illustrated* cover boy. To be certain everyone knew his intent,

Roberto took up a position next to Demetrius at the center circle when the starters went out for the opening tip. Without acknowledging him, Roberto announced: "I got this right here." He then clapped his hands twice and licked the tips of his fingers, the basketball equivalent of a butcher sharpening his blade.

Demetrius had more confidence in his game at that moment than at any point since the eighth grade. During warm-ups, his 3-point shot was falling and he felt bouncy and strong. He was still handicapped, however, by the lingering deficiencies in his game, particularly his ball-handling, and, most of all, by the portly man standing on the sidelines with his shirt tucked into his sweatpants. In the month since Demetrius joined SCA, he had come to understand two truths about how Pat Barrett operated: First, he favored his star, Brandon Jennings, to the point that he could do no wrong. If he took 30 shots in a game and missed 29, Barrett would congratulate him on that one make. Secondly, Barrett didn't know basketball. Total disregard for the teaching of the fundamentals, fixation on dunks and other highlight plays at the expense of a structured offense, defense treated as an afterthought—pick a poison once associated with Keller and it applied to Barrett. "Practices are kinda like what Coach Joe used to run," Demetrius said. "We do a few little drills at the start and then we just play." There were no individual workouts, no drills likes the ones Ryan Smith drew up. After finally freeing himself from Keller's clutches, Demetrius had run directly into the arms of the coach he most resembled. As one rival AAU coach put it: "Demetrius went from one pimp to another."

Demetrius hoped that by joining SCA he would, at the least, be on one of the best grassroots teams in America. The previous year, Kevin Love and Jennings led SCA to titles at the Kingwood Classic, the biggest event of the spring, and the Reebok Big Time, the summer's top tournament. Love moved on to UCLA, and Jennings played for Barrett only intermittently. SCA's success was often cyclical. After a team like the Love–Jennings powerhouse, it took Barrett a few years to restock the cupboard, and in the interim he filled SCA with the best he could find on short notice. Demetrius saw SCA and Barrett as the big-name team he needed to rebuild his reputation. Barrett likely saw him as an adequate placeholder until better players could be found.

Soon after California Hoops won the opening tip, Roberto had the ball on the right side with Demetrius guarding him. He rolled the ball to the left with his left hand, as if he might go in that direction, and when he saw Demetrius adjust his feet, he pounded the ball back to the right and moved hard in that direction. Demetrius was quicker than Roberto, but the combination of being caught off balance and Roberto's strength with the ball overwhelmed him, and Roberto drove in for a clean layup.

The ease with which Roberto got by him changed the way Demetrius played defense for the rest of the game. The crowd's reaction, the collective "OOOOOHHHH!" rising from the stands after Roberto crossed him over, led Demetrius to step back from Roberto the next time down on defense and every time after that. He would give him the outside shot rather than risk being embarrassed again. Roberto identified this instantly, casually made a 3-pointer, and repeated the act twice more in the game's first eight minutes. The one time Demetrius dared to step to him, Roberto drove on him again and pulled up for a 12-footer as Demetrius watched helplessly.

When SCA had the ball, Demetrius stayed near the 3-point line, watching as Jennings took most of the shots. Demetrius scored off an offensive rebound at one point, but he got nothing in the flow of the offense, and he didn't make Roberto work to guard him.

Late in the half, when it looked as if Roberto would win their matchup in a rout, Jennings forced a turnover and sprinted ahead, creating a 2-on-1 break with Demetrius to his left and Roberto as the lone defender. Jennings drove straight at the basket, and as he reached the free-throw line, Roberto stepped toward him, shading to the side Demetrius was on to take away the passing lane. Without stopping, Jennings lofted the ball toward the rim just as Demetrius, in a full sprint, left the ground. He rose toward the rim and turned in midair so his back was to the basket. He met Jennings's pass at the moment the rim was directly behind him, his head several inches above it. The pass was a little low, and so Demetrius had to lean forward to grab it. He snared it with both hands, then scooped the ball up and over his head, slamming it through the net in what was called a reverse alley-oop.

The crowd's reaction almost halted the game. Players ran onto the floor near the benches, people along the baseline slapped hands, and a few leaped into one another's arms. It took several seconds for Roberto to retrieve the ball and then inbound it to a teammate, and the crowd basked in what they had just witnessed: the best dunk of the tournament.

Emboldened by his dunk and the crowd's boisterous response, Demetrius bumped Roberto with his shoulder as they crossed at half-court.

"Man, you suck!" he shouted over the cheering.

"I suck? What does that say about you if I suck and I'm still killing you?"

Demetrius didn't say anything.

"You can dunk, but you can't guard me."

Demetrius remained silent but gave him a push in the chest.

"This ain't middle school no more," Roberto quipped.

Seconds later, Roberto got the ball on the right and made a 3-pointer over Demetrius, catching him on his heels. As he jogged back on defense, Roberto shook his head, as if he was disappointed by how easily he could embarrass his foe.

Early in the second half, with Roberto ahead in their head-to-head battle 16 points to 4, Demetrius moved over to point guard. Roberto picked him up near midcourt, and as Demetrius awkwardly attempted to cross the ball in front of his body, Roberto reached in and tipped the ball free. He picked up the loose ball and raced unabated toward the basket. Roberto would say later, "I had no idea what I was going to do until I did it," but his showmanship seemed rehearsed. He ran at the basket from the right side and then jumped off two feet and twisted his body counterclockwise, completing a perfect revolution before slamming the ball home with two hands, a 360-degree dunk.

Judging by the crowd's response, Roberto's slam ranked below Demetrius's from earlier, but it capped off his dominance of his former rival. Not three minutes of game time later, Demetrius claimed he hurt his knee and retreated to the bench.

A couple of late baskets by Jennings gave SCA the victory, and that, combined with seeing Demetrius feign injury yet again to avoid a challenge, left Roberto unsatisfied. Watching Demetrius shirk away rather than give his best the entire game was not part of the script he'd written in his head. It didn't feel like payback; it felt like kicking a kid when he was down.

"Man, it's just sad. It is like D is waiting for everything to come easy again, like all of a sudden it was gonna be like it was, where he can blow past everybody or jump higher than everybody," Roberto said later. "And, you know, he's good enough. I mean it. He is still a good enough athlete to make it. Did you see that dunk he had in the first half? I can't do that. I can't get high enough to do that. He just needs to work on his game and get his confidence back. After that dunk, he was talking shit and acting like he was confident, but he isn't really confident."

That one game and Roberto's reaction were harbingers of Demetrius's entire grassroots season. He joined SCA to restore his reputation, but as he traveled the nation playing for Barrett, the reaction of the grassroots populace—the players, coaches, and scouting-services types— mirrored Roberto's. Instead of showing people that he was once again a phenom, he reminded them how far he'd fallen. Instead of redemption, he got pity.

31

(NICK KOZA)   (CHRIS WILLIAMS)

Justin Hawkins and Roberto Nelson

When people asked Demetrius what colleges were recruiting him, he rambled off a list that included some of the best programs in the country: Memphis, Villanova, Florida, and UCLA. None of those schools was actively recruiting him, but it was not entirely his fault that he misjudged their level of interest. The recruiting process is confusing, with too many NCAA rules governing the actions of recruiters and with both the colleges and the recruits practicing deception to better their positions. Add in greedy grassroots coaches looking to cash in on their players, and it is not surprising that Demetrius wouldn't know exactly where he stood.

The recruitment of a high school basketball player begins with the simplest of communications: a form letter, sent to recruits sometime after their sophomore season. It is often accompanied by a questionnaire in which a player provides his cell-phone number, email address, his parents' cell-phone numbers, etc. Recruiters are not permitted by the NCAA to send high school players any correspondence before that, but many do, because enforcement is lax. In defense of those schools, the rules governing when it is permissible to write to kids are confusing. In 2006, it was not against the rules for Duke coach Mike Krzyzewski to send a middle schooler a handwritten note—like the one sent to Demetrius when he was in the seventh grade—but sending that same note to a high school freshman would be a violation.

That is one of the many byzantine NCAA bylaws that parents and kids don't understand. Most couldn't tell you whether a certain month was a "Contact" period, meaning coaches were free to call them, or a "No Contact" period, when they were not. They knew only that there were some weeks when their phones rang incessantly and others when they did not.

As their mailboxes filled with letters from colleges, the kids often mistook that as a sign of veritable interest, but no part of the recruiting process is more meaningless. Roberto and Bruce saved every piece of recruiting mail sent to their home in Santa Barbara. Bruce placed a large cardboard box behind a recliner in their living room, and anything they received got tossed into it. That box gave way to another and another and then another. In a twenty-month period, beginning in February of his sophomore year and continuing until November of his senior year, Roberto received 2,171 pieces of mail from fifty-six different schools. These mailings were as pointless as they were wasteful. Of all the mail Roberto received, only 387 pieces, or 18 percent, were ever opened, and Bruce opened the majority; he estimated Roberto looked at fewer than fifty. The sheer volume of mail Roberto received alerted him to the meaninglessness of recruiting letters. But Demetrius, who received fewer mailings, thought a form letter from Villanova or Memphis signaled genuine interest, when it meant only that he was on a mass mailing list.

Recruiters often speak of the prospects they are considering in terms of what tier they are on. There are the Tier 1 kids, the ones with elite talent, like Roberto. A player who really fits a need, such as a big center or pure point guard, can also land on Tier 1, even if he is not ranked as high by the scouting services. Tier 2 consists of players that a school would be willing to take if it missed out on Tier 1 prospects. Tier 2 kids aren't superstars, but they may have a big upside because of their size, like Aaron, or have a signature skill, like Justin's defense, that enables them to contribute immediately in college. Players who fall to Tier 3 have an obvious flaw that could prevent them from being effective college players. They may be too short for the position they play, like Terran, or too slight, like Andrew. Many Tier 3 players overcome their physical limitations and become good college players, but Tier 3 kids can be risky, and recruiters are reluctant to commit to them.

The process gets complicated, because every school slots kids differently and because players don't always know where they stand. USC told Roberto that he was "the number-1 guard" on their list of recruits, but a player a tier or two lower won't hear that he is part of the backup plan.

Iowa State was one of the first schools to aggressively pursue Justin, and assistant coach T. J. Otzelberger spearheaded his recruitment. To an outsider, Iowa State would seem an unlikely school to reach into Southern California for talent, but then, few people knew that Otzelberger had spent a year coaching one of the Pumps' grassroots teams, Double Pump Elite. In the spring of Justin's sophomore year, Otzelberger convinced Carmen to fly out with Justin for an unofficial visit. When they arrived in Ames, Justin was handed a color brochure announcing JUSTIN HAWKINS. UNOFFICIAL VISIT. On the cover was a picture of Hilton Coliseum, where the Cyclones played, and inside was an hour-by-hour schedule of how Justin would spend his two days there, including playing pickup with the current team and meeting the program's academic coordinator. On the back of the brochure was a short bio of Justin, written like those you find in media guides, with lines like: *He ranks as one of the top guards in the state of California for the class of 2009.*

By his second day in Ames, Justin told Carmen he could see himself going to school there. Carmen appreciated the small-town atmosphere and also felt, given her conversations with Otzelberger, that Justin was a priority recruit for the school. Then they met with head coach Greg McDermott.

"We like you, Justin. We like you a lot," McDermott said during a sit-down in his office. "But we are not done taking care of the 2008 class, so we can't offer a scholarship yet."

Translated from coachspeak, McDermott said: *Justin is not a top priority.*

One can see why Carmen and Justin would have been confused. After being convinced by Otzelberger that they were wanted, Carmen spent around $1,000 to get Justin and her to Ames, and then they were fawned over for two days, including a visit to the athletic director's luxury box during halftime of a football game. Naturally, they thought Iowa State wanted Justin. Instead, McDermott merely wanted to keep him "warm" (in the parlance of recruiters) while he waited on bigger fish.

Players and parents were capable of the same trickery. UC Riverside offered Jordan Finn a scholarship right before the start of his junior season, and he and John visited the school twice. Jordan didn't want to attend UC Riverside, however, and he and John went only to keep that school as an option should no others extend Jordan an offer. When UC Riverside coach Jim Wooldridge pressured Jordan to verbally commit during one visit, John told him: "Coach, we really appreciate your interest, but we want to see what success you have recruiting others and see how strong the program gets." That was parentspeak for: *We're holding out for something better.*

Some schools took a shotgun approach, offering scholarships to dozens of kids in the hopes that one would commit. This was more common with smaller programs, like the University of Portland, which had offered a scholarship to six of the former Team Cal kids by their junior seasons. A program like, say, UCLA, had to be more prudent, because so many players would jump at the chance to play for that school. The Bruins recruited Roberto hard—they made phone calls, sent emails, scouted his AAU games—but as his junior year began, he had yet to be formally offered a scholarship. Coach Ben Howland told Bruce he was concerned about Roberto's grades and wanted to see how he scored on the SAT. Howland's hesitancy probably had more to do with wanting to see how Roberto and other players developed: no sense in offering him a scholarship before it was necessary. That didn't stop Howland from committing an NCAA violation regarding permissible contact. In certain months, coaches are allowed to call a recruit or his family only once. In one of these months, and after a UCLA coach had already spoken to Roberto, Howland called Bruce. "I didn't know it was him until I answered the phone, because the number had a Santa Barbara area code," Bruce said. "Ben said he was up in Santa Barbara visiting people, and we talked about maybe getting together while he was in town." Howland had never called Bruce from a Santa Barbara number before. "I guess he knew that if he used his UCLA phone, then people could find out he called me."

Ohio State didn't couch their interest in Roberto. Coach Thad Matta offered him a scholarship when he visited the campus for the Ohio State–Michigan football game in November, and one of his assistants began working with Bruce to make sure Roberto had the course credits he needed to be eligible to play for the Buckeyes as a freshman. He reviewed Roberto's transcripts and advised Bruce on what summer school courses Roberto should take. Like UCLA, Ohio State also violated an NCAA rule in pursuing Roberto: Former Ohio State player and CBS college basketball analyst Clark Kellogg called Bruce and lobbied on behalf of his alma mater. (As a former Ohio State player, he was forbidden under NCAA guidelines from contacting recruits or their families.) "I heard that the missing piece to the puzzle was a kid in California," Kellogg told Bruce. He mentioned that his son, Nick, a guard in the class of 2010, would likely play for Ohio State and said that head coach Thad Matta was building the Buckeyes into a perennial national title contender.

Even if Roberto had wanted to accept the Buckeyes' scholarship offer at that time, he could only verbally commit to the school, an oxymoron of sorts that complicates the recruiting process further. A player can verbally commit at any time, and kids as young as eighth-graders have pledged their allegiance to a school, but either side can break their commitment without penalty. The earliest a recruit can sign a binding letter of intent is in November of his senior year. If Roberto had committed to the Buckeyes in the fall of 2007, it would have left a year for him to change his mind or for another program, like UCLA, to persuade him to switch. If the Ohio State coaches didn't like the way Roberto's game was progressing or found another recruit they liked more, they could simply pull the offer. Some schools had a reputation for being more disingenuous than others, another factor kids had to weigh when selecting a school.

The role played by some grassroots coaches also muddied the recruiting waters. There was a time not that long ago when the top high school players almost always stayed close to home for college. Indiana kids went to Indiana, Kentucky kids went to Kentucky or Louisville, North Carolina players went to one of the schools in the Atlantic Coast Conference. This was due mostly to the fact that only local schools pursued them. A coach in, say, Kansas didn't have the resources to track the prospects in California, and even if he did hear about a top player there, he had no chance of competing with coaches from UCLA or USC, who were better positioned to develop a relationship with a recruit and his family. The rise of grassroots basketball shattered this localism, first by providing coaches an opportunity to scout kids they wouldn't otherwise have seen. At events like the ABCD Camp or the Adidas Superstar Camp and big team tournaments like the Kingwood Classic in Houston, a coach could watch kids from almost every state in a single day. For recruiters, it was like signing on to Amazon.com after spending decades picking through what was available at the corner store.

That alone would not have drastically changed the business of recruiting. Scouting a kid who lived two time zones away was a waste of time if you didn't have a way to establish a relationship with him. Enter the grassroots coaches, the quintessential middlemen. College recruiters quickly devised creative ways to cultivate their loyalty, the most common of which was to hire them as assistant coaches. Adding the right grassroots coach to a staff could open up an entire region's worth of kids.

Not every AAU coach dreamed of moving to the college ranks—for the biggest, it would have required a pay cut—so recruiters devised other means to secure their favor. They paid them to work summer camps and had rich alumni donate money to their nonprofit organizations. One of the more ingenious (and infamous) practices was exposed in 2003, the year that Connecticut paid $22,000 to the Beltway Ballers to play a preseason exhibition game. The Ballers were organized by the same Baltimore organization that operated an AAU team that included Rudy Gay, one of the nation's top 10 players, who Connecticut just happened to be recruiting. Maryland coach Gary Williams, who would lose out on Gay when he picked the Huskies, complained about Connecticut's actions, leading to news stories about how other schools used the same method to line AAU coaches' pockets. Connecticut had paid $25,000 to the Louisiana Futures for an exhibition game the previous year. That team was affiliated with the AAU program of Brandon Bass, another prized recruit.

Any rational person would recognize these maneuvers for what they were: bribes. Money was exchanged in the hopes that the AAU coach would influence a recruit's college choice. The NCAA passed a rule preventing exhibition games like the ones Connecticut had organized, but no one doubted that schools would find new ways to grease the recruiting wheels. The NCAA had no jurisdiction over grassroots coaches. As Pat Barrett once said, "The NCAA can't touch me."

After their visit to Iowa State, Carmen and Justin were unsure whom to trust and jaded by the process. In the weeks that followed, as schools like Arizona, Arizona State, and Cal called and sent emails, Carmen didn't need to temper Justin's enthusiasm. "It's all bullshit until they offer me a scholarship," he said. Early in the summer, when the coach of Justin's grassroots team, the Compton Magic, asked Carmen to call an assistant coach from the University of Nevada, Las Vegas (UNLV), she treated it with the same indifference. UNLV assistant coach Lew Hill, with whom she spoke later, offered the same lines as the other recruiters: UNLV was "interested" in Justin; they would keep an eye on him during the grassroots season.

"Same old shit," she told Justin after the conversation.

In July, Justin played in the Adidas Super 64 with the Compton Magic. All of his games were held on UNLV's campus, either at Cox Pavilion or the Thomas & Mack Center. Before his first game, Carmen noted that Lon Kruger, UNLV's head coach, was in the stands. At subsequent games she saw him as well, and she noted that he always arrived early and never left before the game was over.

Following the tournament, on the first day UNLV could contact Carmen under NCAA rules, Hill called again. He asked if she and Justin would return to Las Vegas for an unofficial visit. Justin was in the process of attending camps at UCLA, Arizona, and Arizona State, all paid for out of her pocket, and Carmen didn't want to waste money like they had on Iowa State. But the Compton Magic coach urged her to make the trip. He had also spoken to Hill and said UNLV's interest was sincere.

In early September, Justin and Carmen drove to Las Vegas for the unofficial visit. Compared to their trip to Ames, it was modest. They toured the campus and met with academic staff, and Justin went to a football game with members of the basketball team. The next morning, they met with Kruger in his office.

"I've been watching you, and I really like your game," Kruger told Justin, and he mentioned his commitment on defense. He then surprised Justin by focusing on what he thought were his weaknesses. "Your ballhandling needs work, and your shot could be more consistent. Also, I think you can be too passive on offense. It is good you look to get others involved, but sometimes a player needs to be selfish."

Had Demetrius or Aaron been sitting across from Kruger at that moment, his bluntness might have turned them off, but Justin knew he was a work in progress.

Carmen would say later that she liked Kruger instantly because he answered her questions with a refreshing directness.

"So how does this all work?" Carmen asked him at one point.

"We would really like to have Justin," he answered.

"But what does that mean?"

Kruger explained how schools had different "levels" of recruits that they were pursuing and that he had to offer scholarships to several kids in the hopes of getting the numbers he wanted. UNLV had four scholarships to give to players in the class of 2009, and he hoped to land two guards and two frontcourt players. Justin was one of the guards they were looking at.

"Who else are you looking at?" Justin asked.

"Anthony Marshall and Elijah Johnson," Kruger responded, naming two guards from the Las Vegas area.

The meeting ended without Kruger offering Justin a scholarship, but the tenor was completely different from that of their conversation with McDermott at Iowa State. Kruger seemed to be saying that if Justin wanted to go to UNLV, he would offer him a scholarship.

At the end of the month, Justin returned to Las Vegas to play at a one-day showcase event where top players were split into teams and scrimmaged. Recruiters were forbidden from attending, but afterward Justin and Carmen visited Kruger again.

"When does a coach really put a scholarship on the table?" Carmen asked him.

"Well, right now we are down to those three guards, and we'll take the first two that commit," Kruger said.

"So are you offering a scholarship?" Carmen said.

"Yes, I am offering Justin a scholarship."

Justin looked at his mom and then tried to hide his smile as he said to Kruger, "Coach, I really appreciate that. Do you mind if I take a little time to talk to my mom and think it over?"

"Of course," Kruger said, and he walked them out of his office.

Carmen and Justin went to a P. F. Chang's near campus. Over orange chicken, they listed the pros and cons of committing to UNLV. It did not have a great academic reputation, but Justin had long talked of running a hotel or restaurant one day, and UNLV offered a degree program in hospitality management. He would be the first player from the 2009 class to commit to that school, and that was risky. If the coaches weren't able to lure other talented recruits, he could be stuck on a bad team. On the bright side, he could help the coaches recruit, steering them toward players he wanted as teammates. The deliberations eventually came down to a simple question: Should Justin take the scholarship in hand or wait on an offer from a bigger school? Committing now felt like the more responsible move. Carmen knew other parents would disagree, saying that Justin was good enough to play in the Pacific-10 Conference, but she had succeeded in getting Justin to this point in large part because of a willingness to do what other parents would not, like moving Justin from team to team and saying goodbye to Team Cal when kids were lining up to join the team. The goal had always been to land a scholarship, and now that scholarship was on the table.

After dinner, Carmen drove to a store near campus and Justin picked out a red hooded sweatshirt with UNLV on the front. She then drove him to the athletic department building.

"What's going on?" one of the assistant coaches said as Justin walked into the basketball offices, wearing the sweatshirt. That coach and others followed him into Kruger's office.

"Coach, I accept your offer," Justin said, and Kruger clapped his hands and scooted around his desk and wrapped Justin in a hug.

"Hold it!" Carmen yelled, trailing Justin into the office. She pulled out her camera and made Kruger pose for pictures.

Many people were surprised that Justin was the first of the Team Cal players to secure a scholarship. They were also shocked that he honored his commitment to UNLV after coaches from Oregon State and other schools later tried to change his mind. "I know I can play in the Pac-10," Justin said when I asked if he was ever tempted. "I don't need to prove it to anyone." No one would say Justin was as gifted as Demetrius or Aaron or many of the other boys, but from the beginning he might have been the surest bet to achieve his dreams.

He was, after all, his mother's son.

In the summer before Demetrius's junior year, Barrett advised him to go to a basketball camp at USC. So-called elite camps were recruiting tools, a way for college coaches to get kids on campus and evaluate them against other players. Demetrius had no offers from major schools when he attended the camp, but he played well there, and on the final day Trojans coach Tim Floyd invited him to one of the luxury boxes at the Galen Center.

"We've been watching you for a while and you are a California kid and we think you fit with our style of play," Floyd said. "So, there is a scholarship waiting for you on the table if you are interested."

The offer surprised Demetrius, and it took him a second to respond. He thanked Floyd, told him he really liked USC, and said that he wanted to talk to his mother about the offer. He wasn't sure he wanted to go to USC, but he left the camp elated nonetheless, because he had what felt like a real offer.

But was it?

Later in the summer, the USC coaches met with Darius Morris, the guard who'd spent a year on Team Cal. He had grown to six foot three and was one of the better players and students in Los Angeles, recruited by Stanford and Michigan, among others. More than most recruits, Darius closely followed the scholarship offers that schools made. Knowing who else recruiters were after gave a hint of how serious they were about him. Before his visit to USC, Darius called other players and was surprised by how many of his peers held an "offer" from the Trojans, including Demetrius, Roberto, and Justin Cobbs, another guard who'd played briefly for Keller.

When Floyd offered him a scholarship during their next meeting, Darius didn't hesitate to raise the issue. "What's the deal with all these guys you're offering?" he asked, and he named Justin Cobbs in particular.

Floyd stumbled through a response. "We had to offer [Cobbs] because, well, he played well at our camp. But we are still evaluating him. It's not a full offer."

Darius looked at his father, shook his head, and before getting up and leaving said, "You can keep your offer, then, because it doesn't mean anything."

The safest way for Demetrius to view his offer from USC was that the Trojans *might* be interested. Another supposed "offer" was even more tenuous. Barrett called Demetrius and said that the UCLA coaches had asked him to pass along word that they wanted to sign Demetrius. This was a fabrication. Upon hearing of this, Bruce called one of the Bruins' assistant coaches, who said, "That's not true. We don't even have Demetrius on our board [of potential recruits]."

One of the few surefire methods for Demetrius or any player to gauge if a school was truly interested was to count the number of times a head coach attended his games. If Tim Floyd took the time to watch Demetrius play over others, his interest was most likely genuine.

In the summer of 2007, the biggest week of the grassroots season came in July, when Nike, Adidas, and Reebok simultaneously held tournaments in Las Vegas. Due to rising operational expenses and criticism over their role in recruiting, the shoe companies did away with big all-star events like the ABCD and Superstar Camps, which had long been the centerpiece of the summer. Now the best time for kids to showcase their abilities to the largest collection of recruiters was in Las Vegas at the Reebok Summer Championships, Adidas Super 64, or the Nike Main Event. Games were held at high school gyms all over the desert, and college coaches in rental cars trekked from gym to gym to scout the kids they favored.

Before the start of Roberto's first game in the Nike Main Event, Bruce pointed across the gym at the coaches from schools recruiting his son: Ohio State, USC, Louisville, Kansas, and Tennessee. It was possible they were there to scout other players, but several had told him in phone calls leading up to the tournament that they would attend Roberto's games, and a few made a point to nod in Bruce's direction when they crossed paths outside the gym. (Coaches were prohibited from talking to recruits or their parents during the tournament.) In contrast, no coaches from major programs were in attendance at the start of Demetrius's first game in the Reebok Summer Championships. Chico State, Boise State, Long Beach State, Cleveland State, the University of San Francisco, the University of Detroit, Missouri State, and the University of Texas at El Paso were represented, but not USC.

"Maybe [the USC coaches] have already seen what I can do, so they don't feel like they gotta watch me again," Demetrius said after that game.

During warm-ups before his remaining games in Las Vegas, he would look out of the corner of his eye at the coaches sitting in the chairs that lined the far wall of the gym. He looked at their shirts, hoping to see the familiar maroon and gold of USC or the colors and logos of the other schools he hoped would recruit him, like Memphis and Villanova. At halftime of Demetrius's final game of the tournament, Floyd walked into the gym, but even that proved little. Was he there to scout Demetrius or to watch Malik Story, the SCA guard from the class of 2008 who had verbally committed to play for the Trojans?

"Man, I don't know what is going on," Demetrius said after the tournament. "USC offered me, so they must be interested, but, man, this shit is confusing. You just never know where you stand with nobody. It's, like, please, just somebody tell me the truth."

32

(JEREMY MYERS)

Demetrius Walker (left) *in one of his first games with JSerra in 2008*

om Stengel sliced into a New York strip steak and announced, "This is perfect." He meant the meat, which he had barbecued moments earlier, but the description also applied to the setting. It was a still July evening, and Tom and his family had gathered at a thick table on the back patio of his new home on the southernmost edge of Los Angeles County, in a city called La Habra Heights. He had recently moved there from Fullerton, and while a departure from Orange County often signified a step down, Tom had upgraded in a big way. His home was more than 4,000 square feet, not including the guesthouse, and was in the midst of renovations that included a completely redone interior, a new pool, and a nine-hole putting course. He would later value the property at $3.75 million.

Perhaps most impressive was the view. The patio looked out over avocado trees that dropped their dark fruit so often that Tom offered them to friends by the bucketful. Beyond the trees was the California sunset, all reds and burnt oranges, made more brilliant by the smog lying thick over the Los Angeles basin. You couldn't see the Pacific Ocean, but you knew it was there.

At the opposite end of the rectangular table from Tom sat his wife, Mary, and to his left were Tommy and his sister, Kelly, who was a year younger but had the same red hair, fair skin, and freckles. Taking up the chairs to Tom's right were two more teenagers who, by the end of the summer of 2007, could accurately be described as dependents. One was Chris Gabriel, a six-foot-eleven South African who had been living in Tom's guesthouse for the better part of a year. He had been brought to the United States by Rick Isaac, the coach of H Squad, in concert with a college assistant coach. After attending a series of prep schools, Chris came to the attention of the coach at JSerra Catholic High School in Orange County. He bonded with that squad's point guard, Tommy, and was invited one night to sleep over. "Then I just never left," Chris said. Tom later helped him secure a scholarship to cover JSerra's $12,000-a-year tuition.

JSerra was a school of 1,000 students in San Juan Capistrano, the Orange County town known for the cliff swallows that are said to migrate between Argentina and the mission there. It opened in 2003 and quickly became, along with Mater Dei, a place where some of the wealthiest families in the Southland sent their children. JSerra's athletic teams were not as dominant as Mater Dei's, which they competed against in the Trinity League, but their facilities were superior. The athletic complex, completed in 2006, cost $40 million to build and covered twenty-nine acres. With almost 500,000 square feet of turf fields, JSerra claimed to have the largest installation of artificial turf anywhere in the country.

The athletic complex was on one side of a busy thoroughfare, the stucco academic buildings were on the other, and a bridge connected the two. Except for the fact that students wore uniforms, JSerra's campus could easily have been mistaken for that of a small college. It also had a strong academic reputation—in one year, 142 of the 143 graduating seniors continued their education after high school.

Lording over JSerra's basketball program was Tom Lewis, a well-known figure in the grassroots basketball world. Lewis starred at Mater Dei and then played for USC and Pepperdine. He was best known among grassroots insiders as Barrett's first prodigy. (It was during the recruitment of Lewis that Jerry Tarkanian branded Barrett "the biggest whore" he'd ever met.) After his playing career ended, Lewis dabbled in coaching, including a stint as an assistant coach with the WNBA's Phoenix Mercury. He took the JSerra job when the school opened and quickly built it into a power program—in no small part because of his relationship with Barrett, who steered players his way.

In addition to Tommy and Chris, JSerra's varsity team featured shooting guard Casey James, who had played a season for Keller. At power forward was six-foot-five Alec Williams, who would go on to earn a scholarship to San Diego State. It was a good team but not talented enough to defeat Mater Dei, which included the North Carolina–bound Wear twins, Travis and David, and Gary Franklin, Jr., at point guard. JSerra needed an athletic wing player capable of beating defenders off the dribble and matching up with bigger guards. It was that need that led Tom to add yet another dependent to his clan, the teenager who sat next to Chris that evening on the patio of Tom's home.

Demetrius.

When Demetrius joined Barrett and SCA, he reunited with Tom, who had become one of Barrett's biggest benefactors. Tom had bought Tommy a spot on a lower SCA team run by one of Barrett's underlings. Combined with his support for the JSerra program run by Lewis (his housing of Chris being his biggest contribution), he was now in deep with Barrett in the same way he had once been with Keller.

For Demetrius to attend SCA's summer workouts in Orange County, someone had to cart him back and forth from the Inland Empire. Tom initially agreed, but he quickly tired of making the drive through traffic. He persuaded Demetrius to stay with Chris in the guesthouse in those weeks when the team practiced every day or on weekends when there was a tournament. He bought Demetrius meals and gave him money to go to the movies with Tommy and Chris. He also paid the trainer who worked them out to train Demetrius as well. Tom's motives, at first, were purely altruistic. He knew better than most what Keller had done to Demetrius and how much he needed help.

It was Barrett who first suggested that Demetrius transfer from Fontana High to JSerra. Demetrius needed to be at a school where he would get more "exposure," Barrett advised, and Tom Lewis had to know more than FoHi's Ryan Smith, since he played Division I college basketball. Tom also saw the possibility of a symbiotic partnership: Demetrius would get a better education, a safer learning environment, and the chance to play on a team that could compete with almost any in the Southland; JSerra would get the kind of athlete it needed to compete with Mater Dei. It also occurred to Tom that if college scouts came to JSerra games to watch Demetrius, they might see something that they liked in Tommy as well. He still thought his son, who had grown to be five foot nine, had the makings of a college player.

Demetrius was an easy sell; he longed to play at a school with a higher profile. Kisha, however, didn't want to move so far from her home, and CIF rules would require her to relocate closer to JSerra. Tom offered to finance a $1,200-a-month apartment in Aliso Viejo, a few miles from the school, and, to further sweeten the deal for Kisha, he offered to pay her a salary for a no-show job with his cement company. Kisha still balked at that arrangement, but then fate intervened. She received a call from the Arizona Department of Corrections with the news that she had been admitted into its training program. Having failed to secure a job in law enforcement in California because of the felonious pasts of Big D and other family members, she had applied to other states and, finally, one had accepted her.

There was surprisingly little discussion about Demetrius moving with her to Phoenix. At the end of the summer, Kisha rented out her house in Fontana and drove east, while Demetrius moved into the Archstone Apartments in Aliso Viejo, into a two-bedroom unit paid for by Tom.

"I don't see what the big deal is," Demetrius said when I asked him whether he thought he should be living alone, a junior in high school. "I've been pretty much on my own my whole life. I've been making my own decisions since I was, like, six years old. What's so different now?"

Late on a Saturday night a few months into his junior year, Demetrius lounged in his apartment, eating pizza and watching the last few minutes of an NBA game on TNT. The apartment was carpeted, with a small kitchen near the front door. A table was tucked into a nook nearby, and some books and a laptop Tom had bought Demetrius were scattered there. Demetrius had taken the master bedroom, and once again his closet was packed from floor to ceiling with shoes. He left all of his trophies in storage, he said, "because I wanted to focus on winning some new ones." The second bedroom was sparsely furnished, only enough to create the illusion that someone slept there. Demetrius told few adults that he lived alone, because CIF transfer rules mandated that a player live with a parent or guardian. If anyone learned that Kisha was living and working in Arizona while Demetrius resided in an apartment financed by Tom, he would surely be ruled ineligible. When a reporter from the *Orange County Register* got wind of his living arrangement, Demetrius told him that he lived with his uncle during the week and his mom on the weekends.

For a teenager living alone, Demetrius kept an orderly house. He didn't clean often, but he kept his clothes put away. He had only one set of dishes, so there wasn't a buildup of dirty glasses and plates; most nights he just ate takeout. He pulled a large garbage can from outside into the kitchen so he wouldn't have to take out the trash very often. As for groceries, Tom or Pat delivered them, or he got money from them and had a schoolmate with a driver's license take him to the store. He had his dog, Sierra, for company, and as the only kid in school with his own place, he didn't want for visitors.

As we sat watching the NBA game, Demetrius talked about life at JSerra. He was doing well in the classroom, with a 3.2 GPA at mid-semester, aided by the tutoring he received from the wife of one of the assistant basketball coaches. He had been instantly popular with the girls because, in Tommy's words, "he was new and black."

Earlier that night, JSerra had been defeated by El Toro High, 65–63, in the La Quinta Tournament. It was an inexcusable loss to an average team, but Demetrius was unaffected. He talked mostly about a cheerleader for JSerra, a light-skinned black girl (one of the few at the school) named Paige. He wanted my opinion on a plan he had to ask her to an upcoming dance. "We have this thing at our school, it's called Lion Wire, and a bunch of kids do, like, these skits and stuff, kinda like *Saturday Night Live* but way stupider. Then every single Friday, during the two different lunch periods, the students watch it. I was thinking that if I could get, like, a little part in it, like at the end, I would just go on there and just say, 'Could I have everybody's attention? There's a special girl in the room that I would like to ask something.' And then I'm gonna say, 'Paige, would you like to accompany me to Winter Formal?'"

Demetrius was encountering much of the normal high school experience for the first time. He debated how popular he was and which teachers liked him and which might give him an A-minus instead of the B-plus he probably deserved. He talked about trying other sports. "Do you think I would be good at volleyball? I think I'd be a beast. No one can jump higher than me." There were numerous clubs at JSerra, and while he hadn't joined any yet, the possibility intrigued him. "They got a club, it's, like, called the Bee Club or something, for kids who take care of bees. No way I'm messing with no bees. I could join the Dance Club, maybe. You know I can dance." The innocence that the grassroots machine had sapped from Demetrius seemed to be returning, and it was the happiest he'd been in years. The only aspect of life at JSerra he didn't like was wearing a uniform. "It's kinda a preppy style, not stuff I would wear normally, but can I tell you something? I look *good*. I mean it. Even the nerdy uniform looks good on *me*." He rolled over on the couch laughing, the first time in a long time his wonderful laugh filled a room.

As for basketball, Demetrius was still fitting in with his new teammates and adapting to Lewis's coaching style. "Coach Lewis is just kinda weird, like awkward socially," Demetrius said. "Like, he never laughs. He might say something funny, but it's, like, he tries never to show people that he laughs. I just can't figure him out." That was less of a concern than how he gave Demetrius free rein, especially at the ends of games. "Coach Ryan at FoHi, if we needed a last-minute shot like we did tonight [against El Toro], he would have drawn something up, something where he would have me coming off a screen or two screens. Coach Lewis was just like, 'Demetrius, do your thing.' He's like Coach Joe in that way." On a positive note, Lewis ran long practices, and the team's conditioning and weight-lifting programs were well structured. Demetrius's fitness level was back where it should have been for a player with his ambitions.

At the apartment, after he finished talking about Paige and the Winter Formal, Demetrius changed the channel on the television to ESPN, to an episode of *Streetball*, a show sponsored by sneaker maker AND1 in which a team of players traveled the country in a bus and challenged teams of local players in different cities. If a local streetballer showed supreme flair and skill, he was invited to get on the bus while someone else was bumped off. It was sort of a modern version of the Harlem Globetrotters, with an emphasis on flashy moves and dunks rather than scripted trickery, and the show was popular with young players. Demetrius knew all the players by their nicknames—"The Helicopter" and "The Assassin" and "Springs"—and this particular episode focused on the newest addition to the touring troupe, a thick point guard nicknamed "Bad Santa."

"He looks familiar," Demetrius said. "I think I've seen him somewhere before."

Bad Santa was Kenny Brunner, one of Barrett's most famous protégés. After his dream of making the NBA finally died, Brunner, once a can't-miss phenom, had remade himself as a streetballer, a basketball clown. Told Bad Santa's identity, Demetrius didn't react immediately, as if he was deciding whether he should feel happy for Brunner that he'd landed a spot on *Streetball* or disturbed that he'd fallen so far short of his dream.

"Man, he used to be good, I hear," Demetrius said. "He played with Tyson, right? I've heard people talk about him, like he was super-quick, I guess. Why isn't he in the league?"

Earlier, Demetrius explained how Barrett recently informed him of more schools that allegedly called to offer a scholarship, including Memphis and Villanova, but none had contacted Demetrius personally or come to see him play. Barrett was surely lying, probably so Demetrius would feel beholden to him.

Schools with genuine interest in Demetrius had found it difficult to establish a relationship with him because of the wall Barrett created. Gregg Gottlieb, an assistant coach at Cal Berkeley, knew Demetrius from when he played with Keller. He had told Cal head coach Mike Montgomery about Demetrius, how he had been used and tossed away, and Montgomery responded, "That kid is the poster child for what is wrong with the system." Montgomery watched Demetrius play over the summer and was very interested in him. "Get him up for an [unofficial] visit," he told Gottlieb. One of the few coaches who spoke with Demetrius directly after having gotten his number from Keller, Gottlieb thought he had a trip lined up, but then Barrett refused to pay for Demetrius to fly to Oakland. He claimed that Cal's style of play didn't

fit Demetrius's skills and that the coursework there would be too difficult for him. When Demetrius asked Lewis about visiting Cal, he said
he would have to spend so much time on schoolwork that it would hin-
der his basketball development.

Unbeknownst to Demetrius, Barrett had been telling people that if
he delivered Demetrius to USC, then someone affiliated with the
school would make a donation to the SCA program. One of the people
he told was Keller, who asked him directly about a rumor that he would
net $200,000 when Demetrius enrolled at USC. "Oh, Joe, you know
how it is, people exaggerate," Barrett answered. "Of course they'll help
out the program, but it's never as much as people say."

Demetrius didn't see the link between Brunner's outcome and his
own situation: Barrett. Demetrius was seventeen years old and his
mother lived 360 miles away, and once again his primary guardian was
a grassroots coach, the man who steered Schea Cotton and Brunner
and many others to grievous ends.

Before the episode of *Streetball* concluded, Demetrius turned off the
television. He stood up and threw the remote on the couch.

"I don't know," he said when asked how it felt watching Brunner. "I
just know I gotta go to bed. I gotta practice tomorrow."

As Tommy dribbled the ball downcourt, scooting across the gym at
Compton Dominguez High as fast as his stubby legs would take
him, something in Demetrius's mind clicked. He was nearly ten yards
behind Tommy, standing beneath the free-throw line at JSerra's end of
the court. Most of the players were content to watch Tommy cruise in
for a breakaway layup just before halftime. Only a single Dominguez
guard, the one who had given Tommy the breakaway by stumbling and
losing the ball, gave chase, and he trailed Tommy by three steps.

In his head, Demetrius saw the likeliest outcome before anyone else.
He had played twenty-nine games with Tommy as a member of the
JSerra varsity team and countless others before that on Team Cal.
Tommy moved like molasses, and that Dominguez guard would close
the gap quickly. He was also taller and could jump higher than Tommy.
While everyone anticipated an uncontested layup, Demetrius foresaw
Tommy's shot being blocked or at least altered to the point that he
missed. So, while the others stood flat-footed, Demetrius suddenly

charged after Tommy and the trailing Dominguez guard. The speed with which he closed the gap reminded me of the first time I'd seen him play, that day in Colton when he weaved around defenders with ease and Keller shot me a glance in the stands, knowing I'd seen the expanse of Demetrius's gifts.

As Tommy neared the basket, he sensed the defender closing in on him. When he finally jumped to lay the ball in, he swung his right arm out wide and lofted the ball up in a manner reminiscent of a hook shot. In one sense, it was the right decision, as the Dominguez guard didn't anticipate it. As he jumped to try to block the ball, it was farther away and higher than he'd expected, and it slipped by a few inches above his fingertips. By releasing the ball in that fashion, Tommy had made an easy shot difficult. The ball touched the backboard too high—about six inches above the painted square—and when it came down it hit the front of the rim, bouncing up and away from the hoop.

Tommy fell to the ground, hoping to draw a whistle for a phantom foul, and as he hit the floor he turned and looked up at the ball, seeing it careen off the rim. Then he saw flash of bright blue. The JSerra uniforms were black with maroon and white trim; Dominguez wore white with red and yellow script. That blue, Tommy knew instantly, had to be from Demetrius's shoes. Whereas every other player wore white or black shoes, Demetrius sported a pair of oversized Adidas the color of the turquoise gemstone most often seen in Native American jewelry. Teammates jokingly called these shoes Demetrius's "moon boots," and in that moment it was the perfect description. He seemed to defy gravity as he caught Tommy's miss with his right hand some ten inches above the rim and then slammed the ball through the hoop. Demetrius grabbed the rim and let his momentum swing him toward Tommy and then back in the direction from which he came, a bit of showmanship with a purpose: It prevented him from coming down to earth on his teammate.

As the crowd at Dominguez's gym roared—even the home fans appreciated a phenomenal dunk—Demetrius landed and then stepped toward Tommy. He reached out his right hand and pulled Tommy up, then slapped him on the butt. "Let's go! Let's go!" he shouted, and then he scowled at the Dominguez player who'd dared to try to block his teammate's shot. "That's right! That's right!" he yelled at him, nodding his head emphatically.

By that brisk night in February when Demetrius and JSerra faced Dominguez in the third round of the Southern Section playoffs, I had seen Demetrius play in a game or practice more than 170 times, including a half dozen instances during his junior season at JSerra. The ways he had changed as a person and a player were too vast to list, but one of the most recent developments was that he cared less about the outcomes of games. He was content to score a lot, as if tallying a high point total was more important than doing what was necessary to get a win. Somebody had to score for JSerra, and he took enough shots that 20 points was the baseline and 30 points was expected. When the team lost—and they did nine times during the regular season—he referred to his point total as proof that it wasn't *his* fault.

In December, in the Ocean View Tournament of Champions, Demetrius had scored 25 points against Compton High, but USC signee DeMar DeRozan answered with 45, a career high, including the game-winning shot with six seconds left. In JSerra's two losses to rival Mater Dei, Demetrius scored aplenty, but it was others who influenced the game. In the second of those contests, a 15-point Mater Dei victory in January, Gary Franklin, Jr., made eight 3-pointers and scored 30 points. He also smothered Tommy defensively, to the point that Demetrius had to bring the ball upcourt to ease the pressure on him. "Man, I scored twenty, it wasn't *my* fault," Demetrius said afterward, which was something Gary would have never said had Mater Dei been defeated.

Against Dominguez, though, a different Demetrius came forth. Perhaps he was shaken by the realization that, if JSerra lost, then the season would be over. Or maybe he was driven by the opportunity to best Jordan Hamilton, the temperamental kid who Gary Franklin, Sr., once kicked off the Runnin' Rebels but who was now six foot seven and ranked among the top 15 players in the country. He was still fiery and good for a few outbursts a game, but he was also a star, headed to the University of Texas if he got his academics in order. (Had Aaron still been at Dominguez, the game would have carried even more weight, but he dropped out of school before the playoffs and his whereabouts were unknown.)

Winning, and only winning, was Demetrius's goal from the opening tip, and he played like it was the seventh grade all over again. He scored 17 points in the first quarter, an average of better than a basket a minute, as JSerra jumped to a 23–15 lead. Most amazing was his efficiency. He took only eight shots, making six, and was fouled on the two misses. At the free-throw line, he converted all four of his attempts. It was as perfect a quarter as anyone could play, and the best part was how he lifted his teammates. When Tommy committed back-to-back turnovers six minutes into the game, Demetrius didn't roll his eyes or look to Lewis to sub him out. He clapped his hands and urged Tommy to continue on. Casey twice missed open 3-pointers that Demetrius created by driving and dishing to him, but rather than sulk, Demetrius sprinted back on defense.

Demetrius's dunk off Tommy's missed layup put JSerra in the lead, 35–30, but the most promising sign was how he helped up Tommy and then stood up for him against the Dominguez guard. He hadn't been given an ideal set of teammates to take on Dominguez and Hamilton; the Dons were far more athletic and could blow past Tommy and Casey and others. But if Chris Gabriel continued to rebound and defend the basket and Demetrius kept scoring, JSerra had a chance.

But working against that chance was Lewis, who over the course of the season had proven himself to be an inconsistent tactician. Going with a zone defense looked, on the surface, to be the right way to overcome Dominguez's athletic advantage, but it hurt more than it helped. It was a matchup zone, meaning one player—Casey—played man-to-man against Hamilton, with the others guarding quadrants of the court. Lewis termed this defense "Rover" and implemented it days before the game. JSerra was accustomed to playing man-to-man or a conventional 2-3 zone, so in addition to taking on a very talented team, they had to learn a new defense. The fundamental flaw in this approach was that Casey simply wasn't athletic enough.

Hamilton was what coaches called a "slasher," and the best way to defend a slasher is to never let him get moving toward the basket. When Taft High played Dominguez during the 2007–08 season, Justin had drawn the task of guarding Hamilton. "You just need to be real physical with him, grab and hold him, and let him know he isn't going to get to the basket," Justin said. "He is in love with his jump shot, so you give him that. He takes more and more three-pointers and, unless he is really hot, that hurts his team." In the second of the two matchups between Taft and Dominguez, Justin held Hamilton to two points in the first half. Dominguez was still in the game to start the second, but then, on three consecutive possessions, Justin forced Hamilton into turnovers. On the last, he picked him cleanly and drove in for a dunk, to which Hamilton responded by pulling off his headband and throwing it onto his team's bench. "I was so in his head that he worried about looking bad," Justin said. "When he gets like that, it's game over."

Casey worked hard and his fundamentals were sound, but he wasn't the same caliber of defender as Justin. If Lewis was intent on playing the matchup zone, Demetrius was the only player capable of marking Hamilton. JSerra needed Demetrius to provide much of its offense, however, so Lewis didn't want him to expend too much energy on defense.

The flaw in Lewis's strategy was exposed immediately. Hamilton got past Casey and into the lane and drove into Chris, drawing foul after foul. Chris was five inches taller than Hamilton, Dominguez's tallest player, and when Chris got the ball on the low block he couldn't be stopped. The only way Dominguez was going to take him out of the game was by putting him in foul trouble, which Hamilton did in the first few minutes. Dominguez might have run away with it, but Demetrius kept JSerra in the lead, and his support of Tommy, Casey, and others elevated their play as well. He was once again the tap from which his teammates drew their strength.

As the second half started, Hamilton got free from Casey and made a 3-pointer to tie the score 35–35. Lewis called the team out of the zone and placed Demetrius on Hamilton. After cruising past Casey for most of the game, Hamilton wasn't prepared for this change. He drove hard to his right, but Demetrius cut him off and Hamilton barreled over him, picking up his third foul. The fans behind JSerra's bench applauded along with Demetrius, as it appeared to swing the momentum to the Lions. Not a minute later, however, Chris picked up his fourth foul when he awkwardly stepped in front of a driving player and was whistled for a trip.

Lewis ordered his players back into the matchup zone, and Hamilton quickly put Dominguez up by 9. Demetrius responded by sparking an 18–4 run to end the third quarter, scoring 8 of those points. He also assisted on two other baskets by Alec Williams, JSerra's burly power forward, including the final score of the quarter on a fast break that put the Lions ahead 55–50 going into the final eight minutes.

Chris reentered the game at the start of the fourth quarter, and for a brief spell he became the focal point, but then he picked up his fifth foul with 5:31 left and JSerra up by 4. Hamilton then scored on back-to-back possessions, both on drives to the basket, to tie the score 63–63 with just under three minutes remaining.

Demetrius had 29 points to Hamilton's 28, and it would have been hard to declare a winner in their individual matchup. Both were electrifying and dogged, and each showed why he was considered a future college player. If anything, Demetrius deserved the edge: He had done more with less, given the limitations of his teammates. The game would come down to which star made the crucial play in the final minutes, and Demetrius was given the first chance. With 2:13 remaining and the score still tied, he got the ball from Tommy on the left side with Dominguez's Myron Green shadowing him. Green had defended Demetrius for most of the game, and he looked worn down by the experience. As Demetrius made his move to the hoop, Green lunged at him, and Demetrius went by quickly. Two defenders rotated over, and Demetrius wisely bounced the ball through traffic to Alec, who was alone on the right side. Rather than simply lay the ball in, Alec tried for a thunderous dunk, but he lost the ball as he brought it down, and it ricocheted off the back of the rim. In the scrum for the rebound, a Dominguez player was fouled, and he made two free throws with 2:11 on the clock, to give Dominguez its first lead since the third quarter.

Demetrius brought the ball upcourt, relieving Tommy of ballhandling duties at this key moment in the game. He patiently got JSerra into its offense and the ball was rotated around, but Demetrius made sure to get it back atop the key as the clock wound down. He dribbled in on Green, and then he turned and began backing him closer to the hoop. For much of the game, this had been an effective strategy, as Demetrius used his leaping ability to hit a turnaround jumper or got Green on his hip and bounced around him. Demetrius got within ten feet of the basket, and then Dominguez coach Russell Otis shouted "Double!" and two defenders moved toward Demetrius. One of them was the player marking Tommy, and as his man rolled toward Demetrius, Tommy moved to an open space just behind the 3-point line. Demetrius waited until the defenders were on him and then bounced a perfect pass to Tommy, who stood wide open.

Tommy's shot still had a bit of a lunge to it—it was nowhere near the textbook jump shot Scott Jaimet wrote about—but his release was solid.

As the ball arced toward the rim, it looked good all the way, yet Demetrius still fought through four Dominguez defenders to get just under the basket. He had a clear look as the ball rattled inside the rim, popped up, then came down against the back of the rim and bounced out and to the left, too far for him to retrieve. He chased after it anyway, as did Alec, and that put both of them out of position as a Dominguez guard corralled the ball and led a fast break that ended with another layup and a 4-point Dominguez edge.

On the ensuing possession, Demetrius refused to give the ball up and drove wildly to the basket. Fortunately, he was fouled, and he made two free throws with 1:17 on the clock to bring the deficit back to 2.

Lewis put JSerra in a full-court press, but Dominguez broke it in eleven seconds, and a guard scored yet another uncontested layup. The ensuing inbounds pass should have gone to Demetrius and he was calling for the ball, but Casey was closer and Alec passed the ball to him. As Casey turned upcourt, he cut quickly and lost the ball out of bounds. JSerra fouled to prolong the game, but Dominguez made their free throws and won 75–68.

As the game ended—as Demetrius's junior season came to a close—fans from both teams flooded the court. One by one, the Dominguez players and their supporters approached Demetrius and hugged him or slapped his hand. He looked each person in the eyes. "Thank you, thank you," he said. He eventually moved past them, reaching the end of the stands where a narrow passage led to a door and the visitors' locker room. He got halfway to the exit but then bent over, placing his hands on his knees. After a few seconds he stood up, and tears were rolling down his cheeks. He quickly took off his jersey and used it to cover his face. He bent over again, holding the jersey over his face with both hands, and his body shook as he wept. Fans in the bleachers above him shouted encouragements. "You did all you could," one said. Another yelled: "You played your heart out, Demetrius."

For several moments he remained there, crying into his jersey, as the praise rained down on him.

(CALEB MAXSON)

Demetrius Walker (#3) huddling with his SCA teammates

The swan song to Demetrius's grassroots experience came in July in Las Vegas. Like the majority of the former Team Cal kids, he played for a team in the Adidas Super 64, one of the three big shoe-company-sponsored tournaments held simultaneously that week. It marked the end of an eight-year passage through the youth basketball machine, and that milestone touched the boys in different ways. Justin was pensive as he talked about his last go-round with Compton Magic. "It would be cool if the last memory we had was of winning this tournament," he said. "But mostly I'm just gonna enjoy playing with everyone one last time. We've been through a lot together." For Demetrius, the finality of the moment brought trepidation. He didn't

have his future sewn up as Justin did, and the Super 64 was his last opportunity to impress the recruiters and the scouting services, a final
lunge toward his dream. He could redefine his legacy with a great week,
completing the phenom-to-flop-to-phenom narrative, but he wavered
at the thought of more judgment. "I wanna play. I know it's important," he said. "But to be honest, I wish it was already over."

Andrew, Jordan, and Terran were also hoping to enhance their
prospects, and there were rumors that Aaron and Rome would be arriving in Las Vegas, said to be playing for one team or another. And then
there was Roberto, who snubbed Nike and joined Justin on the Compton Magic, surrounding himself with players and parents he knew for
his final grassroots event. He would be one of the most watched players
in Las Vegas—the top college coaches would line the walls of the gym
every time he played — and yet he couldn't have cared less. "I shot a
seventy-eight the other day," he said upon seeing me in the gym for his
first game. "I'm playing like Tiger [Woods] right now."

Also among the assemblage in Las Vegas were some nervous grassroots coaches, who spoke with great concern about the future of youth
basketball. Three months earlier, at the Final Four, NBA commissioner
David Stern and NCAA president Miles Brand announced a "youth basketball initiative" and pledged $30 million in seed money to remake the
grassroots game, citing a need to fix the corrupted system. Many AAU
coaches worried that this would drastically alter the landscape in which
they operated. One theory went like this: The NBA would set up basketball youth academies in major cities, tying them to professional
teams, as they do in Europe. The best players would matriculate to
these academies, where they would get good coaching and an education
and be shielded from middlemen like Joe Keller and Pat Barrett. Stern
and Brand did not specifically mention this setup, and their plan was
light on details in general. Other than the promise of a website, they
gave no hint of how they would bring about change. But they swore
that reform was coming, and that scared some of the men whose liveli-
hoods depended on the status quo.

The most savvy among them, however, knew there was nothing to
fear. The greatest indicator that this "initiative" lacked initiative was
that Stern and Brand said they were counting on the shoe companies to
work together to help change the culture of youth basketball. Stern included representatives from Nike and Adidas in summit-like talks on

the state of the game and talked as if those two companies were partners. "They are willing to step back and do something that is not bad
for business but good for basketball," he said. Former Georgetown
coach John Thompson, a member of Nike's board of directors, was "sitting and laughing" when he heard Stern and Brand say they were
counting on Nike and Adidas to work together. "The shoe companies
are businesses. Nike doesn't want Adidas to do well," he said on his
radio show. "They want relationships with players. That's what they
do."

Allowing the shoe companies to help them remake youth basketball
was like asking the beef industry to promote vegetarianism. There was
no incentive for them to change, and so they would not. The wheels of
the grassroots machine, as long as they were greased by shoe-company
dollars, would continue to churn unabated.

Prior to arriving in Las Vegas for the Super 64, Demetrius played
with SCA in several spring tournaments, and he built on the strong
play that ended his high school season. He performed like one of the
best guards in the country, particularly in a tournament in Denver,
where he averaged 33 points a game. His confidence was higher than it
had been in years, as evidenced by the new answer tone to his cell
phone, a song by Lupe Fiasco called "Superstar."

In late April, Demetrius called with news that appeared to confirm
his return to elite status: "Indiana offered me a scholarship!" Unlike
with other supposed "offers" that had been filtered through Barrett,
Demetrius had spoken to Indiana coach Tom Crean. "He said that he
wanted me to come there and be the face of the program. He said that
I reminded him of Dwyane Wade. He said he wants me to be the
Dwyane Wade of Indiana, and that he would convert me to a combo
guard—that I would play shooting guard and some point guard. Indiana is a big-time program. I know they are not very good right now, but
Crean is a good coach and I can go there and play as a freshman. They
need players who can play right away. I know it's a lot of pressure, but
there has been a lot of pressure on my back my whole life."

SCA was scheduled to play in a tournament in Indianapolis in May,
and the plan was for Demetrius to visit Indiana's campus the day after
the tournament and verbally commit on the spot.

"I can't believe it. I can't believe I am going to commit to Indiana," he said. "The more I think about it, I know that it's the perfect place for me. I can get away from [Southern California] and all the shit that people put on me here and just start new. I can't believe it is happening. Man, I'm so excited. I'm going to Indiana!"

SCA traveled to Indianapolis for the tournament, but, for reasons unclear to Demetrius, Barrett never took him to Indiana's campus fifty-two miles south in Bloomington. Upon returning to California, Barrett told Demetrius that the Hoosiers were no longer interested in him. "The [Indiana] coaches thought you were in the class of 2008," Barrett said. "They need guards now, not in a year." Demetrius didn't understand. How could they have thought he was a grade older? And even if they needed guards now, why did that kill their interest in him for later?

A few weeks later, another SCA player, Malik Story, signed a letter of intent with Indiana. Story was a grade older that Demetrius and had once committed to USC, but the Trojans were rumored to have lost interest in him, and so he became the rare kid still looking for a scholarship late in his senior year. Story's father was on Barrett's payroll and was one of his closest associates. "Pat needed to find [Malik] a spot, so he did at the expense of Demetrius," Sonny Vaccaro speculated. Demetrius also suspected foul play, although he didn't immediately finger Barrett. "It doesn't make sense," he said. "Coach Crean was super-interested, and then all of sudden he doesn't want me at all. I know it wasn't 'cuz I played bad [in Indianapolis]. I played good. And I know I played better than Malik."

That setback shattered Demetrius's newfound confidence, and he arrived in Las Vegas dejected and vulnerable. USC remained in the picture, but that was of little consolation. "People hear that you are going to a big-time program like Indiana and they know that you are for real," he explained. "Man, it just sucks. Why does this shit keep happening to me?"

In SCA's opening game of the Super 64 at Rancho High School, Demetrius played like he wasn't completely over the Indiana disappointment. Against Utah Pump N Run, he missed his first four shots and SCA quickly fell behind, 18–8. Barrett hadn't accumulated much new talent, and the few players with promise were younger. It was another rebuilding year, and Demetrius's chances of impressing the recruiters would suffer because of that.

Justin walked into the gym early in the second half, with Utah leading 44–30. The Compton Magic weren't slated to play until later, but he had come to see if the message-board posts and scouting-service reports he'd read about Demetrius's improvement were true. "You know, we beat this team by twenty at a tournament in the spring," he said matter-of-factly. Assistant coaches from a dozen schools, including USC and Cal, leaned against a wall along one baseline, and they saw the same flaws in Demetrius's game that Justin covered in rapid-fire statements. "He's dribbling the ball too high. He's gotten better handling the ball, but it's still not great. . . . He's showing the ball too much. A good defender will take it from him. . . . He's trying to do the same crossover every time. I would take that away from him if I was guarding him." Like most of the SCA players, Demetrius gave little effort on defense, and it was no surprise that SCA couldn't mount a comeback and lost 81–68. "You are supposed to be one of the top teams here and you lose by twelve—jeez. That doesn't look good to them," Justin said, and he gestured toward the recruiters.

Demetrius followed that performance with a better showing against Houston Select, although few college coaches witnessed it. SCA played the late game, and the side of the gym reserved for college coaches was mostly empty. Not even USC and Cal bothered to attend. Demetrius scored 11 points in the first half, including three 3-pointers, and boosted SCA to a 36–31 lead. He got tired in the second half, and Houston pulled ahead, but a late rally cut the deficit to 1 with under a minute left. As the best senior-to-be on the team, the final shot was Demetrius's to take. Barrett might have devised a play beforehand, but it looked as if Demetrius just got the ball out on the wing and improvised. He drove into the lane and slipped between two defenders, then flipped a shot over Houston's center that looked good but rattled in the rim and fell out.

Despite the loss, Demetrius felt good about his performance, which included 21 points and at least seven assists.

In between Demetrius's games, so many of the former Team Cal kids or their parents roamed the gym that it felt like a reunion, complete with gossip about those who weren't present. "I heard Rome is going to continuation school," one parent said. Another said he had seen Aaron a few days earlier: "He didn't look good. Do you think he is doing drugs?" A number of the kids asked me about Keller. "Is it true that he lives in a mansion?"

The boys looked and talked differently from when they were younger and Keller brought them onto his team, but some things remained the same. Watching Jordan Finn take the floor for Double Pump Elite, John bellowed from the stands, "Jordan, be aggressive!" His words bounced off the walls of the gym, and I thought I saw Jordan roll his eyes. Two hours later, as the Compton Magic defeated EBO, Carmen sat with two UNLV fans who had come to watch Justin. She saw them arrive wearing Runnin' Rebels attire and introduced herself; by halftime she had their numbers programmed into her phone and was talking about job opportunities for Justin after college. "Boy, he can sure play defense," one of the men said as Justin forced a turnover. Carmen, forever modest, said, "We're working on it."

Following the Magic's victory, a number of Keller's former players and their parents made their way to another gym to watch IEBP and Andrew Bock take on Indiana Elite. IEBP played smartly and with great discipline, a testament to Keith Howard and Julius Patterson, two good men operating in a den of thieves. The team didn't have enough talent to win the tournament, but they had Andrew, who with each passing game proved more and more how wrong Keller had been about him. Coaches from Stanford and Gonzaga watched him closely, and against Indiana Elite he scored on two drives in the final minute to give undersized IEBP the victory.

Aaron and Rome never journeyed to Las Vegas, and there were other boys absent who had been a big part of Keller's team, but it didn't lessen the nostalgia. Jordan, Roberto, Justin, and Terran sat together watching Andrew's game, teasing Jordan about the iPod he found on the bleachers a day earlier. The type of music downloaded to it strongly suggested that it had previously belonged to a young girl, but the others took turns teasing Jordan about his love for Beyoncé and Rihanna. That scene could have taken place years earlier in Portland or Baltimore or Memphis.

Demetrius's absence from that scene highlighted a less obvious ramification of Keller's influence: the destruction of his friendships. Joe pitted Demetrius against Aaron and Roberto, and he drove away Andrew, Jordan, and Justin. Those boys should have been Demetrius's friends for life, bonded by their accomplishments and their travails. Now, when they crossed paths in the gym or elsewhere, they exchanged a brief hug or just nodded. It was the same greeting they gave to people they barely knew.

They could have been like Seattle Rotary Select, the team SCA played next. Seven years earlier, in Portland at the Nike Invitational, Keller's team had humiliated Rotary Select, winning by 67. That game included the moment that typified Keller's approach: After Seattle's point guard Peyton Siva fell to the ground and cried after turning the ball over in the face of Fist, Keller ordered the boys to press him more, to take out what remained of Siva's heart.

Siva was one of seven players from that team still playing for Rotary Select coach Darryl Hennings. Keller had once talked about keeping his team together through high school; Hennings had done it. "These boys are like brothers," he said. "When we started out, we weren't as good as Joe's team, and we knew we weren't going to be that good for a while. But I liked these boys, and they all got along and played hard. It's hard to take ten superstars and keep them all happy and make them a team. So we took a different approach."

As Demetrius slapped hands with Siva just before tip-off, it was impossible not to contrast them. Once tiny, Siva was now chiseled, with tattoos running up his thick biceps and over his shoulders. He was not tall, maybe five foot ten, but he didn't need to be. Anyone with a rudimentary understanding of basketball could have watched three minutes of action and anointed Siva as the best senior prospect in the gym, and he was headed to Louisville. He was so much quicker than everyone else, and yet he never looked as if he was in a hurry or out of control. He dissected a defense the way Roberto did, always knowing the precise skill to call upon at the right moment. In three successive series early in the game, he ran a perfect pick-and-roll with a teammate that resulted in a layup, made an open 3-pointer, and drove through four players for a score. He tallied 14 points in the first half as Seattle built a 44–32 lead, but he controlled the game to such an extent that I would have sworn he scored twice that amount.

Demetrius scored 8 points in the first half, and he didn't play poorly, but Rotary Select was so dominant that anything positive he did got buried in a slew of open 3-pointers and easy layups by Siva and his teammates.

As the second half started, Demetrius glanced over at the many recruiters who filled the gym. Some of the biggest names in the coaching
business were present, including Ben Howland, Roy Williams from
North Carolina, Rick Barnes from Texas, and Connecticut's Jim Cal-
houn. Among the other schools represented were Michigan, Tennessee,
Arizona State, USC, and Cal. Demetrius would have liked to think they
were there to see him, but Seattle's roster included six-foot-ten forward
Josh Smith, one of the elite prospects in the class of 2010. The majority
of the coaches were surely there to scout him.

Rotary Select continued to dominate in the second half and quickly
built its lead to more than 20 points. Siva and his teammates relaxed a
little on defense, and that enabled Demetrius to pad his stat line as he
scored on several transition layups.

With 10:26 left and Seattle up by 26, Siva began showboating,
adding flourishes to his dribble, like an extra slip of the ball between his
legs or around his back. He tried riskier passes, in the hopes of spring-
ing a teammate for a dunk, and cherry-picked, hoping to get a dunk of
his own.

On one possession, he trotted into SCA's half of the court and then
settled on the right side. His teammates maneuvered underneath the
hoop, and he spied a chance to slip a pass through. He fired the ball
one-handed into the key, but it was deflected by one of SCA's forwards
and then knocked by another out to Demetrius, who stood on the opposite side of the court from Siva.

Demetrius threw the ball out in front of him, beginning a speed
dribble toward Seattle's basket. The only player with a chance of catching him was Siva, who was across the court and a few steps behind. He
could have just let Demetrius go; it was the choice most players would
have made. What did it matter if Demetrius cut SCA's deficit from 26
to 24? But Siva bolted after him, and by doing so he instantly injected
some importance into a game that had lost all meaning.

They covered the ground in seconds, but time slowed down.
Demetrius, with those long strides that he'd inherited from his mother,
needed only five steps before he was at the 3-point line. Siva's shorter
legs churned at an amazing rate, and somehow he closed the gap. After
two more steps for Demetrius and four for Siva, they were dead even
and they both jumped at the same time, Demetrius swooping in from
the right side of the basket and Siva from the left. As Demetrius cocked

his right arm back, holding the ball some three feet above and behind his head, Siva thrust his left arm forward, attempting to get his hand between Demetrius and the basket. The outcome would be decided largely by their God-given gifts: by who was taller and stronger and could leap higher. As special as Siva was, Demetrius had him in all three categories.

Their bodies slammed into each other's at the exact moment that Demetrius brought his right arm down. The force of the collision knocked Siva back, moving him just enough for Demetrius to hammer the ball through the rim. He did so with such force that it shook the backboard, and it continued to rock for several seconds after the boys fell to the floor. Siva landed on his butt and fell backward, and Demetrius almost landed on top of him. He managed to hold his balance, however, and hopped over Siva's outstretched legs.

An official's whistle halted the game—Demetrius had been fouled—but a dunk like that, coming over one of the best players in the tournament, would have stopped the action regardless. People in the stands shouted and slapped hands. "Put that on YouTube!" one woman screamed. The college coaches usually didn't react to anything on the court—they didn't want to look like fans—but many of them covered their faces with their hands. One coach turned around and laughed into the cement wall behind him.

Demetrius did his best to act like it was no big deal. As he walked away from the basket, he shook his head a little and grinned slightly, as if to say: *Peyton should know better.* Siva had a huge smile on his face as he lifted himself off the ground and then jogged back to his team's bench. He knew his teammates were going to rib him for what happened, and he decided to get it over with. He walked into the middle of a scrum of his friends who surrounded him and began pointing at the top of his head. "Ooooonnnnnnn yooouuuu!" they shouted and laughed, turning a humiliating moment into a humorous one.

When the game resumed, Demetrius made his free throw and then was subbed out. He exited the game with 20 points and received a warm response from the crowd. "Maybe he isn't so much better than everyone else, like he was before," said the mother of a Seattle player, "but he's still good."

After the game, Hennings, Seattle's coach, hugged Demetrius as the two teams left the gym. "You played great," he whispered in his ear.

Later, while standing outside the gym with his team, Hennings said, "I am one of the people who knows what Joe did to that kid. He paraded him around and treated him like a star and never taught him the game or how to work. What Joe did was a travesty. Poor kid. And now look: Joe is gone and Demetrius has to deal with people calling him a failure because he is not the next LeBron or whatever Joe and Clark [Francis] and everyone said he was going to be. But how can people say he is a failure? He made it. He did. Kids all over the country are trying to get a college scholarship, and Demetrius is one of the lucky ones. Maybe he'll never make the NBA, but he is still going to get a scholarship. Not many kids achieve that. Not many kids get to be where he is."

Demetrius sprained his knee dunking over Siva, and it swelled overnight. It forced him to sit out SCA's final game, a 69–53 loss that eliminated Barrett's bunch from the Super 64.

Thus, the final impression Demetrius would make on the grassroots game was that dunk, and it was an appropriate ending. It didn't mean anything. It didn't change the outcome of the game, nor would it alone sway the recruiters. As awe-inspiring as it was, it didn't thrust Demetrius back into the realm of future NBA stars. Yet the scouting services wrote glowingly of his "posterizing" dunk over Siva, and one by one they moved him up in their rankings.

In the world of grassroots basketball, Demetrius was a phenom all over again.

EPILOGUE

Like a
Legend

(RALPH FRESO/*EAST VALLEY TRIBUNE*)

Demetrius Walker

A s flawed a person as he might have been, Joe Keller had a gift for identifying special athletes at a very early age. Of the roughly two dozen kids he coached on the Inland Stars/Team Cal, eighteen received Division I basketball scholarships and two others signed to play football. It was a testament to the talent Keller assembled that many of the kids he considered not elite enough went on to play in college. Even his castoffs became stars.

Andrew Bock's expulsion by Keller proved a blessing. While he didn't emerge as an elite prospect according to Clark Francis's rankings, he continued to improve under the guidance of the noble coaches of IEBP, and he received scholarship offers from San Diego State, Creighton, and other mid-major schools. Andrew had grown to a respectable six foot one but was thin and didn't wear his athleticism the way Demetrius or Roberto did. Still, a few bigger programs were intrigued enough to ask Andrew to hold off committing to a school until the end of his senior season, hoping to keep him "warm," while continuing to gauge his ceiling as a prospect. Worried that waiting would jeopardize the offers he already had, Andrew signed a binding letter of intent with Creighton, a school with a history of making the NCAA tournament with players the major programs undervalued.

Andrew led Eisenhower High, which had no player taller than six foot three, to a Division II state title in his senior season, and he was the only one of Keller's former players to be selected to the first All-State team by Cal-Hi Sports. After watching him dominate during his senior season, a coach from a Pacific-10 Conference school who had been reluctant to offer Andrew a scholarship called IEBP coach Keith Howard. "We blew it on Andrew," the recruiter admitted. "He's the best point guard in California."

Other players Keller discarded who went on to earn scholarships included Darius Morris (Michigan), Justin Cobbs (Minnesota), Kendall Williams (New Mexico), LaBradford Franklin (San Diego State), Casey James (Penn), and Chris Cunningham (Santa Clara). Pe'Shon Howard became one of the top-100 players in the class of 2010 and signed with Maryland.

Gary Franklin, Jr. (Cal), and G. J. Vilarino (Gonzaga) proved they were phenoms as well, and their fathers, like Rob Bock, would conclude that the limited time their sons spent under Keller's influence had been key. They weren't around him long enough to be corrupted.

Jordan Finn accepted a scholarship to play at Air Force. John Finn considered sending him to a prep school for a year in the hopes of eventually landing an offer from a Pac-10 team, but Jordan overruled him and John respected his decision. Keller's prediction that Jordan would one day rebel against his father's demanding ways proved incorrect.

Justin Hawkins honored his commitment to UNLV, and **Terran Carter,** his teammate at Taft High, also landed a scholarship, to Cal State Northridge. Terran did not qualify academically, however, and he enrolled at Pierce College, a junior college in Woodland Hills, California.

Roberto Nelson seemed set to sign with UCLA or Ohio State, but then Craig Robinson, Barack Obama's brother-in-law, was hired as the coach at Oregon State. His hiring of former Compton Magic coach David Grace as an assistant coach gave Robinson an in with that program's players, and he quickly got a commitment from Joe Burton, the burly center known as "Indian Joe" when he played for Keller. Like Andrew, Burton had proved Keller's prognostications about his potential incorrect. He had sprouted to a respectable six foot seven, much taller than Keller ever thought, and he was a top-150 prospect.

Roberto admired Robinson, who had a background much like the white men he occasionally golfed with on Santa Barbara's nicer courses, including an MBA from the University of Chicago. Robinson was equally smitten, telling one person during the recruitment of Roberto that, while Oregon State didn't need any guards in the class of 2009, "I am willing to make an exception for Roberto. I think he is that good."

Most top prospects would never have considered Oregon State, as it would do little to boost their profile to sign with a team that had not won a conference game the season before and played in the out-of-the-way hamlet of Corvallis. But Robinson focused Roberto on a consideration far more important than a school's winning tradition or media exposure: playing time. If Roberto went to Oregon State, he would likely be the best player in the program the minute he arrived on campus and play major minutes as a freshman. "How many guards does UCLA have coming back?" Roberto said, knowing well how crowded the Bruins' backcourt was. "And the way I look at it, UCLA will win with or without me. If I lead them to a Final Four, it's no big deal, because that's what is supposed to happen at UCLA. But if I help Oregon State win, well, I'd be like a legend up there."

Bruce Nelson, Roberto's father, wanted Roberto to attend UCLA, but by November, when Roberto signed a letter of intent with Oregon State, Bruce was in no position to counsel him. He was locked up in Tehachapi State Prison after being convicted of sexually assaulting two women he cared for at the rehabilitation facility where he worked. If paroled as soon as he was eligible (in December of 2011), Bruce would likely get to see Roberto fulfill the dream that he never realized: starring for a major college basketball team.

Aaron Moore did not play basketball in what should have been his senior year in high school. He was talked into taking classes at a community college by Barbara and ended up at a school in Oklahoma, placed there by the coaches at Cal State Fullerton. After several months, he returned to Riverside and was promptly kicked out of his mother's home once again. In the final weeks of that school year, when his former Team Cal friends were attending proms and graduation parties, he was squatting in a vacant home in a subdivision in Fontana not far from where his nearly two-year-old son lived with his mother. "I talked to the coach at Riverside [Community] College, and he is setting me up with work-study, and I can get some grants and go there and play for a year or two and then transfer," he said on a rare day when I was able to get in touch with him. "I'll get my school stuff taken care of there and then go to a [Division I] school. I know it is going to work out. I just know it."

Rome Draper, Jr., spent his senior year at a continuation school. The teachers and coaches at Etiwanda High tired of his disregard for classes and practice. When he ran into one of his former teammates at the mall or elsewhere, he often said that he intended to play basketball again, but they only had to look at him, his eyes hazy and his body soft, to know that was unlikely. The coach at Barstow Community College knew Rome from when he played for Keller and convinced Rome to enroll there. Rome told friends he still hoped to land a scholarship to a Division I school.

Joe Keller continued to build his empire, and by 2009 there were 312 Jr. Phenom Camps in five different countries, including Japan, Mexico, Canada, and Puerto Rico. He also operated seven national camps for boys and girls in San Diego and employed thirty-seven people.

Keller contentedly ran his business, but his interest for basketball waned. Though he would not admit it, he missed the way he felt coaching the boys, the best team in America that one wonderful season in 2004, and he missed being the underdog. Now that he was wealthy and comfortable—or, as he would put it, "big-time" all the time—something was missing. The climb up from the bottom, from installing car alarms to becoming a millionaire, was the best part, and Keller couldn't reminisce about those days with the people who had made the journey with him. He was never again close to any of his former players or their parents.

He eventually found a new outlet for his notorious competitiveness: his son Jordan's baseball career. Youth baseball was in the early stages of growing a grassroots system similar to the one for basketball, and Keller dove right in, placing Jordan on a traveling team. At first he resisted the urge to coach Jordan, but he couldn't help himself. He also helped finance the team, worked to lure talented players from other squads, and came up with its catchy name: Team Phenom.

Jordan's team quickly became one of the best in the area, then in the state, then in the country. In the summer of 2008, the group of eight-year-olds won a national tournament, after which Keller called to deliver the news. "National champions!" he shouted over the phone. "Once again Joe Keller brings home a national championship!" I asked him how Jordan had played. "He was the best player in the whole tournament. And he's younger than most of these kids too." Then he lowered his voice, just as he had done eight years earlier when he let me in on the secret that was Demetrius. "I'm telling you, Jordan is the real deal. You should see him. You gotta come down here and see him play. He will blow you away. He's gonna be playing for the Yankees someday. *Sports Illustrated* is going to put him on the cover. . . . I'm telling you, my son is a phenom."

Demetrius Walker verbally committed to USC a week after returning from his final grassroots event in Las Vegas. He heard that the Trojans were hosting two 2009 recruits who, like him, were guards, and he panicked at the thought of losing the one scholarship offer he considered viable. News of his pledge spread quietly among recruiting services and the media that followed USC basketball. Reviewers called him a "solid" get for the Trojans but not a major addition, and Demetrius was equally lukewarm about the union. After informing USC coach Tim Floyd of his decision, he did not call friends with the news or throw a party. "I went out to dinner with my uncle, but it wasn't like we were celebrating or nothing," he said. "We really didn't even talk about USC."

A month later, Tom Stengel pulled Tommy out of JSerra and enrolled him at Mater Dei, the latest move aimed at netting Tommy a scholarship offer. Tom saw no reason to continue supporting Demetrius. If he wanted to spend his senior year at JSerra, Demetrius would have to pay the rent on the apartment in Aliso Viejo and cover the other expenses Tom had fronted.

Demetrius had no choice but to move into the home his mother rented in Surprise, Arizona, a suburb of Phoenix, and he enrolled at St. Mary's, his third school in three years.

Leaving Southern California put some needed distance between Demetrius and his grassroots past. He didn't love Arizona, but he grew to like that his reputation as the failed "next LeBron" didn't follow him to the Valley of the Sun. Coaches and teammates on the St. Mary's basketball team marveled at his athleticism and scoring ability, judging his abilities in the moment rather than by what he was supposed to be. It made the transition to yet another new school easier and also led him to second-guess his decision to play for USC. "I don't know if I want to go back to L.A.," he said. "There, man, it's like people are always talking shit about you, picking you apart. Here I can just be who I am and people are cool with that."

Without Barrett around to lobby hard for the Trojans, Demetrius took an unfettered look at the USC program, and he didn't like what he found. Floyd and the Trojans were under NCAA investigation for alleged infractions involving former player O. J. Mayo, and Floyd was a noted over-recruiter, meaning he always looked for players to bring in who could bump the ones he had out of the way. This was not unusual in college basketball, but Floyd was particularly merciless. For a player like Demetrius, whose confidence was still on the mend, Floyd was a bad fit. "If Demetrius goes to USC, within a year or two he'll be gone, transferred to a school like Long Beach State or Loyola Marymount," Sonny Vaccaro said. "Floyd will run him off."

Demetrius also kept hearing that Barrett advised him to go to USC only so he'd get money from the school. "Pat, Joe, they are all the same," Demetrius said. "They are just out for themselves. Pat doesn't care about me. He cares what he can make off me." It was a simple realization, but for Demetrius it was a watershed. After nearly a decade growing up in the grassroots-basketball machine, Demetrius finally understood the motivation of the men running it.

The NCAA provides a weeklong window in November of a basketball recruit's senior year to sign a letter of intent with a school. If a player doesn't sign during that period, he must wait until the spring. Schools push players to sign in November because they want their recruiting classes set early, and most players don't want to wait either. Demetrius's realization that USC wasn't a good fit came just two days before the start of the November signing period. "I don't think I should go to USC. I know that now," he said. "But I can't wait until the spring to sign. That's too risky. There might not be a scholarship left at a school I like. I don't know what to do."

I asked him if he had heard from any other coaches since he verbally committed to USC (no) or if he had a school in mind that he hoped would take him (no again). "People at [St. Mary's] keep asking me about why I didn't choose Arizona State," he said. "I know a coach from there talked to Pat about me a long time ago, or at least that is what Pat said, but I don't know if that is true of if they would still want me now."

I told him to call Herb Sendek, Arizona State's coach.

As luck would have it, Arizona State had just released one of its recruits, shooting guard Jared Cunningham of San Leandro (California) High, from his verbal commitment because of a low SAT score. Sendek and the Sun Devils had a scholarship available and a need for an explosive backcourt talent. "We would love to get you on campus for a visit," Sendek said, but the soonest that could happen was two days after the signing period began. USC would expect him to sign on the first day, which meant he had to stall the Trojans long enough to visit Arizona State and decide if that school was a better fit.

On the first day of the signing period, officials at St. Mary's set up a table in the lobby of one building for Demetrius and two other players to sign letters of intent. A local television crew and a few reporters showed up to chronicle the moment. Demetrius never joined his teammates at the table, telling his coach that he didn't want to sign that day. He stood in the back of the room while his teammates signed their letters.

It took until that evening for USC to realize something was awry. An assistant coach left Demetrius a message, and Demetrius waited until he knew the coach was out of his office to call him back. The coach left another message the following morning, and then Barrett, who undoubtedly had heard from the Trojans' coaches, called as well. "I'm having second thoughts about USC," Demetrius told Barrett. "I don't think it is the best fit for me." Barrett had panic in his voice as he pleaded with Demetrius to sign with the Trojans, repeating his earlier talking points and again failing to mention the program's obvious drawbacks. He then tried to guilt Demetrius, saying Demetrius had given Floyd his word and breaking his commitment would be dishonorable. Recruits and schools break verbal commitments to one another all the time, and Pat Barrett, of all people, was in no position to counsel Demetrius on integrity. In the past, his words would likely have swayed Demetrius, but not now. "Fuck Pat," Demetrius said after their conversation. "I gotta do what's best for me."

A few hours later, Floyd called.

"So what is that I am hearing about you needing time to make a decision?" he said to Demetrius.

"Well, I couldn't sleep last night, Coach. I was tossing and turning, and my gut feeling was that it just wouldn't be right to sign right now. I need some time to think."

"You've been committed to us for four months," Floyd said. "Why are you having these feelings now?"

"I don't know, Coach. I don't know why I am having these funny feelings, but it's how I feel."

"I don't really have time for this," Floyd said. "There are other guys out there we can recruit. I don't have time to be waiting around for you."

"Well, that's your choice. I don't want you to sign anyone else right now. I'd like you to wait, like, two days, just give me some time to think."

Floyd accused Demetrius of wanting to look at other schools. Demetrius denied it, and then the conversation deteriorated.

"I see what kind of person you are," Floyd said. "You are a liar and you are not a man of your word. . . . I thought you were a player like O. J. Mayo and DeMar DeRozan, not afraid of coming in and competing for a spot, but you'd rather be given a position instead of earning one."

"Coach, I'm not afraid of anybody."

"Yes you are. And I'll tell you this: If any NBA teams interested in you come talk to me first, I am going to tell them who the real Demetrius Walker is."

Before Demetrius could fashion a response, Floyd hung up.

Demetrius was so distraught after the conversation that he had difficulty retelling what Floyd had said. "Can Coach Floyd do that? Can he tell NBA teams not to draft me?" he asked. "If that's true, I'll just sign with SC. I don't want to fuck up my future. Oh, man, this is fucked-up. I fucked up."

I assured him that if he was good enough to make the NBA, teams wouldn't care about the feelings of a man who had never coached him. Still, he was shaken by Floyd's threats, and it dampened the excitement that surrounded his signing with Arizona State a few days later, which was big news in the local press. (The following summer, Floyd resigned as USC's coach, following more allegations of NCAA violations committed by his program.)

As the school year wore on, Demetrius grew more content with his college choice. Away from Barrett and the rest of the profiteers, he played his senior season unencumbered by his past and without worry for his future. The competition in Arizona was a step down from what he'd faced the year before with JSerra, and he dominated most opponents. To see him play during his senior season was to be reminded of his golden days with the Inland Stars and Team Cal, when he played with joy and confidence, surrounded by his friends.

Demetrius ushered St. Mary's through the playoffs and into the 5A Division I state championship game against Gilbert Highland, which was the top seed. "My school has lost in the state finals, like, three times in the last four years," he said. "So for me to deliver a state title would be big."

In his last game before going off to college, Demetrius conjured up a performance reminiscent of the best he'd ever played. On St. Mary's first defensive series, he swatted a player's shot into the stands, and his intensity in guarding Gilbert Highland's best player, Indiana-bound guard Matt Carlino, bled over to his teammates, who played with emotion befitting the most important game of the season. He scored in such a variety of ways that Gilbert Highland had no means to stop him: near the basket, using the post moves he'd learned as a young boy; from the 3-point line by employing the jump shot taught to him by Fontana High's Ryan Smith; on fearless drives to the hoop that showed how he had improved as a ballhandler, the fruits of hours of work in the gym at St. Mary's.

When it was over, after Demetrius tallied a game-high 27 points and St. Mary's won 70–62, he stood in the middle of the court surrounded

by his teammates and looked toward the ceiling of the arena in Glen-
dale. He let out a loud scream, a roar, and he pumped his fists. Moments later he was handed the state championship trophy, a block of
dark wood with a gold ball on top. He walked off the court holding the
trophy over his head, one of the nets draped around his neck, and then
he stopped at the base of the stands where Kisha stood. She walked to
him and they hugged, and he kissed her on the cheek and whispered
into her ear.

"I did it, Mom. I did it."

UPDATE

———

The Dream They
All Harbored

emetrius Walker received a copy of *Play Their Hearts Out* a few months before its publication. Two weeks after it arrived at his dorm room, I called to get his initial impression.

"I haven't started it yet," he said.

Two more weeks passed and I called again. "I've been really busy. Haven't been reading much."

After another month went by, he said: "I'm still kinda at the beginning. Just starting it now."

Three months after receiving the book, he finally came clean. "Look, George, I'm not going to read it. I'm sorry."

Why wouldn't he read it?

"Because some of the things I went through, it's going to hurt reading about those things, living them again. And I know there are other things that I didn't know about, things that went on behind closed doors. Reading those things, that's going to hurt, too, and I just don't know if I'm ready for that."

I asked Demetrius if it would be okay if I read him a few pages over the phone, parts of the book that I felt he might get asked about, and he agreed. Other than those few pages, however, he has not read *Play Their Hearts Out,* and he doesn't intend to do so for some time. "Maybe one day when I have a son and he starts playing basketball, I'll read it to him so he sees what his dad went through and that basketball is a business."

As far as I know, Joe Keller has also not read the book. I sent Keller an advance copy, but he received it after an excerpt of the book appeared in *Sports Illustrated.* The excerpt included the story of how he missed the birth of his daughter to attend the 2003 AAU Nationals. Keller was aware that story would appear in the book—several times over the years I had told him that it would—but it still angered him, as did the general tone of the excerpt. He cursed me and threatened to sue me and said he would "ruin my life." I asked him to read the entire book before passing judgment, but he said he didn't need to read it. "I knew you were going to screw me," he said.

We have not spoken since.

People who associate with or work for Keller have contacted me to defend him. They don't refute what I wrote, but say that Keller has "changed" and that he is doing so much good now that it is wrong to crucify him for past "mistakes." I heard that rationale enough times that I raised the issue with Demetrius: Did Coach Joe just make a few mistakes that should be forgiven?

"I look at it like Joe did what Joe does," Demetrius said. "That is the person he is. If you are that type of person, you don't think you are making a mistake, because that is how you are accustomed to doing things. Deep down, I think he knows that leaving me and letting me crash and burn and have to pick up the pieces myself was wrong. Would he ever admit to it and apologize? I don't know. Maybe. Would it be genuine? I don't know. Maybe. With Joe, I would say that my vision is blurred. He was like a father figure to me, and there was that part of our relationship and some positive things, and then at the end he just dumped me. That sort of blurs everything for me, and I guess I now look at him like two people. The two sides of Joe."

Keller's life, from what I have been told, has changed very little since the publication of *Play Their Hearts Out*. He is still running his camps, still making money, and an August 2011 *Wall Street Journal* article about a middle-school basketball phenom referred to Keller as an "influential figure in AAU circles." Keller told me when we first met that nothing I would write about AAU kingpin Pat Barrett would hurt Barrett's business, and now the same can be said about him. Keller ascended to a loftier place than even Barrett reached, and how he got there matters little to the parents and kids who view him as the nation's premier broker of middle-school dreams.

Unlike Keller, Demetrius is in a very different place, mentally and physically. He played the 2009–10 season for Arizona State, although he didn't play much. He averaged only ten minutes a game, and he did not play or did not score in the team's final nine games. There were some bright moments, like the 14 points he scored in fifteen minutes at Washington, but the Arizona State coaches were unhappy with Demetrius's work ethic in practice and his poor attitude, and that led to less and less playing time.

In the spring of 2010, Demetrius announced that he was transferring to New Mexico. To those who knew his story, the departure from Arizona State was further proof that the grassroots basketball machine produces a certain type of kid. Facing adversity, Demetrius ran to a new school rather than stick it out and compete for more playing time. There is an underpinning of truth to that, but his decision to transfer was an educated one and probably the right call.

Demetrius was never a good fit for coach Herb Sendek's controlled, slower-paced offense. Had he not chosen Arizona State in haste, desperate for an option other than USC in the final few days of the November signing period, he might have learned that and signed with a different school. Typically, a recruit's parent or grassroots coach assesses whether a player is a good fit for a coach's system. Demetrius had no trusted advisers, and so he made a poor choice. It is not uncommon; at Arizona State alone, four players transferred after the 2009–10 season, a stunning exodus.

Demetrius sat out the 2010–11 season per the NCAA's transfer rules. He was out of the spotlight and free to work on his game and catch up with the other players in his class who had more mastery of the fundamentals. He had three minor knee surgeries during that year, but he said at the start of the 2011–12 season that he was healthy and looked to be one of the Lobos' top three guards, along with Kendall Williams, another of Joe Keller's former players.

"That would be cool, Kendall and I starting together on the same college team," Demetrius said. "Kendall, he was younger and so we didn't play together a lot when we were with Joe, but we were together when it all started."

Kendall had a stellar freshman season, averaging 11.6 points per game, and he was named the Mountain West Conference Freshman of the Year. "Kendall really broke out last year, surprised some people," Demetrius said. "I feel like now is my time to do that."

Young people mature after a few years in college, and much of the change I have seen in Demetrius can be chalked up to that. His struggles his freshman year at Arizona State and then seeing players like Kendall and others outshine him led to further reflection, and I think he understands fully how hard he must work even to get close to his dream of playing professional basketball.

He has been buoyed by the reactions from readers of *Play Their Hearts Out*. People approach him on the street or send him messages on Facebook, and their words are overwhelmingly positive.

"Some people say I'm pretty much the poster child for how basketball is all screwed up," Demetrius said. "I don't know what to say to that. It is what it is, I guess. It's my life. I just hope that the kids after me, if they play AAU ball, have a different experience. As long as the system gets better, I'm okay with being the poster child."

Aaron Moore's reaction to the book took me by surprise. He immediately stopped responding to my calls, emails, and messages I sent on Facebook. When I showed up unannounced at one of his games—he played for San Bernardino Valley College during the 2010–11 season—Aaron let me know with a menacing look that I should leave immediately.

Perhaps I shouldn't have been caught off guard by Aaron's reaction. I wrote critically about his mother, Barbara, and that had to upset him. I did try to write about Aaron and what he went through with compassion, to always remind readers that it was irresponsible adults who let him down, but I worry now that he sees me as another of those betrayers.

Most of the players read the book with great interest and came away full of questions. Justin Hawkins, who played a major role for UNLV the past two seasons, summed up the reaction of many when he said: "There was so much that I didn't know was happening. Joe was doing some crazy things. Is all of that true?"

Jordan Finn, who transferred from the prep school at the Air Force Academy to Nevada, and Andrew Bock, who got homesick at Creighton and transferred to Pacific in Stockton, California, reacted similarly. Pe'Shon Howard read the book between classes at Maryland. "When D was little and getting all that hype, I was a little jealous," he said. "I wanted the hype, too. But now I'm glad it wasn't me."

Roberto Nelson, who sat out his freshman year at Oregon State due to eligibility issues, called me several days in a row as he read the book with Joe Burton, his Oregon State teammate and another former Keller player. "Did Joe [Keller] really make all that money?" Roberto asked one night. The following evening, he called again: "Did D really hide in the bathroom?" A day later, after he finished the book, he told me: "Man, I really hope D makes it."

few parents complained that I left out key bits of information, that
I didn't always provide context for some of their decisions. A couple griped that I had portrayed another parent too fondly ("You really love Carmen Hawkins," said one parent). John Finn, with whom I still have spirited discussions about the players and basketball, had small complaints, but in general he said that the book was an accurate version of the events "as a writer might see them." In closing, he said: "It is also probably true that we don't always see ourselves as we are."

In June of 2011, the Los Angeles Lakers selected Darius Morris in the second round of the NBA draft. The many alumni of the Inland Stars/Team Cal were buzzing with the news, as Darius was the first of Keller's many prodigies to fulfill the dream that they all harbored at one time or another.

Not long after Darius landed with the Lakers, Rome Draper enrolled at Pierce College in Woodland Hills, California, and joined the basketball team. Rome had not played organized basketball in over a year and had stopped taking classes; there were rumors that he was running with the wrong crowd. People had given up on him. Suddenly, he was working out and back in school at that community college, and his old teammates were ecstatic.

I asked Demetrius about Darius and Rome. He was happy for Darius, said it gave him hope that if he keeps working he can find the same ending. As for Rome, Demetrius said: "If he keeps it together, Rome can make it. He's got the talent. You know, that would make a great story. How Rome kinda lost it and fell off the map and people forgot about him and then he starts playing again and in the end he makes it. If that happens, you should write that story, George. I'd definitely read *that*."

ACKNOWLEDGMENTS

I was fortunate that this book came to the attention of Mark Tavani at Random House. His understanding and excitement over what I was hoping to achieve inspired me, and he enriched the text with his suggestions. The guidance and support that my agent Andrew Blauner provided as he patiently waited for this book to take shape was invaluable. I owe him a great debt. Terry McDonell, the editor of the Sports Illustrated Group, twice allowed me to take time off work to write this book, and he has always encouraged ambitious projects such as this one. Craig Neff of *Sports Illustrated* has been a great editor and friend.

I would not have a career in writing if it weren't for Emilio Garcia-Ruiz, Bill Dwyre, and Kerry Temple. The friends and colleagues who helped me with this book and over the years are too numerous to list, but a special thanks to Lowell Cohn, Grant Wahl, and Michael Silver.

Richard Sheehan from the University of Notre Dame gave me a crash course in economic theory that enriched several chapters. Walt Harris, Julius Patterson, Keith Howard, Dave Taylor, and Darren Matsubara informed my understanding of the grassroots-basketball system, and Sonny and Pam Vaccaro spent countless hours contributing to and challenging my understanding of youth basketball. I first interviewed Sonny when I was a twenty-two-year-old intern at the *Los Angeles Times,* and in many ways the seeds from which this book grew were planted that day.

I met my wife, Sharon, five years into this project, and without her I would have struggled to finish it. The final stretch included brain surgery (for me), a wedding, and the birth of our daughter, Jessica. During that time Sharon read every chapter, gave smart advice, and was my biggest advocate. I am blessed to have such a committed partner.

Greg and Natalie Dohrmann, Erika and Todd Chapman, Joan

Dohrmann, and my parents, George and Suzette Dohrmann, provided countless hours of dog care during the many days I spent on the road. Maddie and I thank you.

Joe Keller took a leap of faith when he allowed me to follow him and his team, and for that I am grateful. He won't be pleased with everything I have written, but I hope that he will come to appreciate that he has a straightforward and honest account of this period of his life. If I could not visit the Inland Empire and drink Coronas, eat Mexican food, and talk basketball with Coach Joe, it would be a great loss.

Kisha Houston, Carmen Hawkins, Bruce and Roberta Nelson, John and Shelly Finn, Rob and Lisa Bock, Rome Draper, Sr., Sharon Patton, Bill Howard, Gary Franklin, Sr., Tom Stengel, Rachel Carter, Barbara Moore, Violet Keller, Brian Beard, and Gerry Vilarino welcomed me into their homes and into their lives. Thank you for your trust and cooperation.

It would have been impossible to spend so many years around the players and not develop a great affection for them. I fell into the habit of calling them "my kids," and I followed their lives so closely that at times they felt like family. I asked a lot of Aaron, Roberto, Justin, Rome, Jordan, and Andrew, and they were always eager to help, as were Gary, Terran, Pe'Shon, Darius, Tommy, G.J., and Craig. Finally, there was Demetrius, who took every one of my calls and put up with day after day of me at his side, notebook in hand. This is a book about many people, with many themes, but at its core it is Demetrius's journey.

Thanks, D, for letting me tag along.

A CONVERSATION BETWEEN
SETH DAVIS AND GEORGE DOHRMANN
ON THE EXPERIENCE OF WRITING

Play Their Hearts Out

SETH DAVIS is the author of *When March Went Mad*. He is an on-air studio analyst for CBS Sports coverage of NCAA basketball and is an on-air host, reporter, and analyst for the CBS Sports Network. He is also a staff writer at *Sports Illustrated,* where he has worked since 1995, primarily covering college basketball and golf. A graduate of Duke University, Davis lives with his family in Ridgefield, Connecticut.

Seth Davis: What was it about Joe Keller and his program that made it the ideal subject? Was it just his willingness to participate or was it more than that?

George Dohrmann: I think the biggest factor was Joe's ambition. He was just so driven and I knew immediately that he would stop at nothing to succeed. You put him together with a group of kids and their parents, most of whom were very naïve, and it was just logical to think that something compelling was going to occur. As driven as Joe was, he was also a little naïve, with that mix of insecurity and arrogance that I write about in the prologue. I felt that he alone, regardless of what happened with the boys and the team, was at the start of an interesting journey worth charting.

SD: You followed Keller and his players for eight years. How early on did you realize that the story warranted writing a book? Was there any point in the project where you thought you might scrap it?

GD: In the early years I had my doubts that a great story was emerging, and I had some regret that I was spending so much time and money following Joe and the team. During one visit in February of 2004, it dawned on me that I would be spending my second consecutive birthday with Joe Keller. That was a depressing realization. But when the boys reached middle school, there was a short period of time during which Adidas gave Joe a sponsorship deal and Team Cal won AAU Nationals. Demetrius's and Joe's profiles rose significantly, and the shoe deal provided a pivot that allowed me to access the behind-the-scenes stuff with the shoe companies. In short, those two events raised the stakes and elevated the story.

SD: It is never easy reporting on children. How did you handle that ethically?

GD: Early in the book, the story focuses on Joe and the parents and you rarely hear from the kids. That was intentional. The boys were so young that to be quoting them extensively and delving into their feelings seemed inappropriate. I made the decision not to engage with them deeply until they came to me. For example, when Justin was around thirteen he started really questioning some of Joe's decisions. I didn't ask Justin about Joe; he offered his opinions as a way of exploring how he felt. At that moment, I felt like Justin was capable of understanding what was going on and the questions I might ask, and that is when he became a more central character in the book. I didn't want any of the boys to look back and say, "I was so young I didn't know what he was asking me about." I also didn't want any of the boys to feel like they were in the book against their wishes. Terran is an example of a player who was never totally comfortable talking with me. As a result, he never became a major part of the book.

SD: Students in journalism school are always warned against developing personal relationships with people they're covering. You were around these youngsters for eight years. You watched them grow up. Do you consider them your friends?

GD: You can't spend eight years around anyone, especially children, and not open up to them. I could not be some unemotional fly on the wall, unaffected by the highs and lows they experienced. The kids knew that I was rooting for them, and they also knew when I disapproved of something that Joe did or that their parents did. Knowing that, I took two precautions. First, whenever the boys came to me seeking advice, and that happened often in the later years, I did my best not to influence events. If Demetrius asked, "Do you think I should leave Coach Joe?" I would not answer that question. I probably sounded a lot like a therapist, saying over and over, "No, tell me how *you* feel about that." Second, I tried to be honest with readers. I don't think anyone could read *Play Their Hearts Out* and not detect how I feel about certain people. I don't purport to be 100 percent neutral, and I inserted myself into the book at times to make my feelings known, like when I questioned some of Joe's coaching tactics. As for my relationship with the boys, I still speak regularly with Demetrius, Justin, Roberto, and a few others and I hope we remain close for the rest of my life.

SD: There were many emotional moments in the book, particularly with Demetrius. Given how close you got to some of the players, how difficult were those to report on?

GD: I can recall two moments that broke my heart. The first involved Aaron. His mother had kicked him out of the house, and he said she didn't even let him pack any of his clothes. He had one pair of jeans, one T-shirt, and one pair of underwear. That was it. He was a wreck. He was such a smart, soulful kid, and I hated seeing him go through that and hearing him talk about how he still loved his mom and hoped she'd take him back. Another difficult moment was flying down to see Demetrius after Joe dumped him. That quote he gave me, about how he never had a "pops" until Joe found him, that was something that, when I listened to it later on my digital recorder, made me cry. D was so hurt and I knew he would carry that hurt forever because what Joe did was the equivalent of a father telling his son that he didn't matter anymore.

SD: What has surprised you the most about the reaction to the book?

GD: I've heard from people who work for NBA teams and also a couple of NBA players. One front office executive told me that he gave the book to members of his team's coaching staff so that they would better understand the players who were coming into the league. The fact that LeBron James jumped from the Cleveland Cavaliers to the Miami Heat a few months before the book came out led some people to draw from the book an explanation for why LeBron acted as he did. I think that is valid. Most NBA players are a product of the grassroots system, and understanding how that system works will help teams in their dealings with their athletes.

SD: What reaction to the book pleased you the most?

GD: Dozens of high school coaches reached out via email or Facebook to thank me for exposing the actions of the grassroots coaches that they have been battling over the years. Many were happy to now have something they could point to and say, "See, this is how bad it is." I also heard from coaches at small colleges who said that the book reinforced their decision to stay at the lower levels, where you don't have to deal with the likes of Joe Keller and Pat Barrett because you aren't going after the elite prospects.

SD: If you were made the almighty king of the NCAA and grassroots basketball, what changes would you make?

GD: That almighty king exists, and his name is David Stern, the NBA commissioner. He could urge NBA teams to set up the kind of academies that European soccer teams have, which over time would ensure that the best prospects are being coached and schooled properly. It would also minimize the influence of profiteers like Joe Keller. The best kids from the academies would go straight to the NBA and those who weren't ready would go to college. That would benefit both the NBA and the NCAA. Of course, setting up that kind of system would be expensive, and I'm not sure the NBA deems it necessary, which is too bad.

SD: In a more realistic sense, is there anything that can be done to reform this corrupt enterprise? Or is the genie too far out of the bottle for that?

GD: Absent that kind of radical overhaul, I think the situation is too grim to fix. There is too much money at stake and too many greedy people involved in the game for the coaches with the best intentions, like Ryan Smith from Fontana High or Julius Patterson and Keith Howard at IEBP, to win out.

SD: What's the best anecdote you witnessed or wrote about that didn't make it into the book?

GD: I cut an entire chapter that dealt with how girls would do crazy things to get close to the players. One girl faked she was pregnant to get Justin's attention, telling kids at his high school that she was having his baby, when he didn't even know who she was. Girls got into fistfights over the players, sent them naked photos, and so much more. It was a peek into how basketball stardom, even at an early age, leads people to treat you differently and warped how the boys viewed the world. It was tough losing that chapter, but I went into this project knowing that most of what I gathered over eight years of reporting would never make it into the book.

GEORGE DOHRMANN is a senior writer at *Sports Illustrated* and the magazine's investigative reporter. In 2000, while working at the *St. Paul Pioneer Press,* he won a Pulitzer Prize for a series of stories that uncovered academic fraud in a university's basketball program. Dohrmann lives in San Francisco with his family. This is his first book.

Printed in the United States
by Baker & Taylor Publisher Services